absurdly BIG ADULT JOKE BOOK

absurdly BIG ADULT JOKE BOOK

JOHNNY SHARPE

ARCTURUS

Published by
Arcturus Publishing Limited
For Bookmart Ltd
Registered Number 2372865
Desford Road
Enderby
Leicester
LE9 5AD

This edition published 2001

Printed and bound in Scotland
by Omnia Books Ltd

Typography by Alex Ingr

Cover design by Communique

Edited by Paul Whittle

© Arcturus Publishing Limited
1–7 Shand Street, London SE1 2ES

ISBN 1-84193-064-4

Contents

At Home   7

At School   8
In the Money   27
Keep it in the Family   44
Next Door Neighbours   73
With the Ball and Chain   84
A Nod to Confucius   97

At Play   103

Among the Animals   104
At the Movies   122
At the Zoo   130
Down on the Farm   135
In the Park   156
On the Desert Island   159
On the Skids   164
On Their Worst Behaviour   169
Up for a Party   185
Up for a Lark   195
In the Ladies   201

At Work   205

At the Hotel   206
At the Office   210
On the Job   221
In Church   230
In the Restaurant   249
In Uniform   254
On the Road   276
Up in Court   280
Machoman   298

In Love   301

Adultery   302
In Bed   338

On Honeymoon   351
Out of Love   372
Romance   388
Men on Women   416

In Sickness & Health   423

At the Chemist's   424
At the Doctor's   428
In Hospital   458
In the Dentist's Chair   471
In the Grave and Beyond   474
On the Couch   492
Over the Hill   501
She's Gotta Have It   530

On the Field of Play   537

Football   538
Golf   548
Out on the Cricket Pitch   564
Sport in General   568
Smart Alecs   572

Out on the Tiles   583

Down the Pub   584
In the Altogether   612
In the Wild   614
In the Gay Bar   622
On Holiday   630
On the Game   645
Out Shopping   668
Women on Men   677
Lights on – Nobody Home   683

At Home

At School

"Mummy, the milkman's here. Are you going to pay him or shall I go out to play?"

★

A woman was walking along the street with her little daughter when they came upon two dogs humping. When the daughter asked her mother what they were doing, embarrassed mum did some quick thinking and replied, "The dog on top has hurt itself so the one underneath is carrying it."
"Well, isn't that just typical?" said the little girl. "You try and do someone a good turn and all they do is turn round and fuck you."

★

A little girl in a convent school asks her teacher, an old nun, who came first, Adam or Eve.
"Adam," replied the nun, "men always come first."

★

"My dad's got two of those," said little Tommy as he watched his grandfather urinating.
"No, that's not right," replied his grandfather, "you're mistaken there."
"I'm not," replied the little boy, "he's got a little one for weeing with and a great big purple one for cleaning the au pair's teeth."

★

When she was a baby, she was so shy, she used to change her own nappies.

★

I always knew my parents really hated me.
My bath toys were a kettle and toaster.

★

"Mummy, mummy, the au pair is in bed with a strange man.
Ha ha, got you! April fool. It's only daddy."

★

A father was very upset about his young son's betting habits, so went up to school to talk to the boy's teacher, who promised to have a word with him.
"Maybe if he lost heavily on a bet, it would cure him," she suggested. That night after school she asked the boy to stay behind and confronted him about the bad ways he was getting into.
"It's not only me, miss," replied the boy. "You're a cheat; you pretend to be a natural blonde but you've got dark hair between your legs."
"I have not!" she blurted out without thinking.
"Oh yes you have, and I'll bet you my next month's pocket money."
The teacher was in a bit of a quandary. She had promised to help and this could be an expensive bet for him to lose. So she lifted her skirt and dropped her knickers. Having won the bet

she rang the boy's father to tell him the good news.

"Damn it!" he said, "This morning he bet me a tenner he'd get your knickers off before the day was out."

A junior teacher decided to play a little guessing game with her class."Listen everyone, I'm going to turn around and hold something in my hand and you have to guess what it is. Here's a clue, it's yellow and you can eat it."

One of the children guessed a melon but another guessed a banana.

"That's right," she said. "Now I'm holding something red in my hand, and this is also something you can eat." A little girl guessed apple.

"Well done, it shows all of you are really thinking." At this point a boy at the back asked if he could have a turn. With his back to the class he said, "I've got something in my hand that's long and has a red tip."

"Now John, enough of that," said the teacher.

"Actually, it's a match, miss," says Johnny, "but it shows you're really thinking."

★

Little Billy peeped into his big sister's bedroom one day to see her rubbing her hands between her legs, saying, "I need a man, God, I need a man."

The next night he peeped into her bedroom again and was amazed to find a man in bed with her. Later on that night if anyone had looked in Billy's room they would have seen him rubbing his hands between his legs, saying, "I need a Playstation, God, please, I need a Playstation."

★

A woman who lost the top half of her bikini in the sea was running back up the beach with her arms across her breasts when a little boy stopped her.

"Please, miss," he said "If you're selling those puppies, can I have the one with the pink nose?"

★

"Mummy, mummy, why do fairy stories always start, 'Once upon a time...'?"

"They don't always sweetheart, sometimes they start 'Had to work late again...' or even 'Bloody traffic, it took ages...' ."

★

"Mummy, mummy, Bobby's got something I haven't got," said the upset little girl, pointing between her legs.

"Oh don't worry about that," said Mummy relieved, "as long as you've got one of these you'll always be able to get one of those."

★

"Daddy, daddy, are you still growing?"

"Why do you ask, son?"

"Because the top of your head is coming through your hair."

★

Once a week the boy would travel across town to pick up child support money from his father and take it back to his mum. This money had come regularly for 16 years but on the boy's sixteenth birthday his father told him it was the last payment and to tell his mum he wasn't the father anymore.

"That's okay, Dad," replied the boy. "Mum says you never were."

★

The children go back to school after Christmas and are asked by the teacher what they received from Father Christmas.

"I got a brmm brmmm," says one little boy, but the teacher is quite angry and tells him he's not a baby and should use the right names.

"Sorry, Miss, I got a car."

"Well done, Bobby, and how about you, Tracy?"

"I got a woof woof," she said.

Again the teacher had to remind the class to use proper words.

"I got a puppy, Miss," she replied.

"Jason, what did you get?"

The little boy hesitated because he didn't want to get it wrong and make teacher cross with him.

"I, er... got a book," he stuttered.

"Well done," smiled the teacher.

"And what was it called?"

"Winnie The Shit, Miss."

★

"Now try and get to sleep, son. Dream about what you would like for Christmas."

"I wanna watch, Daddy," he replied.

"Well, you can't," retorted Dad. "Now get to sleep."

A woman was breastfeeding her baby in the park when a young boy sat down next to her.

"What does the baby have to drink?" asked the boy.

"Just milk and orange juice," she replied.

After a few moments thought the little boy asked, "Which one is the orange juice?"

"Mummy, Mummy, you can go to bed now because Dad's locked up for the night."

"I don't think so, sweetheart, he isn't home yet."

"But it's true Mum, the police have just been on the phone to tell you."

"Please Miss, I've hurt my finger," said little Rosie to her teacher. "Have you got any cider?"

Puzzled, the teacher asked her why she wanted cider.

"Because I heard my sister telling her friend that when she gets a prick in her hand she always put it in cider."

The parents were so proud when their son John went away to University but all he did was constantly write home for money to spend on books, trips, membership fees and so on. Then halfway through the term he wrote to tell them he had a lead role in the University play but needed money for the costume. All this money was beginning to really annoy the parents but they did as he asked and it was a month later when he wrote again to say thanks.

"The party was fantastic," he wrote. "Everyone thought I looked a real count in the costume."

On seeing this, the father retorted, "Bloody hell, I give him all that money and he still can't spell!"

Mum arrived back from staying overnight with her mother and asked her daughter if everything went alright.

"Oh yes," said little Anne. "Dad took me to the fair and I had some candy floss and an ice cream. It was great. But last night, I had a tummy ache, so I went to look for Daddy and he was in the au pair's room and he was in her bed and...."

"Stop," said Mum angrily, "I want your Daddy to hear this."

When Dad came in, Anne repeated her story while Mum looked on, beside herself with rage.

"Tell us what they were doing!" she demanded.

"The same thing that you and the man from next door were doing last week, Mum," she replied.

Marooned in the middle of the Yorkshire Dales, a man finds overnight accommodation with a local farmer, who tells him he can share a bedroom with his young son. That night, just before retiring, the young boy kneels down at the bottom of the bed and the man is so impressed he kneels down as well.

"What are you doing?" asks the boy.

"The same as you."

"Gosh, my mum's going to go mad. There isn't one where you are."

A little girl was found wandering down the crowded High Street, crying her eyes out. When the policeman asked her what was wrong, she told him she'd lost her father.

"What's your dad like?" he asked.

"Football, beer and fishing," she replied.

"Mummy, do babies come out of the same place that boys put their willies into?"

"That's right."

"So if I have a baby, will it hurt my teeth?"

A little boy was out walking with his mother when they met the new vicar.

"Good morning," he said, and looking down at the young boy he continued,

"And who do we have here?"

"I'm Mr Cole's son," said the little boy.

Later, his mother corrected him on his answer.

"You don't say 'I'm Mr Cole's son'," she said.

"You say, 'I'm Billy Cole'."

A few days later, the little boy was stopped by the local headmaster.

"You're Mr Cole's son aren't you?"

"I thought I was, but Mum says I'm not," he replied.

It was halfway through the English lesson when Miss decided to test her class on spelling.

"I want everyone to tell me what their fathers do for a living and then spell it out to me."

"Johnny, what does your Dad do?"

"He's a farmer, Miss."

"OK, spell that, please."

"F-a-r-m-e-r."

"Well done Johnny. Now Bob how about you?"

"He's a police constable, Miss."

"Very well, please spell that out."

"P-O-L-I-C-E C...U..."

"No, try again."

"CCC-U-S-"

"No, no, you'll have to think carefully about this, go and practise in your book."

"Who's next? Oh yes, Colin, what does your father do?"

"He's a bookmaker, Miss."

"Now can you spell that for me please?"

"No, but I can give you 5-4 on that Bob writes 'cunt' in his book."

Neighbour to little girl: "What's the name of your new baby sister?"

"I don't know; I can't understand anything she says."

"Mummy, Mummy, why has Daddy put his willy in the biscuit barrel?"

"Take no notice, darling, he's fucking crackers."

"Please Miss, I want a wee wee," said little Annie, holding herself.

"Annie, we don't use words like that in the classroom. When you want to go to the toilet just put your hand up and say you want to do number one," said her teacher.

Soon afterwards, Jason yelled out, "Miss, I got to go and do a poo poo."

"Now, Jason, when you want to do that, you say you need to go and do number two."

The rest of the lesson went without any interruption until five minutes before the bell when Gregory put his hand up and said, "Please Miss, I want to fart, would that be number three?"

A concerned father knew his son's pet hamster was dying and felt he ought to try and soften the blow.

"Son, I know your little Brownie is like one of the family but eventually he will die and go up to heaven. We must try not to be too sad. He's had a good life with us, so we must celebrate the happy times and not get too upset when he goes."

"Dad, can we have a party?"

"Yes, that's a good idea. You can invite some friends round."

"Dad?"

"Yes, son?"

"Can I kill it now?"

At a family gathering, a young boy suddenly lets out a noisy fart. "Bobby, manners please, you shouldn't do that in front of your grandma."

"Sorry, Dad, I didn't know it was her turn."

The teacher turned to her class and said, "Today, children, we are going to find out how many of you know the meaning of certain words by putting them into sentences. The first word is 'definitely'. Who can do that one for me?"

"Please, Miss, the sea is definitely blue."

"That's a good try Tracy, but sometimes the sea is grey, or even green depending on the weather, so we can't be that definite."

"I have one, Miss," said John. "Apples are definitely red."

"Well done for trying, but apples can also be green."

"Yes, Tom, do you want to say something?"

"Please Miss, does a fart have lumps?"

"Good gracious Tom, no ... no, of course not."

"Then, Miss, I've definitely crapped in my pants."

"Now, children, tomorrow I'd like you to bring in something connected with your father's work so that we can all learn a bit more about the different jobs people do," says the primary school teacher. The next day, little Jimmy brings in a bus ticket "cos my father is a bus conductor, Miss."
"Well done, Jimmy, and how about you Lucy?"
"I've brought in a betting slip cos my dad's a bookie, Miss."
"Fine...and you, Billy?"
"I've brought in a light bulb and a toilet roll. My dad works at the big car factory and this is what he brings home every night."

★

The teacher told the class to make up a poem about Timbuctoo, to recite in front of the class.
The first child recited hers:
"When I was lying in my bed
I dreamt of a ship with funnels red
A beautiful ship, its hull was blue
I think it was going to Timbuctoo."
"Well done, Lucy. Now let's hear the next." During the morning all the poems were heard, the last one coming from young Billy, a rather disruptive boy.
"As we walked down a road in Kent
We saw two ladies in a tent
I said to Tim, what shall we do?
Then I bucked one and Tim bucked two."
"Get to the headmaster!" roared the teacher.

★

Two kids were arguing in the playground.

"My dad's a better darts player than yours," said the first boy.

"No he ain't," said the second boy "My dad got the highest score last week."

"OK, OK, but my mum's better than your mum."

"Yeah, alright, my dad says the same thing."

★

The boy's father was so disappointed with his son's school report, he decided to go and see the headmaster to find out what had gone wrong.

"Well I have good news and bad news," replied the headmaster.

"The bad news is that your son has discovered he's gay and he spends all his time pursuing the good looking boys instead of studying."

The father was horrified.

"But what on earth is the good news?" he stammered.

The headmaster smiled. "Well the good news is that your son has been voted Queen of the May."

★

Father walks into his son's bedroom to find him lying face down on a life-size picture of Madonna.

"Son, what's going on?" gasps his father.

"It's alright dad, I've got plain Jane from next door underneath."

At the end of the human biology class, the lecturer conducted a quick question and answer session to check that everyone had been listening to his lesson.

"You over there, the girl in red," he said pointing, "which part of the body becomes 10 times its normal size under emotional stress?"

Flushed with embarrassment, the girl refused to answer, so another student volunteered.

"The pupil of the eye Sir."

"Correct," replied the lecturer and he turned to the girl saying,

"Young lady, your refusal to answer my question indicates three things. One, you haven't been listening to my lecture, two, you are obsessed with sex, and three, you are going to be very disappointed."

It was the annual school dance and young Johnny was dancing very close with a girl from the 6th form. After a minute or so she whispered in his ear,

"Why don't we go outside to the car for a while."

"Oh I don't know," he said, "I like dancing."

But the girl continued to coax him and eventually he agreed. When they got outside it was pitch black so the man produced a torch from his pocket.

"Have you had that torch with you all night?" she asked.

"Yes," he said.

"Oh well, in that case let's go back to the dance."

★

Two women, who were at school together, bump into each other 10 years later. The first one is a bit of a show-off.

"Yes, I can't complain. I went for a job on an estate just outside Henley and ended up marrying the Lord of the Manor. Ha Ha."

"Oh, how nice," said the second.

"And Jack darling encouraged me to start a stud farm and we've now got one of the best in southern England."

"Oh, how nice."

"We've got two lovely boys ... at Eton, of course."

"Oh, how nice."

"Anyway, listen to me blathering on! What happened to you?"

"Me? Oh, I went to finishing school after we left, and learnt how to say, 'Oh how nice' instead of 'fuck you'."

The local doctor was asked to give a talk on sex education to the girls at the local high school but, knowing his wife was a bit of a prude, told her he was speaking on hot-air ballooning. A few days afterwards the headmistress met the doctor's wife in the street.

"Please tell the doctor again how much we enjoyed his talk. I think the girls learnt a lot from him."

"Well, I am surprised," exclaimed the wife. "He's only done it twice and the second time he couldn't get it to rise properly."

A very pompous self-made man decided to pay for his son to go to private school and the whole family went up to visit the headmaster.

"I'm Sir Dunwell Bates, this is my wife Lady Bates, my daughter Miss

Bates and my son Master Bates."

"Don't worry," replied the headmaster. "We'll soon put that right."

The pretty young teacher had been form tutor of the Year 8 boys for half a term. Over the past few days she had noticed that one of her pupils had become distracted. Instead of getting on with his work, he would just gaze into space. Eventually she asked him to stay behind for a quiet word.

"Billy, you used to be such a hard worker but something's happened to change all this. What is it?"

"I'm in love, Miss," he replied.

She smiled, sympathetically. "And who is it?"

"It's you, Miss. All I can think about is you."

The young teacher looked embarrassed.

"Oh Billy," she said softly, "sometimes life isn't that simple. I, too, have dreams. I dream of getting married but I don't want a child..."

"Oh that's OK, Miss," he interrupted, "I've brought a condom."

"Cynthia," said her governess angrily, "it didn't look good when you let that strange man kiss you in front of the rest of the class."

"Well actually, Miss, it was better than it looked."

★

The student teacher was sitting in on a religious education lesson in class 4B. Suddenly, the teacher turned to her and

said, "Miss Lustleigh, will you tell the class the name of the first man."

"Well, I could," she replied coyly, "but I promised we'd keep it a secret."

★

The woman was walking down the street when she saw a young boy standing on the corner, drinking a can of beer and smoking a cigarette. "Why, this is disgraceful!" she exclaimed. "You should be in school."

"Piss off," he replied, "I'm only four years old."

★

A little boy started school but was causing a great deal of trouble for the teachers. Each lunch-time, he would be taken to the dining room for dinner but once there, he would refuse to sit down.

"Bollocks to you!" he would shout at the top of his voice, making all the other children behave badly as well.

When he repeated this behaviour, the following day, he was reprimanded but it didn't have much effect. Again, he shouted "Bollocks to you!"

At the end of the week, his parents were contacted and told about his behaviour.

"Well, if that's how the little bugger acts, don't give him any dinner," replied Dad. "Bollocks to him."

★

A little boy was playing pirates in the playground when the headmistress happened to walk by.

"Hello Tommy," she said. "What are you up to?"

"I'm the Captain and me and my men are going to fight all the enemy ships," he said, waving his cardboard cutlass and putting on his eye patch.

"So where are the buccaneers?" she asked, looking round.

"Under my buck'in hat of course," he replied.

"All right class," said the teacher. "Quieten down and each of you tell me in turn what would you like your body to be made of, if you had the choice."

"I'd like my body to be made of £10 notes," said one little girl, "then I could take some off and buy a car."

"Okay," replied the teacher, "who's next?"

"I would like my body to be made of gold," said Josie, "then I'd only need a little bit of it to buy two cars."

"Thank you Josie. How about you, Ben?"

"I'd have my body made out of pubic hair, miss."

The teacher was shocked.

"Whatever for?" she asked.

"Well my big sister's only got a small patch, but there's always plenty of cars parked outside our house!"

The English schoolmistress decided to test her children's knowledge of famous quotes.

"All right class," she said, "whoever gives me the right answer can go home an hour early from school."

She stood before them and began.

"The first quote is 'Tis better to have loved and lost than never to have loved at all.'"

A hand went up immediately.

"Please miss," said Beth, "that's Alfred Lord Tennyson."

"Very good," beamed the teacher. "You may go."

She read out a second quote . "Every dog has its day, and I have had mine."

Mary put her hand up. "Bernard Shaw, miss."

"Well done, off you go."

"Bloody girls!" murmured Tommy, from the back. "Fuck 'em all, the silly bitches."

"Who said that?" demanded the teacher looking round.

"President Clinton," said Tommy quickly, and before she could answer he'd dashed from the class.

Two streetwise kids were walking to school when one said to the other, "Guess what? I found a condom on the patio."
The other replied, "So what's a patio then?"

In the Money

An old spinster walking home late one night was accosted by a burglar. "Hand over your money!" he demanded.

She said she hadn't got any money, but he didn't believe her and started to search her. He frisked her up and down, put his hands inside her bra and also inside her pants. Satisfied there was no money he was just about to go when she said, "Hold on a minute. Keep trying. I can always write you a cheque."

A Rolls Royce pulls up outside the posh Beverley Hills hotel and the doorman walks down to greet the new guests. There are only two occupants in the car. The President of the country's leading bank and his ambitious wife Julia. She gasps when she sees the doorman then smiles and greets him warmly.

"Oh Tom, I can't believe it's you," she says, "how wonderful." They chat for a few minutes and then she and her husband disappear inside. As they take the lift up to their penthouse suite, he asks her about the doorman.

"Oh Tommy was an old boyfriend of mine, many years ago. In fact, at one time we were engaged," she says.

"I bet you're glad you didn't marry him though," he says.

"Why do you say that?" she asks.

"Well, because I'm the President of a National Bank and he's just a lowly doorman."

His wife looks at him for a few moments and then replies

coldly, "What you're forgetting Gerald, is that if I had married Tommy, he would be President now."

★

The Lord of the Bowertree estate was entertaining an important guest for lunch. He asked his manservant to pop down to the station to collect a parcel containing a special bottle of the finest malt whisky and a box of Havana cigars.

"By the way," he told his manservant, "I've run out of snuff. Pop into the tobacconist's, there's a good chap."

An hour later the manservant was returning from the village when he realised he'd forgotten the snuff.

"Bugger," he muttered to himself, looking around for inspiration. Suddenly, he spotted an old cow pat in the grass, it had dried up in the warm sun and turned white and crumbly. Quick as a flash, he picked it up, crumpled it into fine dust and decided to take a chance. After lunch, the Lord called for his manservant.

"Ah, there you are," he beamed, "a little whisky, a fine cigar and a pinch of snuff."

As the manservant did as he was asked, the Lord sniffed the air suspiciously. "There's an odd smell in here," he said, "has anyone brought something in on their shoes?"

"No," came the reply from his eminent guest, "actually I've got a bit of a cold, so I can't smell anything."

"Then take some snuff," said the Lord handing him the casket.

Aftertwo sniffs, the guest sat back and remarked, "That's good snuff, Cecil. It's cleared my nose wonderfully, and I can smell that shit now."

The East End gang boss had always been very careful whom he employed, for fear of being grassed up. He thought he'd been really clever with his crooked accountant who was deaf and dumb. There wasn't much of a risk that he would overhear too much. However, it eventually dawned on the boss that someone was stealing money from him. A lot of money! And it didn't take long for him to discover it was his crooked accountant.

"Benny," he ordered, "Get that bastard down here pronto and get Marty to come with him. He can read the hand signs."

Later in his office, the boss started interrogating him.

"Marty, ask him what he's done with the money."

At first the terrified accountant signalled his ignorance of the theft but when a gun was put to his head, he spilled the beans. With rapid hand movements, he explained that he'd hidden all the money in a trunk in an old derelict factory, two miles from the office.

"So what did he say?" demanded the boss impatiently.

"It's no good boss," replied Marty. He says you haven't got the bottle to shoot him, so you can go and get fucked."

A millionaire had been going out with a croupier from the local casino for two months. They'd had a great time, often out until the early hours of the morning, but both of them knew nothing serious would come of it.

Then one evening the croupier turned to the man and said,

"Why don't we get married?"

The man looked shocked.

"Oh come on Rose, you know that's not possible, when I marry it has to be to a titled family."

"I know," she sighed.

"Then why did you ask?"

"I just wanted to know how it felt to lose a fortune."

Lady Mary strolled down the path to where the young gardener was pruning the roses.

"Hello Thomas."

"Good morning Your Ladyship."

"You know Thomas, ever since you've come to work for us, I've been afraid that you would force me to kiss you," she said.

"Oh Your Ladyship, how could I do that with a pair of secateurs in one hand and a bag of clippings in the other?"

"Well," she mused, "you could put the secateurs on the bench and rest the clippings against that tree."

"Now Suzanne," said the wife to the new housemaid. "I shall be out tonight at Lady Cynthia's so you'll only be serving dinner to my husband. I hope you'll be able to cope if anything unexpected comes up?"

"Oh yes madam," she replied. "I've got a packet of condoms."

A rich couple decided to hire a full-time handyman to look

after the house, all the outbuildings and also the garden. They offered very low wages so it took a while to select a candidate, but out of despair they eventually chose a man from the neighbouring village. The following weekend they left him in charge while they visited friends in the next county. Alas, when they returned, they discovered the man sitting in their lounge with water pouring through the ceiling.

"What the hell's going on?" they demanded. "We hired you to make any necessary repairs. Why haven't you mended the roof?"

"Can't," he replied. "It's raining. It's too wet."

"Well, why didn't you do it while it was dry?" they said in exasperation.

"Couldn't, it wasn't leaking then."

"You look happy this morning Jack," said his mate.

"Yeah, I came into some money last night – a girl with gold caps on her teeth."

★

A woman rings her husband up at work to tell him she's won the jackpot on the lottery and that he'd better start packing.

"Darling that's wonderful!" he shouts with glee. "Where are we going?"

"I'm not bothered," she replied. "Just make sure you're gone by the time I get home."

★

A smart talking man who thought he could charm the birds off the trees met his match one night. The man had just learned that his father only had days to live and then he would inherit over half a million pounds. Overjoyed at the promised wealth, he celebrated at the local wine bar, where he saw a ravishing long legged blonde.

He couldn't wait to brag to her and indeed she was so interested in him, they went back to his house together. The next day she became his stepmother.

Bob suggested to his wife that a good way to save money would be to put £1 in the money box every time they made love. A year went by and Bob decided to empty the money box and see how much money had been saved. He couldn't believe his eyes when he found not only £1 coins but lots of £5, £10 and £20 notes as well.

"How come we've got all these notes?" he asked amazed.

"Well, not everyone's as stingy as you," she retorted.

As it was very windy outside, the lady held onto her hat and took no notice of the fact that her skirt was flying up around her thighs. Realising she was getting funny looks from some of the passing men, she said, "Look lads, this hat cost a fortune and is brand new. What you're looking at is 40 years old."

Down at his local social club, Jack was amazed to see a girl

lean over the table exposing her bare bum. Not only that, but on each buttock was tattooed the number 6. Jack immediately felt it was a sign he was going to be lucky, so he went over to the Treasurer and bought ticket 66 for the prize draw the next night. It was a bonus prize of £1,000. The following night Jack arrived after the draw had taken place and he turned to his mate at the bar, saying, "Was the winning ticket 66?"

"No, sorry mate, you were almost right."

"What was it, then?" asked the disappointed Jack.

"It was 606."

A man went round to his mate's, and the wife answered the door.

"Is he in?"

"No," she said.

"I fancy you."

"Go away."

"How about a quick one?"

"Piss off."

"I'll give you £300."

"Alright, come in."

Later her husband comes home.

"Did Jack come round?"

"Yes."

"Did he drop my wage packet off?"

Legend has it that when a person is born they are kissed by

an angel on the part of their anatomy that will bring them fame and fortune.

There are a lot of men who make excellent Chairmen – I wonder where the angel kissed them.

A man receives a letter ordering him to attend the local tax office for an interview about his last year's earnings. Unsure of what to wear, he asks his mate, who tells him to look very smart, wear a suit and a good pair of shoes to show him that he's an honest man. Later on in the pub he meets another mate, tells him about his impending interview and that he's off to buy a good pair of shoes. But his mate disagrees, telling him he should wear old clothes, look very poor, so the tax man will feel sorry for him. By this time the man is very confused, so on the way home calls in at his cousin's house for advice. His cousin is a wealthy businessman.

"Well, my advice to you is the same as I gave my daughter, Marlene, when she asked me what she should wear on her wedding night – a long bri-nylon nightie or a short skimpy baby-doll nightie. It doesn't matter what you wear, either way you're going to get fucked."

A man and woman walked into a bank with a large sack of coins.

"Did you hoard all this yourself?" asks the bankteller.

"No," came the reply. "My wife whored, I pimped."

"It's no good, sir," said the DSS man to his interviewee. "It's no good saying you feel like 65 – you have to be 65."

★

A rich couple lost all their money, and were trying to think of ways to save money. The husband said to his wife, "If you learn to cook we can get rid of the housekeeper."
And she retorted, "If you were better in bed we could get rid of the gardener."

★

Two friends on a walking tour of Dartmoor get lost in the mist and after many hours of wandering about finally come across a cottage. A widow lives in the cottage and after hearing their sorry story she welcomes them in and gives them some supper and a glass of beer. She tells them she only has two bedrooms so one can sleep in the spare room and one with her. The two men toss a coin and Jack ends up sleeping with the widow. He has a wonderful night and in the morning after breakfast they depart. After a few minutes Bob asks Jack how it went.
"What a night, mate. It was great, but this morning she asked for my name and address so I gave her yours – you know what my wife's like." Bob was so incensed by this that it broke up their friendship and they didn't see each other again for nine months. When the widow died, Bob said, "Hello Jack, you remember that widow? Well, I've had a letter from her solicitor and she's ..."
Jack hastily interrupted, "Look, sorry Bob, my wife would have strung me up by the balls."

"Let me finish," said Bob. "The solicitor's letter said she'd died and left me £1million."

Did you hear about the debutante who wrote home from the States to say she had a beautiful fur coat and it only cost her 200 bucks?
She never could spell!

On the way home to her flat, a young couple passed a jeweller's store. The man stopped and said, "If you're very nice to me tonight I'll buy you that diamond ring."

The girl, who loved material possessions, agreed immediately.

The next day, after a night of passion, the couple passed the shop and went in. But instead of buying her a beautiful diamond ring, he bought her a cheap brooch instead.

Later that day she visited her mother and, between the sobs, told her what had happened.

"My darling," replied her mother. "One thing you must learn – when they're hard they're soft and when they're soft, they're hard."

Two men sitting on a park bench reading newspapers. Suddenly one of them puts down his paper and bursts uncontrollably into tears.

"Excuse me," says the other, "I can't help but notice you're very upset about something. Can I help?"

"I've just read that the richest man in the whole world has died."

"I'm sorry. Were you related to him?"

"No," sobbed the man, "that's why I'm crying."

A randy old financier was bonking his secretary up against his desk when there was a knock at the door. The timing couldn't have been worse. She rushed back to her room and in haste he stuck his dick in the desk drawer. As the door opened the newcomer commented, "Why Mr Large, you're looking pleased with yourself."

Yes," he replied, "I've just come into some stocks and shares."

What's green and takes an hour to drink?
The family allowance cheque.

A jackpot winner on the lottery was asked what he was going to do with his new-found wealth.

"I'm going to travel round the world, visit all the racecourses, spend time in Las Vegas, enjoy myself with the girls, drink lots and buy a super, top of the range sports car."

"And what will you do with any money left over?"

"I don't know, probably just squander it."

"He'll be alright soon," said the doctor, putting the patient into the recovery position. "He's just in shock after seeing his numbers come up on this week's jackpot."

"Oh thank you, Doctor," replied the wife. "Just one thing, how long should I leave it before I tell him I didn't buy a lottery ticket this week?"

★

Flo's husband dies and because he was such a popular fella, she decides to put an announcement in the paper. But not having a lot of money, she tells the local newspaper she wants to keep it as short as possible. "Just put 'Ben Potts dead'."

"Actually Madam, you can have up to six words for the same price. Is there anything you would like to add?"

Flo thinks for a few moments, and then says, "Yes, OK, can you add 'Ferret for sale'?"

★

A man was always thinking up ways of making easy money and one day he thought he was on to a certainty. He taught his parrot to say the 23rd psalm and then took it down the local pub.

"I bet anyone £5 my parrot can recite the 23rd psalm, from beginning to end" he said.

Quite a lot of interest was shown and the money laid on the bar.

"Go on then, parrot, recite the psalm."

But the parrot remained completely dumb and eventually the

man took it home, having lost quite a lot of money.

"Why the bloody hell didn't you do as I taught you, you scrawny old bird?"

"Now hold on," said the parrot. "Think what the odds will be tomorrow when we go back."

★

What's the difference between a Lloyds investor and a seagull?
A seagull can still put down a deposit on a BMW.

★

Was it love at first sight?
No, second. The first time I didn't know he had so much money.

★

At a party to celebrate her 21st birthday, the daughter put all her presents on display including a cheque from her father to buy a new car. During the evening the guests would wander over to take a look at the presents and on one occasion a man was standing at the table looking at the cheque, doubled up with laughter.

"Mum," whispered the birthday girl, "who is that man?"

"Oh him, he's your dad's bank manager."

The rich and elegant old woman stopped to reverse her Rolls into the only free parking space. But as she was slowly backing in, a young girl in a nifty little sports car, came up behind her and nipped into the space.

"You've got to be young and daring to do that," said the girl. The old woman ignored her and continued to reverse into the parking spot, pushing the sports car out of the parking space and down a slope, where it smashed into a wall and burst into flames. The old woman finished parking, then turned to the dumbfounded girl and said,

"And you've got to be old and rich to do that."

The rich boyfriend presented his girlfriend with a beautiful fur coat made out of skunk.

"I'm amazed," she said, "that such a gorgeous coat could come from such a stinking little beast."

"Well fuck off," said the boyfriend. "I didn't expect gratitude but there's no need to get so personal."

A woman has her portrait painted by a local artist and asks him if he would paint her dripping with fabulous jewels. She explains,

"If I die before my husband and he gets married again, I want his second wife to go crazy looking for the stones."

Three brothers are left their father's business in his will. The oldest son says, "Dad left me 48% of the shares so I'm going to be Chairman."

"OK" says the second son "and I'll be in charge of the everyday running of the business because I've got 30% of the shares."

"Now wait a minute" says the third and youngest son. "What about me? Don't forget I've got 22% of the shares."

The other two confer amongst themselves and then reply,

"We've decided you can be in charge of sexual matters."

"What does that mean?"

"When we want your fucking advice, we'll ask for it."

"Hello Bates," said Lady Smythe to the gardener. "Do you think you're a good sport?"

"I believe so, yes ma'am," replied the puzzled man.

"And do you think you're a good fuck?" she asked, opening her dressing-gown to reveal nothing on underneath.

"I think I am, yes," stammered the blushing gardener.

"Well, today's April Fools' Day: fuck off".

The Chairman turned to his secretary and said, "I'll never forget that weekend we spent together in the Cotswolds, will you?"

"I don't know," she replied, "it depends how much it's worth."

There had been an awful car accident resulting in a flashy sports car hitting a roadside tree and badly injuring the two passengers. When the emergency services arrived, the man was screaming hysterically.

"Try and calm down, Sir," said the paramedic, "and we'll try and see what's wrong. At least you weren't flung through the windscreen like your girlfriend."

"Aagh!" screamed the man even more. "Have you seen what's in her mouth?"

★

The poor man was in great difficulties. His business was failing and it looked as if he was facing bankruptcy. As a last resort he popped into the local church and kneeling down he prayed fervently.

"Oh God, please don't let this happen to me, please let me win the lottery."

But on Saturday night, he had no luck.

The following week, the situation got worse. The man lost his house and all his possessions, so once again he went into Church and prayed desperately, "Oh please, please I beg you, please let me win the lottery."

But on Saturday, he had no luck. On the following Monday, his wife and children left him and he was now completely on his own. He ran into church, got down on his knees and pleaded,

"Oh God, all has gone, I have nothing left. Have pity on me, I beg you. Why won't you help me win the lottery?"

At that moment, there was a tremendous thunderclap, a bright flashing light and God boomed out,

"Help me out on this one, Amos; buy a fucking ticket!"

★

The retired colonel is striding out through the village when he is accosted by one of his servants, a little the worse for wear. "Hello, your colonel sir," grins the man. "How the devil are we?" he mimics. Not only drunk but insulting!

The colonel is outraged and bellows, "Drunk as a skunk!"

The man whispers conspirationally,

"Don't worry Sir, your secret's safe with me, I've had a bit to drink myself."

★

Lady Cynthia, a spinster for 60 years was finally forced to get married because of financial difficulties within her aristocratic family.

On the night of the honeymoon, she walked into the bedroom wearing a long white nightdress and a pair of long white gloves.

"What's this for, old girl?" demanded her new husband. "Why are you wearing gloves?" She replied haughtily, "One has been informed by ones Mater that one has to actually handle the so-called member."

★

A rather arrogant social climber liked to impress her friends and relations by putting on sumptuous dinner parties. One night, however, as they were all sitting around the table her stomach took a turn for the worse, and she was unable to contain a fart.

Without turning a hair, she immediately said loudly, "Jeeves,, stop that at once!"

But Jeeves replied immediately,

"Certainly, madam, which way did it go?"

Keep It In The Family

"Dad, Dad," said his son excitedly. "I've done it. I've got a part in the new play."

"Well done lad, what is it?"

"I play an old man who's been married for 35 years."

"That's a promising start. Next time you might get a speaking part."

A little girl was watching her father take a shower . She asked him what his testicles were called.

"They're my plums," he replied.

A little later she told her mother what he had said.

Mum retorted, "And did he tell you about the dead branch they're hanging off?"

A man rushed into a newspaper office saying, "I hope I'm not too late to put an announcement in the paper – my wife has just given birth to a baby girl after 10 years of trying."

"Of course, sir," replied the clerk. "How many insertions?"

"Oh, I can't remember – bloody thousands!"

A man is loading his kids into the car, five squeezed in the back and two in the front. As he gets in himself he's heard to mutter, "Wow, I almost screwed myself out of a seat!"

A simple-minded couple go to the doctor's because the wife is pregnant again with the fifth child in as many years.

"Why didn't you use the condoms that I instructed you to wear?" asked the doctor.

"I'm sorry, Doc," they replied, "but we don't have an organ so I put it over the flute instead."

A very ugly couple were walking along the road with two beautiful children when they overheard a passer-by express amazement at the fact that two such ugly people could have such lovely children. They turned to the passer-by and said, "You imbecile, we didn't make them with our faces!"

A male and female astronaut landed on an undiscovered planet and soon met up with some of the inhabitants. These inhabitants showed them many things, including a baby machine which produced the new offspring. On seeing this, the astronauts were asked how their little ones were made. Rather than explain, they stripped off and gave a full and satisfying demonstration. The inhabitants looked puzzled.

"But where are the new ones?"

"Oh that won't happen for another nine months," they replied.

"Well if it takes that long, why were you rushing so much at the end?"

★

On seeing her friend pregnant, the woman offered congratulations but added sadly, "We've been trying for years

but with no luck."

"Well, do as I did," replied the happy woman. "Go to a faith healer," and then lowering her voice she murmured, "but go on your own."

A husband, his wife and their six children sat down in the restaurant and called the waiter to order their meal. It was obvious the six children were three sets of twins and the waiter couldn't help but remark, "I hope you don't mind my asking, but do you always have twins?"

"Oh no," replied the wife without thinking. "Sometimes we don't get anything."

Did you hear about the woman who had a hard time breastfeeding her baby? She couldn't get her husband out of the way.

What's the similarity between women's breasts and train sets?
They were both intended for kids but it's the dads who keep playing with them.

Two women talking:
"My first pregnancy resulted in triplets and that only happens once every 250,000 times."

"Wow!" said her friend. "I'm surprised you ever had time to do any housework."

★

It was decided to add sex education to the school curriculum and the parents were asked how they felt about this. The majority were in agreement with one proviso – no graphic demonstrations, just keep it oral.

★

Just as the young girl is coming out of the school gates, a car draws up and a man leans over to ask her if she'd like a lift home.
"No, thank you," she replies.
But he asks again.
"Come on, it's raining, you'll be soaked by the time you get home."
"No! Go away and leave me alone."
The man follows her up the road. "Look, get in please, I'll get you some sweeties."
"No!" she yells and starts to run.
"I'll get you some sweeties and your favourite comic."
"No, no, no!" shouts the girl. "Just because you bought the Lada doesn't mean I have to ride in it, Dad."

★

"Look at this," said Flo's friend, holding up the newspaper. "It says here that there are 19 women in the village all expecting a baby on the same day – June 23. Your baby's not due until July is it?"

"No, it's not, but then I didn't go on the Mothers Union trip to Weymouth."

A kindly old curate happened upon three young girls crying in the deserted old graveyard. Taking pity on their distress he invited them into the rectory for a cup of tea and a slice of cake. In the warmth of the kitchen and the smell of freshly baked cakes, the three girls cheered up.
"Now," he said, smiling as he brought over the tea tray, "Who's going to be mother?" and they all burst into tears again.

"John, your dad's not very good at these things, so I wonder if you'd tell your brother about the birds and the bees," asked Mum.
John sought out his brother and said, "Hey Bill, d'you remember what we did last night?"
"Sure, we went down the Palais, picked up a couple of birds, had a dance, then took them round the back of the bus station for a good 'one two'. Why do you ask?"
"Mum just wanted you to know that what you did last night is the same for the birds and the bees."

Poor old Sammy. He was a Caesarean baby and even now, 20 years later, he still goes out of the house through the skylight.

★

Two husbands are in hospital anxiously awaiting for their wives to give birth. One of them is so nervous, the other tries to comfort him, saying, "It'll be alright mate, I've been through this before."

The nervous man asks a lot of questions, finally saying, "Can you tell me how long it will be before I can have sex with my wife again?"

"Are you private or NHS?"

"NHS."

"In that case, you'll have to wait until you get home."

"Doctor, I've only got three weeks to go before my baby is born, can you advise me on the best position for delivering it?" she asked. "Well, the most common way is exactly the same position as when you conceived."

"Oh goodness, you mean in the dark under the stairs, standing on an orange box!"

The young couple have been married for six months and one day when they are in bed he asks her if she is happy.

"Oh yes," she replies. "Everything is wonderful."

"But is there nothing that bothers you?" he persists.

"Well... only a couple of things," she finally condedes.

"You're always picking your nose and we always make love with you on top."

"I can explain that," he says. "When I was growing up my father gave me two pieces of advice which I try to follow – 'Keep your nose clean and don't fuck up.'"

★

Bob and Sheila had a small flat in the city and decided the only way they could have a Sunday afternoon 'quickie' was to send 10 year- old Johnnie out on the balcony and ask him to report on the neighbourhood activities. It was sure to distract him for an hour. The boy began his commentary as the parents got down to business.

"An ambulance has just stopped at old Mrs Jenkin's place, Mr Wales is walking his dog, Mat and Jenny are on their bikes and the Davidsons are having sex."

Mum and Dad sat up in bed astonished.

"What do you mean?" said Dad. "How do you know?" he spluttered.

"Their Billy is standing out on the balcony with binoculars too," replied the son.

Mother receives a telephone call from school telling her they are sending home her son for weeing in the swimming pool.

"But everyone does that," she says.

"Not from the top diving board, they don't."

A young boy at school called Tommy is always in trouble. Stealing, pinching, bullying, his misdemeanours are endless. Then one day, the head teacher calls his mother in to tell her that they have no choice but to expel the boy. This time he's been found wanking in the classroom.

"You know it's a big problem," says the head teacher. "You've got to stop him from doing it."

"How?" she asks.

"Well, tell him he'll go blind if he carries on like that."

When they get home, Mum insists that Dad goes upstairs and has a word with him."

"Go and explain what will happen," she says.

So Dad goes up to his son's bedroom and starts to talk to him in a stern voice, warning him of the dangers of what he is doing, and the awful consequences it can have.

"Hold on a minute, Dad," says the little boy. "I'm over here."

★

Grandpa takes his grandson to Blackpool for the day and they go on every ride in the fair except for the big dipper. But the boy's not satisfied, he wants more.

"Oh please, Grandpa, please, please let's go on the big dipper."

After ten minutes of constant pestering, Grandpa relents and they go on three times.

"Can I have an ice cream now, Grandpa, please, please can I have an ice cream?"

Grandpa knows his mother has said 'No', but it's anything for a quiet life, so he buys the boy a cornet. In the afternoon, they go down onto the beach and the boy has a donkey ride. He loves it. In fact, he loves it so much, he wants Grandpa to buy the donkey.

"No, no, no," says Grandpa, but the boy screams and yells and pesters him that he eventually buys the donkey for £50.

"What are you going to call it?" he asks.

"Tosser," said the boy, "cos he kicks a lot and is always tossing people off his back."

Later on, at 3am in the morning, Grandpa is woken up by the little boy because the donkey has broken his leash and disappeared.

"Grandpa, Grandpa!" cried the boy. "Tosser's off!"

"Now look here boy, I've taken you to Blackpool, you've been on all the rides, I've filled you up with ice creams and bought a donkey. Don't you think I've done enough for one day?"

Daddy is mowing the lawn when his young son comes running out of the house calling to him.

"Daddy, Daddy, what's sex?" asked the boy.

For a moment Dad is dumbstruck but then decides that if his son has asked the question, then he must do his best to answer it. For the next few minutes Dad talks about the birds and the bees, then human relationships, love, the sex act, having babies – in fact he does a pretty good job of covering every aspect. Eventually he comes to a stop when he sees how oddly his son is looking at him.

"Why did you want to know?" he asks.

"Well Mummy said to come out and tell you that dinner would be ready in two secs."

Man to son:

Endeavour to marry a girl with small hands, it'll make your penis look bigger.

★

"Mummy, Mummy, I know how babies are made, I know how babies are made! I saw Daddy put his willy in your mouth last night."

"No, that's not right," replied Mummy, "that's how I get my expensive jewellery."

★

"Hey June, how about a bit of slap and tickle tonight?"

"Sshh John, don't talk like that in front of the children. Let's use code. Whenever you feel like it, just say 'how about turning the washing machine on.'"

A few evenings later, June turned to her husband and said,

"Shall I put the washing machine on tonight?"

"Don't bother love, you looked a bit tired so I did it by hand."

★

"Mummy, Mummy, what are you doing?" exclaimed the little boy as he walked into the bedroom to find her sitting on Daddy.

"Just flattening Daddy's tummy," Mum replied.

"I wouldn't bother, when you go out tonight the au pair will only blow it up again."

★

"Okay kids," said Dad, returning home from work. "My boss gave me a box of chocolates today so I think it ought to go to the person who always does what Mummy says and never answers her back."

"Oh Dad," wailed the four children, "that's not fair, you know that's you!"

The man had been working on the oil rig for three months but now he had a two week break.

"I can't wait to get home," he said, "before the kids forget what I look like."

His pessimistic workmate replied,

"Just make sure you know who they look like!"

★

"You may scoff son," said the father, "but wisdom comes with age. Consider this: A young bull will spot a herd of cows on the other side of the field and rush right over, giving a couple of them a right seeing to. But an old bull will take his time, walk over slowly and fuck the lot."

★

The delicatessen owner was very sad that his forty-year-old daughter had never married. In fact, she didn't even have a boyfriend because she said she wasn't interested. Then one night, her father heard a noise in the shop and creeping down to investigate he spied his daughter masturbating with a large German sausage. The next day, a customer walked into the shop and asked for a selection of French cheeses.

The shop owner fetched Brie, Camembert and some very ripe Roquefort, and laid them out in front of the customer.

"Oh, I'll also have some of that German sausage," he said.

"I'm sorry, sir," came the reply, "that's not for sale. That's my son-in-law."

For the fifth time that week, Jane had arrived home at two in the morning looking very dishevelled. Her parents knew she had an exciting new boyfriend, but her appearance was causing them great concern.

"Janey, Janey," they said the next morning, "this new boyfriend – what's he like? What are his intentions?"

"I don't know," she replied, "he keeps me mostly in the dark."

The tight-fisted couple asked their son what he wanted for his birthday.

"I wanna watch," he replied.

So they let him.

The angry father opened the door to find his daughter canoodling in the porch with her boyfriend.

"It's nearly half past one in the morning," he bellowed, "do you think you can stay here all night?"

"Gosh, I don't know," replied the boyfriend. "I'll have to ring my parents for permission."

★

"How did you get on at school today?" Dad asks his son.

"Okay," he replies. "We had a really hard spelling test, they were such long words."

"Really? Such as?"

"Masturbation," says the boy.

"My goodness!" exclaims Dad, "that is a mouthful."

"No dad," corrects the boy. "A mouthful is a blow job. Masturbation is done by hand."

While his mother was in the kitchen cooking dinner, her young son was playing with his toy garage. For a while, all was quiet and then she heard him say, "Call yourself a bloody mechanic, this fucking car has broken down again."

Then later she overheard him shout, "Hey, you! Get your arse over here and look at this engine."

"Johnny, Johnny," she said, coming into the room. "Enough of that foul language. I won't have you talking like that, now go to your room."

An hour passed and mum let Johnny come back down and continue playing. She smiled as she heard him say, "Bay number 5, sir? That'll be £10 please. Yes, you'll find the carwash around the back. Have a nice day... Oh, good morning Madam, I'm afraid your car isn't ready yet. If you want to know why, go and ask that bloody cow in the kitchen."

★

A father decided to test his 18-year-old son's initiative. He gave him a duck and told him to go into town and come back better off. On his travels, the son met a prostitute and asked for 15 minutes of her time in return for the duck. It was an unusual request, but she accepted and took him back to her flat. After the session, the prostitute was so impressed with his athleticism that she told him she'd give the duck back if they did it again. So later that day, he still had the duck and he'd

enjoyed himself a great deal. Then to his dismay, the duck was frightened by a loud noise. It flew into the path of an oncoming truck and was killed instantly. The driver was so upset he gave the boy £10 compensation.

"So how did it go?" asked the father when his son arrived home.

"Pretty good," replied the son.

"I got a fuck for a duck, a duck for a fuck and £10 for a fucked up duck."

★

A discontented woman had taken her small son for a walk in the woods, but within moments of her looking away, the boy had wandered off. She searched for him for over an hour and it was beginning to grow dark. As a last resort, she looked heavenwards and cried,

"Oh God, please don't let anything happen to my son, please take me instead."

Moments later, she heard crying and there caught in some undergrowth, was her little son.

"Oh thank you, thank you," she said happily, running up to him. Then suddenly she stopped and remarked, "But just before you go, God, he did have his teddy bear with him!"

★

A man and a woman find themselves sharing the same carriage on an overnight sleeper to Glasgow. After half an hour the woman shouts down to the man, "It's quite cold in here, do you think you could pass me another blanket?"

"I've got a better idea," he says, "Why don't we pretend we're married?"

"Well, OK then."

"Good, then get your own bloody blanket."

A father is keen to take his son for an aeroplane ride, but he is unwilling to pay the huge prices charged by most charter pilots. The only person he knows who will do it cheaply is a rather shady stuntman. The stuntman is always looking for a way to make easy money so he suggests that they can have the ride free as long as they don't say anything or make a noise. If they do, then they will have to pay double.

The father agrees and tells his son there must be complete silence or the pilot will not fly.

The next day, the trip takes place and very soon the small plane is soaring high into the sky. The stuntman smiles to himself, certain that once he begins to perform some of his incredible manoeuvres, one of them is sure to make a noise. He loops the loop, flies upside-down, drops like a stone from a great height and many other tricks over the 30 minute period. But not a sound is uttered.

Eventually, admitting defeat, he returns to base.

"That was quite amazing," he says to the father, shaking his hand." I was sure one of you would have broken the silence."

"It was very hard," admits the father, "particularly when my son fell out halfway through the trip."

As the young girl passed her parents' bedroom she saw them both changing to go out. Her father had just come out of the shower and was drying himself.

"Oh Mama!" she cried "What's that?" pointing to her father's well-endowed tackle.

"Ah ha," smiled Mum, "that's something very special."

"Indeed," interrupted her father, "if it wasn't for this you wouldn't be here... Come to think of it, neither would your mother!"

★

The man at the bar looked sadly into his pint of beer and sighed heavily.

"What's up Bob?" asked the landlord. "It's not like you to be so down in the mouth."

"It's my four-year-old son," he said. "The little bugger's got our next-door neighbour pregnant."

"Get away!" exclaimed the landlord. "That's impossible."

"It's not. He punctured all my condoms with a needle."

★

Johnny had been put over his father's knee and given a couple of sharp taps on the backside for swearing at his mum.

"Right son," said Dad sternly, "now tell me why I did that."

"Bloody hell!" replied the boy astonished. "First you whack me and then you don't know why the fuck you did it."

"Now son," said his father. "Let's see how much you've learnt in maths. What's two and two."

After a moment the boy replied, "Four."

"Good," replied his father, "but let's try and be a little quicker. What's four and four?"

This time the boy counted on his fingers and replied "Eight."

"Okay," said Dad patiently, "but try not to use your fingers. Put your hands in your pockets. Now, what's five and five."

After a few moments of fumbling the boy replied, "Eleven."

"Dad," said the young teenager pointing to the different-sized packets of condoms, "Why do they come in different amounts?"

"Well son," replied his dad, "the pack of three is for the lad who gets lucky at the weekends when he goes out clubbing. One for Friday and two for Saturday. Now the pack of six is for the experienced young bachelor who has a date nearly every day of the week. And finally, the pack of 12 is for the married man. One for January, one for February, one for March ..."

"Geraldine, how could you!?" exclaimed her mother, looking at paintings of her naked daughter hanging on the studio wall.

"I can't believe you'd pose nude for your boyfriend."

"Oh Mother, I didn't," she replied. "He must have painted them from memory."

Two hillbillies decide it's time to teach their 20-year-old son about sex.

"Come here, Arnie," calls Pa. "Come into the bedroom, there's something we want to show you."

Arnie shuffles into the bedroom to be greeted by the sight of his parents standing before him stark naked.

"It's time you learnt about sex, so your Ma and I are going to show you. See this hole between your Ma's legs, well watch carefully."

To the boy's astonishment, he watches open-mouthed as his parents get it together on the bed in front of him. Just then, his younger brother walks by and wants to know what all the noise is about.

"Ma and Pa are showing me what sex is," replies Arnie.

"What's sex?" asks Colin.

"Look, I'll show you. See that hole in Pa? Now watch this!"

★

"Mummy, Mummy, what's a pussy?" asked the small boy. His mother went to the encyclopaedia and showed him a picture of a cat.

"That's a pussy," she said.

"Mummy, Mummy, what's a bitch?" continued the little boy.

Again, Mother consulted the encyclopaedia and showed her son a picture of a dog.

But the boy wasn't convinced so he went to his father and asked him what a pussy was. Dad went to his magazine, opened it at the centrefold and drew a circle on the model.

"There you are son," he said, "that's a pussy."

Then the little boy asked him what a bitch was and Dad replied sadly, "Everything outside the circle, son."

A man gets a peanut stuck firmly in his ear and no matter how hard his wife tries, they cannot get it out. Just as they're about to give up, their daughter arrives home with her boyfriend. When they hear what has happened the boyfriend tells them confidently that he knows how to get it out. He sticks 2 fingers up the man's nose and tells him to blow as hard as he can. The man does this and the peanut pops out. Sometime later the parents are talking and mum comments, "Our Vera's got a clever boyfriend there. I wonder what will become of him." "Our son-in-law, by the smell of his fingers," came the reply.

An 18-year old boy says to his father,

"Dad, I keep getting these terrible urges, what can I do about it?"

"I think you'd better go and see my friend Bob, he's a sex therapist, I'm sure he'll be able to help. Pop round to his house this evening."

The boy does as his father suggests but after 5 visits, there's no improvement. The sixth time he goes round the door is opened by Bob's wife who tells him the therapist has been called away on urgent business.

"Can I help at all?" she says.

The boy tells her his problem and within moments she takes him by the hand, leads him upstairs and makes frenzied love to him. The

next day he meets his father who asks him how therapy is going.
"It's great now Dad," smiled the boy. "The therapist's wife has got
more brains between her legs than he has in his head."

**The little girl's mother was entertaining her next door
neighbour when her little daughter walked in.**
"Hello Mrs Crabbit, are you a gardening expert?" she asked.
"No I'm not, why do you ask?" said the puzzled neighbour.
"Mum says if there's any dirt about you'll dig it up."

It was cold and pouring with rain but the boy's mother insisted he go
and feed the animals on their freeholding before he could have
breakfast. The boy went out in a dark rage, kicked the chickens,
punched the cow and threw water all over the pigs. When he got back
inside his mother was furious.
"How dare you!" she fumed. "For that you get no eggs because you
kicked the chickens, no milk because you thumped the cow and no
bacon because of the way you treated the pigs."
Just then, Dad came down the stairs and nearly tripping over the cat,
he gave the animal a mighty kick. The boy turned to his mother and
said, "Are you going to tell him or shall I?"

★

**A little girl went into her parent's bedroom to find her parents
in bed.**
"Well!" she exclaimed. "And you tell me off just for sucking

my thumb."

★

A very rich businessman asked his small son what he would like for Christmas.

"A baby brother please," he replied.

"I'm sorry son, there's no time.. It's only 3 weeks to Christmas."

"Well can't you put more men on the job?" the son suggested.

★

The farmer and his wife were entertaining the local bigwigs when their son runs in and announces to his father in a loud voice.

"Dad, Dad, the bull's fucking the cow."

After a moment of shocked silence, the farmer turns to his son and calmly says,

"Next time son, be a little less explicit. You should have said 'The bull is surprising the cow'.That sort of language comes from associating with riff raff."

Lo and behold, the following week the farmer and his wife are entertaining again when their son rushes in.

"Dad, Dad the bull is surprising the cows."

"Well done, son, you've remembered what I told you, but you should have said the bull is surprising the cow … he can't surprise more than one cow at a time, you know."

"But he can, Dad!" insists the boy. "He's fucking the horse."

★

One evening Father passed his daughter's bedroom and heard her saying her prayers. Smiling to himself, he stopped to listen and heard her say, "God bless Mummy, God bless Daddy, God bless Grandpa, bye bye Grandma."

"How odd" thought Father, but he didn't want his daughter to know he'd been listening so he didn't say anything to her. But tragically, next day Grandma collapsed and died. A few months went by and one evening Father heard his daughter praying again.

"God bless Mummy, God bless Daddy, bye bye Grandpa."

No, it couldn't mean anything thought Father apprehensively, but next morning they received a telegram to say that Grandpa had passed away in his sleep!

The household got back to normal and almost a year passed before father heard his daughter again.

"God bless Mummy, bye bye Daddy."

Absolutely panic-stricken Father stayed up all night, too frightened to sleep in case he didn't wake up. The next morning he walked to work instead of taking the car, in case there was an accident, and spent the day at his desk doing very little but worrying. When he got home that evening he collapsed into a chair, his nerves in pieces, and told his wife all about the nightmare day that he'd had.

She replied, "You're not the only one to have had a bad day. This morning when I opened the front door I found the gasman dead on the front doorstep."

★

Daddy was taking his young son for a walk in the park when they passed two dogs humping. When the boy asked his father what was happening he told him they were making a puppy. A

few days later the little boy caught his mum and dad in the throes of sex and when he asked them what they were doing, Dad replied they were making a baby.

The little boy said, "Well can you turn Mummy over, I'd much rather have a puppy."

A young boy walked into a bar and asked for a bottle of beer and 20 cigarettes.

"Now, now," smiled the barmaid wagging her finger. "Do you want to get me into trouble?"

He replied, "Not at the moment, I just want my beer and fags."

"Mummy, Mummy, are little birds made of metal?"

"Of course not darling, why do you think that?"

"I just heard Dad say he'd like to screw the arse off the bird next door."

The hillbilly couple are out at the drive-in movie, eating hominy grits, drinking beer and doing a bit of serious necking.

"Say Mary-Jo," drawls the boy. "What yew say we get in the back of mah pick-up truck an' have us some real fun?"

"Why Billy-Bob!" exclaims the girl, "how could yew suggest such a thing? An' with mah parents in the pick-up truck next to ours!"

"They're mah parents too!" retorts the boy.

Grandpa and grandson go out together for a days fishing. At lunchtime, the man opens a can of cider.

"Can I have some Grandpa?" asks the boy.

"I tell you what son," replies Grandpa. "Can your willy touch your backside?"

"No Grandpa."

"Then you can't have any cider."

Later on Grandpa gets out his cigarettes.

"Can I have one Grandpa?"

Grandpa replies, "Can your willy touch your backside?"

"No."

"Then it's no to a cigarette."

On the way home, they pass a newsagents and each of them buys a scratch card. Grandpa wins nothing, grandson wins £2,000.

"Are you going to share some of your winnings with me son?" asks Grandpa.

"I'll you what, Grandpa," replies the boy, "can your willy touch your backside?"

"It sure can," replied Grandpa confidently.

"Then go fuck yourself."

★

The little boy's mother had been away for a week's conference and on returning she asked her son how he'd been.

"It was okay," said Ben, "Except there was dreadful thunder and lightning on Tuesday night so me and Daddy snuggled up in the same bed."

"You mean Daddy and I," said his young nanny.

"Oh no," said the boy, "that was Wednesday night, don't you remember?"

★

When Dorothy was expecting twins she interrupted a burglary and got shot twice in the stomach. Fortunately, the babies were delivered safely but the bullets were never recovered. Seventeen years went by when one day her daughter came to her in great distress.

"Oh Mum, I just been to do a wee wee and out popped a bullet."

Dorothy told her it was nothing to worry about and explained what had happened all those years ago. A little later she caught sight of her son, sitting down with his head in his hands. She went up to him, put her arms round his shoulders and said,

"Don't worry, I think I can guess what happened. You went to the toilet and a bullet came out."

"Oh no Mum, it wasn't like that. I was having a wank and I shot the dog."

★

It was an idyllic scene. Little old Grandma was sitting in her rocking chair, knitting a jumper for her granddaughter. On the floor in front of her chair sat her two beautiful grandchildren, quietly looking at some picture books. All of a sudden, the children turned to their grandma saying,

"Oh Grandma, please tell us a story. We love your stories, please, please."

"Well ... I don't know" replied Grandma "I'm a bit tired."

"Oh please Grandma, tell us our favourite story about when you were a whore in Liverpool."

★

"Grandpa, have you got your own football?" asked his grandson.

Puzzled, Grandpa replied, "No, Billy, I don't play football anymore, why do you ask?"

"Because I heard Dad say that when you kicked it, we'd all be able to afford a good holiday."

★

During Sunday school, Tracy turned to her teacher and said,

"Please Miss, I've found out where God lives."

"Really!" smiled the teacher. "Where does he live?"

"At number 12 Beech Street."

"How do you know that?"

"Yesterday, I was passing it on the way to school and I heard a woman from the upstairs bedroom shouting,

"Oh God, Oh God ...."

★

A little boy ran into his mother's room crying hysterically.

"I don't want my willy any more," he wept, "willies are bad!"

"Don't be silly darling," she replied. "Of course willies aren't bad, Why do you say that?"

"Because I've just seen Daddy in the bathroom and he's trying to pull his off."

★

"Daddy, Daddy!" cried little Tom, "please come and look, my pussy cat is lying in the garden with his feet in the air and he won't move."

Assuming the worse, Dad went into the garden to take a look.

"I'm sorry son, I'm afraid Tiddles is dead."

Through his sobs, the little boy asked why the cat's feet were sticking up in the air.

Quick as a flash, Dad replied,

"That's so Jesus can grab hold of them and take him up to heaven."

A few days later, dad comes home from work to find Tom crying in the garden.

"What's happened Tom?" he asked.

"It's Mummy, she nearly died today, like my poor pussy cat!"

"How can that be?" asked dad aghast.

"I went into the summer house a little while back and Mummy was there with her feet in the air shouting 'I'm coming, I'm coming'. Oh Daddy, if it hadn't been for the milkman holding her down, Jesus would have taken her up to heaven!"

A little boy went shopping with his mother and when she began trying some clothes on in the fitting room, he remarked, "You've got big balloons, Mum."

"That's not the right word for them," she replied, "why do you call them that?"

"Because yesterday I saw Daddy blowing up the au pair's."

★

Further down the street, a young girl walked into her parents bedroom to find her mother astride her father. To cover any embarrassment they told her they were playing a game.

"Can I join in?" she asked.

"Of course."

So the girl sits astride Dad as well, jumping up and down, pretending Dad is a horse. As the parents reach a climax, the little girl shouts excitedly,

"Hold on tight Mum, this is where the au pair usually falls off."

★

Mrs Primly is walking down the village street when she sees young Emily pulling a cow by a rope.

"Goodness me!" she exclaims, "What on earth are you doing with that?"

"I'm taking it to the bull," she replies.

"The bull! What a thing to ask a young girl, can't your dad do it?"

"Oh no," replies the girl, "it has to be the bull."

★

Did you hear about the couple who adopted a baby from Spain? They signed up for evening classes in Spanish so that they would be able to understand the baby when it started talking.

★

"Daddy," said the little girl. "May I have a computer for Christmas please?"

"I'm sorry darling, not at the moment, your mum and I have a pile of heavy bills and our new car is costing us heaps of money each month."

The following Spring, the little girl asked her father again for a computer but he repeated what he had told her before. A week later, early in the morning Dad sees his daughter leaving the house with a suitcase in her hand.

"Where are you going?" he asked.

"I'm leaving," said the little girl. "Last night I was walking past your room when I heard you telling Mum you were pulling out and I heard her telling you to wait because she was coming too. So there's no way I'm staying here to cope with all the bills."

★

My mother-in-law and I don't get along.

Take our anniversary for instance. She sent us some monogrammed bath towels.

"Hers and Its."

★

I knew my future mother-in-law didn't like me from the start, when she bit the groom on the wedding cake in half.

★

Next Door Neighbours

Two busybodies were walking through the park slagging everyone off when one says to the other, "Look at her from number 16, breast feeding in public again!"

"My my, that boy's 18 if he's a day, and he's not even her son."

Two neighbours are chatting over the garden wall.
"When my husband comes home from work tonight, he'll probably bring me a huge bunch of flowers."
"Oh isn't that nice, you are lucky."
"No, not really. He'll expect me to take all my clothes off and be on the floor with my legs in the air."
"Oh dear, why's that? Haven't you got any vases?"

Two women talking over the garden fence.
"Why, Beryl, you're looking very pleased with yourself, what's been going on?" asked Mavis.
"Well I've had the most extraordinary week," replied Beryl. "Yesterday I answered the door and standing there was this gorgeous young man who asked me if George was in. When I told him he wasn't, he took me by the hand, led me upstairs, put me on the bed and made love to me all morning. It was fantastic! Then yesterday, he came round again, asked if George was in and when I said no, he took me back up to the bedroom and had me in 3 different positions for more than 3 hours. He never seems to get tired! Then, would you

believe it, he comes back again this morning, asks for George and when I tell him George is at work, he carries me up to the bedroom and takes me time and time again.

Mavis, I can't believe how wonderful it's been. One thing that puzzles me though ... why does he want to see George?"

★

"Billy," said the blonde young neighbour. "I forgot to get some milk at the corner store, do you think you could go for me?"
"No," said the boy, "but I overheard Dad say he could."

★

Two women talking over the garden fence.
"My husband's an efficiency expert."
"What's that then?"
"Well, I'll put it this way. If a woman did it, they'd call it nagging."

★

"Do you know what mothballs smell like?"
"Yes."
"Goodness. How do you get their little legs apart?"

★

Johnny's neighbour, Mrs Morgan, had a celebrated parrot. People from far and wide would come to see the bird because he was such a wonderful conversationalist. There was only one drawback – the parrot was obsessed with ducks. If he saw a duck he had to shag it and unfortunately for Mrs Morgan there was a farm just across the field and the ducks were forever being rogered by her obsessed parrot. One day the farmer came round in a dreadful rage.

"If ever I see your parrot near my ducks again, I'm going to shoot it dead. My poor ducks are worn out and I won't be having it anymore."

Mrs Morgan turned to her parrot angrily.

"You hear that, if it happens again I shall punish you so badly you'll never forget it."

A week went by and the parrot behaved himself but one afternoon when all was quiet he escaped again to do the evil deed.

"That's it!" she screamed, and taking a pair of shears from the garden shed, she cut all the feathers off his head until he was completely bald. The following day, Mrs Morgan was hosting a cocktail party and the parrot was put in the corner and ordered not to move all night. As the guests arrived they were greeted by their hostess and then the parrot in the corner who would say loudly but politely, "Good evening Sir, Good evening Madam."

However, the last two guests to enter were both bald and as soon as the parrot caught sight of them he screamed, "OK, you two duck shaggers, over here in the corner with me."

Three men on the way home from work were moaning about their dull, tedious lives.

"Let's try and liven it up a bit," said one."I know, when we get home, we'll do exactly whatever our wives tell us to do."

They all shook hands and went their separate ways, agreeing to meet up the next morning and swap stories. The following day, on the way to work the first one told them what happened.

"I got in, lit a cigarette and all of a sudden I sneezed. The cigarette dropped out of my mouth onto our new sofa and burnt a hole. 'Why don't you burn the whole house down while you're at it?' my wife said, so I did. I haven't seen her since, she stormed off threatening me with divorce."

The second man looked very downcast.

"My wife's gone home to her mother. When I got in last night I decided to mow the lawn but I went over a pebble which flew up and broke the kitchen window.

She said 'Well done. Why don't you smash them all?' So I did, and that's when she left."

"That's nothing," replied the third man. "My wife's reported me to the police for indecent assault. She'd gone out for the evening and by the time she got home I was already in bed. Of course, when she got in beside me the old todger started to look lively so I put my hand on her pussy but she didn't want to know.

'You can cut that out,' she said, so I did. Does anyone want a toupee?"

What is the definition of a real friend?
One who goes into town and gets two blow jobs, then comes back and gives one to you.

Two women talking over the garden wall. The first said,
"It's no good Beryl, I'm at my wits end. I can't stand the sight

of George any longer. He treats me like shit, he's never at home, he just uses the place as an hotel and I know he's shagging everyone in sight. It's had a terrible effect upon me, I've already lost a stone in weight."

"Leave him Sylvia, leave him and take him for everything you can," replied her outraged friend.

"Oh I will, I will, just as soon as I lose another half stone."

Finding her cooker had packed in, Beryl called up the repair man and arranged for him to come round on Tuesday morning.

"I won't be in," she said, "but I'll leave my key with the next door neighbour. Please leave the bill with her when you've finished and I'll pop a cheque in the post. Oh, by the way. I've a very fierce guard dog named Growler, but you'll be alright if he sees the neighbour let you in. I've also got a parrot but be warned, whatever you do, please don't say anything to it."

Having been given all the instructions the repair man went round on Tuesday morning and soon had the cooker repaired, although the whole time he'd been there he'd had to put up with a stream of obscenities from the parrot. As he was packing up to go his temper finally snapped and he turned to the parrot saying,

"Drop dead, you fucking little shit."

The parrot went very quiet and then with a gleam in his eye rose to his full height and said,

"Growler, kill ...."

A man looks over his garden wall to see his neighbour digging

a hole in the back garden.

"What are you up to?" he asks.

"I'm digging a hole for my dead hamster," he replies.

"Sorry to hear that, but it's a big hole for a hamster isn't it?"

"Of course it is, it's inside your fucking cat!" he yells.

"... and another thing," continued the complaining woman, "I now know what eternity feels like. It's the time it takes between me coming and him leaving."

Two men, who've been good friends for years, go off hiking over the Yorkshire Dales. They walk 20 miles during the morning and stop for lunch at the Travellers' Rest for sandwiches and a few pints of beer. Of course, halfway through the afternoon Bob is dying for a pee and rushes into the undergrowth to relieve himself. All of a sudden Pete hears a mighty scream and rushing over he discovers that Bob has been bitten on his todger by a rare snake.

"Don't worry Bob, I'll go and get help," says Pete and he sets off for the nearest village. The doctor tells him that his mate will die unless he acts immediately.

"You need to suck out all the poison from the wound as soon as possible."

Pete returns to Bob who's lying there in agony.

"What did he say?" asks Bob.

"Sorry mate, the doctor says you're going to die."

Three men go away for the weekend on a hunting trip and as they are sitting round the camp fire on the first night, they start bragging.

The first said, "If it hadn't been for my quick thinking, our next door neighbours would never have survived the fire. I happened to see smoke coming out of an upstairs window, so I immediately rushed into their house and dragged them all from their beds before the whole place went up."

"Very good," said the second man, "but I foiled a daring bank raid. There I was in the bank when these armed men burst through the door and took everyone hostage. With my quick thinking, though, I managed to hide in the utilities cupboard and when all was quiet, I got out and set off the alarm."

The third man said nothing. He just continued stirring the hot ashes with his penis.

★

Three female friends were walking in the country when they stumbled across a very old bottle, half hidden in the earth. On taking the stopper out, a genie appeared and told them he had the power to grant them more intelligence.

The first woman, who was a 'plain Jane' asked for 50% more intelligence and she was turned into a famous surgeon.

The second woman asked for 25% more intelligence and she became a teacher.

The third woman who was a bit of a stunner and one for the men, replied, "I don't think I want any. It's good to be dumb,

men will do anything for you. In fact, I think I'd like to be even dumber."

And on saying that, she turned into a man.

Two old men are chatting over the garden wall.

"I hear old Bates is living with a gorilla," says one.

"Well I never, is it male or female?"

"Female of course. You know old Bates, there's nothing unnatural about him."

Two young girls talking over the garden fence.

"Honestly Joan, my new boyfriend's got submarine hands."

"What do you mean?"

"You never know where they'll turn up next."

★

A very poor uneducated and plain woman found herself in dire straits. She was only 30 but already she had 5 children and her husband had abandoned her. It seemed as if the children would be taken away but a kindly welfare worker took the family on and managed to re-house them, sort out debts and get her a little job. A year went by before the welfare worker saw the woman again, but to her shock and amazement she was 5 months pregnant.

"Oh no, why have you done this, you were just getting back on your feet and building up your self respect. Whose is it?"

The woman looked tearful and replied,

"It's the next door neighbour's. I was just so flattered that he'd actually asked me."

A single man moved in next door to a couple and it wasn't long before he and the wife became attracted to each other, but they managed to keep their feelings in check. Then one hot summer's afternoon, the single man went round for afternoon tea. While there, he noticed the couple's guttering was full of weeds so he volunteered to go up the ladder and clear it for them. While he was up there, the couple lay out on the lawn sunbathing and as the husband rubbed sun lotion on his wife's back, the man shouted down,

"Hey, you two, no sex down there!"

"We're not," they yelled.

A couple of minutes went by and the man up the ladder shouted again.

"Hey, stop all that sex!"

Again, they shouted up, "We're not having sex."

Some time later, the man came down for a rest and the husband said he'd finish off. So up he went leaving his wife and next door neighbour sunbathing on the lawn. The nearness of their bodies was too much for them and soon they were making mad passionate love.

"Well, bugger me," said the husband looking down from the ladder. "Up here, it really does look as if they're having sex."

A couple and their precocious son moved into the close and invited all their neighbours round for a 'getting to know you' cocktail party. Unfortunately, the young son, who should have been in bed, kept coming back down and bothering his parents.

"Don't worry," said the retired Sergeant-Major, "I'll soon get the boy settled."

After a few minutes the guest rejoined the party and nothing more was seen of the son. The party was a great success and everyone left a little the worse for wear.

"Oh, by the way," said the couple to the Sergeant-Major as he was putting on his coat to leave. "Thank you for settling down our son, what is your secret?"

"Oh quite simple really, I just taught him how to masturbate."

Three women were discussing safe sex. The first said she used the pill, the second said she always carried a packet of condoms and the third said she always used a tin with a few pebbles inside. The other two looked at her in amazement.

"How does that work?" they asked.

"Oh, it's easy really. I get the man to stand on the tin and when I hear the pebbles start to rattle I kick it out from under him."

Two women are talking over the garden wall and the conversation turns to money.

"You know, Doris, I've discovered a great way to get more money out of my old man. Last week I wore a low necked jumper when we went shopping and as I bent over the supermarket freezer one of my boobs popped out. You should have seen Bill, he nearly had a blue fit. I told him it was because I didn't have enough money to buy a new bra so he's increased my housekeeping. You ought to try it."

The following week, the two women met up for another chat and Doris was asked if she had taken her friend's advice.

"Oh, it was a disaster!" exclaimed Doris. "We were just about to go down the bingo when I lifted my skirt and told my husband I had no knickers on because I couldn't afford to buy any. The old skinflint, he threw me a quid and told me to buy a comb. 'At least you can look tidy', he said."

With The Ball and Chain

She said bitterly, "When all that is stiff is his socks, take the money and run."

The woman went to the beauty parlour and after her treatment, said to the beautician, "Do you think my husband will think I'm beautiful?"
"I should think so. He still drinks a lot, doesn't he?"

The husband came down to breakfast, holding his head in his hands and moaning.
"So Gerald," said his wife, "have you ever been told you're the most handsome man in town?"
"No dear."
"And have you ever been told you're the best dancer in town?"
"No dear."
"So has anyone ever told you that you're irresistible to women?"
"Certainly not dear."
"Then pray, where did you get all those silly ideas at the party last night?"

"Is that the obituary section of the *Clarion*?" asked the woman.
"Yes, madam, can I help you?"
"I'd like to put a notice in, reporting the death of my husband from

gunshot wounds."

"Good gracious, when did it happen?"

"Just as soon as I find the cheating bugger."

★

The husband was standing on the crowded platform when he thought he saw his wife amongst the crowd. He pushed his way through the people, came up behind her and gave her a big hug and a lip-smacking kiss on the neck.

To his horror, as the woman turned round, he realised it wasn't his wife.

"Oh no, I'm so sorry," he said blushing profusely. "It's just that your head looks like my wife's behind."

★

"Hello Joan. You look happy today, what's going on?"

"Oh Maisie, I am," she replied. "Last night my husband brought home a big tube of KY jelly. He said it would please me greatly. And it did. When he went to the bathroom I smeared it all over the bedroom door and the silly sod couldn't get back in!"

"You're a fool to yourself Ethel," said her neighbour scornfully. "That husband of yours has you running around in circles."

"Oh don't say that," replied Ethel with spirit. "He helps with the housework, you know. He sits in front of the television and gathers dust."

Said the disillusioned woman,
"The only time my husband wakes up stiff is when he's been jogging the night before."

The old couple had just finished lunch when the wife remarked,
"You know James, we're not getting any younger, we've got to accept that it won't be too long before one of us passes on."
"Oh come on Ruby," he replied, "don't let's talk about such things."
"Well okay, but I just want you to know I think I'll go to Eastbourne when that happens."

The old woman turned sadly to her friend and said,
"The spark's gone out of our marriage, Flo. These days, when we're in bed, I bring out the animal in Alfred. He runs to the door, scratching and whining to get out."

An old couple had been married for thirty years, and in all that time no one could remember when he didn't chew tobacco. He was always seen with heavily stained teeth and black gunge dribbling out of his mouth. Now the thing that puzzled their neighbours was how his wife could have stayed with him so long. In her younger days, she had been very attractive and even now, she could turn a head or two. Two

days before the couple's wedding anniversary, her friend finally plucked up the courage to ask, "How could you have stayed with him so long. That awful black, filthy stuff forever dribbling from his mouth?"

"Well I have thought of leaving him on many occasions," she said, "but I couldn't bear to kiss him goodbye."

★

After an hour of playing bridge and getting beaten every time, the husband excused himself to go to the bathroom. As he left the room, the wife turned to her hosts and remarked scornfully,

"This'll be the first time I've known what's in his hand all night."

★

A woman went to the doctor's complaining that her sex life was very unsatisfactory.

"My old man says I'm frigid," she explained.

"Don't upset yourself," replied the doctor kindly. "I think I have the answer. Just take one of these pills an hour before lovemaking and you'll appreciate the difference."

So the woman took the pill and her whole body became electric. She couldn't wait for her husband to get home.

Unfortunately, he went straight to the pub after work and the magic moment was missed. When she went back to the doctor's, he asked her how it had gone and she explained the dreadful disappointment she'd felt and how the lack of fulfilment had made her ill.

"Mmm," mused the doctor, "it's a shame there wasn't another

man to take his place."

"Another man!" she cried. "I don't need pills for other men!"

A worried man went to the doctor's and asked him to come and visit his wife who was ill in bed with a bad chest infection.

"Just one thing in confidence, doctor," he said. "My wife never wears any knickers. I hate it. I beg her to change but she just won't listen to me. I wonder if you could somehow link her illness to her lack of underwear. Maybe it will convince her."

The doctor agreed and accompanied the man home. He examined the wife's throat and her chest very thoroughly.

"I'm afraid it's a touch of bronchitis," he told her. "I'll write out a prescription for you but I would also strongly recommend that you wear some knickers. It won't help your illness, not wearing them."

She looked at him quizzically.

"Are you trying to tell me that just by looking down my throat you could see I wasn't wearing any knickers?"

"Well...er...yes" he answered.

"In that case," she said nastily, "would you mind looking up my arse and telling me if my hat's on straight."

★

The couple had been married for seven years and their life together had lost it's sparkle. Sex was a disaster.

"There doesn't seem to be any passion left," said her husband one day. "Maybe we should part company."

Now that filled the wife with dread because she didn't want to

lose all the comforts of her married life. It would mean she'd have to find a job! That night she was determined to show him what he would miss. She dressed in her sexiest negligee and actively started to move a bit during their lovemaking. Her husband was astonished, but delighted. The only strange thing was that every 30 minutes, she would excuse herself and disappear into the bathroom, then return and continue more passionately than before. Although the husband didn't want to spoil the moment, he got so curious he eventually had to find out what was going on. The next time she went into the bathroom, he sneaked in after her and to his amazement, she was standing in front of the mirror saying over and over again, "He's not my husband...he's not my husband...he's not my husband."

Fed up with his wife's excuse of always having a headache, the husband came up with a foolproof plan. The next time they went to bed she said, as usual, "not tonight, darling, I've got a headache." "Really?" he replied. "Well it's a good thing I've dusted my dick in paracetamol then."

A journalist interviewed a local woman when he heard she'd had four children, all born three years apart on May 20th. "That's astonishing," he remarked, "and what does your husband do for a living?" "Oh, he's a precision grinder," came the reply.

I'm not saying my wife is ugly, but she has to sneak up on her glass to get a drink.

"Doctor, doctor. It's the wife. She's having trouble with her eyesight," said the agitated husband.
"Really?" replied the doctor, "in what way?"
"She keeps having visions of a pearl necklace."

A man walked into his home and yelled at his wife.
"Mildred, I've just discovered our marriage is illegal!"
"How come?" she replied.
"Your father didn't have a licence for that shotgun."

★

"My wife caught a Peeping Tom last night just as she was getting ready for bed. Phew! She was so angry, she beat him black and blue."
"I'm not surprised. It's a dreadful feeling to think that someone was watching you as you got undressed."
"No, no, it wasn't that. It was when he tried to close the curtains."

★

There was a couple who liked to party every night. One day, on the way home from work, having spent his last £5 in the pub at lunchtime, the husband passed an old beggar and threw him his last few coins. Lo and behold, the beggar turned into a genie and granted the man one wish for being so kind to him.

"I could do with a drink," said the man.

"Well I've got just the answer," replied the genie. "Every time you need a pee, you'll piss 5mls of brandy. It'll be the best you've ever had." "Get away with you," laughed the man and continued home. However the incident stayed in the man's head and the next time he went to the loo, he peed into a small container. It smelled like brandy. He sipped it – and it tasted wonderful.

"Hey, Marge, get a load of this," he yelled to his wife and for the rest of the evening they drank to their heart's content. Every day he'd come home, Marge would fetch the glasses and away they'd go.

Then on Saturday night the husband turned to his wife and said, "Marge, bring me one glass please."

She did as she was asked and he peed into it.

"Why only one glass tonight?" she asked puzzled.

"Well my love," he replied, "I thought tonight you could drink straight from the bottle."

★

"Colin," she whispered, nudging him in the ribs to wake him up. "I can hear noises downstairs, I think we've got burglars. Go and see." But Colin refused to move.

"What's happened to you?" she hissed. "You were brave when you married me."

"I know," he replied, "that's what all my friends said."

"Look at this!" exclaimed the angry husband to his wife, "the bank has returned the cheque you wrote last week."

"Oh great," she replied. "I wonder what I'll spend it on next."

Why are men who have pierced ears ready for marriage? They've known pain and bought jewellery.

A man sat staring sadly into his pint of beer.

"Hello Jack, what's wrong?" asked his mate, sitting down next to him.

"It's the wife," he replied. "We had a terrible fight last night and she came crawling over to me on her hands and knees..."

"Oh Lord! That's awful," interrupted his friend.

"...and she said 'come out from under that bed or I'll put you in hospital'."

Percy arrived home in the early hours of the morning, drunk as a skunk. Not wanting to face his wife's wrath, he very quietly tiptoed up the stairs but just as he got to the top, the cuckoo clock cuckooed once.

Percy cursed and thinking quickly cuckooed another eleven times, knowing his wife would have woken up at the sound of the clock.

"You're very late," said his wife, sitting up in bed.

"Oh, perhaps a little," he replied, "it's only 12 o'clock." With that he slipped into bed and was just closing his eyes when

she replied, "Mmm, by the way, you'd better take the clock in for repairs tomorrow. It cuckooed once at four o'clock, said 'Oh fuck', belched, farted and then cuckooed another eleven times."

Two men, both sporting black eyes, found themselves travelling in the same railway carriage.

"Excuse me," said the first man. "I can't help but notice we've both got black eyes. How did you get yours?"

"I just said something by accident," replied the other. "I went to the counter to buy my ticket and there was the most gorgeous blonde you've ever seen. Not only that, she had the biggest breasts ever. I was so overcome, instead of asking for a ticket to Pittsburgh, I asked for a picket to Tittsburgh. Boom! She threw me a right."

"Yeah, I can understand that," mused the first man. "I got mine the same way, by saying something accidentally. It was at breakfast this morning when my wife asked me to pass the marmalade. I replied, 'Get it yourself, you hard-bitten bitch, you've ruined my fucking life'."

★

A man walked into a chemist and asked for a large-size condom. He then went next door to the sweet shop and asked for the condom to be filled with four scoops of ice cream.
The shopkeeper was dumbfounded.
"Excuse me, sir, I have to ask. Why are you filling this with ice cream?"
"Well, it's my wife's birthday," he replied. "Over the years I've

bought her many, many things from jewels and furs to exotic holidays to labour saving devices such as a washing machine, microwave, dishwasher and every conceivable kitchen gadget."

"So?" puzzled the shopkeeper.

"So, tonight, I'm going to give her a deep freeze."

★

Geoffrey found his host in the library.

"I'm very sorry," he began. "I just walked into the bathroom to find your wife having a bath. Do forgive me."

His host looked up sadly and replied, "Bloody skinny bugger, isn't she?"

★

Over a few pints of beer, two men were so engrossed in their conversation that they didn't notice the time. Suddenly last orders were called and the first man cursed out loud.

"Bugger! That's me for the cold-shoulder treatment, I promised the wife I'd be home early."

He looked glumly into his pint and continued, "I just can't win. Whenever I go out I make sure none of the doors squeak, I oil the garden gate, I move anything I might trip over in the dark and then when I get home, I take my shoes off before going upstairs, undress in the bathroom and slip very quietly into bed. And it never bloody works! She still turns over and shouts 'Where have you been until this time of night?'"

"No mate," said the second man, "you're doing it all wrong. When I get home late at night, I swing the garden gate backwards and forwards to make as much squeaking noise as possible. Then I slam the front door, turn on all the lights, and stomp up the stairs into the bedroom. I jump into bed and give the wife a good nudge in the ribs and say 'How about it then love?' and you can bet you've never seen a woman sleep so deeply."

"It's no good!" cried the downtrodden husband. "I can't go on. I'm off to join the Foreign Legion."
"Very well," retorted the wife, "but don't let me find you trailing sand all over my nice new carpet when you get back."

Walter was hammering away in the garden when George popped his head up over the wall.
"Fancy a pint, Walt?" he asked.
"No, I can't," replied Walter sadly. "The wife's ill in bed, so I've got to look after her."
As if on cue, they heard terrible noises coming from the house.
"Is that her coughing?" asked George.
"Don't be daft," replied Walter. "She couldn't get inside this. It's too small. It's going to be a new kennel for the dog."

As John got undressed, ready for bed, his wife turned to him in alarm. "John, why have you got that cork sticking out of your bum?"

"Oh no," groaned John, putting his head in his hands. "If only I hadn't gone to the tip this morning," he continued. "While I was there, I spotted this bottle glinting in the sun. I rubbed off the mud to get a good look and a genie appeared. He said he'd grant me anything I wanted."

"Well, what did you say?" asked his wife impatiently.

"I said, no shit."

★

A man went to the doctor's complaining that he could no longer satisfy his wife's sexual desires.

"We'll soon put that right," said the doctor, "take two of these pills before bed and you'll see a great difference."

That night, the man got out his bottle of pills and took two. Then he thought to himself "the wife's got a good sexual appetite" so he took two more. What an evening! The man had never felt so virile. He took his wife to bed and satisfied her time and time again until she fell into an exhausted sleep. Around three in the morning, she woke up to find her husband wasn't in bed. So she went in search of him. At the bottom of the stairs, she found the cat, purring contentedly, then in the kitchen she found the dog wagging its tail enthusiastically. But there was no sign of her husband. Suddenly, she heard a noise from the shed and when she peered through the door, there was her husband with his todger in a vice and some sandpaper in his hand. "George, what are you doing?" she gasped.

"Listen Doris, you're satisfied, the cat's satisfied, the dog's satisfied, so I'm not going to leave the budgie out of this!"

★

A Nod to Confucius

Did you hear about Santa Claus going to the psychiatrist? He didn't believe in himself.

"How do you say 'screw you' in agent talk?"
"Trust me."

There had been such heavy snow overnight that the poor little bird was unable to find adequate shelter and fell to the ground in a dead faint. As time passed, a cow ambled along and dropped a cow pat on top of it. The dung was so warm, the little bird began to thaw out and was so overjoyed at his surprise rescue that he sang at the top of his voice. Unfortunately for him, a mean old cat came along, heard the singing, discovered the little bird and ate it.
So, people, beware.
Not everyone who drops shit on you is an enemy and not everyone who gets you out of shit is a friend. Even more importantly, when you find you're in deep shit, keep your mouth shut.

What's the difference between 365 days in a year and 365 condoms?
One's a good year and the other's a fucking good year.

An ornithological meteorologist is a man who looks at birds and can tell whether...

★

I went to this discussion group on premature ejaculation. In fact, I was five minutes early, but it was all over.

★

The man was so fat he used to rock himself to sleep trying to get up.

★

He's not only unlucky, he's also very short. Yesterday he walked under a black cat.

★

I wish I hadn't bought that cheap suit. Yesterday I went out. It was only cloudy but it shrank three inches.

★

Why do bald men have holes in their pockets? They like to run their hands through their hair.

★

Why is the Irish pound called the punt? Because it rhymes with bank manager.

★

There's one thing wrong with oral sex – the view.

★

Have you noticed how cars only break down on the way home and never when you're going to work?

★

Did you hear about the unhappy atheist?
He had no one to talk to during orgasm.

★

Did you hear about the drug addict?
He started on heroin, went onto curry, progressed to madras, then vindaloo, and now he's in a Korma!

★

What's better than roses on your piano?
Tulips on your organ.

★

Why do Scotsmen wear kilts?

So the sheep won't hear the zip.

★

A bad football team is like an old bra.
No cups and very little support.

★

What have a diamond ring and David Beckham got in common?
Both come in a posh box.

What's the difference between like and love?
Spit and swallow.

A dangerous lunatic escaped from the mental institution and raped a washer woman before making his escape.
The headline in the local paper read, "Nut screws washer and bolts."

What's the difference between a vulture and your mother-in-law?
A vulture waits until you're dead.

Old proverb:
Girls who look for trouble often get a belly full.

Wise old saying:
Girls who use their heads can stop the population explosion.

Words of wisdom from a philosopher:
"It all comes down to the same thing in the end. Live life like a dog. If you can't eat it or fuck it, then piss on it."

★

Old saying:

May your organ never quit while you are halfway through your favourite piece.

★

What do you get if you merge Xerox with Wurlitzer?
A company that makes reproductive organs.

★

Which one is the odd one out: Luncheon meat, soya bean or a vibrator?
Luncheon meat; the other two are meat substitutes.

★

Did you hear about the two cannibals who caught a clown?
As they began eating it, one side to the other
"Hey wait a minute, do you taste something funny?"

★

At Play

Among the Animals

A man took his dog to the vets and asked for its tail to be completely removed.

"But why?" asked the vet. "That's a bit drastic."

The man replied,

"My mother-in-law's coming to stay next week and I want to make sure there are no signs of any welcome."

The dog auditioned for a part in the new summer show. He told half a dozen jokes, using different accents, tap-danced and closed with a song.

"What d'you think?" the owner asked the agent.

"Well, I don't know," replied the agent, shaking his head. "The delivery's good but the material's very weak."

As the stranger walked into the store, he saw a sign that read 'Beware of the Dog'. The next moment he saw an old sheep dog sprawled out on the floor, fast asleep.

"Is that the dog referred to on that sign?" he asked the storekeeper.

"Yes, it sure is," came the reply.

"Well, it's hard to believe the dog is so dangerous. Why did you put the sign up?"

"Because since I've put the sign up, people have stopped tripping over him."

Just as the man was going into the bar, a crocodile tapped him on the shoulder.

"Fancy making some quick money?" he hissed.

"Bloody hell, a talking crocodile!" he exclaimed. "I can't believe it."

"Sshh," whispered the crocodile, "now listen to me. We'll go into the bar and you bet everyone in there that I can talk. It can't fail."

The man was delighted with the idea, so he carried out the plan, took everyone's money and then asked the crocodile to speak.

Silence. It didn't say a word. Eventually the man had to pay out hundreds of pounds before storming out of the pub, seething with rage.

"You fucking wanker," he yelled at the crocodile, "you've cost me a fortune and I'm going to make a handbag out of you, RIGHT NOW!".

"Calm down, calm down," replied the crocodile. "When we go back in there tomorrow, just imagine the odds we'll get."

After fifteen years of service in the house of Lord and Lady Muck, the cook was asked to leave to make way for someone younger and more dynamic. On the day of departure, she received her final wages, only to discover that the stingy pair had thrown in a meagre £10 extra as a 'thank you' for loyal service.

"Well, I never!" she exclaimed, throwing the money at the dog.

"Why on earth did you do that?" they demanded.

"At least I'll show proper appreciation to those who've worked hard. That's to say thanks to the dog for helping me clean all the dishes over these past fifteen years."

★

The woman went along to the dog behavioural centre to tell them about her problem pet.

"He keeps chasing cars," she explained.

"Well, not to worry. It's quite normal and in time the dog will grow out of it."

"But you don't understand," she wailed. "He keeps burying them in the back garden."

★

The man was very proud of his guard dog, which he would leave outside his house to warn off any would-be burglars. Then one day, there came a frantic knocking at the door and on opening it, the man saw a distressed woman.

"Is that your dog outside?" she cried.

"Yes," he replied.

"Well, I think my dog's just killed it."

"What!?" roared the man. "What sort of a dog have you got?"

"A peke."

"A peke!" he exclaimed.

"How could your dog kill my big guard dog?"

"I think it got stuck in his throat," she replied sadly.

"Hey, come over here," hissed a voice. Looking round the man could see no one but an old mangy greyhound.

"Yes, over here," said the greyhound. "Look at the state of me. I'm stuck here in this shed when I should be out winning more races. I was a triple champion in my time, you know."

The man was dumbfounded. A talking dog! He could become famous. Everyone would want to see it. Millions could be made. He went to look for the dog's owner.

"I'd like to buy your dog," he said, "is it for sale?"

The owner shook his head and said,

"No mate, you don't want that old thing."

"Oh but I do," persisted the man. "I'll give you £100 for it."

"Well all right, but I think you're making a great mistake."

"Why's that?"

"That dog's a bloody liar. He's never won a race in his life."

A variety show producer is on the look-out for a new act, and one day he happens to be walking round a country fair when he notices a group of people huddled around one particular stall. As he approaches, he sees a chicken dancing up and down on an old ceramic pot. The audience are obviously enjoying the act, so the producer asks the man if the chicken is for sale. After a lot of hard bargaining, they eventually decide on a sum of £1,500 and the producer goes off happily, with the chicken and the pot safely under his arm. However, two days later he storms back in a very angry mood.

"You double-crossing bastard!" yells the producer. "You tricked me, that chicken hasn't danced a step since I bought him."

"Mmm," mused the man, thoughtfully. "Did you light the candle under the pot?"

The baker's shop was quite empty when the dog walked in with a basket in his mouth, a list and money tied round his neck. The assistant looked at the list, filled the basket with two loaves of bread, three doughnuts and a treacle tart, and the dog left swiftly. Every Tuesday afternoon the same thing would happen. The dog would arrive at the quietest time, get the basket filled and then disappear. The assistant became more and more intrigued. One Tuesday, she decided to follow the dog and discover where it went when it left the shop. Having got permission for some time off, she closely followed the animal. He crossed the busy high street, took a short cut up an alley, walked across the park and strolled into the council estate. Five minutes later, he turned into a garden and walked up to the front door where he rang the bell.

All of a sudden, the door was flung open and the dog was booted back down the path. Outraged at this behaviour, the assistant called from the road,

"What do you think you're doing? This is a very special dog, don't treat it in such a cruel way."

"Keep out of this!" snarled the man. "This bloody dog's got to learn. That's the second time this month he's forgotten his keys!"

A man tried to smuggle a puppy into the country to avoid the quarantine laws, but accidentally drew attention to himself as he tried to walk casually through customs. He had put the dog down his trousers but every time he took a step, his whole body would shake and he kept making little moaning sounds.

"Excuse me sir, is there anything wrong?" enquired the customs official.

"Yes Officer," gasped the man in a strangled voice. "I tried to smuggle a puppy into the country by putting it down my trousers."

"Oh yes?" smiled the officer knowingly, "you've just discovered it's not house-trained, have you?"

"No," replied the agitated man, "I've just discovered it's not weaned."

"I'm sorry Doreen," said her husband gently. "Old Rover's getting very old, he can hardly walk and he doesn't hear so well anymore. I think you have to prepare yourself for the worst."

"Nonsense," replied his wife, "there's nothing wrong, look I'll show you."

"Come on Rover," she called. "Come here Rover, and sit."

"Oh dear," sighed her husband. "I told you his hearing was affected. I'll go and get the mop and bucket."

"Just give me a shandy," said Bob to the landlord.

"Blimey, you must be bad," replied the landlord, shaking his head. "I've never known you to order anything less than a double scotch."

"No. I'm on the wagon," replied Bob sadly. "I got so drunk last night, I went home and blew chunks."

"Oh come on!" said the landlord. "Everyone does that now and again."

"No, no, you don't understand," groaned Bob. "Chunks is the name of my dog."

Why do dogs stick their snouts in blondes' crotches?
Because they can.

A man walked into a country pub with a flea bitten old dog on a lead. The bar was full of wise old country folk, most of them had big dogs lying at their feet. He addressed the crowd.

"See here," he said, pointing to his dog. "This dog understands everything I say. Not just command words like "sit", "lie", "beg" and all that crap, but proper sentences. I'll wager anyone £2 that he'll do exactly as I say."

The customers looked down at the mangy old dog and one by one they took up the bet until there was nearly £100 in the kitty.

"Okay," said the man, putting up his £100. "Watch this". He picked up his dog and threw him on the open fire. "Patch, get off that fire!" he yelled.

Before the race meeting had begun, some of the horses were boasting about their achievements.

"Well I've won over half the races I've been in, and I've been placed in the rest," said the bay horse.

"I've won 18 races out of 24," said the black.

"I've only lost one race in the whole of my career," said the white.

"Excuse me," interrupted a greyhound who'd been listening to them, "I've won 20 races out of 20."

The horses looked down on him in astonishment.

"Bloody hell," said one, "a talking dog!"

A woman was walking through the park when she spotted a man and a dog playing chess. She watched the game for a few minutes and then remarked,

"I can hardly believe what I'm seeing. A dog playing chess. What a clever animal!"

"He's not that clever, madam," replied the man. "I've beaten him four games out of six."

This man loved his pet ferret so much he never went anywhere without it. One night he went to the cinema but was told that ferrets were not allowed in. Unperturbed, he went round the corner and stuffed the ferret down his trousers, then bought his ticket and sat down to enjoy the film. However after half an hour the ferret became very restless, so the man opened his flies to give the animal some air. Two girls were sitting next to him and suddenly one turned to the other and whispered urgently, "Tracy, that man next to me has got his willy out!"

"Never mind, just ignore it," replied her friend.

"I can't," she gasped, "it's nibbling my knee."

A motorist was having trouble with his car and stopped to see what the problem was. He'd been peering under the bonnet for a few minutes when a voice behind him said,

"That's your carburettor, that. "

Startled, the motorist looked around but all he could see was an old cow in the nearby field. He felt spooked out by the whole episode so jumped quickly back in the car and headed for the nearest garage. Later, as the mechanic was inspecting the car, the motorist recounted his experience.

"Was it a black and white cow with a crooked horn?"

"Yes, it was," he replied.

"Oh, you don't want to listen to her," says the mechanic, "doesn't know the first thing about engines, that cow."

"What have you got there, Bob?" asks his mate.

"It's an elephant that fucks cats."

"Get away, that's impossible!"

"Look, I'll show you. See that cat over there?" And as he looks the elephant goes over and stamps on it. "See, I told you so.".

A man went to the pet shop to buy a parrot but the only one on offer cost £500.

"Why is it so expensive?" he asked.

"Ah well, it's a very special parrot, it lays square eggs," said the pet shop owner.

"How very odd. OK, I'll take it, but just one thing – does it talk?"

"Well, it can do, but up to now all I've heard is 'Aagh, oooh, bugger...'."

A man walked into a club with a pet snake under his arm.

"Hey, you can't bring that snake in here, he might bite one of our members," said the Manager.

"Oh that's no problem, you just get a friend to suck the poison out."

"But what if he bites someone up the backside?"

"Well, then you really find out who your friends are."

A man goes into the vet's.

"Say 'aaah'...." says the vet.

"Why?" asks the man.

"Because my dog's just died."

A man was desperate to buy a singing canary, but none of the shops for miles around had one in stock. Eventually, he was advised to buy a mavi bird.

"If you file the bird's beak down by 3/8", it'll sing just like a canary," he was told. "But be very careful, any more than that, and the bird will die because he won't be able to eat."

So the man went to the hardware shop and bought a file and a steel tape measure. A few weeks later, he happened to go back to the shop for some nails and the storekeeper gave him a friendly greeting.

"Hello sir, I remember you. You had a mavi bird, how is it?"

The man looked downcast and answered, "He's dead, poor thing."

"Oh, I am sorry. Did you file too much off the beak?"

"Oh no. He was dead when I got him out of the vice."

Three rats meet up in the underground sewer and start boasting about their toughness.

"I'm not scared of anything," says the first, "I'll raid any house, take what I want and they never catch me."

"That's nothing," replies the second scornfully. "Whenever I see rat poison I just chew it up and spit it out." They wait for the third to speak but he gets up and starts to move away.

"Hey, what's up, where are you going?"

He replies haughtily,

"I ain't got time for this, I'm off to fuck the cat."

A woman was given a parrot for her birthday but the bird had grown up with a bad attitude and some of the foulest language she had ever heard. Try as she might – teaching it new words, soothing it with music – she could not get the parrot to change. One day, he was even worse than usual. She got so angry that she put him in the freezer and closed the door. The bird could be heard squawking, kicking and screaming, and then all went quiet. Frightened that she may have harmed him, she quickly opened the door and the parrot calmly stepped out.

"If I've offended you in any way, I'm very sorry," he said. "I promise it will never happen again. By the way, what did the chicken do?"

A man buys two dogs from the pet shop and no matter what he does he can't stop them from shagging each other. He tries throwing cold water over them, putting pepper on their backsides, and then changing their diet, but nothing works. In desperation he rings the vet in the middle of the night to tell him the problem.

"Here's a good idea," says the vet. "Why don't you take the telephone over to the dogs and give each of them a ring."

"Will that really work?" replies the astonished man.

"Well it damn well worked for me," says the vet as he slams down the phone.

A man goes to buy some rat poison. The shopkeeper gives him a bottle of powder and tells him to sprinkle it round his hole.

Exasperated, the man replies, "If I could get that close I'd step on him!"

A woman is left a pair of parrots in her aunt's will and immediately rings the vet to ask him how she can tell which was the male and which the female.

The vet tells her to creep down first thing in the morning and try and catch them mating; the one on top would be the male and she should mark him with some tape. This the woman does and on catching them in the act she puts a white tape around the male bird's neck. A couple of days later the vicar comes to tea and on seeing him the male parrot says, "Oho, caught you too, did they?"

A man and a parrot find themselves sitting next to each other on a plane. As the stewardess comes along the man asks for a coffee, at which point the parrot shouts, "Get me a brandy and be quick about it!" A little upset by his attitude, the stewardess goes off and returns with the brandy but not the coffee.

"Excuse me miss, you've forgotten my coffee," he tells her.

"Oh sorry," she replies, and is just about to go when the parrot shouts even louder, "And get me another brandy you incompetent cow!"

This time she's very upset but returns quickly with the brandy having forgotten once again to get the man's coffee. Maybe if I take the same attitude as this parrot I might get results, he thinks to himself.

"Hey, coffee, and be quick about it, you dozy bitch!" he shouts.

In no time at all the stewardess returns with two male colleagues who drag both the man and the parrot from their seats and throw them out of the emergency hatch. As the man passes the parrot on the way down, the bird turns to him and says, "You know, you've got a real attitude for someone who can't fly."

In another part of the parish a woman has a parrot who uses such foul language she has to keep him covered up when visitors call round. One day the vicar comes to tea and on hearing about her problem suggests he take the parrot back to his house where he has a female parrot who is forever on her knees praying. Maybe she can change his ways. The woman agrees and the parrot goes back with the vicar. As soon as he is put in the female parrot's cage, his awful behaviour begins. "C'mon girl, let's get to it, get them little parrot knickers off." Lo and behold, before the vicar or the lady can intervene, the female parrot replies, "At long bloody last, my prayers have been answered."

★

Two mates are out walking when one suddenly rushes behind a bush to have a pee. Unfortunately there's a snake hiding in the undergrowth and when Jack gets out his penis the snake bites it. Hearing Jack's screams, Bob rushes over and seeing what has happened rushes off to the doctor's.

"You'll have to hurry, otherwise your friend will die," says the doctor.

"Cut a small incision in the wound and suck out all the poison, but be quick."

Bob goes back to his mate who's looking very pale and weak.

"What did the doctor say?" he whispers.

"I'm sorry mate, you're going to die."

★

A man comes home from work one day to find a rat shagging the backside off a cat in the garden. The next evening he returns home to find the rat doing the same thing to a bull terrier. Unable to believe his eyes, he takes the rat into the house to show his wife but as soon as she sees it she screams, "Aahh, get that sex maniac out of here."

★

Three dogs meet up in the vet's. The Alsatian tells the other two he's being put down for biting his next door neighbour. "Same here", says the second dog – a Rottweiler – "I've scared too many children at the local school."

The third dog, a Great Dane, says, "I'm here because yesterday my gorgeous blonde owner got out of the bath, bent down to dry her feet and without a second thought I mounted her and did what comes naturally."

"So you're being put down as well," ask the other two dogs.

"No," replies the Great Dane, " just having my nails cut."

A man goes into a bar with a giraffe and they both get horribly drunk until the giraffe collapses in a dead faint on the floor and the man gets up to leave.

"Hey," says the bartender. "You can't leave that lying there."

"It's not a lion, it's a giraffe," says the man.

Three friends are sitting round the fire talking about their dogs. The first one tells them his dog is called Woodman.

"Let me show you why. Woodman, go boy."

At that, the dog takes a log from the side of the fire and carves a beautiful statue of a bird. Then the second explains why his dog is called Stoneman.

"Go boy, go." Immediately the dog jumps up, takes part of the stonework away from the front of the fire and trims it into a stone carving of an Indian.

Finally, the third friend says, "My dog's called Ironman. Watch this." The man heats the fire tongs until they are blisteringly hot and then tells his mates,

"I'll just touch him on the balls with this and you watch him make a bolt for the door."

"Hey, does your dog bite?" asks the man sitting down next to a guy with a dog at his feet.

"No," he replies. But a moment later, the dog takes one almighty bite out of the man's ankle.

"Hey, I thought you said your dog didn't bite!" he says angrily.

"That's right," says the dog owner, "that there's not my dog."

Two men are sitting on a park bench watching a dog licking its balls. One says, " I wish I could do that."

The other replies, "Give him a bone and he might let you."

★

A goose goes into the local job centre and joins the back of the waiting queue. When his turn comes he goes up to the interviewer and asks what's on offer.

"My goodness!" gasps the interviewer. "You can talk."

"Well, of course," retorts the goose. "I'm not bloody stupid."

"OK, let me see, come back on Thursday and I'll have something for you."

After the goose has gone, the man rings the circus and persuades the owner to take on the goose, with 5% of the profits coming to him.

Thursday arrives and in waddles the goose.

"So what have you got for me?" he asks.

"Well, I've got you a great job in the circus," he enthuses. "Good money and full board."

"No, that's no good to me," says the goose. "I'm an electrician."

★

"What are those marks on your knees?" one girlfriend asks another.

"Oh, that's from making love doggie style", she replies.

"It looks painful to me, don't you know any other way?"

"Oh yes, I do but my dog doesn't."

★

What do you do if a pit bull terrier tries to mount your leg?
Fake an orgasm.

★

Two ducks meet in the hotel bar, have a few drinks and decide to book into a room for the night. But ever mindful of safe sex, they ask room service for a packet of condoms. A few minutes later the condoms arrive and the waiter asks the male duck,

"Shall I put it on your bill Sir?"

"Certainly not!" snaps the duck. "What do you think I am, some sort of pervert?"

A man rang the vet in some distress.

"It's an emergency! My dog has swallowed a condom! What shall I do?"

"No need to get too alarmed, just keep him in and I'll get back to you at the end of surgery."

Half an hour later, the vet rang back. "How's it going?"

"Oh, it's alright now, we found another condom in my wife's handbag."

At the Movies

A sleazy young man went to the cinema and sat next to a pretty girl. As the film started, he put his hand on her leg but she slapped him away. A little later, he tried again and put his hand on her knee, only to be pushed off again. Then when he put his hand on her thigh, she turned to him angrily and said, "You've got no chance. You're just wasting your time. I'm Picasso's daughter and what you're looking for is on the back of my neck!"

Did you hear about the film at the Soho sex club?
It was very emotional, there wasn't a dry fly in the place.

At long last the Cisco Kid is captured by the Sioux Indians, who bury him up to his neck in the sand to face a long and painful death. Out of respect for the 'Kid' the Indians grant him one last wish and he asks them to free his old trusty horse.

So the horse is freed and the Cisco Kid whistles him over and whispers in his ear. The horse then runs away but appears an hour later with a beautiful girl on its back. The girl gets off, comes over to the Cisco Kid and lifts her skirt to show she has no knickers on. She then sits on his face and wiggles around.

As the Cisco Kid comes up for air he shouts to his horse, "You silly bugger, I said go and get me a posse."

It was a glamorous Hollywood party and a beautiful, curvaceous blonde came up to one of the show business agents and said, "Wow, you really turn me on, let's go somewhere less busy and I'll make mad, passionate love to you all night."

The agent replied, "I don't know, what's in it for me?"

★

Little Red Riding Hood is walking through the woods when she spots the big bad wolf hiding behind a tree.

"Come out, come out, I can see you, Mr Wolf!" she shouts.

"How can you see me?" he asks.

"I saw your big bushy tail sticking out."

Mr Wolf turns and disappears deeper into the woods but a few minutes later, Little Red Riding Hood shouts, "Come out, come out, Mr Wolf, I can see you behind the rocks."

Out comes the wolf and asks, "How can you see me?"

"I saw your big ears sticking out," she says.

The wolf runs further into the woods but again hears her shouting.

"Come out, come out Mr Wolf, I can see you behind that bush."

"How did you see me this time?"

"I saw your long nose sticking out."

"Just who are you anyway?" asks the wolf angrily.

"I'm Little Red Riding Hood."

"And what are you doing here in the woods?"

"I'm going to visit my grandma."

"Well go and fucking visit her then!" yells the wolf, "and let me have a shit in peace!"

★

Two girls are watching a film in the local cinema when one turns to the other in panic.

"Tracy, the man next to me is masturbating."

"Well, just ignore him."

"I can't, he's using my hand."

★

Snow White was asked to leave Fairyland last week.

She was found sitting on Pinocchio's face saying, "Tell a lie, tell the truth, tell a lie, tell the truth...."

★

An usherette in the local cinema was known to be an 'easy-going' girl and one night she gave her favours to the cinema manager. After an hour of humping, he was about to leave when he gave her two passes to the film premier of a much advertised new drama. But instead of being grateful, she complained, "This isn't going to put food in my childrens' mouths."

"If it's food you wanted, you should have fucked a grocer," he retorted.

★

The film had only been on 20 minutes when a woman came rushing out into the foyer of the cinema looking very upset.

"I've been interfered with!" she complained to the manager. He eventually managed to calm her down and took her to another section of the cinema. However, a short time later another woman ran out complaining of the same thing.

This was too much for the manager, so he took his torch and went to investigate. Lo and behold the torch picked up a bald-headed man crawling along on all fours.

"What's going on?" he demanded.

"I've lost my hairpiece," said the man. "I put my hand on it twice but it got away."

A reporter from the Hollywood gutter press was interviewing one of the industry's hottest starlets.

"Will you be telling all in your memoirs?" he asked.

"Oh yes, but the book won't be published until after my death."

"Oh great, I hope it's soon."

Taking his girlfriend to the cinema, the man's wig fell off when they were canoodling in the back row. As he felt around trying to find it, his hand accidentally went up his girlfriend's skirt.

"Oooh ..." she moaned. "Go on, go on, that's it."

"No, it can't be," he said. "I part mine on the right."

Why did the Lone Ranger kill Tonto?

He found out what 'Kemo Sabe' meant.

Little Red Riding Hood was walking through the woods when she was suddenly attacked by a huge wolf.

"At last, at last," laughed the wolf, "I'm going to eat you all up."

"Oh sod it," said Little Red Riding Hood. "Doesn't anyone fuck these days?"

While on holiday, the Seven Dwarfs visit the local convent to buy some souvenirs.

They meet up with the Mother Superior and Dopey stops to talk to her.

"Excuse me, your holy one, do you have any short nuns here?"

Mother Superior is quite puzzled by the question but replies "Not very short, maybe one or two around 5'."

"Are you sure there aren't any nuns about 3' in height?" he persists.

"No, no, no one like that."

As the dwarfs leave, the Mother Superior follows them quietly down the road to try and discover the reason for such an odd question. She overhears the other dwarfs asking him what was said, and he replies,

"She said they don't have any."

On hearing this, the dwarfs fall about laughing and chanting, "Dopey's fucked a penguin, Dopey's fucked a penguin."

The Lone Ranger and Tonto are riding along a narrow canyon, when suddenly an arrow comes flying through the air and thuds into the ground in front of them. They look up quickly, to see both sides of the canyon lined with hostile Indians, and even as they watch, more appear in front of them, at the end of the canyon.

They turn their horses around to get the hell out of it, but there are hundreds of Indians coming up behind them, and it is obvious they have ridden into a trap.

"Well, old friend," says the Lone Ranger, turning to Tonto, "looks like we're really in trouble this time."

"Oh yeah?" replies Tonto, "what d'you mean 'we', white man?"

How did Pinocchio find out he was made of wood?
His hand caught fire.

Sherlock Holmes and Doctor Watson went on a camping trip to Dartmoor and as they lay down for the night Sherlock Holmes said,

"Doctor Watson, my old friend, when you look up into the darkness, please tell me what you see."

"Well, I can see a very clear sky, there are no clouds and the stars are out in their millions. I can see the Milky Way and I believe that extra bright star over there is the planet Venus which you can see at this time of the year. I would also deduce that being such a clear night will mean that it will get quite chilly."

Watson laughed and said,

"But knowing you, Sherlock, I'm sure there are many things I have missed. What have you deduced?"

There was a moments silence and then Holmes replied, "Somebody's nicked our tent."

★

The Lone Ranger and Tonto have just spent a month riding through the desert, after escaping from a canyon full of Indians. Eventually, they come across Prickly Gulch Creek where they go into the saloon for a much needed drink. They've only been in there a few minutes when a man runs in asking if anyone owns a big white horse.

"That's mine" replies the Lone Ranger, "Is there anything wrong?"

"Sure is, the animal's collapsed" said the man.

The Lone Ranger and Tonto go outside to see poor Silver lying prostrate on the ground, but after giving him some water he seems to revive a bit. The Lone Ranger turns to Tonto and says, "Will you just run around it for a few minutes so it can feel a breeze and that'll soon put him right."

Tonto starts to run around Silver while the Lone Ranger goes back inside to finish his drink.

A moment later another man rushes in asking who owns the white horse outside.

"Bloody hell!" says the Lone Ranger. "That's mine, now what's wrong?"

"Oh your horse is alright," says the man, "it's just that you've left your injun running."

★

Did you hear about the cowboy who arrived in town wearing a paper shirt, paper trousers a paper hat and paper boots?
 The sheriff arrested him for rustling.

★

A man walks into a saloon, draws his gun and shoots the piano player dead.
"I've been itching to do that for a long time" he says, "that bloody noise has been driving me mad."
The barman beckons the man to one side.
"Mind if I give you a bit of advice, Mister? If I were you I would file off any sharp edges on your gun and grease the barrel."
"Is that supposed to make me a better shot?" asks the cowboy.
"No, but you'll find it'll make things easier for you. That piano player you just killed has two big, mean brothers and when news gets to them about what you did, they'll shove that gun right up your arse."

★

At the Zoo

Her husband was so ugly, every time he went to the zoo he had to buy two tickets – one for going in and one for getting out.

A rather shy girl is visiting the zoo when suddenly as she passes the monkey house, a huge ape grabs her, pulls her over the moat and gives her a good seeing to. Afterwards she is taken to hospital in a state of shock and it is almost a week before she is allowed any visitors. When she does eventually have friends to see her and they ask how she is, she replies, "Terrible, he hasn't phoned, he hasn't written…"

★

The man had only been working at the zoo for a week when he was asked to show round a group of foreign tourists. One of the women asked him what the difference was between echidnas and porcupines.
"The echidnas' pricks are longer," he replied.
The answer caused great discomfort amongst the group and once they had gone the boss took him to one side and asked him to be more careful with his choice of words in the future.
"It's quills," he said, "use the word quills."
A couple of weeks later another group of tourists were doing the rounds.
"Hey, look at that porcupine," said one of them.
"No Sir," corrected the zoo keeper, "it's an echidna. It's smaller, not so dark and it's quills are longer than a porcupine's … but their pricks are about the same size."

★

A female elephant is having an awful time with flies who keep biting her on a part of her back too far away for her to shoo them off with her tail. When a little mouse sees this he quickly runs up her leg onto her back and within a minute has eaten up all the flies.

"Oh thank you so much!" cries the elephant. "If ever you need a favour doing, please don't hesitate to ask."

"Well, actually," says the mouse, "I did often wonder what it would be like to shag an elephant. Would you mind?"

The elephant is a touch surprised at this, but agrees and the mouse is soon humping away. Suddenly a bunch of bananas fall off a tree and hits the elephant on the head. "Ouch!" she says. "Yeah, take it all, bitch!" says the mouse.

★

This is the story of the three bears. One of them married a giraffe. The other two put him up to it.

A gorilla has escaped from the local zoo and taken refuge at the top of a tree in a neighbouring garden. The householder rings the zookeeper who arrives 10 minutes later with a pair of handcuffs, a Doberman pincher, a stick and a shotgun.

"Okay," says the zookeeper to the man. "I'm going to go up after him and poke him with this sharp stick. When he falls to the ground, the dog will go for his balls and as the gorilla puts his hands over them to protect himself, you slip on the handcuffs."

"That sounds easy enough," replies the man, "but what's the shotgun for?"

"Now listen carefully, this is most important. If I fall out of the tree before the gorilla, shoot the fucking dog!"

Once there was a small private zoo that was dependent on public contributions to pay for its upkeep. However, times were tough and the zoo was losing money hand over fist. Somehow the owner had to raise some cash. He came up with a brilliant idea. The next day, notices went up that anyone who could make the most ferocious lion jump straight up in the air would win £1,000. The entry fee would be £50. Many people tried, but no-one succeeded and much to the owner's delight, a lot of money was raised. Then, two days later, a small rather insipid man arrived at the zoo and offered his £50 to take up the bet. Feeling quite safe, the owner took him over to the lion's cage and called for witnesses. When a crowd had gathered, the man produced a wooden truncheon from within his coat, swung it around in the air and hit the lion in the balls as hard as possible. With an almighty growl, the lion jumped three foot into the air. Very dispirited, the owner handed over the £1,000 prize. A couple of months passed and the owner was forced to think up another bet. This time he decided to challenge people to make the lion shake his head from side to side within 15 seconds of meeting it. It was a roaring success and the financial situation started to improve. Alas, to his horror, the small insipid man appeared one week later and handed over his entry fee. He went over to the lion and whispered, "Do you remember me?"

The lion nodded apprehensively.

"Do you want me to do the same as I did last time?"

And the lion shook his head vigorously.

Two old ladies visiting the zoo land up at the giraffe enclosure and are amazed to find the giraffe's testicles just inches from their faces. One of the old ladies can't help herself and leans through the fence squeezing one of the testicles in her hand. All at once the animal jumps into the air, clears the fencing and gallops off into the distance. The zookeeper rushes out to find out what has happened and when he hears the two old ladies explain, he immediately drops his pants.

"Here, you'd better do the same to me, I've got to catch that son of a bitch!"

The elephant keeper at the zoo was grooming his animal when a man stopped to ask him the time. The keeper got down on his knees, swung the elephant's balls to and fro and replied, "Half past four."

Amazed, the man caught up with his friends and urged them to return with him to see this extraordinary occurrence. They agreed and all went back to the keeper. "Excuse me, do you know the time, please?" said one of the friends. Again the man got on his knees, gently handled the elephant's balls and replied, "Four forty-five."

After the party moved on, the first man's curiosity got the better of him and he returned to the keeper.

"I'll give you £50 if you show me how you can tell the time."

"If you insist," said the keeper. He beckoned the man to get down on his knees as well, then moved the elephant's balls to one side and said, "You see that clock tower over there?"

Down on the Farm

Three blokes were talking in a pub in Wales about the best way to shag a sheep.

The first two agreed it was the back legs down the wellies and the front legs over the wall. But the third said, "No, it's the back legs down the wellies and the front legs over the shoulders."

"Doesn't that make it difficult?" said the other two. "What's wrong with our way?"

"What! And miss out on all the kissing?"

Walking through the village, the local vicar spotted young Billy with a herd of bullocks.

"There's a fine looking herd," he remarked.

"Yeah," replied Billy. "Dad made 'em."

"Oh no, son," said the vicar, "God made those bullocks."

"No," said Billy. "God made them bulls, dad made them bullocks."

A man who had done a lot for his village was complaining about the lack of respect he received from the rest of the inhabitants. "For instance," he said, "see all those beautifully mown lawns, the abundance of flowers, the avenue of trees? I did all that, but do they call me John the Horticulturist? No, they bloody don't. And look at the stunning new village hall and the ornate wall around the church. I did all that but do they call me John the Builder? Not bloody likely! I shag one sheep ..."

★

Two farmers are talking over a pint.

"I'm glad to see you and your wife are on better terms. Solved the eternal triangle problem, did you?"

"Oh yes," replied the other. "We ate the sheep."

★

A local nymphomaniac is out walking in the country when she spies two brothers harvesting the wheat. Now the two boys are ideal specimens of manhood, but not very worldly.

"Hi boys, why don't you take a break from work and we can all have a good time. But you'll have to wear these condoms because I don't want to get pregnant."

The boys are entranced by her and immediately agree to anything she suggests.

A year goes by and one day one of the brothers says, "Our Jack, do you remember the time we met that girl in the cornfield?"

"I do that," he replied dreamily.

"Well, do you care if she gets pregnant?"

"No, not anymore."

"Nor me. Let's take these things off now."

★

A man walking along a country road comes across a shepherd with a huge flock of sheep. He says to the shepherd, "I'll bet you £150 against one of your sheep that I can tell you the exact number of sheep in this flock."

There's a pause for a moment while the shepherd thinks it

over but he feels quite confident because the flock is so big.

"OK," he says. "You're on."

"964," says the man.

"My God, that's amazing!" splutters the farmer. "You're absolutely right. You'd better take one of the sheep."

The man picks one up and begins to walk away, when the shepherd cries, "Hold on a minute, will you give me a chance to get even? Double or nothing, that I can guess your occupation."

"OK," replies the man.

"You're a government economist," says the shepherd.

"I'm amazed," responds the man. "That's absolutely right, but tell me, how did you deduce that?"

"Well," says the shepherd. "Put down my dog and I'll tell you."

As the man parks his Rolls Royce in the village car park, one of the locals comes up to him, and says admiringly, "That's a lovely car you have there; how much did it cost?"

"About £200,000."

"Blimey, how much petrol does it take?"

"29 gallons."

"And how many miles does it do to the gallon?"

"About two miles. I work for Cunard you know."

"Well, I work fucking hard as well, but I still can't afford a Rolls Royce," he retorts.

It was market day in the small town and towards the end of the day a vet approached one of the old farmers.

"Have you ever considered artificial insemination for your herd of cows, Mr Woodall?"

"No thanks, I'll stick to the old fashioned way, if it's all the same to you."

"OK, but if you change your mind, give us a ring and we'll take it from there."

On the way home, the farmer pondered the vet's words but couldn't imagine how a cow could be serviced without a bull. His curiosity eventually got the better of him and he rang the vet asking for his cow to be serviced as soon as possible.

"OK", replied the vet. "If you can get a few things ready. Wash down the cow's backside, put down some clean straw and have a bucket of hot water and a stool ready."

When all was ready, the vet arrived.

"Have you done everything I asked?"

"That I have," replied the farmer. "I've even hammered a nail in the door for you to hang your trousers on."

A farmer was getting less and less eggs from his hens and decided he would have to replace the old rooster who wasn't carrying out his job properly. So he bought a new rooster. Later in the henhouse the old rooster turned to the new rooster and said, "Look, let's make a deal. Let me just have three of the hens and I'll leave the rest to you."

"No way," came the reply. "This is all mine now."

"OK," said the crestfallen rooster, "but let me have some pride. Let's have a race across the farmyard and back, winner takes all."

"All right," said the new rooster, thinking there was no way he was going to lose to this tired old bird.

They set off, but just as the new cock was about to overtake, the farmer burst out of his house and shot him dead.

"Christ, that's the third queer rooster I've bought this month."

★

Over a pint in the local pub a farmer was telling his neighbour about the trouble he was having with his chickens. They weren't laying, they weren't breeding. Hearing this, his neighbour told him not to worry because he had a cockerel that was forever on the job, in fact he'd worn his chickens out, so he was quite happy to sell him. The transaction took place and the rooster went home to the new farm. In no time at all he was servicing all the chickens with amazing results, and not only that, the ducks were looking a lot livelier, as were the geese. The farmer was overjoyed.

However, two days later the farmer couldn't find his prize rooster anywhere and it took a lot of searching before he was eventually discovered behind the barn, lying stiff with his legs in the air.

"Oh no," said the farmer, "the poor bugger, all that work's killed him."

"Sshhh!" whispered the rooster. "See those vultures up there...?"

139

A farmer taking his driving test is asked to make a U turn.

"Fetch me my wellies, I'll make her eyes water."

★

A man's car broke down in the middle of nowhere and he ended up seeking refuge at a farmer's cottage.

"Well, we've only got two bedrooms," he said, "but you can share a bed with my daughter as long as you don't bother her." The man agreed and not wanting to disturb her, slipped into bed without turning the light on. In the morning he thanked the farmer for his hospitality and commented on how cold his daughter was.

"Oh yes," replied the farmer sadly. "We're burying her this morning."

★

A ventriloquist was being shown around a farm by a local yokel.

As a joke the ventriloquist made the bull look as if he was saying, "Hello there."

The yokel did not react. So he then made the hen say, "This man has been stealing all my eggs."

At which point the yokel got very flustered and said, "When we get to the sow, don't believe a word she says."

★

A farmer stopped work to have a midmorning snack and as he sat there he watched the cock chasing the chicken around the farmyard.

Having finished, the farmer threw his scraps on the ground and immediately the cock ran over to gobble them up.

"Bloody hell!" he said. "I hope I never get that hungry."

A stranger walked into the bar and asked for a pint of beer. Now it was a very close knit community, and the locals were always suspicious of outsiders, so they elected Jack from the nearby farm to find out who he was.

Some minutes later after Jack had chatted to the stranger about the weather, he asked the man what he did.

"I'm a taxidermist," replied the man, "and I've really enjoyed spending time in these parts. Yesterday I stuffed a prize winning sheep dog, then I mounted Mrs Smith's goat and today, I'm going to have a go at her old pig."

Jack returned to his mates who were dying to know what had been said.

"It's alright lads," he replied to their questions. "I thought he said he was a taxi driver but in fact he's really a shepherd like us, on holiday."

★

At the summer fayre, Farmer Brown has brought along his favourite horse and is making a lot of money by taking bets on anyone who could make him laugh.

One cunning-looking local comes up and takes up the bet. He whispers something in the horse's ear and the animal starts to laugh uncontrollably.

Not to be outsmarted the farmer offers him double or nothing if he can make the horse cry.

The local goes round to the other side of the horse, out of sight of onlookers, and after a moment the horse starts to cry uncontrollably.

As the farmer pays up, he asks the man how he managed to make the horse laugh and then cry.

"Well, first I told him my knob was bigger than his, and the second time I showed him."

Finding himself lost, a motorist stops to ask a farmer for directions and as they are talking he notices a pig with a wooden leg.

"Why's that pig got a wooden leg?" he asks.

"Oh, that pig is a real hero. Do you know he's been a life saver. About four months ago our barn caught alight and if it hadn't been for that pig alerting us by his noise, we'd have lost all our horses."

"Very good," replies the motorist, "but why has he got a wooden leg?"

The farmer continues, "And do you know, not long after that I fell into a fast flowing river and he saved my life by running for help."

"Yes, I see, but that still doesn't explain why he's got a wooden leg."

"Oh come on, sir, a pig like that, you don't eat him all in one go."

Backing out of the farmyard on his milk float, the milkman drove over and killed the prize rooster. Feeling very bad about it, he sought out the farmer's wife to tell her the bad news.

"Excuse me, madam, I'm so sorry but I've run over your prize rooster and I would like to replace it."

"Well, that's fine with me," she said. "You'll find the chickens behind the barn."

How can you stop a rooster from crowing on Monday morning?
Eat him for lunch on Sunday.

A local crop dealer is on his way to visit a farm out in the middle of nowhere. It's a long distance to travel, so he puts his foot down and is going at 60mph when he's passed by a three-legged chicken that soon disappears into the distance. He gets to the farm, carries out his business when he suddenly remembers the chicken and asks the farmer about it.
"Oh yes, that's our three-legged chicken. We raised them ourselves. You see there's me, my wife and our John and we all like the legs but it was a waste when we had to kill two chickens for our Sunday lunch."
"And are they tasty?" asked the crop dealer.
"I don't know, we haven't caught one of the buggers yet!"

A little girl was walking along the street pulling a cow by a rope. She passed the old village busybody, Mrs Seebad, who said, "My dear child, where on earth are you going with that animal?"
"I'm taking it to the bull," she said.
"Oh fancy asking you to do a thing like that. Can't your dad do it?"
"Oh no, it has to be the bull," she said, smiling sweetly.

★

"Don't worry about the cow," said the vet to the farmer. "It just needs a pessary up its backside. Take this tube, simply insert it in the cow's bum and blow."

When the farmer returned to his farm, he explained the method to his cowman and left him to it.

Half an hour later, the cowman came looking for him.

"I'm sorry, Mr Brooks, I can't seem to blow the damn thing up."

Farmer Brooks went back to the cow shed, took the tube out, turned it round and re-inserted it. He then blew the pessary up first time.

"Mr Brooks, why did you turn the tube round?" asked the cowman.

"Well, I'm not sucking the end that's been in your mouth!" he replied.

★

The vicar's out for his morning constitution when he sees the local farmer in the field, shagging a pig. He walks further on and sees the farmer's son, shagging a sheep. Then just behind the barn he spots the grandfather tossing off. Unable to contain his anger, he goes up to the farmhouse and knocks loudly on the door. When the wife opens it, he yells, "It's absolutely disgusting, your husband's shagging pigs, your son's shagging sheep and then what do I see behind the barn but your father tossing himself off!"

"I know," she says sadly, "but, you see, dad's too old to go chasing the animals anymore."

★

An Australian tourist travelling through Wales sees a farmer with the back legs of a sheep stuck down his wellingtons.
"Are you shearing that sheep?" he asks.
"No bloody way!" comes the reply. "Catch your own."

★

The old farmer wasn't a very friendly man; in fact, most of the time he was downright rude. One day a travelling salesman stopped by and as they were talking a fly landed on the man's chin.
"Is there something on my chin?" he asked.
"Ay," said the farmer. "It's a fanny fly – you usually find them on cows."
"Are you trying to infer that my chin looks like a fanny?" he demanded.
"I ain't saying that at all," said the farmer and then added, "but you can't fool the fly."

A man knocked on the door of a farmer's cottage and said, "I happened to notice you had some canary grass down in that bottom meadow, would you mind if I picked myself a few canaries?"
"Go right ahead, but you won't get any canaries," replied the farmer.
A little while later, the farmer spotted the man heading for home and was flabbergasted to see he had a cage full of canaries. Some weeks later, the man returned.

"Would you mind if I took a walk down towards the stream? Only I've seen some toadflax down there, and I'd like to collect a few toads."

"That's OK," said the farmer, "but you won't get any toads from toadflax."

An hour later the farmer couldn't believe his eyes when he saw the man had a bag full of toads. The following week the man knocked at the door again.

"Good morning, I've just noticed that you have some pussy willow near those woods...."

"Just a moment, sir, I'll get my boots, I'm coming with you."

Johnny goes to work on a farm and is put in charge of the sheep. To his dismay he cannot get them to lamb so seeks advice from an old mate, brought up in country ways.

"Get your sheep in the tractor, take them up to the top of the moors at the dead of night and shag them yourself," said the friend. "Then in the morning if they're lying down they'll be pregnant."

So that night Johnny does as he's been told, takes them up to the moors in his tractor and gives them all a good shagging. Next morning he looks out of his window but they're all standing up. So next day he tries again, takes them up the moors in his tractor does the business, but the next morning they're still all standing up. The following night he goes through the routine again but the next morning he's woken up by a terrible noise.

"Bloody hell!" he curses, and looks down into the farmyard to see the sheep sitting in the tractor sounding the horn.

★

A pompous upper class prat went duck hunting but no matter how hard he tried, it was more than 6 hours before he managed to shoot one down. Delighted at his sudden luck he searched for the fallen duck and found it in a nearby field. As he was about to pick it up a farmer appeared and said aggressively, "What the hell do you think you're doing?"

"I'm getting my duck," he replied.

"Oh no you ain't. This here's my property so it's mine."

"But I've spent all day trying to get a duck and you're not taking it away from me," he spluttered.

And so they argued on until the farmer suggested,

"Look here, there's one way we could settle this argument. We'll take it in turns to kick each other in the balls and the last man on his feet gets the duck."

The hunter agreed, and the farmer went first because, as he said, it was his idea. Wearing steel capped, hob nailed boots he aimed carefully at the hunter and gave an almighty kick. His poor victim turned a sickly white, his eyes disappeared and he gave out the most agonised cry. It took at least 5 minutes for him to come to his senses but he bravely stayed on his feet.

"Right!" he gasped. "Now it's my turn."

"Don't bother, you can have the duck," replied the farmer.

★

Jack, from the neighbouring farm, happened to see his mate Bill gathering in the harvest without any trousers on.

"Hey Bill, how come you're out here with no trousers on?"

"Well Jack, it's like this. Last week in that hot sun I was out all afternoon without a shirt on. Bloody hell, I suffered the next day. My neck was as stiff as a plank ... so this is my wife's idea."

Farmer Bob went along to a meeting of the local Paranormal Society at the Town Hall to hear guest speakers talk about their strange experiences. Sitting at the back, he couldn't hear all that was being said and he began to doze off when one of the speakers asked loudly, "Now come on, don't be shy, there must be someone here whose had a relationship with a ghost?" Without thinking, Farmer Bob put his hand up and was asked to come down to the front.

"Ladies and Gentlemen, this gentlemen here has kindly volunteered to tell us about his intimate relationship with a ghost. Please give him a warm hand."

But Bob had come to a sudden halt.

"Ghost!" he exclaimed. "I thought you said goats."

★

The man sat at the bar looking morosely into his pint of beer. No matter how hard he tried to ignore it, a little voice inside his head kept on and on at him, saying, "How could you Bob, how could you sleep with one of your patients!"

As a few more pints disappeared down his throat until he began to feel a little better – even the voice inside his head began to mellow.

"OK Bob, I suppose you're not the first person to sleep with one of their patients and no matter what they say, you're still the best vet in the district."

A flirty young farmer's daughter took her father's prize cows over to the neighbouring farm to be serviced by their bull. The handsome farmhand brought in the bull and before long there was a flurry of activity.

"Cor, I wish I was doing that" said the farmhand feverishly.

"Well it's alright by me," replied the girl, smiling coyly.

"Thanks" he said, "but maybe the cow wouldn't like it."

Two shepherds are driving a lorry full of sheep back to their hillside farm when suddenly the brakes fail as they come hurtling towards a sharp bend in the road.

"Quick!" shouted one of the men. "Jump for it."

"What about the sheep?" shouted the other.

"Oh fuck the sheep!" he yelled the first shepherd.

"What!" cried the second, "do you think we have time?"

★

The electricity man called round at number 63 Ramtop Drive to turn on the power for the new tenants. After knocking at the door for some time it was eventually opened by a small boy.

"Where's your mum, son?" he asked.

The little boy didn't answer but just pointed at the stairs. So,

thinking there was something wrong he went up the stairs and walked into the bedroom. There on the bed was a woman being shagged by a huge billy goat. He rushed back down the stairs, badly shaken by what he had seen, and stammered at the little boy.

"Son, son, do you know what's going on up there, do you know what they're doing?"

The boy just looked at him and then said,

"Na-a-a-a-a-a."

The farm inspector was on his annual tour of the county and had arrived at Farmer Giles' place.

"So how many sheep do you have?" he asked.

"I don't know," replied the farmer, "every time I try to count them, I fall asleep."

A motorist was driving through farm country when he got a terrible urge to have a shit. He spotted a man up ahead ploughing the field, so he told him his predicament and the farmer pointed to some outbuildings 200 yards away.

"You'll find a privy up there," he said, "but watch out for..."

But the man was off and running and didn't hear the end of the sentence. Sprinting up the field behind him the farmer turned the corner, only to see the poor man had fallen into a trench.

"That's what I was trying to warn you about," he said.

"It doesn't matter," said the man. "I wouldn't have made it anyway."

★

"That bloody bull's going to the knacker's yard!" yelled the farmer. "It's nearly killed me three times."

"Oh give him one more chance," replied his wife.

★

The young man had been brought up in the city. He'd never seen the countryside, he'd never come across any of the animals. It so happened that one weekend he was invited to go camping with some friends. He set off early in his car and arranged to meet them at the farmer's field. Alas, just half a mile from his destination, a goat ran out into the road and he ran over it, killing it stone dead. Overcome with shock, he finished his journey and sought out the old farmer.

"I've just run over something, back there down the lane," he said pointing. "But I'm not sure what it was."

The farmer asked him to describe it.

"Well, it had two tits and a beard and it smelt dreadful."

"Oh no," wailed the farmer, "you've just killed my wife."

★

A kindly man came across a young boy whose cart had shed its load of manure.

"Come back with me," he said, "we'll get you cleaned up, have a spot of lunch then I'll bring back my two sons to help you clear the road."

The boy hesitated, "I'm not sure," he faltered, "my dad might not like that."

"I think your dad will be pleased you're doing something about it," said the man and eventually the boy was persuaded.

A couple of hours later, they returned with his two sons to begin clearing the load.

"By the way, where is your dad?" asked the man.

"Under the manure," came the reply.

Two chickens were standing at the side of the road. One said to the other,

"For goodness sake, don't cross that road, or everyone will want to know why."

Three bulls had serviced the farmer's herd of cows for more than five years. During that time they had split the herd between them, each having an amount appropriate to their size, so the biggest bull had 20 more than the smallest.

Then one day, the bulls discovered a fourth bull was going to join them.

"Sod that," said the biggest bull, "he's not having any of my cows," and the others agreed they were not sharing either. The following morning a huge lorry arrived at the gate of the field and out stormed the largest bull they had ever seen, who began snorting loudly and glaring menacingly over at them. "Oh well," said the biggest bull nervously, "I guess he can have a few of my cows. It'll be nice not to have to work so hard."

"Yeah, I agree," said the middle-sized bull, "there's no reason why we can't share a bit. He can have some of mine as well."

Suddenly the smallest bull started snorting and stamping his feet on the earth, sending up clouds of dust.

"Hey, listen mate," hissed the other two, "I wouldn't go up against him, just let him have some of your cows."

"He can have all my fucking cows," replied the small bull. "I'm just making sure he knows I'm a bull."

★

A travelling salesman was returning home very late one night when his car broke down on the middle of Dartmoor. He needed to use a phone and as he peered across the huge desolate landscape he spotted the silhouette of a farmhouse nestling in a valley.

The salesman headed off towards the house but as he got closer, he suddenly had doubts.

"Oh bugger," he thought. "The farmer's not going to be too pleased to see me at this time of night, he's probably asleep."

He continued on and had ever darker thoughts, "…might even think I'm a burglar and turn his gun on me."

By this time, he'd reached the door and rung the bell. After a short time, he heard footsteps coming down the stairs and he thought again, "Shit, he might just set the dogs on me."

In the silence of the night came the sound of the key turning in the lock, and as the door started to open, the traveller said loudly, "Oh fuck your bloody phone."

★

The President was driving through Republican country when his driver knocked over and killed a pig that suddenly strayed into the middle of the road.

"You'd better go and tell the farmer," ordered the President, "and offer to pay for it."

"Yes sir," replied the driver and off he went.

It was almost four hours later when he returned with a satisfied look on his face.

"Where the hell have you been?" demanded the President angrily.

"Well, I did as you said. I went up to the farmer's house and told him what I'd done. He invited me in, gave me a fantastic meal and then invited me upstairs to shag his daughter."

"But why?" puzzled the President.

"I've no idea," replied the driver. "All I said was that I was the President's driver and I'd run over the pig."

What's the difference between a sheep and a Lada?
You don't feel quite so embarrassed being seen getting out of the back of a sheep.

"Now listen, sons," said daddy hedgehog. "You're old enough to leave home and there are many dangers out there, the worst one being that busy road. If you ever need to cross it, but a car comes along before you get to the other side, just make sure you're standing in the middle of the lane and it will go over you without hurting you. Look,

I'll show you."

The hedgehog went out to the middle of the lane and waited for an on-coming car.

"Here comes one!" he shouted. "Now watch how its ..." but that's all he had time to say before there was a sickening crunchy sound and poor dad was flattened.

"Oh dear," said one of the sons, "I meant to ask him about three wheelers."

What do you call a flock of sheep tied to a lamp post in Wales? A Leisure Centre.

What can cows do that women can't?
Stand up to their tits in water without getting their fannies wet.

★

In the Park

Two naive young men were sitting in the park talking.

"Tell you what Jake," said Maurice. "Let's go down the new pub tonight, 'The Crown and Sceptre.' I've heard it's right good. After you've bought the first drink, the rest are free for the whole night. And," he grinned conspirationally, "then you goes out the back and has sex."

"Are you sure?" asked Jake doubtfully.

"Oh yeah, it was my sister what told me. That's what happened to her when she went down there the other night."

It was so cold in the park last month that the local flasher was reported to be describing himself to the women he met.

A man came staggering through the park well and truly pissed when he saw a man doing press ups. After watching him for a minute, the drunk started to laugh.

"What's so funny?" asked the man angrily.

"I think you ought to know your woman's left you," replied.the drunk.

A Scotsman, on the way home from a heavy drinking session with his mates collapses onto a park bench and falls into a very deep stupor.

Some time later two girls walk past and on seeing him debate

whether he has anything under his kilt. They decide to look and discover he's stark naked.

"We really ought to leave him a record of our visit," one says to the other, so giggling with delight they tie a blue ribbon round his willy before moving on.

Finally the Scotsman comes round and staggers behind a bush bursting for a pee. When he sees the ribbon he smiles and says to it, "I don't know where you've been, or what you've been up to, but I see you've won first prize!"

Two old men sitting in the park. One says to the other "When I was young I never slept with my wife before we got married. Did you?"

"I'm not sure," says the other. "What was her maiden name?"

A man walked up to a policeman with a tiger trailing behind him.

"Excuse me, officer," he said. "I found this tiger earlier today, and now he just keeps following me around. What should I do with him?"

"Hmm," said the policeman, "I think really you should take him to the zoo."

The man agreed that this was a good idea, and off he went, with the tiger in tow.

Next day, the policeman was walking his beat through the park again, when he saw the same man, who still had the tiger with him.

"Here," said the policeman. "I thought I told you to take that tiger to the zoo?"

"I did," said the man, "and we had a great time. Now we're going bowling, and tonight we're off to the cinema."

On the Desert Island

A man is abandoned on a desert island. After six years, a beautiful, shapely blonde in a wet-suit gets washed ashore, and they get into conversation.

"How long have you been here?" she asks.

"Six years," he says.

"That's a long time. Would you like a drink?"

"I'd love one," replies the castaway eagerly.

With that she unzips a pocket in her wet suit and gets out a bottle of Scotch. The blonde then asks if he would like a cigarette.

"Yes, please!" he replies, so she unzips another pocket to produce a packet of cigarettes and a lighter.

"How long did you say you'd been here?" she asks again.

"Six years."

"Ah... then would you like to play around?"

The castaway is astonished. "Don't tell me you've got a set of golf clubs in there as well!"

Only two people survived the sinking of the luxury liner and separately they managed to make it to a desert island. The man who had been travelling economy class couldn't believe that his companion was none other than one of Hollywood's most famous starlets.

At first they remained on platonic terms but as the weeks passed natural desires took over until one night they tore each other's clothes off and did what comes naturally.

The next day he turned to her and asked whether she would mind doing him a favour. Would she dress up in some of his clothes? He had a pair of trousers and a shirt.

Puzzled, she agreed and when they met up later he patted her on the back and boasted, "Hello mate, you'll never guess who I fucked last night!"

A Kiwi oilrig worker on his way out to an oil rig was stranded on a desert island, with only a pig and a dog for company. After some months of watching the pig scurry around, with its sexy little wiggle and cute little curly tail, his frustration began to get the better of him, and he decided that in the absence of a woman, the pig would have to do. So picking a moment when the pig had its face in its food, he crept up on the beast, and was just about to grab it, when the dog rushed up, barking its head off, and the pig naturally bolted.

This happened repeatedly; every time he got near the pig, the dog would rush up and ruin everything.

Then one day his prayers were answered: a beautiful girl was washed ashore. He looked after her until she'd recovered her strength and in gratitude she asked him if there was anything she'd like him to do.

"Too right there is, mate," answered the Kiwi. "Hold that bloody dog, will you?"

A bloke found himself stranded on a desert island with six women. To keep it fair, it was decided he would service a different woman every night and have Mondays free. After a

few months the man was exhausted, realising how tiring it was to perform constantly every night except one. Then one day to his joy, he found a man washed up on the beach who would be able to take some of the workload from him. However, his hopes were shattered when the man's first words were "Hi, gorgeous, how about the kiss of life?"

'Oh fuck,' thinks the man, 'there goes Mondays.'

A man was stranded on a desert island and one day found a bottle washed up on the beach. Inside the bottle was a genie, who was so grateful for being let out that he said he would grant the man one wish. After some thought the man said he had always wanted to visit the Far East, so could the genie build a road from the island to the Great Wall of China.

"My goodness," replied the genie. "I'm not sure I can do that. Imagine all the work involved in building across oceans, and mountainous landscapes, all the materials ... no, I don't think that's such a good idea."

"OK," said the man. He thought for a moment and said, "Another thing I've always wanted is to understand women. I want to know what makes them laugh, why they get so angry, why they cry ..."

"About this road," replied the genie, " do you want a motorway or will a dual carriageway do you?"

After two months of being shipwrecked on a desert island, the man sees a barrel floating towards the shore and holding onto

the barrel is a stunningly beautiful naked woman. As he rushes down to meet her she says, "I think I have something you want." The man's eyes light up. "I don't believe it!" he gasps. "You've got beer in that barrel!"

The man had been stranded on a desert island for two years. One afternoon, looking out to sea, he shouted excitedly to himself, "Oh boy, oh boy, a boat's coming and there's a beautiful, young, voluptuous blonde on board, and she's stark naked ... and she's waving to me, blowing me kisses and rolling her hips..."

By this time, he had a mighty erection which he suddenly grabbed with both hands.

"Fooled you, fooled you," he laughed. "There ain't no fucking boat."

Three men had been marooned on a desert island for three months when one day a man-made raft was washed ashore, carrying a beautiful young girl.

"She's mine," said the Frenchman. "Look, she's got a red, white and blue blanket covering her."

He pulled the blanket away to reveal a pair of tartan knickers.

"There," said the Scotsman triumphantly. "She was made for me." And saying this he pulled them off.

"Aaah!" said the Indian, falling to his knees. "Behold, the sacred beard of our Holy prophet..."

A man had been stranded on a desert island for two years when he experienced severe shaking of the ground and noticed a great tidal wave bearing down upon him. "Oh Lord, please help me," he prayed. Suddenly, a boat appeared and a man aboard shouted to him urgently, "Quick, get on board, before the tidal wave comes!"

"No, no, I have faith in Jesus," said the castaway. A few moments passed and another boat appeared.

"Quick man, don't be silly, get on board, there's not much time left."

"No thank you, I have faith in Jesus."

With only seconds to go, another boat appeared and a voice called out in panic, "If you don't get over here right this minute, it'll be too late!"

"No thank you. I have faith in Jesus."

The next moment, the tidal wave hit the island, smashing everything to pieces. The poor castaway drowned.

Later in heaven the man met Jesus and said reproachfully,

"I had faith in you. I can't believe this has happened."

"What do you mean, you can't believe it!" cried Jesus "I sent three bloody boats, didn't I?!" .

A man and his dog got stranded on a desert island, and as time went on, they ran out of food and things looked pretty grim. "I'm sorry Rex," said the man, "one of us has got to eat," and with that he killed the dog and put him in the cooking pot. For three days, he dined well, until there was nothing left of Rex but a pile of bones. The man looked at them sadly and said to himself, "It's a pity old Rex isn't here. He'd have loved those bones."

On the Skids

A tramp was roaming the streets when he suddenly came across a £10 note lying on the pavement. Picking it up, he looked down at his old worn out shoes and said, "Feet, I'm going to get you some new shoes." A little later he looked at his tattered clothes and said, "Legs, I'm going to get you some new trousers." A little later he noticed his willy had grown into a right big stonker. "Oh, oh," he said. "Who told you we'd come into money?"

A frustrated young lady heard that men with big feet also had big members, so when a tramp came to the door with the biggest feet she'd ever seen he was invited inside. After wining and dining him, she then took him to bed. The next day, as he was leaving, she called out crossly, "In future try and wear shoes that fit you!"

The down-and-out man had spent his morning begging from street to street. He hadn't done very well and was just about to give up when he noticed a very posh woman walking up the private road to her mansion.

"Excuse me, madam," he said as politely as possible. "Can you spare a bob or two?"

"I'll do better than that," she said. "How are you with a paint brush?"

"Erm, okay, I suppose," he replied, puzzled.

"Good, there's a can of orange paint here. If you paint the porch round the back, then I'll pay you a decent day's wages."

The tramp disappeared and nothing was seen of him for the next three hours when he reappeared with an empty can.

"All finished?" she asked.

"It is," he replied, "but just one thing," he added helpfully, "it's a Ferrari round the back, not a Porsche".

A couple of old tramps who haven't eaten for many days suddenly come upon a dead dog. The first tramp cries out, "At last, food!", and he starts to eat the dog. "Don't you want any?" he asks his mate, who replies, "No thanks mate, not at the moment."

When the first tramp has finished, they go on their way but after a few minutes the tramp that ate the dog groans in pain and vomits it up.

"Oh great!" exclaims the second tramp. "At last, just what I've been waiting for – a hot meal!"

Walking down the street, a man is approached by a tramp who begs him for some money.

"Let me give you a drink," said the man.

"I don't drink," replied the tramp.

"Then let me give you a cigarette."

"No thanks, I don't smoke."

"How about this betting slip for the 2.30 at Cheltenham tomorrow?"

Again the tramp refused, saying, "I don't gamble either."

Suddenly the man had an idea. "Why don't you come back with me and I'll cook you a 3-course meal with all the trimmings?"

"Look," said the tramp. "Couldn't you just give me the money?"

"Maybe, but I want my wife to see what happens to someone who doesn't drink, smoke or gamble."

Two down-and-out alcoholics had run out of money and were unable to buy any more grog. It was sending them completely round the twist, until one of them came up with a great idea. They just had a few pence left, enough to buy a sausage, which Bert shoved in Dick's flies.

"OK, Dick, now watch this." The two men went into a bar, ordered drinks which they soon polished off, and when the barman asked for the money Bert got down onto the floor and started sucking the sausage.

"Why, you disgusting buggers!" shouted the barman, "Get out of here or I'll have the law onto you."

All day they repeated the trick and drank until they were sozzled.

"You know, Dick, my knees are bloody sore from kneeling on the floor so often."

"That's nothing," replied Bert. "I lost the sausage after the second pub."

★

Did you hear about the two old tramps at Christmas?

Not able to buy turkey and stuffing, they bought two budgies and a pair of chest expanders.

A man is sitting quietly in the café having a cup of tea when an old tramp comes and sits beside him. After a few minutes, there's the most awful smell and putting his hand over his nose, the man turns angrily to the tramp and says,

"You dirty bastard, have you crapped yourself?"

"I have," replied the tramp.

"Then get out of here and go and do something about it."

"I can't," came the reply. "I haven't finished yet."

★

A tramp, wearing only one boot, was shuffling down the street when he was stopped by a busybody woman.

"Do you realise you've lost a boot?" she said.

"Oh no," he replied. "I've just found a boot."

★

Two tramps are so hungry, they haven't eaten for days and are beginning to get quite desperate.

"John," said one, "I've got to have a crap; I'll just go behind that bush." So off he goes.

Meanwhile, John remains where he is and he suddenly hears a very strange noise.

"Bob, what's that funny noise I can hear? It sort of goes oh.. oh.. oh.. oh.."

"How should I know, I can't hear anything." And he squats down again.

"Bob, Bob, it's that noise again. Look, I'll have to come round and see what it is."

So John goes behind the bush trying to locate the noise 'oh... oh... oh... oh...'

"Oh, I see," he says triumphantly, "it's just your arse eating the grass."

★

An old tramp walks into Social Services with a pig on a lead. "Can you find somewhere for me and my pig to live?" he asks. "Just a bed if that's all you've got. My pig can sleep underneath it."

"But what about the smell?" asks the official.

"Oh, the pig don't mind."

★

On Their Worst Behaviour

A man fishing off the end of the pier is suddenly amazed to see an old wizened woman in a wheelchair hurtling down towards the edge. To his dismay he realises she is determined to go over, so just in time he stops her and asks what's wrong.

The old woman, who's wrinkled, half bald and toothless, starts to cry and tells him she's nearly 90 and has never been kissed. The man looks at her, hides his repulsion and gives her a kiss, although it's almost too much to stomach when she sticks her tongue down his throat. However she goes away happy. But a couple of hours later he sees her again, hurtling down towards the pier's edge.

"What's wrong now?" he asks.

Tears streaming down her face, she tells him she has never been hugged. So he closes his eyes takes a deep breath and just manages to give her a big hug. The man returns to his fishing and after another hour he hooks a very big fish. At that crucial moment the old woman returns, hurtling down the pier, and losing concentration for a moment he loses his prize catch.

He turns to the tearful old hag who, this time, tells him she's never been fucked. So the man gently lifts her out of the wheelchair, and smiling toothlessly at him she tells him to lie her on the sand under the pier where they won't be disturbed. The man agrees, takes up two loose planks from the floor of the pier and drops her through to the sand below. The woman laughs excitedly, again saying, "I've never been fucked before."

Well you will be now," replies the man. "The tide comes in in 15 minutes", and with that he walks away.

A dirty old man picked up a beautiful young girl in the local pub and invited her out for dinner. To his surprise she accepted and they went off to the most expensive restaurant in town where she ordered all the most expensive food and drink on the menu. Astonished, the man asked her if she always had such a big appetite.
"Only when someone wants to get into my knickers," she replied.

Three men are discussing how best to drive women wild. The first says he nibbles their ears and their toes and it really turns them on. The second says he kisses them all over and it drives them mad. The third says that after he's made love to them he wipes his cock on their curtains – now that really does drive them wild!

"It's about time you got married, son."
"But why, dad?" he replied, "Why should I buy a book when there's such a good lending library in town?"

★

Nursing one almighty hangover, Lady Ponsonby decided to get a breath of fresh air and take a walk around the grounds. After a few minutes she met her husband's manservant and casually mentioned to him that she was feeling under the weather after last night's riotous hen party and couldn't remember getting to bed.
"I helped you, madam" replied the manservant. "I took off your dress

and hung it up so it wouldn't get creased."

"But I woke up totally naked," she replied.

"That's right, madam, I removed your underclothes because I thought they might be a little uncomfortable."

"Gosh, I can't remember anything," she said, "I must have been really tight."

"Not after the first time, Your Ladyship."

"If you want an extra bit of sport in bed," said one bloke to the other, "mount her from behind and whisper in her ear: 'This is how I do it with your best friend'. Then try and stay on for 10 seconds."

Two men fell overboard when they were out at sea and only Jim could swim.

"Jump on my back, John, and we'll try to swim for shore," Jim said.

For the next 2 hours Jim swam towards land. Twice he was ready to give up but urged on by John they eventually made it.

"Bloody hell, I'm fucked," panted Jim as he crawled up the sand.

"Yes, sorry about that," said John "It was the only way I could hang on."

I says to my mate, "I like your hair, how do you get it like that?"

He replied, "My girlfriend strips and I rub my head between

her tits and my hair goes like this. Try it."

"I will."

Next day, we meet up and he says, "Did you try it?"

"Yeah," I says. "And you've got a lovely house as well."

Left stranded after falling off her horse some miles from home, a young cattleman's daughter was rescued by an Indian who brought her back to the ranch on his mount. When the father heard the sound of hooves he went out to meet them and helped his daughter down from the back of the horse.

"How did you manage to stay on?" he asked her.

"Well, it was difficult at first but then he told me to hold on to the saddle horn."

"Saddle horn?" asks the rancher "But Indians always ride bareback!"

A boy and girl stop for a kiss while walking through the park. "Mmm, you smell nice," says the girl. "What have you got on?"

He replies, "I've got a hard on but I didn't realise you could smell it."

Three men are discussing what to buy their wives for their birthdays. "I'm going to get my wife some sexy underwear and a pair of Italian shoes, then if she doesn't like one, hopefully she'll like the other."

"That's a good idea," says the second man.

"I'll get my wife two presents as well and maybe one of them will be alright. Let's see – I think I'll get a gold necklace and an evening dress."

"What about you Jack?" they say, turning to the third man who has remained morosely quiet.

"Oh, I know what I'm getting Doreen, a mink coat and a dildo. If she doesn't like the coat she can go fuck herself."

Into a bar comes a man grinning all over his face. He says to the bartender, "I'll have three rums, one bourbon and two double Scotches, please."

The drinks are lined up before him and he downs them all straightaway.

"Hey, what's the big occasion?" asks the bartender.

"I've just had my first blowjob," replies the man.

"Oh right, was it OK?"

"It will be, once I get rid of the taste."

For quite some time this man has been living next door to a beautiful young girl and they have never done more than just say hello on meeting.

One day, however, the girl comes out wearing a flimsy dressing gown and invites him over to her door. It's obvious she's making out to him and he becomes very hot under the collar. All of a sudden she urgently whispers to him, "Let's go inside, I hear someone coming..."

He blindly follows her indoors and once inside she drops her dressing gown to the floor and stands there stark naked.

"So honey," she coos, "what do you think my best attribute is?"

The man stutters, "It's, er.... It's got to be your ears."

"My ears!" she gasps. "Why? Have you ever seen such flawless skin, have you ever seen such beautiful breasts, have you ever seen such a gorgeous arse? Why do you say my ears?"

"Well, it's like this," he explains. "When we were outside and you said you heard someone coming... well, that was me."

A conman bought a pet shop and put an advertisement in the window saying he had a very special dog, ideal for spinsters. Sure enough, the ad attracted a lot of attention and one woman came into the shop asking for more details.

"It's a big alsatian, miss," he said, "and it keeps women warm on cold nights – if you know what I mean." (wink wink)

The woman bought the dog but a few days later rang the pet shop complaining that the dog had done 'nothing special'.

The man went round to the woman's flat and found her in bed while the dog was asleep on the floor.

"Come on, Rover," he said, taking his clothes off, "How many more times do I have to show you!"

Ever since the new cook had arrived at camp, he had been treated miserably. They'd thrown away his clothes, turned his bed upside down and hidden his post. Eventually, however, they grew bored and told him there would be no more tricks.

"You really mean that?" he said.

"Yes," they assured him.

"OK, good, then I'll stop pissing in the soup."

Did you hear about the girl who swallowed a razor blade? The doctor decided to let it come out naturally but during the time it took for that to happen, it gave her an appendectomy, badly lacerated her husband, cut out the tongue of her next door neighbour and damaged the hand of a casual friend.

"I'm really fed up with my wife's slovenly ways," complained Bob. "This morning, I went to piss in the sink and it was full of dishes!"

"But if I give you oral sex, won't you lose respect for me?" "Not at all," he replied. "Not if you're good at it."

Did you hear about the man who entered his dog in the local pet show? He got three months.

The beautiful blonde whispered to the handsome doctor, "Oh kiss me again, please kiss me again." "It's ethically wrong you know," he said. "I shouldn't really be fucking you in the first place."

A very famous Member of Parliament was walking through the park when he suddenly got a huge erection and had to dash behind a tree to relieve himself. Unfortunately, a passer-by caught him in the act and took a photo of him. Extremely alarmed at the bad publicity this would bring, he offered to buy the camera and film from the stranger. It took a great deal of haggling but they finally agreed on £500. Walking back to his office a little later with the camera slung over his shoulder, the MP met one of his colleagues.

"Is that a new camera?" he asked, interestedly. "How much did you pay for it?"

"£500".

"Christ, he must have seen you coming!"

A miserly old woman was always trying to find ways of saving money and came upon the idea of feeding her husband cheap dog food. It took a few days for him to get used to it but when she insisted it was the best minced steak he had no reason to be suspicious. Three months went by when one afternoon she received a phone call from the local hospital to say her husband had been brought in following an accident. She arrived at casualty 20 minutes later and asked the doctor on duty how he was and what had happened.

"Just a few broken bones, really. An odd accident, though. It seems he was hit by a car when he suddenly sat down in the middle of the road and tried to lick his backside."

The rush hour train was packed to capacity and standing pressed up against a pretty young girl was a creepy looking man.

"Will you stop pushing that thing at me," she whispered angrily.

"It's only my wallet," he replied.

"Well, you must have a bloody good job," retorted the girl. "You've had three rises since we left Waterloo."

★

A man out walking with his dog is amazed to see his doctor down on all fours with his fingers halfway down a rabbit hole. As he continues to watch, the doctor withdraws his hand and a moment later a rabbit pops his head out. The doctor knocks it out and puts it in his bag. After watching him catch ten rabbits this way he goes over and asks what the secret is.

"It's very simple," replies the doctor. "Before you come out put your hand between a woman's legs; when the rabbits smell it they can't help coming up for more. That's when you get them."

"I can hardly believe it," says the man. "Are you sure?"

"Of course, you can trust me, I'm a doctor."

The man ponders the doctor's words on the way home and when he sees his wife bending over the oven he quickly puts his hand between her legs. Without looking round, his wife says, "Hello doctor, off rabbit hunting again?"

★

Three hikers stop for a rest in the Yorkshire Dales and looking over into an adjoining field they see some sheep.

"Hey, I think that sheep's smiling at you," jokes one of them. "I wish it was Cindy Crawford."

The second says, "I wish it was Sharon Stone."

The third says, "I wish it was dark."

An Australian DJ on one of the local radio stations decides to launch a new competition. He asks people to ring in with a word used in everyday speech but not found in the dictionary. If they're successful, they win a prize. It's not long before a man rings up with the word 'goan'.

"Well thanks for that word, I'll just check it's not in the dictionary … no, it's not. So how would you use this word?"

"Goan fuck yourself," came the reply.

Lost for words, the DJ quickly puts on some music.

An hour later, he gets another call and this time the word is 'smee'. He looks it up and it's not there.

"So how would you use this word?" he asks the caller.

"It's smee again; goan fuck yourself."

Three blokes were talking in a pub in Wales about the best way to shag a sheep.

The first two agreed it was the back legs down the wellies and the front legs over the wall. But the third said, "No, it's the back legs down the wellies and the front legs over the shoulders."

"Doesn't that make it difficult?" said the other two. "What's wrong with our way?"

"What!" exclaimed the third man. "And miss out on all the kissing?"

★

"You look happy this morning Jack" said his mate.
"Yeah, I came into some money last night – a girl with gold caps on her teeth."

★

"You will still love me now we're married, won't you?" asked the newly wed girl.
"Oh, even more," he replied, "I've got a thing about married women."

★

A poor simple young girl went to the doctors and was told she was pregnant.
"But how come?" she said. "I haven't been with a man."
Patiently, the doctor explains the birds and bees to the young girl.
"Oh no," she gasped, "the first aid teacher told me it was artificial respiration."

★

Jack and Flo had a distant cousin staying with them and one night when she was taking a bath, Flo went in to give her some more towels and noticed she didn't have any pubic hairs.
"Really," said Jack, when Flo told him about it later. "That's very odd, you must be mistaken."
"No, I'm not," said Flo. "You can see for yourself."

Flo told him that the cousin usually had a bath on his darts night. As they had a bungalow, he could nip back, look through the window and see for himself. The darts night came around and sure enough the cousin went for her bath. A little later, Flo walked in and this time felt compelled to say something.

"Why haven't you got any hair on your fanny?" she asked.

"I didn't know I was supposed to," said the naive girl.

"Oh yes, look I'll show you," And with that Flo lifted her skirt, pulled down her knickers and showed the girl her thatch.

Jack came home 30 minutes later in a very angry mood. "What the hell were you thinking of, exposing yourself like that!" he shouted.

"Oh don't be silly Jack, you've seen me hundreds of times."

"Maybe, but the bloody darts team haven't!"

Have you heard about the two spinsters in the shower? One said, "Where's the soap?" and the other replied, "Yes it does, doesn't it?"

Lucy's mother looked so young that many people mistook them for sisters. Now it just so happened that Lucy was courting a local dairyman but, unknown to her, the dairyman was also seeing her mother. One day, Lucy came home in tears.

"What's wrong?" asked her mother.

"William and I stopped seeing each other a month ago because I'm sure he was being unfaithful. But I've just seen him in the High Street and I still love him!" she cried.

"Never mind, you'll find someone else. You'll just have to forget about him. Did you return all the presents he gave you?"

"Yes I did and what's more I put tiny pinpricks in all his condoms – that'll teach him ... Mother, are you alright?"

★

What two other purposes have hill farmers found for sheep? Wool and meat.

★

How can you tell if a woman is wearing pantyhose?
When she farts her ankles swell up.

★

A young man was meeting his future in-laws for the first time at their large mansion in the country, and was understandably feeling quite nervous about the prospect.

They sat down to lunch and the first course went by without incident but just as the young man was about to tuck into the roast, he was unable to stop a small fart escaping.

"Jasper!" exclaimed the hostess to the dog.

Unfortunately, less than five minutes later, another, larger fart began to build up until, try as he might, he was unable to contain it any longer.

Again, the hostess shouted, "Jasper!"

Feeling pleased that the dog was getting blamed, the young man relaxed but in doing so he let out a rip roarer that fairly rattled the crockery.

"Jasper, get the hell over here quickly before that bugger dumps on you." shouted his hostess.

A bloke was walking home late one night when he was set upon by two muggers who beat him up and stole his wallet.

They also managed to break his top set of dentures. Lying on the ground battered and bruised, he was found by a kindly gentleman and helped to his feet.

"You look as if you could do with a stiff drink," said the gentleman. "My house is just round the corner, you're welcome to come and sit for a while until you're feeling better."

So some time later and two large whiskies later, the man started to recover and in doing so realised his dentures were broken.

"Wait a minute," said the gentleman, "I think I can help you out."

He disappeared for a few minutes and came back with a selection of different dentures.

"See if any of these fit," he said.

After trying on six different pairs the man found one that seemed to be perfect.

"I can't thank you enough," he said. "You rescue me from the pavement, help me to recover my wits and on top of all that you're a dentist as well."

"Oh no," said the gentleman, "I'm an undertaker."

★

Did you hear about the girl who said she'd do anything for a mink coat?
Now she can't do it up!

"Your kisses really burn."
"Sorry, perhaps I ought to put my cigarette out!"

Why do Australian men come so quickly?
Because they can't wait to get down to the pub to tell their mates.

What does a prat call his best friend's wife?
A really good fuck.

The Head of State would just like to say in defence of the sexual harassment charge against him, that the woman must have been slightly deaf. What he did say was, "Hold my calls and sack my cook."

★

The man was so drunk, he slipped and fell as he came out of the pub causing one car to swerve out of his way and plough into the back of a bus which caused a two-mile tailback. As the drunk was helped to his feet, one of the crowd asked him what had happened.
"I don't know," he slurred "I've only just got here myself."

Well, I've stuffed the turkey. All we need to do now is kill it and buy some apple sauce, and we'll have a great Christmas dinner.

A woman was being taught how to swim by the local swimming instructor, Sleazy Sid, who was holding her up in the water.
With an astonished look on her face she said, "Will I really sink if you take your finger out?"

★

Up for a Party

On her way home from an all night party, the girl was stopped by the traffic cops and breathalysed.

Looking at the results one of the policemen said, "You've had a few stiff ones tonight, Miss."

"That's amazing," she said. "I didn't know you could tell that as well."

A fellow went to a dance and as he was going round on the floor he said to the girl, "Your name's Hyacinth."

"How did you know?" she said.

"By your scent," he replied.

Later he danced with another girl and this time guessed her name was Rose. Towards the end of the dance his new partner was overheard to say, "But how did you know my name was Fanny?"

A party of game shooters stopped overnight at an hotel in the middle of Dartmoor. They'd had a very successful day so were in the mood to celebrate and by the time they retired to bed, many were unsteady on their feet.

Charles staggered into his room and was just about to collapse on the bed when he realised he hadn't cleaned his gun for the next day's shooting. As he sat down to the task, in his befuddled state he didn't realise it was still loaded and all of a sudden the gun went off in his hand, and fired a shot which went straight through the ceiling.

The following day at breakfast, the manager came up to him quite upset.

"I hear you had an accident with your gun last night. In fact it went straight through the ceiling and into the room of a young honeymoon couple, badly damaging the man's finger."

"What!" exclaimed Charles, "that's a damned poor show. Do convey to them my sincere apologies."

Then after a moment's pause, the manager continued, "Still it could have been worse; another few minutes and you'd have shot his head off."

A man was very embarrassed about having a wooden leg and a bald head, so when he received an invitation to a fancy dress ball, he panicked because he didn't want people to notice his problems. His friend advised him to write to a fancy dress company and explain his dilemma. A few days later, a huge parcel arrived and on opening it, he found a pirate's outfit. The enclosed letter informed him that the spotted handkerchief would hide his bald head and the wooden leg would be ideal for him to take on the character of Long John Silver. The man was outraged and wrote a strong letter back complaining that all they had done was draw even more attention to his wooden leg.

Some time later another parcel arrived, this time it contained a monk's habit. The enclosed letter informed him that the habit would hide his leg and the bald head would fit the part perfectly. The man wrote an even angrier letter back, pointing out that now the costume would emphasise his bald head. By return of post he received a small packet and a note which read, "We enclose a tin of treacle. We suggest you pour this over your bald head, stick your wooden leg up your arse and go as a toffee apple."

Just before the famous comedian is due to appear on stage at a cabaret dinner, a stranger comes up to him and says, "Hey, Jim, you're the tops with me, I'm your biggest fan and tonight I've got a red hot date. I'd really like to impress her and wondered if you would pretend to know me and come over and say hello. My name's Jack and I'll be sitting on the first table."

And indeed the comedian remembers the stranger's request and halfway through his act comes over to Jack's table.

"Hello, Jack, good to see you, hope you're okay."

"Fuck off, Jim, can't you see I'm busy?" replies Jack.

After a really wild party, two girls wake up the next morning and one says to the other, "Ugh, my mouth tastes like the inside of a bird's cage."

"Well, I'm not surprised," said the second girl. "You did have a cock or two in there last night."

★

Three sisters, named Flora, Fiona and Fanny lived in the same village in Yorkshire and were renowned for their beauty, although all of them had extra large feet. One evening, Flora and Fiona went to the local village bop and were soon chatting to some lads from the next village.

"By gum," said one of the lads. "Haven't you got big feet!"

"Oh that's nowt," they replied. "You should see our Fanny's."

Have you heard about the girl who gave up 10-pin bowling for sex? She found out the balls were lighter and she didn't have to wear shoes.

A rather shy man was dancing with a very shapely redhead when suddenly one of her earrings came off and dropped down the back of her dress.

"Would you mind getting that for me?" she asked him.

"Of course," he said, but the earring had dropped down a long way.

"Er..." he said embarrassingly, "I feel a perfect arse."

"My tits are alright too," she purred.

Two girls – one out for a good time, the other more staid and religious – go out clubbing for the night. Julie thoroughly enjoys herself, but Monica is not at all happy. As the club closes, they are approached by two boys who offer to walk them home. It's not long before the boys make their move – arms round the shoulders and a little nibbling of the girls' ears.

"Oh no!" gasps Monica, "dear Lord, please forgive them for

they know not what they do."
"Leave it out," hisses Julie, "mine does."

★

It was the night of the summer ball and all those attending were dressed in their very best. DJ's for the men, evening gowns for the women.

Halfway through the event, Alistair noticed a young woman sitting on her own, so liking what he saw, he strolled over to ask her for a dance.

"Thank you for asking," she said, "but I'm afraid I shall have to say no, because I have no legs."

The man was terribly embarrassed but she was so sweet, he sat down next to her and the rest of the evening passed in pleasant conversation.

"Would you mind if I took you home?" he said much later, and she quickly took up his offer.

When they arrived at her house, he kissed her goodnight and was surprised to find how passionately she returned his advances. It wasn't long before he was completely carried away with the situation and he whispered to her urgently, "How much I would like to make love to you! But this car is too awkward and I don't know how we'd manage."

"Oh, that's no problem," she replied. "Under my dress there's a big hook strapped to my back. If you place that over the top of the garden fence, I'm sure it would work."

So he carried her over to the fence and they were soon in the throes of extreme passion.

Now Alistair was quite a decent bloke and after it was all over, he felt somewhat ashamed of his behaviour. He took her down from the fence and carried her into the house.

"I'm awfully sorry," he said, "I feel a bit of a heel."

"Oh not at all," she assured him. "You've been the perfect gentleman. Most of the others usually leave me hanging on the fence."

Jack was fanatical about his special racing bike and he would clean it mornings and evenings, rubbing a special lubricant over it to stop any rust.

One day, he was invited to dinner at his girlfriend's house and went round on the bicycle but was told he couldn't bring it inside, it would have to remain round the back of the house.

After the meal, the mother said she wasn't washing up, she'd done the cooking.

"Well, I'm not," said the daughter.

"And I'm not," said the father.

"Neither am I," said Jack. "It looks like rain and I've got to see to my bike."

They seemed to have reached a stalemate so the father shouted, "Right, the next one who speaks will do the dishes!"

It was so quiet you could hear a pin drop, but Jack was getting very agitated as he looked through the windows at the storm clouds gathering. He needed to get the lubricant on the bike.

In sheer desperation to make someone speak he suddenly jumped on top of his girlfriend and rogered her there and then on the dining-room floor. The parents were utterly shocked

but no word was said. So as he saw the first few spots of rain he jumped on the wife and gave her a good seeing to as well. But still nobody spoke.

As the rain started to fall Jack knew he had failed, jumped up and said, "It's no good, I've got to use the lubricant."

At which point the father shot out of the room saying, "OK, I'll do the dishes."

A man went for an audition at the local club.

"You'd better not be a hypnotist, they're not welcome here."

"No, I'm a singer," he replied, "but what's wrong with hypnotists?"

"Well, we had one here a couple of days ago. He had 12 people on stage in a trance when he tripped over the microphone wire and shouted 'Shit'. We've been cleaning the place ever since."

Overheard at a fancy dress party:

"I'm a turkey," said the girl, "What are you?"

"Sage and onion," he replied.

The lift was packed solid with people as the doors closed and the attendant called out, "Which floors please?"

A man standing at the back shouted out, "Ballroom!" and a lady in front of him cried, "Oh I'm so sorry, I didn't know I was crushing you that much."

★

It was the church social and everyone was having a good time singing and dancing. Suddenly at a lull in the noise, Mrs Riddler shouted over to the vicar,

"What is it a man stands up to do, a woman sits down to do and a dog lifts up his leg to do?"

Blushing profusely, the vicar replied that he didn't know and amidst peals of laughter she cried, "Why, shake hands of course!"

A rather toffee-nosed couple moved into the area and to show off their new house invited the neighbours in for a cocktail party. They sent their adolescent son to bed and told him not to bother them but he kept coming down on any excuse – stomach ache, thirsty, couldn't sleep. Eventually, one of the guests, a retired colonel, suggested he take the boy back up to bed and he would soon get him settled.

Ten minutes later, the Colonel reappeared and they had no more trouble for the rest of the evening. As the party was breaking up, the couple took the Colonel aside and asked him what the secret was.

"Oh, simple really. I taught him to masturbate."

"I'm sorry you can't come in here, you have to wear a tie" said the bouncer at the night-club.

The man goes back to his car but can only find a set of jump leads. He slings them round his neck and walks back to the club.

"Will this do?" he asks.

"OK, but don't start anything."

It was the night of the grand fancy-dress party and on arriving, everyone was announced.

Shortly after 8pm, Jack arrived at the door wearing only his underpants.

"What are you?" insisted the announcer.

"I'm premature ejaculation," replied Jack.

"What! I can't say that, there are ladies present."

"OK, well just say I've come in my underpants."

It was a busy night in the Club and the crap table was doing a roaring trade. On one such throw a lot of money had been bet and as the dice landed, a beautiful brunette opened her coat to reveal she had nothing on underneath as she shouted, "I've won." She collected all the winnings and walked away.

"What did she throw?" asked the croupier afterwards.

"I don't know," everyone replied. "We weren't looking at the dice either."

★

A man arrived at a party half way through the evening to find most of the guests in the middle of a frenzied party game.

"What's going on here?" he asked.

"Oh come and join in," he was urged. "It's a great game. All the girls are blindfolded and they have to go round guessing who the men are by feeling their private bits."

The man hesitated.

"Oh I'm not sure about that," he said.

"Don't be daft," came the reply, "your name's been called out four times already!"

★

After a wild party the night before, both husband and wife woke up with dreadful hangovers.

"Last night in the garden, was it you I made love to?" asked the befuddled husband.

"I don't know," replied the wife. "What time was that?"

★

Up for a Lark

What do you call a group of twelve men with large willies? A hung jury.

★

What do you call a man with a 4" penis?
Norm.

★

The arrogant man had been thrusting away madly for more than five minutes when his date for the night turned to him and said,
"You remind me of Valentino."
"The great lover, you mean," he said smugly, "but... isn't he dead?"
"Exactly," she replied.

★

An arrogant man was walking in the park when he saw a pretty girl approaching with her dog.
"Hello darling," said this would-be stud.
"Nice day for it," he added, winking. The girl ignored him but the dog got an erection.
Puzzled, the man engineered another meeting with her a few minutes later and the dog reacted in the same way.
"What's going on here?" he asked. "Why's your dog getting so frisky every time I talk to you."
"Easy," she replied haughtily, "he knows a cocksucker when he sees one."

★

"Come on girl," whispered the boastful man, "how about coming back to my place and letting me give you six inches."

"No thanks," she replied. "I don't think you've got the energy to get it up three times."

★

As she left the room, the sweet young girl said to her boss, "Oh just one more thing Mr Arno, you've left the barrack doors open."

It wasn't until later he understood what she meant when he looked down and realised he'd left his flies undone. He pressed the intercom and said, "Maureen, can you come in here for a moment please?"

As she walked in he said proudly,

"When I left the barrack doors open this morning, did you see a soldier standing to attention?"

"Oh no," she replied sweetly. "I saw a shell-shocked veteran who'd seen better days."

An arrogant man asked his wife if she would like some ice cream he'd bought back from the supermarket.

"How hard is it?" she asked.

"About as hard as my dick," he boasted.

"Okay, pour me some then."

A husband and wife are admiring their newborn baby son.

"My goodness, just look at the size of his willy," said dad proudly.

"Yes sweetheart," answered his wife, "but at least he's got your nose."

★

A man goes to the doctor's because his penis is a massive 60 inches long.

"It's ruining my life," complained the man. "Is there anything you can do?"

"I'm sorry, there isn't," said the doctor, "but I think I have an answer to your problem. I've heard there's a deep pond in the middle of Crossways Wood. When you find it, you will see a frog sitting on a lily pad. You must ask it to marry you and when it says no, your penis will shorten by 10 inches."

However absurd the story, the man is so desperate, he sets out for the wood. Sure enough, there's a frog sitting on the lily pad.

"Hey frog," he shouts, "will you marry me?"

"No," replies the frog and the man's penis shrinks by 10 inches.

The man is overcome with happiness. Two more times he asks the frog to marry him and it shrinks another 20 inches. Wonderful, thinks the man, just once more and it'll be perfect.

"Hey froggy, will you marry me?"

By this time the frog is so annoyed with all the pestering that he shouts back,

"I'm fed up with telling you, no, no and no again!"

A male visitor to a country golf club ended up in the female locker room by mistake. He was unaware of this mix up until halfway through his shower when two ladies entered and he could hear them talking across the way. In a panic, all he could think of was to escape without being recognised. He wrapped a towel round his head and in a sudden dash, ran naked from the room.

"My goodness," exclaimed the first woman. "That certainly wasn't my husband."

"Nor mine," said the second.

"In fact," continued the first, "he's not even a member of this club."

The woman's husband had been chosen as opening batsman for the local cricket team. She was so concerned he might injure himself that she immediately went out to buy him a box for protection.

"What size would that be?" asked the young saleswoman. "They come in different sizes."

"Well, I'm not sure," replied the woman blushing.

"Okay, no problem," replied the assistant, holding up her little finger. "What about this?"

"Oh no, bigger," replied the wife.

The assistant held up two fingers.

"No, bigger than that," came the reply.

Eventually, she held up all five fingers.

"Yes, that's it," said the wife triumphantly.

So the assistant put all five fingers in her mouth and declared with some expertise, "Fine, that's a size 4 then."

Marvin went into the chemist for a packet of condoms but when the girl asked him what size he needed, he shook his head in bewilderment.

"I've no idea," he said.

"Oh that's no problem," replied the girl kindly. "If you'd just like to come in the back with me a moment."

Once there, she took off her knickers and asked him to enter her. He was astonished but delighted.

"You're a size 4," she said after a moment. "Now please take it out."

They went back into the shop and he bought a packet of size 4. On his way home, he bumped into his sleazy friend Maurice, and recounted his amazing experience.

"Cor! I need a bit of that!" sleazed Maurice and off he went looking for the chemist.

"A packet of condoms please, Miss," he said, moments later.

"Certainly sir, what size?"

"Oh, I don't know," said Maurice.

"Okay, if you'd like to come in the back with me."

He did as she asked and he received the same service.

"You're a size 5," she said. "Now take it out please. How many packets do you want?"

But sleazy Marvin refused to stop until he was completely satisfied, and then zipping himself up he said to her grinning, "None today, thanks, I just came in for a fitting."

★

A woman went to an alternative healer to find out if anything could be done to make her breasts bigger.

"No problem," said the healer. "All you have to do is recite 'Mary, Mary quite contrary' and you will soon notice the difference."

Walking through the park on the way home, the girl couldn't stop thinking about the amazing treatment and sitting down on a bench, she started to recite the verse. She was staring down at her breasts in amazement, as they slowly began to fill out, when all of a sudden, a man appeared behind her. "I bet I know where you've been," he said, "Hickory, dickory, dock..."

The year was 2900 and advances in medicine had resulted in special body part shops appearing all round the country. One morning, a young man walked into one of these shops and requested a new penis.

"What size sir?" came the reply. "We have 6-inch, 8-inch and 10-inch."

As the man looked at the different sizes he remarked, "Have you got the 10-inch in white?"

In the Ladies'

Have you heard the mating call of a blonde?
"Oh I'm soooo drunk."

What did the Jewish lady say to the flasher?
"You call that a lining?"

"Oh Patsy, you know that gorgeous man across the road, he was banging on my door for almost an hour last night."
"Well, why didn't you open it?"
"I didn't want to let him out."

Two girls are walking along the prom when a holiday photographer steps forward.
"Hold on Jean, he's going to focus."
"What! Both at the same time?"

A woman said to her friend, "Do you smoke after sex?"
"Gosh, I've never looked," she replied.

★

Three girls were talking on a bus about safe sex.
The first said she always carried a packet of condoms in her

bag; the second said she was on the pill; and the third said she used a tin with a few pebbles inside. The other two looked at her in amazement.

"How does that work?"

"Oh, it's quite simple. I make him stand on it and when it starts to rattle I kick it out from under him."

Two women were chatting on a bus:

"I've got a dreadful sore throat," said one.

"Oh you poor thing! When I've got a sore throat I suck on a Life Saver."

"Ah, that's easy for you to do. You live near the seaside."

Two women are talking on a bus and one says to the other,

"I was so embarrassed this morning. I met my son's new teacher. What a hunk! He made me go weak at the knees and instead of telling him I had come about our Billy, I said I'd come about his willy."

"Never mind," replies the other. "Sometimes we all say things we didn't mean to say. For instance, this morning I made my husband his breakfast and accidentally told him I hated his guts and that was why I was sleeping with his best friend."

Two ladies talking in the laundrette:

"Has your husband been circumcised?" said one.

"No," replied the other. "He's always been a complete dick."

★

Two women talking:
"How do you keep your youth?" said the first.
"I lock him in the cupboard," replied the second.

★

Two girls talking on a bus:
"Last night I had three orgasms in a row."
"That's nothing, I had over 50."
"Golly, he must be good."
"Oh, you mean with just one guy?"

Two women talking on a bus:
"No, Doreen, you've got it wrong. If you think the way to a man's heart is through his stomach, you're aiming too high."

★

Two girls talking:
"What do you think of the new salesman? He dresses fashionably."
"And quickly too," replied the other.

★

Overheard on the top deck of a bus:
"My husband's away at sea so much, when he comes home he's like a stranger."
"Oh you lucky thing, how exciting."

★

"I've been out with every player in the rugby team and I haven't bonked one of them," said the girl.

"Oh, I know who that'll be," replied her mate. "It's that scrum half, isn't it? I reckon he's gay."

★

"But Joan, if sex is a pain in the arse, you're doing it wrong."

★

At Work

At the Hotel

Three girls arrive at the hotel to be interviewed for the job of a chambermaid. The manager asks each of them in turn what they would do if they found a £10 note.

The first said, "Finders keepers."

The second said she would hand it in and after three months, if it had not been claimed, would take it herself.

The third answered the same as the second, except that with the money she would buy everyone who worked in the hotel a drink and then give the rest to the local hospice.

Now ... which girl got the job?

The one with big tits, of course.

★

"I can't sleep in that room," said the angry man to the receptionist. "It stinks in there."

"I'm sorry sir," she replied, "the last occupant had a skunk with him. Perhaps if you opened the windows..."

"What?" he interrupted, "and lose all my pigeons!"

A difficult customer complained that there was a hair in his venison stew.

"I don't expect to find this in a top class hotel," he said angrily, "so I'm not paying for it."

Later, the waiter met the man again when he was asked to take up room service. This time, he found the man with his head between a young woman's legs.

"Aah," said the waiter, still angry from their earlier confrontation. "I see you don't mind hair in your mouth now."

"No, I don't," retorted the man. "But if I find any venison stew down here, I won't pay for this either."

The phone rang and a voice at the other end said, "Mr Smallman? We have one of your employees staying at our hotel. He has run up quite a large bill and I'm checking to see that it will be paid."

"How much is it?" asked Mr Smallman.

"£550," came the reply.

"What?" he spluttered. "For three days! That's impossible."

"I've got the chits here," said the hotel man.

"You've got the chits! What do you think I've got?"

★

A salesman was amazed to see a lot of very expensive cars in the hotel car park and commented on it to the hotel owner, a beautiful blonde, as he was signing in.

He asked her who owned all the cars, and she replied, "Actually, they are all mine."

"Gosh, you must have a very successful business to afford all those cars."

"Not necessarily," she said, "I've won them all in bets I've had with the men who've stayed here. You see, I bet them that they can't do what my eight year old nephew can do."

"Well, of course I can," he replied. "Any man could do what an eight year old boy can do."

So the bet was agreed with the car and the hotel as the stake.

First the blonde called the boy over, took out one of her ample breasts and asked him to kiss it. The boy did as she asked and then the amazed man did the same. Then she dropped her panties and asked the boy to kiss her down below. He did and the man followed. At this point the man thought he had won the bet and gleefully asked for the key to the motel.

"Just a minute," she said, and she turned to her nephew, saying, "Last thing, Johnny, bend your willy in half and ask the gentleman for his car keys."

A man goes for an audition as a pianist in a local hotel night-club. He starts by playing a stunning blues number which has everyone stopping work to listen to it. When he's finished the club owner is delighted and asks him about the music.

"I wrote it myself," said the man. "It's called 'I Want To Shag You Long And Hard'."

After a stunned silence, the owner asks him to play something else and this time it's a funky jazz number. Absolutely superb, there are cheers all round the bar. The man tells them he also wrote it and called it 'Lick My Love Pump, Madame Hot Pants'.

After some embarrassment the owner comes to a decision.

"You've got the job, on one condition; you never ever tell the audience the titles of the music you play."

Although not too happy about it, the man agrees. After all, the pay is good.

Some weeks go by and the club's popularity goes from strength to strength. People come from miles around to hear the pianist and his reputation spreads like wildfire. The night after a particularly successful session, the pianist staggers off to the toilet. He's been given free drinks all night by the admiring public and is feeling a bit the worse for wear. In fact he's so far gone he forgets to do his flies back up. On the way back to the stage a lady taps him on the shoulder.

"Excuse me, do you know your fly is open and your dick is hanging out?"

He replies, "Know it? I wrote the fucker!"

At the Office

Secretary to her boss: "Excuse me Sir, the invisible man's here."
"Tell him I can't see him."

★

His secretary was absolutely naff.
"Why don't you answer the bloody phone?" he said in
exasperation.
"Because I'm damned well fed up," she replied. "Nine times
out of ten it's for you."

★

"Hello Mrs Palmer, I'm your husband's boss and I'm just calling to
say he'll be late home tonight."
Eager to keep her husband's boss happy, the wife invites him in for a
coffee but when he starts to suggest they go upstairs she quickly
refuses.
"Come on," says the boss. "I can show you a good time and I'll even
give you £300 for the pleasure."
They were short of money so eventually, after some more
persuading, the wife agrees and the deed is done. Later that night,
the husband returns home and asks his wife if she has had any
visitors.
"Just your boss to tell me you'd be late home," she replies.
"Oh good," he says. "Did he drop off my wage packet?"

★

The ambitious P.A. went out for dinner with her boss and when the bill arrived she said, "I must insist we go Dutch. You pay for dinner and the rest of the evening will be on me."

★

"You can use my Dictaphone," said the office Casanova to the new secretary.

"No thanks, I'll use my finger if it's all the same to you," she replied.

★

The interview for secretary had been going well until the boss asked, "How good are you on the typewriter?"

"Pretty good," she replied "but I'm better on the floor."

★

Jack and his work colleagues were off on their annual sales conference and relaxing in the bar afterwards, they began recounting their most embarrassing moments.

"What about you, Colin? asked Jack.

Colin hesitated and then said "I suppose it was when my mother came unexpectedly into my room and found me playing with myself."

"Well that's nothing to worry about. Young boys often do that sort of thing," said Jack somewhat disappointed.

"Yes, I know," replied Colin, "but this was only last week."

★

The young girl arrived for an interview to become a trainee executive.

"So Miss Brightly, what are your qualifications?"

"Well I graduated from Oxford with a first class honours degree, having achieved the highest marks ever. I then spent a year in the States, running the day to day business of a small airline and in my spare time wrote a textbook on 'modern business practices'."

"Well, that's wonderful," enthused the interview panel. "Is there anything you wish to add?"

"Yes, I'm a pathological liar."

The young girl couldn't believe her luck when her flashy boss took her out to dinner. They wined and dined at the most expensive restaurant in town and then went back to his penthouse apartment. Later, in bed, he turned to her and said, "What would you do if you found you were pregnant?"

"Oh the shame. I could never tell my parents. I'd kill myself," she replied.

"Good girl, that's what I like to hear," he said happily.

As the new office manager walked into the building, he noticed a youth sitting down on a stool, reading a magazine.

"Hey, you," he called, throwing him £200. "That's a week's wages, pack up and get out immediately... and don't come back."

As the astonished boy left the site, the boss turned to the under manager and said, "That's the way to treat idle buggers like that, just

get rid of them on the spot. So how long had he been working here?"
"He hadn't," replied his assistant. "He just popped in to deliver lunch from the deli, and he was waiting for his change."

The boss called his handsome executive into his office and handed him a bowl.

"Bob, I want you to go next door and masturbate into this bowl."

So the executive, hoping for promotion in the near future, did not question his boss' request but went next door and did as he was asked. A few minutes later he returned and said

"Here it is Mr. Grimes."

"Good. Now here's another bowl. Go and do it again."

So the executive carried out the request for a second time. Over the next hour, the boss told him to do it time and time again until the poor man was so knackered, he begged for a rest.

"Yes, I think that will do fine, Bob. Now you can drive my daughter to the airport, she's got to catch a plane at six."

After the job interview, the post was given to a voluptuous young girl.
"You'll be expected to do the same things here, as you did in your last job," said her new boss.
"Oh that's fine by me," she replied, "as long as I can kneel on something soft."

★

The young girl was being interviewed for the job of personal assistant. As she looked across the desk at her would-be boss, he suddenly said,

"Yes, I think you're exactly what I'm looking for. The pay is £4 above the going rate but that's because I expect my personal assistant to be just that. Very personal, if you get my drift?"

"Oh yes," she replied. "I understand and I'll take the job on those terms."

So, the following Monday morning, the girl arrived bright and early, ready for work. At 9 o'clock, the boss walked in, smiled and said,

"Come on Sandra, let's get personal. I feel like a good fuck."

So she left her desk and went into his office where they did the business. Afterwards she remarked,

"Gosh, you don't waste much time, do you?"

"I don't waste money, either," he replied. "You're fired."

Maurice had died at the untimely age of 53. He had been a very boring man. All he'd lived for was his work so there wasn't a lot of grief at his funeral. Workmates took up a collection and a headstone was bought with the money. Unfortunately, the stone was erected before the soil had settled and it began to tilt. As a temporary measure, the cemetery attendant wired it up to a nearby tree. Later that week, some of his old friends came to see the finished headstone and one immediately remarked on seeing the wire, "Well bugger me, good old Maurice, still working I see. He's got the phone connected now."

The young man was obsessed by the beautiful secretary in his office. He just had to kiss her and maybe cuddle her and ... One day, he plucked up the courage to speak to her.

"I think you're so gorgeous, if I paid you £250, would you come into the storeroom with me so that I can kiss you and rub my hands up and down your body?"

Now the girl liked money a lot, so she agreed and they disappeared into the storeroom. For the next 10 minutes, he showered her with kisses, unbuttoning her blouse and ravishing her breasts, but all the time, he kept murmuring, "I don't know, I don't know."

Eventually, she asked, "Why do you keep saying 'I don't know?'"

"Well, I don't know how I'm going to pay you", he replied.

★

"Excuse me, sir, may I have tomorrow afternoon off? The wife wants me to go shopping with her."

"Certainly not."

"Thank you, sir, I knew you'd understand."

★

The phone rings and it's a man asking to speak to Bob Wankbreak.

"No, I don't think we've got anyone here by that name, just a mo, I'll ask. Is there a Wankbreak here?"

"Wankbreak?" came the reply. "We haven't even got time for a tea break!"

The local bank was held up by four masked gunmen, and customers and staff were ordered to lie face down on the floor. Everyone did as they were told except one young girl who lay down on her back.

"Don't be silly, this is a bank robbery not the office party," whispered her friend. "Lie down the other way."

It was the young girl's first day in her new job as P.A. to the company director. Before she was called in to his room one of the other secretaries took her aside.

"I think I ought to warn you that your new new boss is a right old randy devil. He'll rip your dress off at the first opportunity."

"Thanks's for warning me," replied the girl. "I'll remember to wear an old dress in future."

The company was losing money and the boss had no other option but to get rid of one of his staff – either Jack or Beryl. He decides to tell them straight away and spots Beryl putting on her coat ready for going home.

"Hello Beryl," he says hesitantly, "there's something I've got to tell you. I need to lay you or Jack off."

"Then Jack off," she replied angrily. "I've got a headache."

★

The morning after the office party, the husband put his head in his hands and groaned loudly.

"Oh bloody hell, what a party last night, I can't remember a

thing about it. Did I make a prat of myself?"

"You sure did," replied his wife.

"You put your hand up the skirt of your boss's wife and told your boss to piss off."

"Shit! What happened?"

"He sacked you."

"Well fuck him, the bastard."

"I did," replied the wife, "and you've got your job back."

The ambitious City type lived for his work, nothing else mattered. Every night and all weekend he would bring papers home to work on. Then one day he left some important papers at home and in a panic rushed home to get them. As he was leaving his spare room he saw his wife and boss in bed together.

Later that day he mentioned what he had seen to a colleague.

"Why, that's appalling, are you going back tomorrow to try and catch them at it?"

"Good gracious no, it was lucky he didn't see me this time."

"Jenkins, what on earth do you think you are doing?" said the boss to his employee when he found him in the toilets masturbating. Jenkins thought quickly and said, "Oh that! It's not what it seems."

"Really, then what does it mean?"

"Well, sir, I've got ESP and I'm just bonking my girlfriend in Bristol."

★

The multinational company was looking for a new Director General and three men were up for the job. They were famous for demanding absolute loyalty from their employees, but also for being extremely generous when it came to salaries, bonuses, holidays and the like.

To test their undying loyalty to the company, they were all asked to do the same thing.

"Go into the other room and shoot your wife," they ordered the first man, handing him a gun.

"Oh no," gasped the man. "My wife means more to me than anything, I can't do it."

So he was dismissed.

The second man was given similar instructions.

Handing him a gun they ordered him to go next door and shoot his wife dead.

"I can't do it," replied the ashen-faced man. "Tomorrow is our 25th anniversary and we've lived a very happy life."

So the second man was dismissed.

The third man came in, a gun was passed to him and he was told to go into the next room and kill his wife. The man did as he'd been instructed and went next door. At first there was complete silence but all of a sudden they heard an awful scream, furniture falling over and then all went quiet. A moment later the third man returned.

"What happened in there?" they asked.

"Some prat put blank cartridges in the gun, so I had to strangle her," he replied.

Two businessmen are travelling home on the train. One turns to the other and asks how his business is doing.

"Very well, very well indeed, ever since I've taken on this new salesman. Sadly there's just one problem. He's seduced both my wife and my daughter and made two of the office girls pregnant."

"Good gracious, what are you going to do?"

"Don't worry, I'm watching him very closely and if he tries to fiddle the books, I'll sack him on the spot."

★

It is the conference season and three dentists and three bankers find themselves together at the railway ticket office. The dentists each buy a ticket but the bankers buy one between them.

"How are you all going to travel on one ticket?" ask the dentists.

"You'll see," they reply.

On boarding the train the dentists take their seats but the bankers all cram into the one toilet. The conductor comes round shouting "Tickets please!", knocks on the toilet door and a ticket is passed to him. The dentists are impressed and decide to do the same on the return journey. They only buy one ticket but to their amazement the bankers don't buy a ticket at all.

"How come?" ask the dentists.

"You'll see," the bankers reply.

They all got onto the train, the three dentists crammed into one toilet, the three bankers get into another.

A few minutes later one of the bankers leaves his toilet, knocks on the other toilet door and shouts, "Tickets please!"

★

A man rings up his boss to tell him he won't be in to work.

"I'm sorry, I'm sick," he tells him.

"Sick again," says the boss angrily. "This seems to be happening a lot. How sick are you?"

"Pretty sick," replies the man. "I'm in bed with my sister."

★

On the Job

Two men were painting a bridge over the River Severn. One was in a cradle at the top and the other was in a second cradle further down, steadying the ropes.

"Throw me up some paint thinner!" shouted the first man.

"Oh thanks," said the second man, who was hard of hearing. "I've been on this diet a month now."

"No, I said throw me up some thinner."

"Yes thanks, I've had my dinner."

"Listen, you stupid prat, I said PAINT THINNER!" bellowed the first.

"Oh right!" and the second man threw him up a bottle of paint thinner which unfortunately hit him on the head causing him to fall out of the cradle and plunge into the icy waters never to be seen again. The following month, an inquest was held and before the verdict was announced the coroner asked whether anyone present had anything to say.

His mate got up and replied,

"Just one thing, Mr Coroner, sir. I think his accident had something to do with sex."

"Really? Why's that?"

"Well, as he passed me going down I heard him shout 'Cunt!'."

★

Did you hear about the promising young actress who had to perform live sex on stage?

By the end of the performance, there wasn't a dry handkerchief in the house.

★

"I want to open a new bank account, NOW!" yelled the nasty customer.

"Of course, sir," replied the teller, "but there's no need to shout."

"Just open the bloody account," he replied.

"Okay, just one moment."

"NOW!" he shouted, "get off your fat arse and get on with it."

Upset at the language, the bank teller walked off and returned with the manager.

"For fuck's sake, I want to open a bank account, I've just won £20 million on the lottery," he said.

"Immediately, sir," replied the manager and he turned to the teller, saying,

"Get your fucking arse into gear and open an account."

★

An actor went into the theatrical outfitters and asked for an RAF uniform, one that Douglas Bader would have worn in the Second World War.

"I'm sorry sir, we haven't got an exact match at the moment," said the shop assistant, " but we do have one from a slightly later era."

"No, no," replied the man. "It has to be absolutely correct. I'm a perfectionist and I'm playing Douglas Bader at the Princes Theatre in six weeks time."

"In that case, sir, if you come back next Monday, I may be able to help you."

"I'm afraid that's no good, I'm having my legs off next Monday," he replied.

★

An ageing, out of work actor, received a phone call from his agent telling him to be in Leeds the following Friday for a part in the Christmas panto. The actor was thrilled. At last, he would be treading the boards once again! However, his joy turned to despair when he realised he didn't have enough money to travel to Leeds. Then he had an idea. Early next morning he went down to the canal and engaged a bargee in conversation.

"Excuse me, bargee," he said. "I am to appear in Pantomime at Leeds Theatre next Friday and I wondered if anyone was going my way?"

"As it happens, I am," replied the bargee. "I set off at six o'clock in the morning, and we'll make it by Thursday as long as we get through the locks without a mishap."

True to his word, the bargee set off at six the next morning with the ageing actor on board. As the first lock came into view, the lock keeper shouted down,

"Hello there, what are you carrying?"

"I'm carrying 10 ton of pig shite and the actor Cyril Carstairs," replied the bargee.

At the second lock, the lock keeper asked the same question and again he got the same reply.

"I'm carrying 10 ton of pig shite and the actor Cyril Carstairs."

So the journey continued until they came to the outskirts of Leeds and the final, 22nd lock. As they approached, the actor tapped the bargee on the shoulder.

"Excuse me, bargee," he said " We're coming to the final lock, and I wonder, just this once, if I could have top billing?"

★

The local journalist had been sent to interview a woman who had eleven kids. They were all boys and she was hoping to start up her own football team.

"So Mrs Haverlot, this is your eldest son. What's his name?"

"Bobby," she said. "After Bobby Charlton."

The journalist scribbled in his notebook.

"And this lad here, what's his name?"

"Bobby," she replied.

He looked puzzled, but continued, "What about this one?"

"Bobby," she replied.

The journalist laughed. "You'll be telling me next that they're all called Bobby."

"That's right," she said.

"But how do they know who you want when you call one of them?"

"Oh that's no problem," she said, "they've all got different surnames."

★

It was Saturday morning and the newspaper deliverer was touring the estate, collecting the week's money. When he got to number 74 Prospect Road he rang the bell but got no answer. Just as he was about to move away, he suddenly had a feeling that someone was standing just behind the door. He put his ear to the wood and could hear a great deal of panting and gasping.

"It's the newspaper man," he called.

A voice was heard from the other side,

"Can you come back in 10 minutes, I'm just paying the milk bill."

★

A couple moved into a new house, close to a busy main road. Unfortunately, every time a bus trundled by, the wardrobe door would fly open so the woman rang up a local carpenter who came round that afternoon. He inspected it closely but could find nothing wrong. "I'll just have a look inside," he said, but as he disappeared through the doors, her husband walked into the bedroom.

"What's going on here?" he demanded, opening the wardrobe door.

"You'll never believe this," said the carpenter sheepishly. "I'm waiting for a bus."

★

A group of men were out on a pheasant shoot when they suddenly came across an extraordinary sight. Scampering through the forest was a beautiful, naked young girl being chased by four men in green uniforms. One of the men was carrying a concrete pole. In a matter of seconds they had disappeared into the undergrowth only to re-emerge ten minutes later. "Excuse me," shouted one of the shooters. "What's going on?"

One of the men stopped to explain.

"We work at the local psychiatric hospital and this is one of our patients. She just loves to escape outdoors and run around naked."

"I see," replied the shooter, "but why is that man carrying a concrete pole?"

"Oh that's his handicap. He caught her yesterday."

Jack went down to the Job Centre and as he was scanning situations vacant, he spotted a card asking for a film scene assistant. The successful candidate would need to have a steady hand to be a bikini line shaver on the latest series of an English version of Baywatch. Drooling at the very thought, he took the card over to the desk and told the employment officer he was interested in the job.

"Very well," she replied, not batting an eyelid. "You'll need to go to the service station, two miles out of town."

"Really? Is that where they're interviewing?"

"No, that's where the end of the queue is," she replied.

Jack was a plumber. He worked for himself and had just finished a job for Mr. Crabtree on Gowan Avenue. As he left, he handed him a bill. "Prompt payment would be greatly appreciated," he said.

However, a couple of weeks went by without payment, so Jack sent a reminder. Another month went by and still no sign of a cheque, so he sent a second reminder. After another four weeks, he wrote a letter and enclosed a picture of his wife and two children, writing on the back,

"This is the reason I need money – to feed my family."

Lo and behold, two days later a letter arrived in the post. It was from Mr. Crabtree. But alas there was no cheque. The envelope contained just one photo. A picture of a voluptuous blonde, wearing a bikini and standing next to a zippy little sports car. On the back of the photo was written,

"And this is the reason I can't pay."

★

The young man was selling encyclopaedias from door to door. He had one set left as he knocked at the cottage door and a voice called out,

"Hello?"

"I'm selling the latest, most up-to-date encyclopaedias," he called back.

"Okay, can you come round the back?" came a voice.

So the man walked around the side of the house, to the back door, where he saw a voluptuous woman wearing a see-through nightie and smiling at him seductively.

"Well, hello," she said sexily.

All of a sudden the man burst into floods of tears.

"What's wrong?" she asked, alarmed at his behaviour.

"I've had a terrible week," he sobbed. "My wife left me on Monday, the house burnt down Tuesday, yesterday someone stole my car and now today I'm going to be fucked out of my last set of encyclopaedias."

The milkman delivers the milk the day before Christmas and rings the bell of number 11, hoping for a festive tip. As the door opens, he sees a beautiful woman standing there wearing a see- through nightie. She takes him by the hand and guides him upstairs where she makes mad passionate love to him. At the end of the session, they return downstairs where she cooks a delicious fried breakfast and hands him £1.

"I don't understand," says the puzzled milkman. "What's going on?"

She replies,

"When I asked my husband whether I should give you a £5 tip, he replied 'Fuck the milkman, give him £1'. The breakfast was my idea."

A man walked into the barbers shop and said he wanted his hair to be styled completely different to everyone else.

"Can you part my hair from ear to ear?" he asked.

"If that's what you want," replied the barber doubtfully, but the man was given what he wanted.

However, that afternoon he walked back into the shop.

"What's wrong?" asked the barber. "Are you tired of the style already?"

"No," he replied angrily, "I'm just fed up with everybody whispering in my nose."

Johnny was looking for his mate Bob Cox and thought he might be having his hair cut. He popped his head round the barber shop door and called out

"Bob Cox in here?"

"Sorry, no," replied the barber, "we only do shaves and haircuts."

★

Bill, the local barber, had a secret remedy to restore hair and on the odd occasion he would pass it on to his very special customers.

One such customer came in and asked Bill to give him the

remedy for £1,000. After some thought Bill agreed and told him all he needed do to restore hair to his bald patch was apply some female secretions.

"But how do I know it works?" replied the customer. "You've still got a bald patch on your head."

"Maybe," said Bill. "But have you ever seen a better moustache?"

★

The simpleton's car broke down and the garage man arrived to take a look at it.

"Oh yeah, shit in the carburettor" said the mechanic.

"Really?" asks the simpleton. "How often will I have to do that?"

★

In Church

It was Saturday night and Ted and his two mates were all dressed up ready to paint the town red. But first, as usual, Ted popped into church for confession.

"Forgive me father, for I have sinned. I slept with a woman who was not my wife."

"I suppose it was Christina from the dairy."

"No Father."

"Don't tell me it was Stacey at the Kings Arms?"

"No Father."

"Then it must have been that brazen hussy Marie from the newsagents?"

After the priest had given out the penance, Ted went back outside to meet his friends. He smiled at them saying,

"It's worked again lads, I've got the names of another three ravers!"

The young priest was about to hear his first confession. Sitting further away was the old priest to keep an eye on him. After it was over, the young priest asked how he had done.

"Not too bad," replied the old priest. "In future, however, a bit less Really! Never! Cor! and Wow! and a bit more tut-tutting might be better idea."

A vicar went into a pet shop looking for a nice pet that would keep him company while he wrote his sermons.

"I've got just what you need," said the pet shop owner. "Take a look at this parrot. Not only does it talk but if you pull the string on his left leg he'll sing 'Rock of Ages' and if you pull the string on his right leg, he'll recite the Lords Prayer."

"That is truly remarkable!" exclaimed the vicar, "but what happens if I pull both strings at the same time?"

"I fall off my bloody perch, you wanker!" screeched the parrot.

A simple minded man was sitting opposite a priest on the train.

"Excuse me, why do you wear your collar back to front?" asked the man.

"It's because I'm a Father," replied the priest.

"But I'm a father too," said the man, "and I don't wear my collar back to front."

"Aah, but the difference is, I'm a father to thousands."

"Well in that case," retorted the man, "it's not your collar, it's your trousers you should wear back to front."

★

The local Catholic priest rang up his opposite number in the Church of England asking him for a favour.

"I'm supposed to hear confessions in half an hour but something unexpected has come up and I have to be the other side of the diocese by 2 o'clock. Will you take over from me here?" asked the priest.

"What! but I've never done it before."

"It's quite straightforward," said the priest. "Sit in with me for half an hour before I go and you'll soon get the hang of it."

So the vicar agrees and is soon hidden away within earshot of the confessional. The first person to enter is a woman.

"Father I have sinned."

"What have you done my child?"

"I have been unfaithful."

"How many times have you been unfaithful?"

"Four times Father and I am truly sorry."

"Very well, Put £2 in the box and say 10 Hail Mary's and you'll be absolved." Not long after another woman comes in.

"Father, I have sinned."

"What have you done my child?"

"I have slept with a married man."

"How many times?" "Twice."

"Then put £1 in the box, say 5 Hail Mary's and you'll be absolved."

Moments later the priest whispered to the vicar. "You see how it works? Take over from me now, I have to go."

So the vicar seated himself comfortably in the confessional and immediately a woman sat down on the other side.

"Father, I have sinned" she said.

"What have you done my child?"

"I have committed adultery."

"How many times?"

"Only once, Father."

"Well you'd better go back and do it again."

"What! You want me to do it again?"

"Yes, its two for £1."

★

"Hello Bob, how did you get that black eye?" asked John.

"In church. As we stood up to sing, a large lady in front of me had her dress stuck in the cheeks of her bum, so I pulled it out but all I got in the way of thanks was a black eye."

The following week the two men met again and John was amazed to see Bob had now got two black eyes.

"Don't tell me you got the other black eye in church as well?" he said.

"Well that I did," said Bob. "I was in church with my son and when we got up to sing, the same woman had her dress stuck in the cheeks of her bum. Before I could stop him, my son had pulled the dress out. Now I know she didn't like that so I put it back in... and that's when she hit me."

★

Mother Superior was talking to one of her young nuns.

"Sister, if you were out late at night on your own and a man attacked you, what would you do?"

"I would lift up my habit," she replied.

"Goodness me, and then what would you do?"

"I would tell him to drop his pants."

"Oh Lord save us," uttered the shocked Mother Superior, "and then what?"

"I would run away as fast as I could, and I can run much faster with my habit up, than he can with his trousers down."

A man goes into the confessional and says, "Forgive me Father for I have sinned. Yesterday, I cursed badly, using the F-word."

"Why was that?" asked the priest.

"I was playing a round of golf, all was going well until I reached the 10th hole when my tee shot ended up in thick undergrowth."

"Is that when you said the F-word?"

"No, I stayed calm, took my time and hit a clean shot out of the rough, down the fairway but at the last moment it hit a small branch and veered off into the bunker."

"I like a game of golf myself," said the priest, "and that really is annoying. Was that when you used the F-word?"

"No, I tried not to let it get to me. I took my time and hit a beautiful ball up onto the green only 2 inches from the hole."

"How frustrating, is that when you used the F-word?"

"No Father, I still remained calm …"

"Don't tell me!" interrupted the priest. "You didn't miss the fucking putt!!"

★

"Come in George," said the Mother Superior to her gardener. "I hear you've got a complaint."

"That I have," he replied, "one of your nuns has been doing press-ups in my vegetable garden."

"Well surely there's no harm in that."

"Aah, but you've not seen my cucumbers, they're all ruined."

★

A young girl went into confession and told the priest she had slept with four different men over the past week. Jack on Tuesday, Bill on Wednesday, Peter on Thursday and Chuck on Friday.

"Well my child," said the priest, "on your way home tonight buy two lemons and suck on them."

"But Father, will that cleanse me of my sins?" she asked.

"No, but it'll wipe that damned smile off your face."

Two nuns were walking back to the convent late at night when they saw a suspicious man coming towards them.

"Quick," whispered one of the nuns. "Show him your cross and he may leave us alone."

"Good idea," replied the other and raising her voice as loud as possible she shouted, "Fuck off, you bastard!"

A drunk staggers into church and wanders up the aisle moaning to himself.

"Jesus Christ, I'm in agony!"

Eventually, he makes it into the confessional and all goes quiet. After a few minutes the priest decides he'd better find out if everything is alright so he says

"May I help you my son?"

"I don't know," comes the reply, "it depends on whether you have any paper in there."

In fact the story of Adam and Eve has become slightly mis-told over the years. As it happens, Eve was created first and God gave her three breasts. But after a while she complained that she was in some pain because they kept bumping against each other, so he agreed to take the middle one away. Time passed and Eve began to get bored so she asked God if he could make her someone to play with.

"Of course," replied God. "I'll call him man ... now where did I put that useless tit?"

The vicar knocked at the door and a boy of 14 answered, beer in one hand, a cigarette dangling from his mouth and girls hanging off his arms.

"Excuse me son," said the vicar somewhat taken aback, "is your mum or dad in?"

"Piss off!" sneered the boy, "does it fucking well look like it?"

An old vicar was retiring and selling his horse so he put an ad in the local newspaper. It wasn't long before it was bought by Bob who decided to ride it home. But when he mounted up, the horse wouldn't move.

"I trained this horse from a little foal," said the vicar. "He only moves when you say Jesus Christ and stops when you say Amen."

Bob thanked the vicar and sure enough when he said Jesus Christ, the horse set off. However on the way home they were caught in a ferocious thunderstorm and the horse bolted when there was a particularly loud crack of thunder. By the time Bob had recovered his wits, the horse was galloping madly through the countryside and it took him a moment or two to remember to say Amen. Immediately the horse came to a standstill, teetering right on the edge of a deep canyon.

"Jesus Christ!" he said.

A group of young boys were always getting into trouble on the estate so the local vicar decided to intervene and speak to each of them about their behaviour. When it was Johnny's turn to go in, he sat down nervously wondering what was going to happen. As with the other boys, the vicar decided to find out how much the boy knew about God and whether he understood the difference between right and wrong. The vicar began with the question, "Where is God?"

Johnny stared at him in amazement but did not answer. Again the question was asked, this time more forcibly.

"I said, where is God?" he bellowed.

Frightened out of his skin, Johnny raced from the room, ran all the way home and hid in the wardrobe. His older brother followed him upstairs and shouted through the door, "What's happened?"

"Oh Tom, we really are in trouble this time. God has gone missing and they think we did it."

★

"I don't know what's going on," said worried Bob to his mate. "Last month we moved parishes and I left our church which had a message pinned up outside saying 'Sex is your worst enemy' only to get to the new church and read 'Make your worst enemy your best friend.' "

What do you say to a girl who can suck an olive through a straw?
Will you marry me?

The young man was so nervous on meeting his future father-in-law that he blurted out,
"Sir, may I have your daughter's hole in handy matrimony?"

Johnny looked around the church and turned to his best man, saying, "You know Jack, apart from my wife-to-be's two sisters, there's not a woman in this church that I haven't had."
Jack replied,
"Well in that case, between the two of us we've had them all."

★

There were some doubts about his wedding. On the great day his future father-in-law said to the vicar,
"Why do you rope off the aisles?"
"So the groom can't get away," replied the vicar.

★

Chuck and Jan arrived at the Registry Office to fill in the forms required for their wedding in two weeks time. As Chuck wrote his name, the clerk told him he could not accept a nickname. He had better go next door to the Births, Deaths and Marriages Department to check out his full Christian name. So Chuck went next door and a few minutes later came back and duly filled in his name as Charles. But then it was Jan's turn and she was also told to go next door and confirm her full name. In this case it was Janette.

"It's a good thing I'm thorough," said the clerk smugly, "or this marriage wouldn't have been legal and any kids you might have had would have been technical bastards."

"What a coincidence," said Jan. "That's exactly what the bloke next door said about you."

★

The groom was so ugly he had to wear the veil!

★

A vicar was walking through the shopping arcade when he saw a scruffy man sitting on one of the benches. Overcome with pity, he went up to him and put £5 in his hand.

"Here you are, young man, have faith do you hear, have faith."

A week later, he was walking through the arcade again when the same scruffy man ran up to him.

"I've been looking for you," he said. "'Have Faith' came in at 16/1, here's your winnings," and he put a wad of notes in the vicar's hand.

★

A young man sits down next to a nun in the park and they strike up a conversation. Some time passes and the young man confesses to the nun that her habit really turns him on and that he would dearly like to make love to her.

"Are you a Catholic?" she asks.

"Yes," he replies.

"OK, let's go behind those bushes."

They do as she suggests and the nun satisfies him with a blow job. Afterwards, feeling very guilty the man tells the nun that in fact he isn't a Catholic.

She replies, "Well, I have something to tell you as well. My name is Bob and I'm on my way to a fancy dress party."

★

Thousands of pounds worth of repairs were needed to make the old church tower safe. But funds were low and it would take the small congregation a lifetime to raise such a great amount of money. It so happened that the village was home to a multi-millionaire who would take up residency two months every year and make the odd appearance at church. The vicar decided to approach the man and invited him down to see for himself the bad state of the building. As the millionaire walked round the outside of the tower, a piece of crumbling stonework fell off and hit him on the head.

"Ouch," he cried, rubbing his head.

"I see what you mean, vicar, it does need something doing. Here, take this cheque for £100. As the man turned away to

go back to his car, the vicar turned his eyes heavenward and cried, "Go on, Lord, hit the old skinflint again."

★

The party was in full flow when the priest knocked at the door.

"Oh come in Father," said the hostess, holding a large glass of whisky. "Come and join the fun. I'm sure you don't mind a few adult games," she said winking at him coyly. "In fact, I think you'll like this one. The men are all behind a sheet which has just one hole cut out. Each of them in turn sticks their willy through and the women have to guess whose it is. It's great fun. Do come and join us."

The priest looked shocked.

"My goodness! I can't condone such behaviour!" he exclaimed.

"Well I don't see why not. Your name has come up at least four times," replied the woman haughtily.

★

A devout churchgoer and her 16-year-old daughter attended church every Sunday without fail. On this particular Sunday, the vicar was waiting to greet his parishioners as they left church and happened to notice a slight bulge on the daughter's stomach.

"Good morning Mrs Dogood," he said smiling, "it looks as if your daughter is putting on a little weight."

The woman blushed with discomfort.

"Oh, nothing to worry about," she replied, "just a little wind."

A few months later, the vicar noticed the girl had got even larger.

"Are you sure everything's all right?" he asked.

"Of course, vicar," replied the woman, "just a little wind."

The next time the vicar saw the two women, they were walking down the High Street, pushing a pram. He stopped to say hello and bending down to look in the pram, remarked,

"So that's the little fart, is it?"

★

A wife is so distressed at her husband's excessive drinking that she decides to try and scare him into stopping. After pub closing time that night, she waits for him in the church graveyard, crouched down behind one of the tombstones. Sure enough, he takes the short cut home and as he staggers past her, she jumps up in full devil's costume and shouts,

"Beware, beware, Arthur Chivers, carry on drinking as you are, and you'll soon be joining me down below!"

"What!" he exclaimed, somewhat befuddled, "who are you?"

"I am the devil himself!" she boomed.

The drunk began to smile and held out his hand to greet him.

"Well I never," he says, "you'll know me then, I'm married to your sister."

★

The bishop was not looking forward to his meeting with the new vicar. The latter had only been in his parish a few weeks, but already there were many complaints.

"So why did you decide to enter the ministry?" asked the bishop.

"I was called," replied the vicar. "The Lord appeared to me in a vision and told me to become ordained.

"Mmm," mused the bishop. "Are you sure that's what he said?'

A couple were enjoying the concert when two nuns came and sat down in front of them, their hats totally obscuring the couple's view.

"If we were watching this in Holland where there aren't many nuns, we probably wouldn't get any in front of us," complained the man loudly.

"China would be even better," replied the woman.

They continued muttering for five minutes until one of the nuns turned round and said calmly,

"Why don't you both go to hell, you won't find any nuns down there."

The vicar is preparing for the morning service when he spots a woman, in a very short skirt, sitting in the front pew. He beckons to his deacon and asks, "Isn't that Fanny Blue?"

"Oh no, I don't think so," replies the deacon. "It's just the way the light is reflected through the stained glass window."

"The Canon's here to see you, Bishop."

"Tell him he's fired."

A nun met a man walking along with a number of game birds slung over his shoulder.

"I'm afraid all the pheasants are taken," he told the nun, "but you can have this bugarin bird, here."

"Oh!" exclaimed the nun, horrified, "please don't curse in that way."

"No, no," replied the man quickly, "that's what this bird is called. It's a bugarin bird and it's very tasty."

So the nun took the bird back to the convent and showed it to the Mother Superior.

"Look what I have," she said. "It's a bugarin bird and it'll make a good meal when the priest comes round tonight."

"Sister, how could you!" exclaimed the Mother Superior, "how dare you use such filthy language!"

"Oh no, I didn't swear," assured the nun. "That's its name, a bugarin bird."

So the bird was taken to the kitchen for cooking.

That evening, the nuns sat down to dinner with the priest as their guest.

"What a delicious bird," he commented.

"Thank you," they replied.

"I was given the bugarin bird by one of the local hunters," said the nun.

"And I thought the bugarin bird would be a welcome change to this evening's meal," said the Mother Superior.

"And I cooked the bugarin bird," added another nun.

The priest was greatly shocked by their conversation and replied angrily, "Well let's eat the fucking thing, shall we?"

★

"Okay, girls," said the priest at confession, "one at a time please." The first girl went in and confessed she'd kissed a man the night before. She was told to wash her lips in Holy Water.

The second girl went in and confessed she'd touched a man's penis. As she left the confessional, she told the others she had to wash her hands in Holy Water.

Suddenly an almighty row broke out between the remaining two girls and the priest came running from his box.

"My goodness!" he exclaimed, "girls, girls, what's going on?"

One of the girls retorted hotly, "If I'm going to have to gargle with Holy Water, I'm sure as hell going to do it before she puts her arse in it!"

★

The curvaceous woman arrived at the church door topless.
"I'm afraid you can't come in here," exclaimed the vicar.
"But I've got a divine right!" she protested.
"I agree," he said, "and a divine left as well, but I can't let you in."

★

The priest and the C of E vicar bumped into each other in the public library.

"What a coincidence," said the vicar. "I had a dream last night about a Catholic heaven. It was full of people, drinking, singing and dancing."

"Really?" replied the priest. "I had a dream about a protestant heaven. It was very peaceful, beautiful countryside, gorgeous gardens and gently flowing streams."

The vicar smiled contentedly. "And what were the people doing?"

"What people?" replied the priest.

★

A vain middle aged woman went to confession. "Forgive me Father for I have sinned. I spent an hour this morning in front of the mirror admiring my beautiful body. Will I have to do a penance?"

"No, no," said the priest. "You only do a penance when you have done something wrong. Not for a mistake."

★

For as long as he could remember, the priest had tried to get his next door neighbour to come to church.

"It's no good, Father," he would say. "I just don't believe and nothing you can say will change my mind."

It just so happened that one day the priest and his next door neighbour found themselves aboard the same flight to Rome. Unfortunately, an hour out of Heathrow, the plane developed engine trouble and the situation looked very dangerous. The priest immediately crossed himself and began praying. But then he was astonished to see his neighbour cross himself as well. Happily, the situation was not as grave as anticipated and the plane made a safe landing. As they left the airport, the priest turned to his neighbour and said "Even though you've always told me you don't believe, when the chips are down, you turn to God."

"Oh no, not at all," replied the neighbour. "I'm a door-to-door salesman and before I face any unknown situation I always check I'm prepared – glasses, flies, money and pen."

★

The new vicar set out on his parish rounds to introduce himself to the congregation. At his second stop he came across a cottage standing alone, with six children of all ages, running around madly in the garden. He knocked at the door, but getting no answer, peered through the dining room window.

"Oh goodness!" he exclaimed, moving away hurriedly from the sight of two naked bodies writhing around in ecstasy. Blushing profusely, he moved on to the next cottage where he met a friendly man hanging out the washing. After a few moments of chat, he commented on the people next door.

"They really love children, don't they?" remarked the vicar.

"You can say that again," replied the man, "his wife's just gone into hospital to have her seventh, so my wife's gone round to see if there's anything she can do to help."

★

The Mother Superior lay very ill in bed. Three doctors had visited but failed to make her better. Eventually, they called in a Chinese medicine man who told her she was suffering from a lack of sexual activity and unless she released these pent up frustrations, she would die.

"Oh, but I can't," she gasped. "It's against everything I stand for."

But again, the medicine man warned her of the consequences and eventually she gave in.

"I must insist on three conditions," she said. "First, he must be blind so that he will never recognise me. Secondly, he must be dumb so that he can never speak about it."

"As you wish," said the Chinese medicine man. "But what is the third condition?"

There was a long pause and then she said,

"He must have a big dick."

★

"Excuse me vicar," said the man as he walked into church. "I've had my bicycle stolen and I wonder if you would mention in your sermon today how wrong it is to steal."

"Why certainly," replied the vicar. "As it happens, I shall be talking about the ten commandments so that will fit in nicely.

"And so I say to you, remember what God taught us. Thou shalt not kill, thou shalt not steal..." Later that week the vicar bumped into the man again as he was wheeling his bicycle down the road.

"Ah, I see my sermon must have worked," remarked the vicar.

"Oh no, it wasn't that," replied the man. "It was when you got to the bit about not committing adultery I remembered where I'd left it."

★

In the Restaurant

A man walks into a restaurant, sits down at a table and studies the menu. A couple of minutes later he looks up to see a beautiful waitress standing in front of him. She is so gorgeous that he gasps with pure lust.

"What would you like?" she asks.

"A glass of claret and a quickie please," he replies, drooling at the mouth. The waitress is so disgusted she storms off but returns a few minutes later when she has calmed down. Again she asks,

"What would you like?"

He smiles and says,

"A glass of claret and a quickie please."

"That's it!" she yells, gives him a sharp slap across the face and stomps off.

The man sits there dumbstruck when from the next table a fellow diner leans over and whispers,

"I think it's pronounced 'quiche'."

★

He went for a meal in a kosher restaurant and said to the waiter.

"Excuse me, do you have matzoballs?"

"No sir," he replied. "The chef's just kicked me in the bollocks."

★

"Waiter, I see on the menu that you have a chicken tarka. Shouldn't that be chicken tikka?"

"No, sir, it's like chicken tikka only a little 'otter."

A woman in a very chic French restaurant suddenly sneezes and her boobs pop out of her evening gown.

Moments later, her waiter is taken aside by the Manager.

"Pierre, please remember this is a high class establishment. Next time use warm spoons."

A couple popped into the local hotel bar for a drink but when the man went to the gents he found it infested with flies. Returning to the bar, he complained to the barman, who said to him reassuringly, "Don't worry, sir, the bell for lunch will be rung in five minutes."

"How will that help?" asked the puzzled man.

"They'll all come up to the dining room," he replied.

The lift was packed solid with people as the doors closed and the attendant called out, "Which floors please?"

A man standing at the back shouted out, "Ballroom!" and a lady in front of him turned round and said, "Oh I'm so sorry, I didn't know I was crushing you that much."

★

"What on earth is that?" said the woman to the waiter.

"It's pressed tongue Madam."

"Good gracious! I could never eat anything that came out of an animal's mouth. Bring me a boiled egg please."

★

A woman was so dreadfully upset about being flat-chested that she travelled to deepest Africa to see a witch doctor. When she told him of her plight he gave her a simple spell to make and told her that when she returned home her boobs would grow every time a man said 'Pardon' to her.

A few days later, she was shopping in the High Street when a man came up to her and said, "Pardon me, Miss, could you tell me the way to the Post Office?"

After she had directed him she noticed with delight that her boobs had grown an inch. The following week she was coming out of the bank when a man bumped into her.

"Pardon me, Miss," he said.

Again her boobs grew an inch and she was very pleased with the way things were turning out.

The next night, she and her mates went for an Indian and as the waiter was serving up their meal, he tripped and dropped some madras curry on her clothes.

"Oh Miss, I am so sorry, a thousand pardons to you."

Sadly the restaurant was cleared due to an obstruction.

A businessman visited a very up-market restaurant in Paris and ordered moules marinières, duck à l'orange and a sorbet ice cream. When the first two courses were served, he noticed the man had his thumb stuck in the dishes, but not when he brought out the sweet.

"Garçon, tell me please, why did you have your thumb in the first two courses of my meal, but not when you brought out the ice cream?"

"Certainly, sir, I have bad rheumatism in my thumb and something warm helps relieve the pain."

At this, the businessman was outraged. "It is appalling that in such a restaurant as this, customers have to put up with these disgusting habits. Go shove it up your bum."

Unperturbed, the waiter replied, "I only do that in the kitchen."

A man walked into a restaurant and asked the waiter for a bowl of chilli.

"I'm sorry sir, we've run out," replied the waiter. "The customer on the next table had the last helping."

Disappointed, the man ordered a coffee only and as he sat drinking it, he noticed the man on the next table had not touched his chilli but was eating a steak instead. So he leaned over and said "Excuse me, are you going to eat that chilli?"

"No mate," came the reply, "you're welcome to have it."

Delighted, the man tucked into his chilli and had eaten half of it when he noticed a severed rat lying on the bottom of the bowl. Shocked at the disgusting sight, he retched and puked up the chilli he'd eaten back into the bowl. At this, the man on the next table remarked, "Yeah, that's about as far as I got too."

An Englishman walked into a French restaurant and ordered a bowl of soup, but when it arrived there was a dead fly floating in it. He called the waiter back and spoke to him in French. "Pardon, regardez le mouche."

The waiter replied, "Not le mouche, monsieur, la mouche."

"Good gracious!" exclaimed the man, "you must have wonderful eyesight."

The man had had a bad day and it got no better when he sat down in the restaurant for his lunch. He ordered the roast chicken and as it arrived, he was just about to tuck in when the head waiter rushed over to his table.

"I'm so sorry," said the waiter, clearly agitated. "There has been some terrible mistake. There is only one portion left and this was meant for the man over there." He pointed to a gorilla of a man sitting in the corner looking very angry.

"Well tough," said the man, still in a bad mood. "It's here now and I'm going to enjoy it."

Again he picked up his knife just as the gorilla walked up to his table. "Listen punk," he snarled, "that's my chicken, touch that and you're dead. Whatever you do to that chicken, I'll do to you. Cut off one of its legs and I'll cut yours off, pull off one of its wings and I'll pull off one of your arms."

The man hesitated a moment and then slowly stuck his finger up the bird's backside, pulled it out and licked it.

★

In Uniform

In one of the remotest parts of Outer Mongolia, high up in the mountains, is an outpost of an old regiment. The men have been on duty for six months without a break and only themselves for company. A new recruit joins them and he's only been there a few weeks when a sudden roar goes up from the look-out.

"Hurry, they're coming!" he shouts.

A might roar goes up and all the troops desert their posts and charge out of the gates. The newcomer turns to his mate and says, "What's going on? It's only a herd of goats. What's all the fuss about?"

"If you'd been out here six months without a break, and without female company, you'd know alright," replies his mate.

"But why all the rush, there seems to be plenty to go around?"

"Oh yes, but you don't want to get stuck with an ugly one!"

In a distant outpost of the Foreign Legion, one of the more recent recruits confides to his sergeant that lack of female company is driving him round the twist.

"No need to let that worry you, son. Here, let me show you. See that barrel over there, the one with the hole in the side? You'll find that will help relieve the pressure. You're free to use it on Tuesday through to Sunday."

"That's great, thanks. Er..but... what's wrong with Monday?"

"Well, fair's fair; if you're using it six days a week, then on Monday, it's your turn inside the barrel."

A new sergeant major arrived at the base and the retiring sergeant major, who had one more week to go, said to him, "If you've any problems just come and see me."

The next morning a man was brought to him on a charge of homosexuality.

The new sergeant major, not sure what to do, popped in to see the old sergeant major and said, "Sir, what do you give for cock sucking?"

"Oh, not more than a fiver," he replied.

Two retired colonels were bemoaning the younger generation over drinks at their gentlemen's club.

"You'll never believe this," said the first colonel. "When I told my grand daughter that her grandfather was killed at Waterloo, she wanted to know on what platform it happened!"

"Oh, how ridiculous," replied the second colonel. "As if it mattered what platform he was on."

Two old colonels were talking over their port about a third...

"I say, did you know old Smithers has started living in sin with a monkey?"

"By Jove!" replied the other. "Is it a male or female monkey?"

"Now steady on, female monkey of course. Nothing unnatural about Smithers."

An army unit was crossing the desert when one of the camels stopped and refused to move, so it and its rider were left behind. They were stuck there for four hours and nothing the soldier did would move him. Eventually along came an ATS driver who listened to the problem, saying, "Don't worry, leave it to me."

She put her hand beneath the camel's belly and within seconds he jumped up and disappeared at a rate of knots.

"That's amazing, miss. What did you do?"

"I just tickled its balls."

"Well, you'd better tickle mine, I've got to catch the bugger."

A new commanding officer had just arrived at the foreign legion outpost and decided to tour the base immediately. In one small shed he found a camel and when asked why it was there the private replied hesitantly, "It's for the men to use if their carnal desires get the better of them, sir."

The C.O was outraged.

"Get rid of it immediately, from now on, nothing like that goes on here."

However, six months later and painfully missing the fair sex, the C.O asked his batman if the camel had indeed gone.

"Well, no sir, I'm sorry," came the reply.

"Then let me go and have another look," and he went back to the shed, dropped his trousers, stood on a bucket and gave the camel a right seeing to.

Afterwards he said to his batman, panting, "Is that how the men do it?"

Embarrassed he replied, "Well, no, sir, actually the men ride the camel to the nearest brothel."

★

An old army colonel was awaiting news of the imminent arrival of his son at the exclusive Harley Street Clinic.
"How do you know it will be a son?" asked the doctor.
"Of course it will be, family tradition, man!"
And in fact it was a son. On hearing the news, the colonel asked for him to be circumcised.
"Family tradition," he said.
Later the doctor called to say the baby was ailing.
"Give it some brandy, don't argue, just do it."
Some time later the doctor rang again to say the baby was no better.
"I'm coming over," said the Colonel. "Meanwhile, put him on the breast."
By the time the Colonel arrived the baby was doing well.
"Excellent!" he chortled, "You see this is a real father's son. Mouth full of tit, belly full of brandy and a sore cock."

★

The troops were behind enemy lines, holed up in the basement of an old chateau. Look-outs were placed in strategic points around the grounds and it was one of these that gave the alarm signal just before dusk on the sixth day.
"Quick, everyone below," whispered the troop leader. "Get into the cellar and stay very, very quiet."

They all hid in the basement. All as quiet as mice except for the constant sound of clink, clink, clink.

"What's that bloody noise!" exclaimed the leader. "Hobbs, see to it pronto."

A few minutes passed, the noise stopped and Hobbs returned.

"What was it?" they asked.

"Mitchell, sir, in the old toilet, wanking," replied Hobbs.

"Good man Hobbs. You stopped him then?"

"No sir. I removed the brass buttons on his cuffs."

A youth walked into the public conveniences and saw a man in a uniform, washing his hands.

"Hey, are you a sailor?"

"Yes, son," replied the man, "from the warship moored in the bay."

"Oh wow!" exclaimed the youth, his eyes shining with enthusiasm. "I've always wanted to join up."

"Here," laughed the sailor, "try my hat on for size."

Just at that moment another naval man appeared. "Are you on the warship as well?" he asked.

"Yes," he replied, "Why? do you want to suck my dick?"

"Oh no," replied the boy quickly. "I'm not a real sailor, I'm only trying on the hat."

A visiting general was inspecting the troops out on manoeuvres. As he passed a group of soldiers, disguised as trees, one of them made a sudden movement.

"Now soldier," said the General sternly, "if you move like that, you'll blow the cover of everyone."

"Sorry sir," stammered the distressed soldier. "Yesterday, I stayed stock still when two crows started to build a nest in my top branches. Today, I didn't move a muscle when a dog peed up against my trunk, but General, sir, when I heard two squirrels say let's get the two nuts and take them back to our nest, I just had to do something."

General Carruthers and his wife were hosting the summer ball. All was going well until a rather distressed woman took the General aside and complained.

"Really Maurice, your wife has all but accused me of being a lady of the night."

"Take no notice, Lady Charlotte," he blustered. "I left the army fifteen years ago and she still calls me General."

Three generals out on manoeuvres were boasting about which of their regiments showed the greatest courage.

"Now look here," said General Smythe.

"Watch this. Hey you, private, jump across that ravine."

"Yes sir," came the reply, and the private attempted to jump over the ravine but missed and plunged to his death.

"There," said the General smugly. "That's what I call courage."

"No, no, my dear man. Watch this," said the second General and he called to one of his men.

"Bates, take this message to HQ. It's urgent, so you'll have to go through the minefield."

So Bates set off, but unlucky for him, just as he was halfway across, he stood on a mine and was blown to pieces.

"Now that's what I call courage," said the second General.

"Wait, wait," protested the third General. "Just listen to this."

"Corporal Jones," he shouted. "Take that raft and make your way to the other side," he said, pointing to a fast flowing river that was only 200 yards from a steep waterfall.

"Oh bugger off General," came the reply. "You must be joking, you've been at the whisky again."

"Now gentlemen," said the third General, smiling at his two colleagues. "That's got to take the greatest courage of all."

The regiment had travelled further into the mountains than anyone had gone before. On the third day, they were confronted by a small group of savages.

"Take cover," yelled the colonel, "and get me my red jacket."

It was only a small skirmish and the hunters quickly saw off the retreating savages.

A few days later, they were confronted by a larger band of savages and again the colonel shouted out, "Okay men, shoot at will, and can someone get my red jacket."

The soldiers fought bravely and were finally victorious, sustaining only two minor injuries.

That night round the campfire, they talked over the week's events.

"Thanks to our leader, we've defeated the enemy every time. It won't be long before we reach our destination and we'll be famous."

"Here's to the Colonel!" and they drank a celebratory toast.

"By the way, sir, just out of interest, why do you always ask for your red jacket as we go into battle?"

The Colonel replied "If I wear the red jacket and get wounded, no one will see the blood and lose confidence."

The men were very impressed. They continued their journey to the heart of the mountains but disaster struck the following evening. As they came over a high ridge, they were confronted by a band of savages, at least 500 in number.

"Fight for your lives!" yelled the Colonel, "and someone fetch me my brown trousers."

An old Desert Rat was telling fellow members of the regiment's club about his solution to loneliness when he was so far from home.

"Superb idea, if I say so myself," he began. "Each time I travelled to distant lands I would take a life size picture of the latest pin up. I'd get a hole drilled in the right place and whenever I felt like letting off steam, I'd get out the picture and relieve the tension, so to speak. Kept me going for months."

Just at that moment, the old man's chauffeur arrived and one of the men who had been listening to the story commented

"Your old Colonel certainly had some good ideas, didn't he?"

"Mmm," snorted the chauffeur. "I was his personal assistant on these trips and I bet the old fart didn't tell you how he always made me bend over behind the picture."

A wounded soldier was caught behind enemy lines and sent to the local internment camp. While there, his wounds became badly infected and it was decided that his leg would have to be amputated. The soldier turned to one of the guards and said, "I know you've got a twenty four hour pass coming up. Would you mind sending my leg home in a parcel so that it can be buried in my own country?"

Out of sympathy, the guard agreed. However, the solider got worse and more limbs had to be amputated. One hand, another leg, and one arm were sent back to his own country in separate parcels, each time the guard had time off. Then one day, the commanding officer called in the guard and asked him what was going on. After listening to the explanation, he responded angrily,

"Are you all stupid? Don't you realise he's trying to escape?"

★

The troops were out on manoeuvres in the Himalayas, when one of the animals carrying their supplies collapsed and died.

"You two men there," shouted the Corporal, "bury this animal immediately."

As the men dug the hole, one remarked to the other "Poor old donkey."

"That's not a donkey, that's a mule," said his mate.

Neither would agree so they asked the opinion of a third soldier.

"Trust me lads," he said, "that's an ass."

Some time later, just as they were finishing off the hole, a passing

Colonel stopped to speak.

"Is that a foxhole you're digging men?" he asked.

"No, sir," replied the men saluting, "we're digging an asshole."

★

The court martial pronounced the private guilty as charged and ordered him to be taken from the court to a place where he would face the firing squad.

As the troops escorted the prisoner on the two-mile trek to the execution area, the heavens opened and it rained furiously.

"Bloody awful weather," moaned the prisoner. "All this bloody way, soaking wet, freezing cold, just to be shot."

"Shut up, will you," replied one of the soldiers. "At least you don't have to walk all the way back in it."

★

The group sergeant was showing the young recruit round the camp and was just telling him about the entertainment facilities.

"On Mondays, it's film night," he said, "and you can put in a request for anything you'd like to see."

"I don't go to the cinema," said the recruit.

"Well, on Tuesdays, it's darts night and there's always a prize for the overall winner."

"Sorry, sir, I don't play darts."

"Then on Wednesdays," continued the sergeant, impatiently, "we have a snooker tournament."

"I don't like snooker, sir," replied the recruit, shaking his head.

"Well, on Thursdays, the girls from town come up for a social evening."

"No time for girls, sir," he said.

"What! Don't tell me you're gay?"

"Oh no, sir."

"Damn, you're not going to like Friday nights then,either."

A colonel was posted to the Far East and after three months his wife came to join him. On the first morning she decided to stay in bed, still feeling tired from the plane trip, but at 10.00am the colonel's manservant appeared unannounced, and threw back the bedclothes, saying, "Come on, miss, time to be off. Go get yourself some breakfast and then be on your way."

A unit of soldiers returned to base after spending four months in the war zone. The base also had a squad of women soldiers and the colonel in charge of the men took the leader of the women aside and warned her to keep her ladies under lock and key as his men hadn't seen a woman for months. The women replied, "It's all right, there'll be no trouble," and tapping her head she continued, "My girls have it up here."

The colonel retorted, "I don't care where they have it. If my men start looking they'll find it."

The drill sergeant was known for giving his new recruits a hard time. One night he ordered them all to line up on parade immediately without giving any of them time to get dressed. As

he walked along the line of naked shivering soldiers he noticed that one of them had a real stonker on him. As he passed he swiped the man's dick with his stick but the recruit never batted an eyelid.

"Good man!" said the sergeant, and he turned to the rest of the squad, saying, "That's the sort of soldier we need in this man's army; the sort who can take a blow like that without flinching!"

The man looked at the sergeant and replied,

"Sir, that's not my penis, it's Private Johnson's, standing behind me."

★

The situation looked bad. The platoon had suffered many fatalities and the men were very dispirited. The C.O. felt it was time to give them a pep talk.

"Right, chaps, listen to me. You've done a sterling job, couldn't have asked for better but we have been outnumbered. But we'll fight on, for King and country, until the very last bullet has been fired. When that happens, you have my permission to make a run for it ... by the way, I've got a bad knee, so I'd better set off now."

★

A pompous Sergeant Major spends the night with a German prostitute and the next morning he turns arrogantly to the girl and says, "My dear, after last night, you'll have a baby in nine months' time and you can call it Toby, after me."

She replies, "In two days time, you'll have a rash; you can call it German measles."

To avoid being called up for active duty two men pulled all their teeth out before going in for their medical examination. On this particular morning there were just 3 of them – the two friends and a dirty looking tramp. The first friend stood before the doctor and told him he had no teeth. The doctor put his finger in the man's mouth, ran it around his gums and agreed that he was not fit for active duty. The doctor then turned to the tramp who told him he had very very painful piles.

"OK," said the doctor, "drop your trousers and turn round so that I can examine you."

The tramp did as he was told and the doctor stuck his finger up the man's arse and felt around.

"Mmm, they are bad," said the doctor. "You've failed the test as well."

He then turned to the second friend and said,

"What's wrong with you?"

The man looked at the doctors finger and shook his head vigorously.

"Nothing, nothing at all doctor."

Walking along the street, a policeman came across a young man kicking an older man and he stepped in to break it up.

"It's okay Officer, I asked him to do it," said the older man. "Many years ago I was in the flat of this beautiful young girl when she suddenly removed her dress saying she was feeling hot. So I turned the fire off. Then she stripped off completely, so I thought I'd better leave. As I walked out of the door she said that one day I'd remember this and then ask the first person I saw to kick me. Well I've just realised what she meant."

"Keep kicking," said the policeman.

A man walked into a police station to report that his wife had gone missing.

"She went out about four hours ago and she hasn't been back to cook my dinner so I know there must be something wrong."

"OK sir, let's not panic. I'll just take down some details. Can you describe your wife, what she was wearing when she left the house?"

"No, but I did see her walking down the road with our next door neighbour and she's not back either."

"I don't suppose you can give us a description of her?"

"Oh yes, she's about 5'6", black shoulder-length curly hair, 36-24-36, wearing a red mini skirt and a red and white jacket."

This particular evening, the traffic cop was determined to crack down on drunk and disorderly drivers. He parked near one of the toughest, noisiest and rowdiest bars in town, sat back and waited. A little later, a man staggered out of the bar, tripped over and then attempted to open three cars before he eventually found his own. The man got in and immediately fell asleep. Feeling very pleased with himself, the officer waited all evening until everyone left the bar, got into their cars and drove away. Finally, the sleeper woke up, started the engine and began to pull away.

"Got you," said the police officer to himself and he pulled the driver over and administered a breathaliser test. He was astonished to find the man passed with a zero blood alcohol reading.

"But how can that be?" he said.

"Well, you see, officer," said the man, "tonight I'm the designated decoy."

Police have announced that they would like to interview a man wearing high heels and black lace knickers, but the Chief Constable has stated they must wear their uniforms instead.

Last week, a policeman stopped me driving the wrong way up a one-way street.

He said, "Didn't you see the arrow?"

"No," I replied. "Honestly, Officer, I didn't even see the Indians."

A policeman, his dog and a policewoman were on night duty. It was very cold and the policewoman shivered.

"Are you alright?" asked the policeman.

"Yes," she replied. "I just forgot to put on my black woollen

knickers before coming out."

"Don't worry," said the policeman "My dog's well trained. Let him sniff between your legs and we'll send him back to the station to get them."

Some time passed before the dog reappeared with the desk sergeant's hand between his teeth.

★

A policeman on night duty thought he heard a noise up an alley and when he shone his torch he saw a woman with her blouse undone and her knickers round her ankles, eating a packet of mints.

"What's going on?" he asked.

"Blimey, has he gone?" she replied.

★

Driving home from the pub one night a couple were stopped for speeding.

"You were doing 40mph in a 30mph zone," said the officer.

"Oh no, you're wrong," said the driver.

"I assure you, Sir, that my instruments are very accurate and that you were driving much too fast."

At that point his wife leant across and said to the officer. "It's no good arguing with him now, not when he's had a drink."

★

A simple young man got very drunk one day and was caught short on the way home so he relieved himself in the local river. At that moment a policeman came along and shouted to him, "Stop that immediately, put it away and go home you drunken sod."

The man stuck his dick back inside his trousers and started to laugh.

"What the hell are you laughing at?" demanded the policeman.

"Ha, ha," replied the man, "I really tricked you this time. I put it away but I didn't stop."

One day while on traffic control, a policeman flags down a car for speeding. As he walks up to the car he sees it is being driven by a beautiful brunette.

"Excuse me Miss, did you not see the signs? This is a 30mph zone and you were going at least 50mph. I'll need to see your licence and insurance please."

"Oh dear," replies the dizzy girl. "Do you mean these officer?" and she hands him some documents from her bag.

"That's right Miss, won't be a moment." and with that he walks over to his car to radio in the details.

"I think I know this woman," comes the reply. "Is she a dizzy brunette?"

"Yes, why?"

"Just go back over and take your trousers down."

"What the fuck are you talking about?" says the policeman in amazement.

"Don't worry, just do as I say, it'll be fine."

So the policeman returns to the woman's car, hands back her documents and drops his trousers.

"Oh no," she replies, "not another breathalyser."

A music hall entertainer is stopped by the police for having a faulty break light and on the back seat of the car.

The policeman spots a whole set of knives. He asks the man why he has them – doesn't he know it's against the law to carry knives?

The man explains that the knives are used in his act – he juggles them.

The policeman insists the man gets out to show him so he gets out and stands at the roadside performing his act. Just then, another car drives by and the driver turns to his wife saying,

"Thank God I gave up the drinking, those tests just get tougher every day!"

★

A man stumbles into the police station yelling that his car has been stolen.

"Can you tell me where you left it Sir?" asks the duty sergeant.

"On the end of this bloody key!" he screeches.

Now it had been a difficult evening and the duty sergeant's temper was at boiling point. He retorted,

"Listen here, you wretched little man, you're so bloody drunk, you can't remember anything and your whole behaviour is disgraceful. Why, you've even left your flies undone!"

"Fucking hell!" slurred the drunk. "They've stolen my girlfriend as well."

★

The traffic police flag down a car for driving erratically and ask the driver, a young girl, to step out of the car and take a breathalyser test.

As they look at the results, the policeman turns to the girl and remarks severely,

"You've had a few stiff ones tonight Miss."

"Oh my goodness," she exclaims, blushing. "I didn't know it told you that as well."

A very drunk man was walking down the street, one foot on the pavement and the other on the road.

"I shall have to arrest you for being drunk," said the policeman.

"Drunk?" said the man. "How can you tell?"

"You are walking with one foot on the pavement and the other on the road," replied the officer.

"Oh that's wonderful!" cried the drunk. "For a while I thought I had one leg shorter than the other."

The traffic police spotted a man staggering towards his car and opening the driver's door. They stopped and confronted him.

"Excuse me sir, but I hope you are not intending to drive the car?"

"Of course I am officer," he slurred. "I'm in no state to walk."

★

A naive young man found himself in the wrong part of town late at night, and got attacked by a gang of muggers. He put up a terrific fight but was eventually overcome and lay bleeding on the ground. When the muggers went through his

pockets, all they found was a handful of loose change.

"You went through all that just to protect a few coins?" they asked amazed.

"Oh I see," said the man. "For a while I thought you were after the £500 hidden in my shoe."

★

"What's wrong miss?" asked the kindly policeman when he saw the girl crying.

"A thief has just stolen £20 I had hidden inside my knickers" she sobbed.

"Did you try to stop him?"

"I didn't know he was only after my money."

★

The traffic police flagged down the car.

"Excuse me Sir, you've just hit four parked cars and driven straight over the middle of the roundabout. It's obvious you are very drunk."

"Officer, thank you so much for telling me. I thought the steering had gone on the car."

★

The ticket inspector was checking tickets on the 4.30 to Croydon when she stopped by a man who opened his raincoat and flashed his tackle. "Oh no, that's no good," she replied with vigour. "I want to see your ticket, not just the stub."

"Ladies and gentlemen," announced the airline pilot, "due to a loss of power in one of our four engines, we will now land in San Francisco an hour late. Our apologies for any inconvenience caused."

Five minutes later, he made another announcement.

"A second engine has failed but please be assured that the plane can fly on the two remaining engines. It will just mean a further delay of another thirty minutes."

Then later still, he made a third announcement.

"Due to the failure of a third engine, we will now be landing at San Francisco three hours later than scheduled."

At this point, one of the passengers exclaimed loudly

"Let's hope we don't lose the fourth engine, otherwise we'll be up here all bloody night."

The plane is about to taxi down the runway when passengers see the pilot and co-pilot walking up towards the cockpit. Both look as if they are virtually blind, carrying white sticks and bumping into everyone. At first, the full plane of passengers cannot believe what they have just seen, but as the plane taxis to the end of the runway and turns to pick up speed, a slight panic begins. By the time it's hurtling down the runway, there is ever increasing panic and as the plane lifts into the air an earth shattering scream goes up from the cabins. This sudden change in pitch is followed by the plane rising into the sky.

"Aaah, thank goodness," says the pilot to his colleague. "Safe again. You know, one day the passengers aren't going to scream and then we're really done for."

A fireman comes home from work with a new idea to spice up his sex life. He tells his wife, "Tonight when we go to bed I'll shout First Bell and you take all your clothes off. Then I'll shout Second Bell and you jump into bed and then on the shout of Third Bell we'll make love all night."

So the following day, the fireman comes home from work, shouts First Bell and she strips off, Second Bell into bed, Third Bell and away they go. But five minutes later, the wife calls out, "Fourth Bell."

"What's that mean?" asks her puzzled husband.

She replies, "It means more hose; you haven't got to the fire yet."

A man was working on the sewage farm when he suddenly lost his footing and slipped in.

"Help, fire, fire, fire!" he yelled.

In no time at all the fire engine responded.

"Where's the fire then?" asked the chief fire officer.

"There isn't one," replied the worker. "But if I'd shouted 'shit, shit, shit', no one would have rescued me."

★

On the Road

A travelling salesman is on the train travelling home late from work when he falls asleep and misses his stop. He wakes up to find himself fifty miles from home, no more trains running and not enough money to get a taxi. However, he sees a taxi waiting by itself in the station forecourt and hopes the driver will be sympathetic to his story. But no, the taxi driver won't take him on trust, so the poor man has to hitch-hike, getting home at three in the morning. A few days later he travels to the station again and is relieved to see four taxis waiting for fares, one of which is the bastard from the other night. Leaving this man until last, he goes up to the other three in turn and tells them he hasn't got enough money for the fare but if they take him home, he'll give them a blow job. All three tell him to piss off. Then he goes up to the fourth taxi, tells him the destination, gets in and off they go. Satisfied at his success, he passes the other cabbies, grins at them through the window and gives the thumbs up sign.

The salesman of the year was determined to sell the cheap suit to the hesitant customer.
"But the left trouser leg is shorter than the right," he remarked.
"But that's why it's so cheap sir. All you need do is bend the right knee a bit and no one will notice the difference."
"But look at the two sides of the jacket, one's two inches longer than the other."
"Not to worry, sir, just pull this side up a bit and tuck it under

your chin. Now they're equal. And remember, the suit's very cheap, so lift up your left shoulder and then the sleeve won't hang over your hand."

Eventually the customer was satisfied and he bought the suit, choosing to wear it home. As he left the shop, he passed two doctors coming in and when they saw the man limping along with his shoulder in the air and his chin tucked down on his chest, one remarked to the other,

"Poor man, he's got a terrible affliction."

"Indeed," agreed the other, "but they've managed to fit the suit perfectly."

A truck driver walked into a transport café and looked at the menu which read: "Leg of pork, bacon, black pudding, pigs trotters and pork sausage."

He ordered his meal and also asked for a glass of water.

"Certainly sir," replied the owner, "it'll be water from the bore."

"Bloody hell!" exclaimed the trucker. "Don't waste any of that pig, do you?"

"Hey! That bottle of magic potion you sold me was supposed to make me more intelligent... I'm beginning to think it's a big con."

"There, you see! You're more intelligent already."

Two travelling salesmen were travelling in the same carriage of an old rickety rural train which did not have toilet facilities. Suddenly, one of the men said to his companion, "I'm sorry, I find myself in the embarrassing position of needing the toilet very urgently. Would you mind if I just went on this piece of newspaper?"

The other gave his permission, the act was performed and the paper then thrown out of the window.

Meanwhile the travelling companion, unable to stomach the noxious smell had lit a cigarette.

"I say," said the first man, sitting back down, "this is a non-smoking carriage, you know."

★

Three men are sitting in the same railway carriage when suddenly the phone rings. The first man puts his thumb to his mouth and forefinger up to his ear and carries on a conversation, explaining afterwards that he's got microchips implanted in both digits, so he doesn't need to carry around a phone. Some weeks go by and the three men find themselves in the same carriage again. A phone rings and this time the second man starts to talk seemingly to nothing but afterwards he explains he has two microchips, one in his ear and the other in his mouth. Even better than using the finger and thumb technique. Suddenly, the third man gets up, groans slightly and bends over with his legs apart.

"Excuse me," he says "I think a fax is just coming through."

The woman looked with disgust at the slovenly bloke sitting opposite her in the railway carriage. His tie was askew, his clothes rumpled and he had a huge beer gut.

"You're a disgrace," she said, addressing him. "If that stomach was on a woman, she'd be pregnant."

The man smiled smugly and replied "It was ... and she is."

The Euro Express had just entered the tunnel when all the lights failed. In one of the front carriages sat an old woman, a young model, a policeman and a travelling salesman. As they were plunged into darkness, they heard the sound of a loud kiss, followed by a sharp smack. Moments later, the lights came on and each one sat there as if nothing had happened. The old woman looked at the young model and thought:

"Good for her, how dare that copper think he can get away with such awful behaviour."

The young model thought:

"Ugh, fancy that horrible looking bloke, kissing the old woman."

The policeman thought angrily:

"I didn't do anything; why do I get my face slapped?"

and the salesman sat there contentedly thinking:

"Fooled 'em all. I don't often get the chance to kiss a model, slap a policeman and get away with it!"

★

Up in Court

The tribunal was in session and it was the turn of the defendant to state his case. His legal representative got up to speak.

"Now Mr. Hodges, we have heard that your manner and words to your secretary were so upsetting, she had to take three weeks off work on medical grounds. I wonder if you could give us any mitigating circumstances?"

Hodges got up to speak.

"That morning the alarm failed to go off so I was an hour late getting out of bed. As I jumped up, I saw a note on the pillow from my wife, telling me she'd packed her bags and left with the next door neighbour. I ran down the stairs, tripped over the cat and broke an expensive vase standing on the hallway table. I tried to make myself a cup of coffee but the water had been turned off because of repairs in the street and when I eventually left the house, I noticed the car had a puncture. After another twenty minutes, I set off, only to be caught behind a demonstration march against the building of a new by-pass. So by the time I walked into the office, I was two hours late, having missed an important transatlantic business call, and lost a button off my best suit.

"So," he said, shrugging his shoulders in defeat, "when my secretary cheerfully strolled in and asked me where she should put a new batch of fork handles..."

A man is up before the courts for walking down the High Street completely naked.

"Is it true that you didn't have a stitch on?" asks the Judge.

"That's right, Your honour."

"Well, have you no shame? Are you married?"

"Yes, Your Honour."

"And how many children do you have?"

"16, your Honour."

"Release this man, he was only in his work clothes."

★

"You have been brought before this court to answer the allegation that you stole a young woman's bicycle. How do you plead?"

"Not guilty m'lord," said the young man. "I was walking down the lane when this lady cycled by, stopped when she saw me and asked me to kiss her. Then she took all her clothes off and said I could have anything I wanted. Well, your Honour, I don't wear ladies' clothes, so I took the bicycle."

★

"Mrs Mopps, you are up before the court for beating your husband black and blue. Do you have anything to say for yourself, before I pass sentence?"

"Yes, m'lud. Our Jack came home so drunk I locked him out of the house because of his disgusting behaviour. But he was hammering on the door, and said he was sure I'd open up if I knew what he was knocking with. So I opened the door m'lud and he gave me a box of chocolates. That's when I hit him."

★

Judge to husband, "I'm awarding your wife £300 a month."

"Well, that's very generous m'lud, I'll try and chip in a couple of pounds myself."

"Madam, you are up before this court for driving on the wrong side of the road. Do you have anything to say in your defence?"

"Yes m'lud, the other side was full."

When a witness was asked if a certain event had surprised him, he replied, "Why, you could have buggered me through my oilskins."

The barrister approached the judge and said, "I think he means he was taken aback, my Lord."

★

A young girl was in the witness box giving evidence against her boss for his sexual advancements towards her.

"And what did he say?" asked the barrister.

At this point, the girl was too embarrassed to repeat it, so it was suggested that she write it down for the jury and the judge to read. First it was passed to the foreman, who read, "Get your knickers off and meet me in the basement."

The foreman then handed it to Miss Wantin, an elderly spinster who had fallen asleep and had to be woken up. She read the note, gave the foreman a wink and a toothless smile, and put the note in her pocket.

★

"Good morning, I'm a criminal lawyer," said the man to his new client. "Oh well, at least you're not ashamed about describing yourself," came the reply.

★

A crafty barrister was defending a beautiful, shapely blonde accused of fraud and in his final address he turned to the all-male jury and said. "Gentlemen, are we going to see this poor, very friendly woman spend the next few years in jail or should she return to her private and secluded flat at 48 Green Walk, telephone number 491 7360?"

★

"Before I pass sentence have you anything to say?" demanded the judge.
"Fuck all," came the reply.
The judge turned to one of the court officials and said, "I didn't hear that; what did he say?"
"He said 'fuck all', m'lud" whispered the official.
"Oh, that's odd. I was sure I'd seen his lips move."

★

A man was up before the court on a charge of vagrancy. He had lost his job, house and family and fallen on hard times. The judge found him guilty as charged and looking down at him said, "Young man, it is drink and drink alone that has brought you before this court today."

On hearing this, the young man cheered up considerably. "Oh thank you m'lud, everyone else says it's my fault."

A man was up in court on a charge of soliciting. He had approached one of the principal bass singers in the local opera company, the judge was told.

"If that's so, then case dismissed," replied the judge. "I've heard the singers and in my opinion they all need fucking."

A young boy of 12 was in court charged with being the father of a new born baby.

In his defence, counsel asked the boy to show the court his penis.

"There," he said triumphantly. "Such a small, limp exhibit." And taking it in his hand he tossed it from side to side, saying, "Consider, members of the jury, whether this immature penis could possibly ever have fathered a child."

At this point, the young boy tapped his defence counsel on the shoulder and whispered, "If you don't let go, we're going to lose this case."

When the man was found having sex with his girlfriend in the railway carriage, the police charged him with having a first class ride in a second class carriage.

★

"John Smith and Mary Owen – you are up before the court today for seriously causing a breach of the peace and very nearly forcing the number 49 bus off the road. Have you anything to say in your defence?"

"Yes, Your Honour. We're very sorry for our behaviour but we were the victims of circumstance. Mary collapsed in the middle of the road and I knelt down to give her mouth to mouth resuscitation, but before we knew what was happening, passion took over and away we went. All of a sudden, I was coming, she was coming, and the bus was the only one that had brakes."

A woman got a divorce on the grounds that her husband's penis was too big. Two years later she was up before the same judge, this time requesting a divorce because her husband's penis was too small. Her divorce went through but as she was leaving court the judge gave her a few words of warning.

"Madam, this court will not look too favourably upon you if you appear before us again with a third husband. We have more important things to do than sort out the right fitting for you."

★

The judge addressed the defendant, a sickly 65-year-old man. "You have been charged with kerb crawling on September 4 of this year; how do you plead?"

"Guilty, Your Honour," said the man going into a coughing spasm.

"You are also charged that on September 21, you were found in an illegal club watching pornographic films; how do you plead?"

"Guilty, Your Honour," replied the man suffering another bout of bad coughing.

"And finally, last week you were found with a prostitute in a compromising position in a dark alley; how do you plead?"

During a bout of coughing that shook the man's whole body, he replied, "Guilty, Your Honour."

In a sudden moment of compassion, the judge said.

"Look, before I pass sentence, would you like to suck a fisherman's friend?"

"No, thanks. Don't you think I'm in enough trouble already?"

A simple man was accused of stalking a beautiful young girl and was told he would have to line up in an identity parade. When they took the girl along the line, he shouted loudly,

"That's her!"

"Mr Makepiece, you are up before this court for possessing a counterfeit press. Although no money can be found, I pronounce you guilty of intent to produce counterfeit money. Do you have anything to say?" asked the judge.

"Just one thing your honour. You'd better find me guilty of adultery as well because I have the equipment for that too."

★

The judge turned to the farmer and said,
"Mr Brown, you are in this court to claim damages against this truck driver, for the awful injuries you sustained at the time of the accident. And yet, Mr Brown, at the time of the accident you were heard to say to the policeman that you'd never felt better. Kindly explain."
"It's like this your honour," replied the farmer.
"At the time of the accident the policeman went over to my dog, and seeing it was so badly injured, he shot it. Then he went over to my two cows and when he saw they had broken legs, he shot them as well. So when he came and asked me how I felt, I thought it was a good idea to tell him I'd never felt better."

★

Instead of sending two convicted drug dealers to jail, the judge decides to give them both 250 hours of community service.
"You will work in a drug rehabilitation centre, explaining to those poor addicts the evils of drug abuse. After your sentence you will return to me with a full report of your work."
The two drug dealers carry out the judge's wishes and return to him at the end of their sentence.
"How did it go?" the judge asks the first man.
"I managed to get 30 people off drugs," he replies.
"Well done, and how did you manage that?"
"I drew two circles – one large and one small. I told them the large circle was the size of their brain before drugs, and the small circle was what their brain would be like after drugs."
The judge then asks the second man how he did.

"I got 200 people off drugs," he replies.

"But that's staggering!" says the judge "How did you manage that?"

"Well, I drew two pictures – a small circle and a large circle. I showed them the small circle first and told them that was their arsehole before going into prison ...."

★

The judge turned to the woman and asked

"I see you're divorcing your husband on the grounds that he is a slob and uncouth. Can you give me any examples of this?"

"Yes your honour. Whenever we go out he always drinks tea with his pinkie sticking out."

"But there's nothing wrong with that," said the judge. "It's considered good manners in some circles to drink tea with the little finger sticking out."

"I wasn't talking about his finger," she replied accusingly.

★

Three country lads were out in the big city when they were attacked by a mugger.

"Give me all your valuables" he hissed, "or I'll inject you with AIDS."

Immediately, two of the lads handed over their wallets and then ran away. The third lad, however, refused so the mugger injected him. Later, when the three lads met up the two who had handed over all their money looked at their friend aghast.

"Don't you realise what he's done? You've been injected with

AIDS."

The third lad smiled.

"No, no, it's alright, I'm wearing a condom."

"You are up before this court for the hideous crime of making love to your wife after she had died. Do you have anything to say in your defence?"

"Yes, your honour. I didn't know she was dead, she'd been like that for years."

"You are up before this court for entering a dog in the local pet show," said the judge. "You will go to prison for 3 months."

The little man was found guilty of fraud and sentenced to three years in prison. When he arrived, he was put in a cell with a huge gorilla of a man who was doing thirty years for murder. The "gorilla" looked at the little man with relish and said,

"My name's Digger and what I need to know is whether you're going to be the husband or the wife."

Choosing what he thought was the lesser of two evils, the terrified man chose husband.

"Good," snarled the big man. "Now get down on your knees and suck your wife's dick."

"And where do you think you're going at this time of night?" the police officer asked the staggering drunk.

"To a lecture," he replied.

"Come off it. It's one o'clock in the morning. Who'd be giving a lecture at this late hour?"

"My wife."

Did you hear about the humiliated flasher?

His case was heard in the Small Claims Court.

An explosion at the chemical factory meant that everyone in a five-mile radius had to be evacuated. They were sent to community centres to spend the night on an assortment of mattresses. Around midnight, the local police checked out the people and one officer said

"Are there any pregnant women here?"

"Have a heart," a woman replied, "we've only been here a few minutes."

★

A young police officer was being shown his new beat. After a couple of hours driving around, he and his sergeant stopped for coffee at a local café. They'd just finished when in walked a stunning woman. Her figure was like an hourglass and left very little to the imagination.

"Wow!" whistled the copper under his breath, "who's that, Sarge? I've never seen anything like her."

"They call her 999."

"Yeah? Why?"

"Every time she calls, a copper comes."

★

"Maurice Highton, you are up before this court for shooting your wife. Do you have anything to say?"

"Yes M'lud," he replied, "She called me a dreadful lover."

"And you killed her for saying that?"

"No," he answered, angrily. "I killed her for knowing the difference."

★

"Mr. Merino, you are up before this court for the serious crime of assault against one of your neighbours. Before I pass sentence, can you tell me the circumstances behind this attack?"

"Yes, Your Honour," replied the defendant.

"That low down skunk called my wife an ugly old bag. He said she had a moustache bigger than his, bad breath and legs like tree trunks. I had to defend her honour."

"Mmm," mused the judge, "and is your wife here to testify?"

"Well, the thing is, er... Will it affect your judgement if the allegations are true?" he asked.

★

Our town was so lawless, if you went to buy a pair of tights, they'd ask you for your head size.

★

"Luigi, Luigi," shouted the children as they lined up outside the ice cream van. But Luigi was nowhere to be seen. The motor was running, the music was playing but no-one was serving.

"Stand back kids," said a policeman attracted by all the noise. "What have we here?" The policeman peered inside the van and caught sight of Luigi lying on the floor. He was covered in chocolate sauce, mixed nuts and fresh cream.

"Sarge," he said, speaking into his radio. "This is PC Mann, I need some back-up at Luigi's ice-cream van on Prospect Street. It's Luigi; he's topped himself."

★

A policeman was patrolling the streets late one night when he spotted a car parked up a side alley. He shone his torch through the back window and saw a young couple playing Scrabble.

"What's going on here?" he demanded.

"We're just playing Scrabble," replied the boy.

"That's an odd thing to do at this time of night," he said, looking suspiciously at the girl.

"And how old are you?" he asked.

She looked up at the church clock and replied happily, "In 10 minutes time I'll be 16."

A man was caught short and so relieved himself in the bushes just as a policeman walked by."What the hell are you doing," he demanded angrily. "There's a public toilet just down there."

"It may be big," retorted the man, "but it's not a bloody hose pipe."

★

"You didn't stop at the last junction," said the policeman to the motorist. "I'll have to breathalyse you." The officer held up the bag.

"What's that?" asked the driver.

"This tells you if you've had too much to drink," he replied.

"Well I never!" he exclaimed "I'm married to one of those."

★

The police car indicated for the motorist to pull up.

"Did you realise, sir, you were doing 55mph in a 30mph area," he said, pulling out his notebook. May I have your name please?"

"Malenovich Salkonovichiski," came the reply.

"Okay, well just don't do it again," replied the officer, closing his book and walking away.

★

"I want a divorce," said the woman to her lawyer.

"And can you tell me why?" he asked.

"Because each night in bed my husband let's out this bloodcurdling scream every time he reaches a climax."

The lawyer blushed profusely and said "But ... er ... surely that's quite normal, isn't it?"

"Not when it wakes me up every night," she retorted.

★

The trial was going badly for the defendant. He was charged with murder and although the body had never been found, there was enough evidence to convict him. As a last desperate effort, the defending lawyer decided to play a trick. He stood up, looked at the jury and said "Ladies and gentlemen, I have an announcement to make. In exactly 30 seconds, the person presumed murdered will walk into this courtroom."

There was stunned silence as all the jury looked towards the door, but nothing happened.

The defending lawyer continued "So members of the jury, although I made that last statement up, because you all looked at the door proves there is an element of doubt. Therefore I put it to you that you have no other course than to find the defendant not guilty."

A short while later the jury retired to consider their verdict and it was only 20 minutes before they returned.

"We find the defendant guilty," they proclaimed.

"But how can that be?" protested the lawyer. "You all looked towards the door, you must have had some doubt."

The foreman of the jury replied, "That's true, we did all look towards the door. But your client didn't."

A group of firemen from the amber watch division went to Blackpool on a works' outing. They made full use of all the resort had to offer and stayed overnight in one of the seaside hotels. Then at two in the morning, there was an awful hullabaloo and as the guests looked out of their doors, they caught sight of a naked man running down the corridor,

chasing a girl who was screaming at the top of her voice. Naturally the man, who was one of the firemen, was taken to court for lewd behaviour, but it was the brilliance of his barrister that got him off without a blemish to his name. The barrister simply quoted from the service handbook which stated, "A member of the fire service need not wear his uniform at all times as long as he is suitably attired for the sport in which he is involved."

★

On his travels abroad, a judge visited a court in a new third world developing country. His guide informed him that the court and its proceedings had been based on the English judicial system, and sure enough the judge and barristers were wearing wigs and gowns and all the proceedings were conducted in an English manner. Suddenly he was astonished to see a youth, wearing white gloves, run through the room feeling all the women's breasts. The extraordinary sight was ignored by everyone.

"Why isn't that boy expelled from the court?" demanded the visiting judge.

"But we're only following English traditions," replied the guide. "He's the Court Titter. We've read about him often in the court accounts – 'A titter ran through the crowd.'"

The court adjourned while the judge considered the appropriate sentence for an old street whore down on her luck. Unable to come to a decision, he rang his colleague.

"Clive, Donald here. What would you give an old, down-and-out prostitute?"

Quick as a flash the reply came, "Not more than ten quid."

The shopaholic 'money-mad' woman told the judge she couldn't serve on the jury because she didn't believe in capital punishment.

"But madam," replied the judge patiently. "This is not a murder trial, it's a simple case of a husband reneging on his promise to buy his wife a new sports car."

"Okay, okay," she conceded. "Maybe there is a case for capital punishment after all."

The judge said to the drunk, "Please stand, Mr Havermore. Before passing sentence, I need to know if you are sober enough to understand you have been brought here for drinking."

"Oh, that's very kind, your Honour, but I won't if you don't mind. I'm trying to give to give it up, you see."

★

There had been so much trouble in the border settlement, that a curfew had been enforced from 10pm. Two men set out to patrol the eastern part of town and were walking down either side of the main street. Suddenly a shot rang out and the first patrolman ran over to find his partner holding out his smoking gun and a man lying dead at his feet.

"Why did you shoot him?" he asked. "There's still 20 minutes before curfew."

"Maybe," replied his partner, "but I know where this man lives and he would never have got home in time."

A man was in court for killing his wife. When he saw the jury – only two men and the rest women, he felt his chances of getting off were very slim. Now he was quite a handsome man, so in desperation he thought he would try to seduce one of the women on the jury and persuade her to drop the murder verdict to one of manslaughter. He succeeded and when the trial came to an end the following Monday, the jury left to consider their verdict. A few hours later they returned and found him guilty of manslaughter. He sighed with relief and later managed to speak to the woman to thank her for all she'd done.

"Well, it wasn't that easy," she replied. "The others wanted to acquit you."

★

Machoman

A vain man who thought he had a body to die for gave his girlfriend a photograph of himself, posing in the nude.

"What are you going to do with that?", he boasted.

"Mmm", she replied. "I think I'll get it enlarged."

"If you want an extra bit of sport in bed," said one bloke to the other, "mount her from behind and whisper in her ear: 'This is how I do it with your best friend'. Then try and stay on for 10 seconds."

Did you hear about the vain man who was trying to impress his new girlfriend? When he stood in front of the mirror admiring himself, he said, "I had to fight hard to get this body."

"Really?" she replied. "I'm sorry you lost."

The vain young man lay back contentedly on the bed after making love to his new girlfriend.

"How was it for you?" he asked.

"Oh, pretty painless," she replied. "I never felt a thing."

Some of the guys out west are so mighty they can run in the three-legged race without a partner.

"What are you doing?" he asked excitedly as she put her hand down his trousers.

"Oh nothing," she said. "I thought it might have been the start of something big."

★

As he stood at the mirror yet again, admiring his good looks and muscular body, he turned to his long suffering wife and said, "There can't be that many men who are so well endowed."

"One less than you think," came the mumbled reply.

★

Did you hear about the man who had an audition with the Chippendales?

He was put on their short list.

★

Out on their first date, an arrogant man took the girl back to his flat for coffee.

"You don't talk much," she said.

At that he dropped his trousers and proudly said, "This does all my talking for me."

"Well, that doesn't have much to say either," she retorted.

★

A body builder went down to the local antique shop to find a mirror to hang on the back of the bathroom door, so that in the

mornings after a shower he could admire his fine physique.

"There are plenty of mirrors to choose from," said the shop owner, "but don't have that one – it's evil."

Well, nothing would satisfy him until he had bought the evil mirror which he took home and hung behind the door. Next morning he looked at himself and realised he wasn't as well endowed as he would like. Knowing the mirror had magic powers, he said, "Mirror, mirror, on the wall, make my tool touch the floor."

And his legs fell off.

After leading him on for a while, the girlfriend suddenly moves away, telling him, "If you want to go all the way with me, you'll have to have a sports car and a ten inch dick."

"OK, but I'll be back," he tells her.

And indeed he arrives on her doorstep the following week in a gleaming white sports car.

She is very impressed.

"And that's not all," he says "As far as my dick's concerned, my doctor says he can cut it down to any size you want."

In Love

Adultery

A man went to the doctor's complaining that his wife had such a vigorous sex drive that she was wearing him out. The doctor suggested he bring his wife into the surgery for an examination so they both turned up the following week.

The wife was told to go into the other room and strip off, but when the doctor went in, he was overcome by her beautiful body and the way she started to tempt him over.

"It's no good, I can't help myself!" gasped the doctor and he stripped off frantically and jumped on top of her.

After some time, the groans of pleasure attracted the attention of the husband so he opened the door to see what was going on.

"What the hell do you think you're doing?" bellowed the husband.

"I'm.. er.. taking your wife's temperature," replied the flustered doctor.

Taking a gun from his pocket, the man says, "When you take that thing out, it better have numbers on it."

A tall dark handsome man pops into the vets and asks the receptionist how long he will have to wait.

"Oh, about 30 minutes, Mr Wellbeing has two cats and a gerbil to see."

"Thank you," replies the man and walks out. Over the next few weeks the man appears several times, asks the same question and then leaves. By this time, the receptionist is so intrigued, she tells the vet and he suggests that next time the

man comes in she should follow him when he leaves.

So the receptionist does as she's asked and on returning says to the vet, "Well, it's very strange. All he seems to do is go straight round to your house."

★

"How do you like my new suit?" said Steve to his friend.

"Wow! that must have cost a lot of money."

"I don't know, it was a present from my wife. When I arrived home early yesterday afternoon, it was hanging over the bottom of the bed."

★

"Mabel, that milkman will have to go," said the enraged husband. "He's so cheeky, he reckons he's slept with every woman on this street, except one."

"Oh, I know who that'll be," replied his wife, "that'll be that stuck-up cow at No.32."

★

"I'm sorry to hear your Bert's in hospital, I heard it was his knee."

"That's right, I found a blonde sitting on it."

★

Bob had not long left for work when he realised he'd left some important papers at home, so he drove back and on entering the kitchen, found his wife bending over the cooker. Quick as a flash, he lifted her skirt and unzipped his flies, just as she said without turning round, "Hello Fred, you're early this week."

★

The phone rings and the husband answers it.

"No mate, you want the Met. office."

"Who was that darling?" asks the wife.

"I don't know, I think he wanted the weather forecast, because he asked me if the coast was clear."

★

A man went to the doctors in an awful state. Cuts and bruises to his face and a suspected broken arm.

"What happened to you?" asked the doctor.

"It's my wife, she had one of her dreadful nightmares."

"Do you mean she did this to you while she was asleep?"

"Oh no doctor, it was when she shouted out in her sleep 'Quick, get out, my husband's coming home,' that, without thinking, I jumped out of the window."

"You never make a noise or cry out when you have an orgasm," he complained.

"How would you know? You're never there," she retorted.

Following a night of fantastic sex with a woman he picked up in the pub, the man is afraid to go home and face his wife.

"I have a great idea," says the woman. "Stick these darts in your back pocket and tell her the truth. Trust me, it will be alright."

So, with trepidation, the man returns home to find his wife in the kitchen waiting for him.

"Okay," she hisses, "where the hell have you been this time?"

"I've been making wonderful love to a beautiful woman, all night long," he replies.

"You bloody liar, pull the other one. You've been with your mates playing darts, I can see them in your back pocket."

★

"What the hell's going on here?" yelled the angry husband, on finding his wife and the gardener canoodling in the summer house."

"You see," said his wife scornfully, "I told you he was stupid."

★

Two men were chatting over the garden wall. The first said, "You'll never guess what happened this morning, Bob. My wife was suffering from a hangover, so I went downstairs to make her a cup of tea. Because it was cold, I grabbed the first thing I saw to put on which turned out to be her dressing gown. I was just bending over the fridge to get the milk, when the window cleaner walked in, put his hand up me and grabbed my bum. You can imagine the embarrassment when he realised who I was, it was just an astonishing coincidence that his wife had a dressing gown exactly the same."

★

Doris had been staying with her sick mother for over a month and on returning home, she discovered her husband had been having an affair. She confronted him, shouting loudly,

"Was it Joan, from next door?"

"No."

"Was it Beryl?"

"No."

"Then it must have been Sue."

"No, you stupid woman. Don't you think I have any friends of my own?"

★

The angry woman marched round to her next door neighbour's house and confronted her with a set of photographs.

"Look at these, you common tart, this is proof that you've been seeing my husband. There's one of the two of you in bed, this is a picture of you and him in the back seat of the car and this one shows you sitting on his knee. What do you have to say for yourself?"

For a few moments, the next door neighbour looked through the photographs and then said, "Mmm, not bad, I'll have two copies of the first picture and one each of the other two."

★

It was the same routine every night. Fred would arrive home from the coal mine and jump into the bath that his wife always had ready for him, and then she would lovingly wash his back. However, one evening it all changed. When Fred got into the bath, his wife took a brush to him and scrubbed him till he was red raw.

"Hey woman!" he yelled. "What's going on?"

"You tell me," she retorted. "For as long as I can remember you've always walked into the house dead on 6 o'clock, black from head to toe. But tonight, you're 45 minutes late and a small part of you is white."

★

Old Jake only had moments to live. At his bedside were his family – his wife and four sons, three of which had blonde hair, the other ginger.

"Mavis, I've always wondered why one of our sons had red hair. Tell me truthfully, is he really my son?"

Mavis put her hand on her heart and swore fervently that, yes, he was his son.

"Oh thank goodness," croaked the old man and he died with a smile on his face.

As the family left, the room, the wife sighed deeply,

"Thank heaven he didn't ask about the other three."

★

A man takes the afternoon off work and comes home unexpectedly to find his wife lying on the bed, naked and out of breath.

"What's going on?" he asks.

"I think I'm having an asthma attack!" she gasps.

He rushes to the phone to ring for a doctor when his son runs in.

"Daddy, daddy, Uncle Bill is in the wardrobe and he's got no clothes on."

"What!" shouts the man, and back up the stairs he rushes to find his brother hiding naked in the wardrobe.

"You silly sod!" he shouts angrily, "here's my wife having a severe asthma attack and all you can do is play hide and seek and scare the kids!"

★

A man went to an old furniture shop to buy an antique kitchen table. Almost at once, he saw the table he wanted to buy and asked the price.

"£2,000 sir."

"Never!" exclaimed the man, "that's unbelievably expensive."

"That's true," replied the assistant, "but this is not just any antique kitchen table, this piece of furniture has special powers."

"Get away! Show me."

The assistant went up to the table and said,

"How many floors are there in this building?"

Immediately, the table jumped into the air four times, and indeed there were four floors in the building.

The man wasn't totally convinced.

"OK, ask it how much money I've got in my wallet."

The question was asked and the table jumped up eleven times.

"That's incredible" said the man "it's true, I've got two £5 notes and a loose £1 coin. I must have that table."

So the man paid £2,000 and the antique kitchen table was delivered the next day. While it was being installed, his mate popped over and remarked on the piece of new purchase.

"It's very special" said the man. "Here, I'll show you." He

thought for a moment and then said

"How much money has my wife got in her bank account?"
The table went completely berserk. It started jumping up and down and was still going 30 minutes later.
"But how can that be?, where did she get all that money?" he said flabbergasted.
Suddenly, the table stopped moving, its legs fell apart and its drawers fell to the floor.

★

"Doctor, doctor, I'm having trouble with my todger, can you do anything for me?" said the distressed man.
After a thorough examination the doctor told him that he must have been so sexually active in the past that he's almost worn it out. The fact is that he's only got the use of it for another 25 shags. The young man went home to his wife and told her what the doctor had said.
"Oh no!" she cried "we mustn't waste any of them, we'll have to draw up a carefully planned timetable."
"I've already done that on the way home," he said, "and there isn't a slot left for you."

★

The couple had been married a year when the husband was called away on business on the other side of the country. It would mean he would be away for a month so the wife's friend moved in to keep her company. As it happened, the job finished earlier than expected so he jumped on a plane and on landing rang his wife from the airport. Her friend answered the phone to say that Tracy was in the bath.

"OK, can you tell her I'll be there about midnight so if she can wear something sheer and sexy we'll make it a night to remember."

"OK," said the friend "and who shall I say called?"

The old farmer married a young girl of 18 and after a few months of idyllic married life, he went to see his doctor.

"The problem is I'm having to work many hours on the farm but I have to keep breaking off when I get the urge, to run back to the house, jump into bed and do the business. Then it's back to work, and it's knackering me."

The doctor suggested that his wife should come to see him out in the fields.

"Every time you get the urge," said the doctor, "fire a shot from your gun to let your wife know you're waiting for her. A few months passed and then the doctor met the old farmer in the high street.

"How's the shotgun plan working?" he asked.

"Oh it was very good at first, but then the duck shooting season started and I haven't seen her since," he replied sadly.

The man rang his wife to tell her he had the afternoon off and would be coming home. The phone was answered by a small boy.

"Hello son, can I speak to Mum?"

"No," said the boy, "Mum's in bed with the milkman and

they've told me to stay downstairs."

The man was stunned by the news but after a moment or two he said to the boy,

"Son, go and get my shotgun from the garage, load it with two cartridges and go and blast them."

After an agonising 10 minutes the little boy came back onto the phone.

"I've done it Dad," he said.

"Well done son, I'll finish off when I get back. Go and have a swim in the pool to clean yourself up and I'll see you later."

"But Dad, we don't have a pool," said the boy.

"What! Hold on, is that 0397 46461?"

After months of trying, the Office Manager finally managed to persuade his beautiful secretary to come out to dinner with him. Afterwards they went back to her flat and after some coffee and a little foreplay, they jumped into bed. Alas, no matter how hard he tried, he could not get an erection and full of apologies and acute embarrassment, he went home. He got into bed next to his big, fat ugly wife who was snoring her head off and as his body touched her naked flesh, he got a huge erection. Jumping out of bed he looked down at his swollen organ and said sadly,

"Now I know why they call you a prick."

A man comes home early from work to find his wife in bed with another man.

"Who the bloody hell's this?" he shouts angrily.

"Good question," she replies. "Say lover, what's your name?"

A man came home early from work to find his wife in bed with another man. The man's head was laying between the wife's voluptuous breasts.

"What the fuck are you doing?" shouted the husband.

"Listening to some good music," replied the man calmly.

"Get off, let me hear," demanded the husband, but when he put his head between her breasts he couldn't hear anything.

"Of course not," replied the man arrogantly.

"You're not plugged in."

★

A woman was in bed with her lover when she heard her husband open the front door.

"Quick!" she whispered urgently.

"It's my husband, hide in the wardrobe."

"Ooh, it's dark in here," said a little voice.

"Who's that?" gasped the man.

"That's my mum you've been with and I'm going to call my dad."

"Now, now, son, not so hasty, I'm sure we can work this out."

"OK," said the small boy. "But it's going to cost you."

"How about £5?"

"I'm going to call Dad."

"Well £10 then."

"I'm going to call Dad."

"OK, let's say £20."

"No, £30."

"Well that's all I've got, here you are." The man handed over the money and made his escape when the coast was clear.

A few days later Mum took the little boy to church and as she knelt to pray he wandered off and crept into the confessional.

"Ooh, it's dark in here," he said.

"Oh no, don't start that again!" replied the agitated priest.

The little boy's mum had shaved off all her pubic hair, ready to wear her skimpy bikini when they went on holiday.

"Where's all your hair gone?" asked her son.

"I've lost my sponge," she replied dismissively and told him to go out to play. Sometime later he returned with a big smile on his face.

"Mummy, Mummy am I a good boy for finding your sponge?"

Puzzled, Mum asked him where it was and he answered her proudly, "The lady across the road is washing daddy's face with it."

Saturday morning was the time for all the milk accounts to be settled and the task of collecting the money fell to a young man who accompanied the milkman. Number 47 Acacia Avenue was opened by a bored and lonely woman who suggested that instead of paying the £6 bill, she might pay him in sex. The young man agreed, stepped inside and they went into a back room. As she removed her clothes, he dropped his trousers to reveal the biggest todger she'd ever seen. But as she watched, he took a number of washers out of his pocket and slipped them over his massive hardware.

"You don't have to do that," she said. "I can take anything you can give me."

"Maybe," he replied, "but not for a small bill of £6 you can't."

The man came home early from work to find his wife lying naked on the bed, crying, her eyes out.

"What's wrong?" he asked.

"I've got nothing to wear to the dance tomorrow night," she sobbed.

"Oh come on now! You've plenty of clothes" and with that he went over to the wardrobe.

"See here, there's the nice pink dress, the pale blue skirt, the yellow cocktail dress, hello John, the green silk gown ....

The simple man was beside himself with anger when he discovered his wife in bed with another man.

"How could you!" he yelled, and taking a gun out of the bottom drawer of the bedside table he placed it to his head and cocked the trigger.

"Don't Jim, please don't," sobbed the woman, "put the gun down."

"Say your prayers, you're next," snapped the man.

After partying most of the night a young couple woke up the next day with awful hangovers.

"I'm sorry, love," said the husband, "but was it you I made love to last night in the spare bedroom?"

"I don't know," she replied. "What position did we use?"

What the bloody hell do you think you're doing?" said the angry husband when he caught his wife in bed with another bloke.

The wife turned to her partner and said, "You see, I told you he was stupid."

A duke and duchess were not getting on very well; in fact, the duchess believed her husband to be having an affair with the housemaid, so she decided to test her theory.

The duchess sent the housemaid away for the night and when her husband made an excuse to leave his bed, she rushed down the back stairs and got into her housemaid's bed. Lo and behold, in he came and had his wicked way before she turned the lights on.

"You didn't expect to find me here, did you?" said the duchess.

"Indeed not, madam," replied the butler.

A man turns to his friend and asks him why he's looking so puzzled. He replies, "I've received this letter today and it's from a man who says he'll beat me senseless if I don't stay

away from his wife."

"So what's puzzling you?"

"Well, he hasn't signed it."

When a man arrives home from work one evening he's greeted by his wife, who's got a bottle of hair conditioner in her hand.

"What's that for?" he asks "My hair's OK."

"Yours maybe, but this is for your girlfriend whose hair keeps coming out all over your shoulders!"

A man came home early from work to find his wife in bed with a strange man.

"Let me explain," she said. "He came to the door looking for something to eat, so I gave him the breakfast you didn't want this morning. Then he asked if there were any clothes I didn't want, so I gave him your old blue suit that was going to the jumble sale. At that point he asked if there was anything else you didn't use."

"Did you sleep with my husband last night?"

"No, not a wink."

★

The inevitable happened. A man came home from work early, and as his wife heard the key in the door, the lover jumped out of bed, grabbed his jacket and leapt into the wardrobe. The husband, on seeing his wife in bed shouted, "I know there's a man here somewhere. Come on, where is he?" He looked under the bed, "No, he's not here." He looked out of the window, "No, he's not here." And he looked in the wardrobe. But seeing a man holding a gun he shouted, "And he's not here either."

"Do you talk to your wife when you're making love?"
"Only if she rings up."

"How many wives have you had?" asks Jack to Rob.
"Mmmm, about 12, including my own."

★

A jealous wife suspected her husband of being unfaithful, so when they were both invited to a fancy-dress party she feigned a headache and told him to go on his own. So off he went in his spacesuit costume and an hour later she followed in her own masked outfit. When she got there she spied her husband chatting up every female at the party, so after a while propositioned him herself to see what the response would be. Lo and behold, he had her outside quicker than you could say Jack Robinson and screwed her against the tree. Not long after she left and the next morning at breakfast was ready to confront him with his supposed unfaithfulness.
"How was the party?" she asked.

"Not really my scene," he replied. "I went up to the den to play poker with the boys and lent my spacesuit costume to Freddie Parker."

A man comes home to find his wife in bed with his best friend. The husband goes to the bed and says to his friend, "I have to …. but you?"

Two men are getting dressed in the changing room. One puts on a girdle. "Since when have you been wearing a girdle?" the other asks. "Since my wife found it in the glove compartment," he replies.

"When I came home from work last night, I found my wife in bed with another man. How can I stop this happening again?" "Work more overtime."

My best friend ran away with my wife, and do you know – I miss him.

A businessman away for the week at a conference sends a telegram to his wife saying he'll be home Friday night and is bringing a colleague with him. Friday night comes and he arrives home only to find his wife in bed with a stranger. The businessman goes completely berserk, threatening to kill them both, but his colleague eventually manages to calm him

down by saying there's probably some explanation and they'll sort it out in the morning. Sure enough, the next morning the colleague says to his friend, "You see, there was a good explanation. She's just told me there was a postal strike on Friday, so she didn't get the message."

A man comes home early from work to find his wife in bed. He's immediately suspicious and opens the wardrobe to find her lover hiding amongst the clothes, stark naked.

"What are you doing in there?" demands the angry husband.

"I'm the local pest controller," stumbles the man, "and we've heard there's an infestation of moths about..."

"So how come you're bollock naked?" shouts the husband.

"Well bugger me!" replies the man in amazement as he looks down at his body. "This infestation's worse than I thought!"

What is a vindictive pregnancy?
Someone who's had it in for you while you've been away.

"I want to divorce my husband," said the shapely brunette to her solicitor.

"On what grounds?"

"Infidelity, he's not the father of my child."

Two men in the barber's, a colonel and a sergeant.

"Shall I put some aftershave on, sir?" asked the barber of the colonel.

"Good gracious man, no. My wife would think I smelled like a brothel."

The barber turned to the sergeant, "What about you, sir?"

"Certainly, my wife doesn't know what a brothel smells like."

Coming back from work one day, a husband sees his wife wearing a stunning diamond ring. When he asks her where she got it, she tells him she's won it in a raffle. In the following two weeks his wife is also seen wearing a beautiful fur coat and carrying a crocodile handbag. Again, she tells him she won them in a raffle. The following Thursday she informs her husband that she's going out again and would he be kind enough to turn the shower on for her.

"Oh, I don't think so," he said. "You don't want to get your raffle ticket wet."

In the back seat of a car, a couple are having it away time and time again. Every time he finishes she asks for more. Eventually he tells her he's just got to go outside for a breather. While he's standing there he sees a man looking in a shop window at some car stereos.

"Listen, mate," he says. "I've got a spare radio which you can have for free if you'll do me a favour. I've got a girl in the back seat of my car who's sex mad. She wants it time and time again and you'd be doing me a favour if you took over for a while." The man agrees and gets into the car. A little while later a traffic cop comes along, shines his torch through the car window and asks what's going on.

"I'm making love to my wife," he replies.

"Well, can't you do it at home?" asks the policeman.

"Until you shone the light through the window, I didn't realise it was my wife!"

Two men talking in a bar. "Listen, Jack, we've been mates a long time. I'd like you to do something for me. I've got to go out of town for a few days and I'd like you to keep a close eye on my wife. I have suspicions that she's up to something."

A few days pass and they meet up again in the pub.

"I watched your wife carefully, Jack," said Bob. "On the second evening a man knocked on the door and she opened it in a see-through night-dress. They kissed passionately and then went upstairs to the bedroom where I saw him put his hand between her legs – but then they closed the curtains and I saw no more."

"Oh dear," said Jack. "You see, the doubt remains."

A man walked into a bar and ordered a double Scotch, drank it down in one gulp and immediately ordered another.

"You don't look so good," remarked the bartender. "Is it bad news?"

"Yes," replied the man "I just found my wife in bed with my

best friend."

"Oh no," said the bartender "Here, have the next one on me. What did you do?"

"I told her to pack her bags, get out and never come back."

"And what about your best friend?"

"I went right up to him and said 'Bad dog!'"

Two men talking in a bar. One says, "I've got such a clever wife, why she's even found a burglar-proof way of protecting her clothes. Sometimes when I come home from work there's a man in the wardrobe looking after them."

Jack lived his life to a strict routine and would go out for a pint every Monday, Wednesday and Friday. However, one Friday night he didn't feel very well, so decided to stay in and watch television with his wife. Half way through the evening the phone rang and his wife heard him say, "Why the hell are you ringing me? Call the bloody Met Office!" and he slammed down the phone.

"Who was that?" she asked.

"Some silly bugger asking me if the coast was clear."

Same man talking in a bar:

"And do you know, she loves me so much. Last week I was off sick. Every morning she was so glad to have me home, she'd run out into the street when the milkman or postman arrived, shrieking, "My husband's here, my husband's at home!"

★

A wife who was forever left at home on her own because her husband worked late at the office insisted they go out to the best club in town for her birthday. She was determined he wouldn't get out of it, so that night he was dragged along. At the door the bouncer greeted her husband in a familiar way, "Hello, Bob, nice to see you."

Quickly Bob explained that the bouncer worked in his office during the day and he worked at night for some extra money. In they went and left their coats in the cloakroom at which point the girl in charge also greeted Bob in a familiar way. "Hello, Bob, how are you tonight?"

Again, he remarked that the girl used to work in his office before changing jobs. However, it all went horribly wrong when the stripper also greeted him.

"That's it!" roared the wife as she stormed out and hailed down a taxi. "I could just about accept the explanations about the bouncer and cloakroom attendant but you'll never convince me that the stripper works as a secretary through the day. No way!"

Hearing this the taxi driver turned round and said, "Christ, you've picked a difficult one tonight, Bob."

★

Jack and Bill are in the urinals, and on seeing Bill's prick, Jack exclaims, "How the heck did you get such a huge prick? It's a real stonker."

"Oh that's easy," replies Bill proudly. "Every night before I get into bed I knock it five times on the bottom of the bed."

That night Jack decides to do the same and before getting into bed knocks his prick on the bottom of the bed five times.

Awakened by the noise, his wife whispers, "Is that you Bill?"

Why did the unfaithful man buy a dog?

If his wife overhears him saying, "Lie down, roll over, give it to me and I'll give you a bone," she thinks it's the dog he's talking to.

What does the unfaithful man say to his wife after having sex?
"Sweetheart, I'll be home in half an hour."

A woman goes to her doctor's for a check-up,

After examining her, he gives her the unwelcome news that she is pregnant. She is shattered by this, and immediately rings her husband.

"I'm pregnant, you bastard, why didn't you wear a condom?" she yells.

"Now, hold on a minute," he replies. "I always wear a condom. Anyway, who is this?"

Jack Carter, chairman of an international company, is outraged one morning when he sees that someone has peed in the snow outside his office window. Not just peed but formed the words, " Jack Carter – big arsehole."

He immediately calls in his private secretary and demands that the culprits be discovered.

Later, the secretary returns and rather nervously gives him the news.

"Sir, the urine belongs to the deputy chairman, but ... er..."

"But what, man, come on, but what?"

"Well, sir, the handwriting belongs to your wife."

Betty's walking down the street when she comes upon her hated neighbour, Doreen.

"Hey bitch, how dare you say my John's got a wart on the end of his dick?"

"I said no such thing," replied Doreen. "I said it just felt like he had a wart on the end of his dick."

Husband comes home from the office and sees his wife in the garden.

"Sarah, I have some good news and some bad news to tell you. I'm leaving you for Molly."

"I see," says the wife, "and what's the bad news?"

"That was a wonderful weekend we spent in Paris," said the

**Director to his Secretary. "Will you ever be able to forget it?"
"I don't know," she replied. "What's it worth?"**

Drowsing contentedly after an afternoon of bonking in bed, suddenly there's the sound of a car pulling up outside. Dreamily, the girl whispers, "Oh, oh, quick get moving, that's my husband."
Quick as a flash, the man jumps out of bed, rushes to the window and suddenly stops dead.
"What d'ya mean?" he bellows "I am your husband!"

**A couple are having it away on the sofa when the phone rings. After answering it, she replaces the receiver and turns to her lover, saying, "It was only my husband."
"Oh, no," replies the man "I'd better get out of here."
"Don't worry, he won't be home for hours, he's playing pool with you and two other mates."**

Bob was off on his usual three day inspection of garden centres when he realised he'd left the house without his new seed catalogue. Returning quietly, he saw his wife in the kitchen, bending over, looking inside the fridge. Unable to resist, he crept up behind her, lifted her flimsy nightdress and was just about to do the business when she said, "Only six eggs this week Jack, Bob's away till Friday."

The chief executive of an international company pulled up in his Rolls outside a pub where two men were drinking.

"Hey, Jack, you see that man in the Rolls? He was trying to get me for months."

"Really?" said Jack, "Whose company were you with at the time?"

"His wife's."

Jack and Bill spent the night drinking heavily in the pub and got so drunk that Jack missed his bus home.

"Never mind," slurped Bill. "Come on home with me."

They staggered back to Bill's house and went inside.

"I'll just show you where everything is," he said. "There's the kitchen and if we go upstairs... there's the bathroom, you can kip down in here and this is my bedroom."

Bill opened his bedroom door. "And there's my wife and the man next to her is me!"

★

A man partners up with a new member of the Golf Club and they've played nine holes when he comments, "I see you've got a club in a special leather case, but you haven't used it yet."

"Oh no, that's not a club," explains the man. "I'm a freelance hit man, so I carry my gun around with me at all times in case someone needs my services."

They continue playing another 2 holes when suddenly the man

turns to him urgently.

"I've been thinking of what you've been saying and I'd like to hire your services. Do you see that house across the fifteenth fairway? That's my house, and if I'm not mistaken my wife is having it off with the next door neighbour. How much do you charge?"

"A thousand pounds a bullet," says the hitman, and the golfer agrees to this."Right, let's take a look," says the hit man and he gets out the high-powered rifle, adjusts the telescopic sight and aims at the bedroom window.

"Does the man have red hair and a moustache?"

"Yes, yes, that's him" he says excitedly.

"Shoot them both. Shoot his balls off, and shoot her in the head, the cheating bitch."

The hitman continues to stare through the sights of the rifle, moving the barrel around from time to time.

"Come on, come on," urges the man. "Shoot the bastards, will you?"

"Now just hold on a minute," says the hit man, "I'm trying to save you a grand."

Guns don't kill people; it's husbands that come home early.

"Mum, dad, I have something to tell you. I'm getting married to Julie from the post office, she's agreed to be my wife."

"That's wonderful news," says Mum.

"Er... yes ..." says dad, a little hesitantly.

Later, when they are on their own dad confesses to his son that during his marriage he did have one teeny weeny extra marital affair and that in fact Julie is his half sister. The boy is devastated. He breaks off the engagement but it takes over two years before he can ever look at another girl. Then one day, he comes home again.

"Mum, Dad, I've asked Tracy to marry me and she's accepted."

Mum's delighted, she's been so worried about her poor boy, but once again dad doesn't say much until later.

"I'm sorry son, I did have one other fling and I'm afraid Tracy is also your half sister."

The boy is devastated once again at this news, but then gets angry, and decides to tell his mother the awful truth.

"Don't you worry about your father," she says. "Go ahead and marry Tracy. What he doesn't know is that he's not really your dad."

But I can't believe it!" exclaimed her husband, "pregnant? How can that be? I've always been so careful."

"Now, now," she said comforting him. "What makes you think it's your fault?"

"I guarantee sir," said the pushy salesman, "that this machine will give you the answer to anything you want to know".

"Mmm," mused the company director, "we'll see." He thought for a moment and asked. "Where's my father?"

"He's in the Dog & Duck on Fetter Street, drinking his third pint of lager," said the machine.

"Ah ha," said the director triumphantly, "it's wrong. My father died two years ago."

The salesman looked astonished. "But it's never wrong," he blustered. "Let me try."

"Where is Mr Pettigrew Senior, this gentleman's father?"

The machine replied immediately,

"Mr Pettigrew senior died two years ago and is buried in South Heighton Cemetery. But this man's father is down the Dog & Duck, just ordering his fourth pint."

★

A woman was determined to impress her husband's business associates by inviting them to a lavish dinner party. Early in the morning on the day of the do, she instructed her husband to visit the high class deli on the high street and pick up some live snails – that way they'd be fresh until the last minute. Cursing under his breath, Eric set off for the shop but on the way he noticed his sexy-looking neighbour, beckoning to him.

"Hello Eric," she cooed, standing there in a skimpy negligee. "I'm so scared of ladders, would you be a dear and change the light bulb in the hall for me."

A little overawed by her presence, Eric changed the bulb, stopped for a cup of tea and before he had time to realise what was happening, found himself upstairs giving her his all. Time after time, they romped between the sheets until they both fell asleep exhausted. Suddenly, Eric sat bolt upright, looked at the clock and realised he only had 15 minutes to get to the shop before it closed. He rushed out and got there just in time, bought the snails and hurried home. However, in his haste, he caught his finger in the garden gate and with a cry of agony, dropped the snails all over the path.

"Where the hell have you been?" bellowed his wife from the bedroom window.

Eric looked at his wife's snarling face, then he looked down at the snails and said,

"Come on boys, we're nearly home."

Knowing her husband wouldn't be home till late, the woman brought her lover back to the house for some frolics.

"Hold on, I can't," her lover said suddenly, "I've forgotten to bring the condoms."

"Oh that's all right, my husband's got some."

But after searching for them for five minutes, she returned angrily to the bedroom.

"The bugger's taken them with him, I knew he didn't trust me."

★

A man was in bed with his mistress when he heard his wife arrive home early.

"Quick," he whispered, "get over in the corner."

As she stood there, he covered her in talcum powder, draped a silk scarf around her private parts and told her to act like a statue.

"And what's that?" asked his wife casually, as she walked into the room.

"Just a statue darling," he replied. "It's nice, isn't it – a bit like the one in our neighbour's bedroom."

Later that night, once the man had fallen asleep, his wife disappeared downstairs and returned with a cup of tea. She walked over to the statue and hissed,

"Here, take this, I bet you're feeling thirsty, I certainly was, stuck all that time in our neighbour's bedroom!"

The poor woman was so neglected by her husband that she decided to buy a pet to keep her company. As she walked round the shop, she suddenly saw a poor old parrot, stuck away in the corner of the shop in a dusty old cage. The parrot had lost his feet so nobody wanted to buy him. The poor woman's heart went out to the little bird and she walked over to his cage.

"Hello, old thing," she said. "You look a bit lonely."

"I am," he replied. "I like talking to people. I've got a lot of interesting things to say, but no one's interested because I haven't got any feet."

"But how do you hang on to the perch?" she asked.

"With my dick," he replied.

It only took the woman a moment to decide that the parrot was exactly what she wanted, so she paid for him and they went home. Over the next few months, they would spend hours in deep conversation, and the woman was so happy, she hardly noticed her husband's neglect any more. Then, one afternoon, she arrived back from the shops to be greeted by a very serious bird.

"I've got something bad to tell you," he said. "While you were out, your husband came home with his secretary. They sat on the sofa, kissed and cuddled, then he took her blouse off and started to fondle her breasts."

"Oh no!" she cried. "What happened next?"

"I don't know," he screeched. "I fell off my perch."

The man's wife was in labour, and he rushed her into the new maternity unit where he was asked if he would take part in a special experiment. He was told that they had perfected a way to transfer some of the labour pains to the husband, so that both partners could share the experience. He readily agreed and they began. Some hours went past and because the husband felt well, more pain was transferred over to him, until he took it all and left the wife to have the baby with complete ease. The following day, they took the baby home to find the gasman dead on the doorstep.

Alfred was extremely suspicious of his wife's sudden enthusiasm for golf, so he hired a private detective to follow her and see what was going on.

A few days later, the private detective reported back.

"It would seem that your wife spends a great deal of time in the rough with one of the young golf instructors," he said.

"Oh no," wailed Alfred, his head in his hands, "how long do you think this has been going on?"

"Well sir, considering the number of freckles he has on his backside, certainly for the last month during this hot spell of weather."

A man was going away on business for a month. Highly suspicious that his wife would get up to no good while he was gone, he hired a private investigator to follow her wherever she went. On his return, the P.I. confronted him with his wife's infidelity. All the evidence was on video. The man was shown film of his wife at glamorous parties, dancing the night away at exclusive nightclubs, intimate dinners with one of his work colleagues, overnight stays at luxury hotels...

"Well," gasped the man, "I can hardly believe it."

"Is it because she's involved with one of your colleagues?" asked the P.I.

"No, no," replied the man. "I just didn't believe my wife could be that much fun."

Lady Sylvia became very suspicious of her husband, when every morning at 4 o'clock he would get up and disappear downstairs saying he was going to check the boundaries of their estate, after reports of strangers in the area. Lady Sylvia was convinced her husband was having an affair with their pretty maidservant, so she devised a scheme to catch him out.

Unbeknown to her husband, she gave her maidservant the weekend off to spend with her relatives. That night when he got up again at 4 o'clock and went downstairs, she quickly jumped up and ran down the back way to the maid's bedroom. Quick as a flash, she jumped into the maid's bed, and it wasn't long before she heard the window being opened and a shadowy figure come into the room. Determined not to say anything but surprise him afterwards, she submitted to his lovemaking.

Afterwards, she spoke. "So you'll be off to check if there are any suspicious people about?"

"Not likely," came the reply. "The master and his wife want the gardens looking their best for the May Day celebrations on Monday."

Two old friends were talking over a pint of beer.

"I must say," said Malcolm. "You're the Catholic, you're not allowed to use birth control and yet you have only two children and I, who can use anything, have five kids. I don't understand."

"Oh, it's quite simple really," replied John. "We use the safe period."

"What's that then?"

"Every other Tuesday, when you play darts."

Connie was devastated. Today she'd discovered her husband was having an affair with their next-door neighbour.

"But why George? What's she got that I haven't? You could

hardly call her God's gift to women."

Tired of these questions, he decided to be brutal, but honest. "The thing is, Connie, she's different in bed. You just lay there like a sack of potatoes, but she moves around and moans a lot. It really turns me on!"

That night, Connie was determined to put on a good show. She wore her sexiest negligee (not seen since the honeymoon) and five minutes into his thrusting she started to move about and moan, "George, it's been an awful week. First the milkman got our monthly bill wrong, then the car ran out of petrol, I think I'm going down with a bad cold..."

Gerald was feeling guilty. He'd had a dreadful argument with his wife before leaving for work, and he'd said some unforgivable things. Not least that she was no bloody good in bed. He decided to ring her up and apologise.

It took ages for her to answer the phone, in fact, he was just about to ring off when he heard her say "hello?"

"Oh June, it's me," he said. "Where were you?"

"I was in bed," she replied.

"In bed!" he exclaimed, "in the middle of the day! Why?"

She thought for a moment and replied, "I was just getting a second opinion."

Every Saturday morning, without fail, Derek would get up at 6 o'clock to go down to his allotment. If the weather was bad, he'd potter about in the greenhouse. However, this particular Saturday there'd been a bad car accident and the road had been closed, so he was unable to get there. He returned home nd decided to surprise his wife with a cup of tea. As he entered the bedroom, he whispered lovingly, "Here you are darling, a nice refreshing cup of tea. It's a lovely morning, the sun's really quite hot."

His wife, still half asleep, mumbled from beneath the duvet.

"Is it? I expect Derek will be down there by now getting sunburnt, knowing him!"

An artist and his sexy model were canoodling in the conservatory when they heard her husband's car drive up.

"Quick," whispered the artist. "Take your clothes off so it looks like we're working."

A mafia boss arrives home early from work and discovers his wife in bed with one of his bodyguards.

"You no good motherfucker," he bawls. "I'm going to shoot your bollocks off."

"Oh give us a chance, give us a chance," pleads the bodyguard frantically.

"Okay," says the boss, "swing 'em."

In Bed

A man shouted to his wife, "Lisa, come here a minute and have a look at my grandfather clock."
Lisa walks in to find her husband with his trousers round his ankles and his dick standing to attention.
"What are you playing at?" she demands. "That's not a grandfather clock."
"It will be when you put two hands and a face on it," he replied.

It's late at night and the husband and wife are in bed. She's just about to fall asleep when he whispers in her ear,
"How about a little loving then?"
"Oh no," she replies. "I have to see the gynaecologist tomorrow so I don't want any foreign bodies."
A couple of minutes go by and he nudges her again, saying,
"You don't have a dentist appointment tomorrow, do you?"

Did you hear about the man who had "I love you" tattooed on his dick?
That night in bed, he turned to his wife and said,
"What do you think of this Beryl?"
"There you go!" she exclaimed, "always trying to put words in my mouth."

"Come on Josie," said Jack. "Let's have an early night, I've got a full head of steam here."

Josie wasn't too willing but in the end agreed and they went up to bed. Josie put on a long nightdress.

"Come on Josie, take that nightgown off," pleaded Jack but just at that moment the phone went and Jack went down to answer it. Quick as a flash, Josie barricaded the door and jumped into bed. When Jack returned and found he couldn't get in, he yelled with anger.

"Come on Josie, let me in or I'll break the door down."

"Oh yeah?" sneered Josie. "You and who else? You can't even manage to take a nightgown off and here you are threatening to break down a door!"

Adam was all alone in the Garden of Eden and as he was wandering about he came across two rabbits, one humping the other.

"What are those two rabbits doing?" he asked the Lord.

And the Lord replied, "They are making love."

A little later he came across two doves, one mounted on the other.

"Lord, what are those two birds doing?" asked Adam.

"They are making love," came the reply.

Adam thought for a moment and then said,

"Why am I all alone? Why don't I have someone to love?"

"OK Adam, when you wake up in the morning, you won't be alone any longer."

So the next day when Adam awoke, Eve was lying next to him. He immediately jumped on top of her but a moment later he asked,

"Lord, what's a headache?"

A young couple had been married for less than six months but the bride was obsessed with knowing how many women her husband had slept with.

"If I tell you, it'll only make you angry and upset," he said.

"No it won't," she assured him. "I just need to know."

Eventually the man gave in.

"OK, now let's see. One … two … three … four … five … six … seven … eight … you … ten … eleven …"

★

Mavis is at the end of her tether. Her husband is out of work and all he does is sit or lie in front of the TV drinking beer.

One day, the washing machine breaks down and she asks him to take a look at it.

"Leave it out," he says. "Who do you think I am, a washing machine expert?"

As luck would have it, later on in the day the vacuum cleaner packs up and again she asks him if he would have a look at it."

"Don't be daft woman, do I look like an electrician? Now leave me in peace."

And because things always come in threes, next morning the back door gets stuck and won't open. Feeling very fed up she confronts her idle husband and tells him about the door.

"Bugger off," he replies, "do I look like a chippie?"

That's it. She's had enough. She gets three different tradesmen in and all is repaired. In the evening, when she tells her husband about the repairs, he asks her how much the damn thing is going to cost.

"Well, they told me I could either pay by baking a cake or having sex," she replies.

"So what cake did you bake?"

"Don't be silly," she says scornfully. "Do I look like Delia Smith?"

The young couple arrived back from a wonderful honeymoon to begin their married life in a little terraced cottage. After his first day back at work, the husband returned home to find his wife in floods of tears.

"What's wrong darling?" he asked.

"Oh Ben, I wanted everything to be so perfect for you, but I've gone and burnt the dinner."

The man took her in his arms, consoled her and they ended up in bed. The next day, he arrived home to discover the dinner had been spoilt again, so after comforting her, they ended up in bed a second time. This continued all week but when he arrived home on Friday night, instead of seeing her in tears, he found her sliding down the bannister stark naked.

"What are you doing?" he exclaimed.

"I'm just keeping your dinner warm," she replied.

★

On the day of their marriage a man said to his new wife,

"Everything I have is yours. You can do anything you like in the house but you must never look in the top right hand drawer of my desk."

27 years passed when one day during spring cleaning she couldn't resist opening the drawer. In it she found three golf balls and £1,000.

When her husband came home, she confessed she'd looked in the drawer and couldn't understand why he had never allowed her to look. "I must be honest," he said. "I decided that if I was ever unfaithful I would put a golf ball in the drawer."

"Well, that's alright," replied the wife. "Only three times in 27 years."

"But I have to say that every time I got a dozen golf balls, I sold them," he said.

It was their wedding night and they were spending it in a four-star hotel. As she went upstairs to their room to prepare herself, he stayed downstairs for a final drink. However, as he thought of what awaited him upstairs he abandoned his drink and soon followed her up. But as he entered the room he found her stark naked on her back with the night porter fondling her breasts and the elevator boy down below.

"Darling, how could you!" he wailed.

"Oh come on, Ron, I always told you I was a bit of a goer," she said.

She can remember when she got married, and where she got married, but she can't for the life of her remember why.

A disgruntled man broke the flies on his trousers when he was putting them on and turned to his wife, saying he'd still wear them just to show his mates what he had to put up with.

"Oh no," replied his wife. "I'll mend them, I don't want them to know what I have to put up with."

She took him up to her bedroom and while he waited for her to slip into something more comfortable he noticed her room was piled high with all sorts of cuddly toys. But that was soon forgotten once they got down to it and made love. After it was over he turned to her and said smugly,

"How was it for you?"

"Not bad I suppose," she replied, "you can pick anything from the bottom shelf."

"You look a bit down in the mouth mate, what's wrong?"

"The wedding's off."

"No! what happened?"

"I was in the park with my fiancee, when I saw a dog scratching his back. I said when we were married she could do that for me, and she stormed off."

"But why was she so upset about that?"

"By the time I'd finished speaking the dog was licking his balls."

The two young lovers are in the back of the car parked in a quiet country lane.

"Julie," asks the man, "how about giving me some oral sex?"

"Oh no!" she replies forcefully. "If I do that you'll never respect me again."

A year goes by and during that time he asks her for oral sex on a number of occasions but she always refuses. Eventually they get married and on the honeymoon night he asks her again for oral sex but she replies,

"No, I know you'll never respect me again."

Many years go by and the couple are now in their fifties. One day in bed the man turns to his wife and says,

"Julie, after all these years of happily married life, a beautiful house, big car and two successful children, do you think you could give me oral sex. You know I will always respect you."

So at last Julie gives in and does what he asks.

Sometime later as they're relaxing in bed, the front doorbell chimes. He turns to her and says,

"Hey cocksucker, answer that."

Two girls boasting about their boyfriends.
"Jack's unbelievable," said the first girl. "He walks right up to me and puts it straight in."
"That's nothing," said the second girl.
"Bob puts it in and then walks straight up to me!"

A tomcat was running frantically about the base of the tree while a female cat was giving him the come on from one of the branches.

"Get up there and give her one!" suggested a fellow cat walking by.

"Have you ever tried climbing a tree with a hard on?" retorted the tomcat.

★

The boastful man said to his girlfriend,
"Darling, I'm going to fuck you so hard tonight you'll never forget it."
Later on in bed she turned to him and tapped him lightly on the head with a feather.
"What's that for?" he murmured.
"Well, I guess in comparative terms I'm beating you severely round the head!"

★

A young man met his match when he picked up a girl in a bar and took her back to his place. They were soon in bed doing the business – time and time again she called for more. After a couple of hours the poor bloke was knackered and to gain a short reprieve he said he had to go and put the car away for the night. Once inside the garage he thought he'd better inspect his poor overworked friend so he put his hand down his trousers but couldn't feel anything. In panic he pulled his trousers down and there it was all shrivelled up. He whispered gently to it,
"It's all right, you can come out now, she's not here."

★

Did you hear about the arrogant man who was making love to his new girlfriend?

She whispered, "Please be careful, I have a weak heart."
"Nothing to worry about," he replied. "I'll be careful when I get up to your heart."

★

Jack went to the psychologist complaining of insomnia.
"Don't worry," came the reply. "Just start at your toes and slowly relax all your body bit by bit and then you'll fall asleep."
That night Jack did as he was instructed.
"Go to sleep toes, go to sleep feet, go to sleep ankles, now you knees, go to sleep legs ...."
But just at that moment his wife walked into the bedroom wearing the skimpiest and most sheer of nighties.
"Wake up everyone!" he shouted.

★

A woman went to her vicar to seek advice on her forthcoming wedding. This was to be her third husband and she was not sure how to tell him that she was still a virgin.
"But how can that be?" exclaimed the vicar. "You've already had two husbands."
"That's true, but my first husband was a psychiatrist and all he did was talk about it, my second husband was a gynaecologist and all he did was look. But this time I'm sure it will be different. This time I'm marrying a lawyer so I'm sure to get screwed."

★

What's the similarity between Kodak and condoms?
They are both there to catch those special moments.

★

"Hello, hello, is that the vet?" said the distressed man. "Our dog has just swallowed a condom, what can I do?"
"Calm down Sir, nothing to get too alarmed over, just keep the dog rested and I'll be over after surgery."
Surgery ended and the vet decided to ring first.
"Hello, it's the vet here, how are things?"
"Oh everything's alright now," replied the man. "My girlfriend found another condom in the bathroom cabinet."

★

A husband and wife booked into an hotel only to find their room had two single beds. In the middle of the night, the husband whispered over, "Oh darling, sweetheart, how about coming over here so I can make love to my beautiful wife."
The wife slipped out of bed, but as she crept over to him, she knocked the bedside table and upset a glass of water.
"Never mind darling," he cooed, "it's not your fault, it's just too dark in here."
After a passionate session, the wife returned to her own bed but on the way back she hit the bedside table again and knocked over the lamp.
"Watch out you clumsy bitch!" yelled her husband.

"Billy, I'm pregnant and if you don't marry me, I'll kill myself!" wailed the girl.

"Oh June, you're a brick, not only are you a good fuck, but you're a good sport as well."

A vicious burglar breaks into a house late at night, orders the couple out of bed and ties them up. Now the husband is a big sissy, afraid of his own shadow, so he whispers to his wife,

"Darling, do whatever he says. If he wants sex with you, then let him have it, otherwise he might hurt us."

"Whatever you say," replied his wife. "By the way, he told me he thought you had a cute little arse."

A young man asks for shelter for the night when his car breaks down in the middle of nowhere. The old couple invite him in, apologise for only having two bedrooms – one for them and the other for their unmarried daughter – but offer him the sofa for the night. Round about 4 o'clock, it turns bitterly cold and the old woman comes down to see if he's alright.

"Would you like our eiderdown?" she asks.

"Oh no, no thank you!" he exclaims "She's been down twice already."

A man comes home one night to find a nasty big rat humping a cat. The next day, he finds it humping a dog. Amazed at the sight, he

takes the rat indoors to show his wife.

"Hey, Doris, you'll never believe what this rat ...."

but before he can finish, she interrupts him with a scream,

"Get that bloody sex maniac out of here!"

"How dare you ask me if I've been to bed with anyone else, that's my business!" she said angrily.

"I'm sorry, I didn't know you were a professional." replied the young man.

Taking a short cut home through the park one night, a spinster was confronted by a mugger.

"Give me all your money and jewellery!" he demanded.

"But, I haven't got anything," she replied.

Not believing her, the man started to search her body. His hands moved everywhere, inside her blouse and up her skirt until he was satisfied she wasn't hiding anything. He was about to go when she said to him coyly, "Go on, keep trying, I can always write you a cheque."

★

The man was a prat. On his first date with a rather large lady, he commented arrogantly,

"My dear, I have climbed some of the highest mountains in the world, but getting on top of you is going to be quite a challenge."

"Oh really!" she retorted. "I would have thought it all depended on the length of your rope."

★

All night long, the man had been bragging to his girl friend about his many talents, but when he said cheekily,
"You know, it's a well known fact that men with big dicks have small mouths," she had finally had enough.
"So that explains it," she quickly replied " I could park a 10 ton truck in your gob."

★

Two sperm were swimming along when one says to the other, "How long do you reckon it'll take us to get there?"
"I think we've got quite a long way to go yet, we've only just passed the oesophagus."

"It's no good, it's over," said Julie. "You are so bad in bed."
"Oh come on!" said the man affronted. "How can you tell after 15 seconds?"

"Gosh, your knees look very sore," said Joan to Daisy.
"Yes they are, it's from making love doggie style."
"Well why don't you change your position?" suggested Joan.
"I would," replied Daisy, "but the dog doesn't like it."

★

On Honeymoon

The honeymoon couple couldn't wait to get to their bridal suite. As soon as the door closed they tore their clothes off and dived into the bed. But suddenly the bride began to shake.

"I c-c-c-can't help it."

She explained she had a curious ailment which only happened once a year but it meant she had uncontrollable shakes.

Quickly, the bridegroom had an idea. He rang for room service and asked them to send up four waiters. When they arrived he got them each to take either an arm or a leg and hold her down on the bed. Then he inserted his todger and shouted, "OK lads, let her go!"

It was decided that the newlyweds would spend their honeymoon night with her parents. But the walls were very thin and mum and dad were disturbed by all the humping noises.

Eventually the father had a good idea.

"I know," he said, "every time they do it, so will we."

After an hour, the honeymooners went quiet and everyone fell asleep. But two hours later they started again and after 45 minutes, quiet was restored and the parents fell into an exhausted sleep. However, around dawn activity began again and the father was forced to shout out, "Stop it, you're killing your mother!"

★

A young hillbilly returns alone from his honeymoon and when asked where his new wife is, replies, "I found out she was a virgin, so I shot her."

"Quite right," comes the reply. "If she wasn't good enough for her family then she sure ain't good enough for ours."

After a wonderful first night of their honeymoon, the man came down to breakfast in the hotel dining room. Looking through the window at the magnificent scenery one of his fellow guests greeted him warmly.

"Good morning, a delightful spot sir."

"Oh yes," replied the man, "and so well concealed."

A young couple got married but on the first night of their honeymoon quarrelled about politics – she's Liberal, he's Conservative. Sometime later, having turned their backs on each other, she said, "Sweetheart, there's a split in the Liberal Party and I think it's a good time for the Conservative Party to get in."

"Well, it's too damned late. The Conservative stood as an Independent and now he's lost his deposit!"

On the morning after their honeymoon night, the husband came down to breakfast to find just a lettuce on his plate.

"What's this?" he asked, puzzled.

"I just wanted to see if you ate like a rabbit too," she replied.

In Love

A middle-aged couple went to Las Vegas for their second honeymoon but unfortunately lost all their money gambling and didn't have enough left to pay the hotel bill. Feeling quite desperate, they happened to pass a poster advertising a visiting rodeo. Enormous prizes could be won for staying on the bucking bronco. The husband decided to have a go even though many had gone before him and all had fallen off. To the amazement of the onlookers he managed to stay on and won $ 30,000.

The wife was dumbfounded.

"How did you manage that? You've never been on a horse in your life."

"I know, but don't you remember when we went on our honeymoon and you had that dreadful cough?"

Two friends get married at the same time and go on honeymoon together. They decide to have a bet on who would perform the most times on the first night. They would put the score up outside the bedroom door.

John performed twice and notched up ll outside the door.

Next morning, when Bill staggered down after seeing John's score, he said, "Well done, mate, eleven, you beat me by two!"

★

A young newly wed couple were staying with his folks but when they went to bed that night they were unable to allow their passions to erupt for fear of making too much noise and waking them up.

"Let's go to a hotel," he suggested.

So they packed the suitcase but had trouble closing the lid.

Next door, the father heard her say, "Let me sit on it" and a moment later he heard his son say, "Let's both sit on it."

Amazed, the father jumped out of bed and rushed to the door saying, "I've just got to see this!"

The night before they are due to get married, the intended groom suffers a very bad accident and the part of his body most affected is his willy.

When the doctor realises the man's getting married the next day, he bandages up the injured member as carefully as possible and surrounds it with little splints.

The following night in the bridal suite his wife starts to strip for him. She takes off her top, exposes her boobs and says, "These have never been touched by any other man."

Then she takes her knickers off and says, "And no man has ever seen this."

At that point the man opens his dressing gown and says, "Well, look at this. It's still in the original packaging."

"Darling, what's wrong?" asked the newly married husband of his tearful wife.

"Didn't you like last night?"

"Oh yes," she sobbed, "but look at it now, we've used it all up."

★

A 90-year-old man and his 19-year-old wife came back from their honeymoon and the man was asked if he'd had a good time.

"Not bad, I suppose," he said. "Trouble is, have you ever tried putting a marshmallow into a child's piggy bank?"

★

A girl married a quiet, humble man and after one week, he came home rather flustered.

"When I got to work this morning, I found a pencil tied to my willy."

"That's right," she said. "I thought if you couldn't come, at least you could write."

★

A couple on their honeymoon ask for a suite in the local hotel. The clerk asks them if they want the bridal.

"No, that's alright," replies the groom. "I'll hold onto her ears until she gets the hang of it."

★

A 75-year-old man and 19-year-old girl get married. On their wedding night he gets into bed and holds up four fingers.

Surprised, the girl says, "You want to do it four times tonight?"

"No, no," replies the old man. "I meant pick a finger."

★

It is a special honeymoon hotel and on the big night three men find themselves stranded on their balconies.

"Bloody hell," complains the first man. "She's pushed me out here and locked the door just because I slapped her on her backside and said she had a beautiful big arse."

"Same here," groans the second man. "I just said my wife had great big tits."

They look over at the third man and one of them says, "I guess you've put your foot in it as well?"

"No," retorts the man, "but I sure as hell could have."

On their honeymoon night, he stripped off and his wife exclaimed, "Oh, what a cute dinky winky!"

"Doreen," he said sternly, "that's no dinky, winky, that's my cock."

"Oh no," she replied, "a cock is big and fat and long."

Have you heard about the miserly man who got married and went on honeymoon to Cornwall on his own? His wife had been there before.

It was their honeymoon night. The Reverend Johns and his new wife retired to the honeymoon suite and he disappeared into the bathroom to get ready. When he came out, his wife was already in bed.

"Oh Mabel, I thought you'd be on your knees," he said.

"Oh we can do it that way later. For the moment, I just want to see your face," she replied.

★

A five times divorced woman is convinced that the only way she will be happy is if she marries a man who has had no sexual experience with women. For three years she searches the country and eventually finds a strapping young man in Wales.

After a short courtship, they get married and retire to the honeymoon suite. She disappears into the bathroom to make herself as sexy as possible and when she returns, she's astonished to find all the furniture has been moved over to one wall.

"What's going on?" she asks astonished.

"I've never shagged a woman before, but if it's anything like a sheep, I want as much room as possible," he replies.

★

Three couples get married on the same day and find themselves in the same hotel for their wedding night. When the girls have gone up to bed the men have one more drink before following them and they agree to swap stories of their night of passion the next morning after breakfast.

The next day they meet up and the first man describes the wonderful night he and his wife had.

"We made love five times, I can't wait for tonight."

The second man agrees.

"Neither can I, last night we made love seven times, every which way we could think of."

The third man was strangely quiet.

"How about you?" asked the other two.

"We made love once," he said.

"Once! What did your wife say?"

"It's nearly breakfast time, let's get some sleep."

★

A couple went down to the registry office to arrange a date for their marriage.

"Names please," said the official.

"My name's Robert Smith and this is Jenny Smith."

"Any connection?" she asked.

"Only once," blushed the girl. "Behind his dad's barn last Sunday."

★

After only one month of marriage, the tearful young girl confided in her friend that she was leaving her husband because he drank too much.

"But why did you marry him in the first place if you knew about his drinking?" she asked.

"Ah, but I didn't, not until he came home sober three nights ago."

★

"It's very simple," said the newly wed husband to his bride. "I don't want to be too demanding, so if you want sex tug on this twice. If you don't want it, tug on it a couple of hundred times."

★

"Now you've just got married, let me tell you about sex," said the man's father.

"You go through three different stages. First of all, when you're newlyweds, you have sex anytime, anywhere – the kitchen, the bedroom, the garage, whenever the urge takes you. But then, when you've been married for a while, you usually keep sex to the bedroom – that's stage 2. Stage 3 comes after many years of marriage, it's when you pass each other in the hall and say, 'Fuck you!' "

What did you have for breakfast this morning?
Oh, the usual argument.

"Doreen, ring for the vet, I feel terrible."
"But why the vet?"
"Because I lead a bloody dog's life."

A wife went to the doctor's complaining that her husband couldn't make love. The doctor gave her some pills to give to him and told her to let him know whether there was any improvement. The following week, he met her in the street.
"How did it go?"
"Oh wonderful doctor, thank you. On the first day we did it in the morning, on the second day in the morning and in the evening and only yesterday he did it five times before he died."

"Darling," said the blushing bride on her honeymoon night. "What is a penis?"

Her husband, joyful that she showed such innocence, dropped his trousers to show her.

"Oh that," she said disappointed. "It's just like a prick, only smaller."

It was seven days into their honeymoon and the young bride staggered downstairs to breakfast looking knackered.

"My goodness," said the waitress. "You don't look so good, but aren't you the bride with the older husband?"

"Yes I am, he's 75, but I've discovered he's pulled a dreadful trick on me. When he told me he had saved up for 50 years, I thought he was talking about money."

Two friends talking over the garden wall.

"Did you do as I suggested?" said Doreen. "Did you feed him a dozen oysters on your honeymoon night?"

"Oh I did," replied the other, "but only 10 of them worked!"

"You'll never believe this, Johnny," said the simple friend. "My wife's a bit backward. Why! on our wedding night she put the pillow under her arse instead of her head."

★

In Love

Two couples get married on the same day and end up in the same hotel for their honeymoon. One evening, the girls having already gone to bed, the two men have a couple of drinks together in the bar. As time went on the men started to get boastful and Geoff claimed he could make love to his wife more times than John.

Fired up with booze, John accepted the challenge and they agreed to meet the following morning with the results.

"Last night, I made love to my wife 3 times," said Geoff at breakfast time. "What about you?"

John replied, "34 times."

"What!!" exclaimed Geoff. "OK, double or nothing, let's see what happens tonight."

The next day Geoff arrived in the dining room looking knackered.

"7 times" he said to John.

John laughed, "You lose again, 48 times for me."

"Well that's unbelievable, how do you manage it?"

"Listen, I'll show you. Put your hips back, then push forward quickly. That's one. Now, pull your hips back again and push forward quickly. That's two ...."

★

Jack and Dora were retracing their steps and visiting all the places they saw on their honeymoon, 30 years previously.

"Look Dora, isn't that the little stream we paddled in, and over there ... do you remember I sat you on that wall and we made love. Come on, let's do it again."

So he put Dora on the fence and they got down to business, but this time Dora went absolutely wild.

"Gosh, Dora, that was incredible, you didn't do that last time we were here."

"No," she replied, "but back then, the fence wasn't electrified."

A middle aged man and a young girl had just got married and were now in the honeymoon suite. The man took his trousers off, handed them to his new wife and said,

"Here, put these on."

Puzzled, the girl replied,

"But these won't fit me."

"That's right," he said. "I just wanted to be sure that you knew who would be wearing the trousers in this marriage."

"Oh really!" she sneered, took off her knickers and threw them at him.

"Put these on," she said.

"Don't be silly, I can't get into these."

She replied,

"Too bloody right you can't, and you never will if you start spouting that chauvinist crap at me."

The new husband and wife were having a last drink in the bar before retiring to the honeymoon suite.

"I'll go up and get ready" smiled the wife and she went upstairs. Ten minutes later, her husband followed, but when he walked into the room, he found his wife in bed with the hotel porter and a male guest from across the corridor.

"What's going on here?" he spluttered.

"Oh don't look so surprised darling," she said. "I always told you I could never say no to a party."

A man marries a young naive country girl and on their wedding night, he shows her his tackle and tells her he's the only man to have such a thing. Time goes by and after a couple of months, they're in bed one morning when she grabs his willy and remarks.

"You were fibbing when you told me you were the only man to have one of these, I've discovered that Mr Biggun across the road has one as well."

The husband thinks quickly and replies,

"Oh yes, that was a spare one I had, so I gave it to him."

"Oh darling," she sighs, "Why did you give him the best one?"

★

Three daughters all got married on the same day and all spent the first night of their honeymoon in their parents' house.

As mum locked up, turned out all the lights and went up to bed she passed her daughters' rooms.

In the first room she heard her daughter laughing, in the second her daughter crying, but in the third room not a sound.

Next morning at breakfast she asked her daughters about what she had heard.

The first said, "Well you always told me to laugh when

something tickled me."

"And you always told me to cry when something hurt me," said the second.

"And you always told me not to speak when I had my mouth full," said the third.

★

Only one month into their marriage, a young girl finds her 80-year-old husband cheating on her with a woman of 65.

"Why are you doing this? Can't I satisfy you, what has she got that I haven't?," she complains.

"Patience," he replies.

★

The wedding had taken place in the outback and now the reception was in full flow. A couple of hours had passed when the bride's father called everyone to attention.

"Ladies, gentlemen and the rest of you. The wedding's off. We've run out of beer and er... oh yes, the bride's been raped by one of the guests."

A loud groan went up only to be followed by cheering a couple of minutes later.

"It's all right everyone," shouted the bride's father. "Problem over. Another 10 barrels of beer have arrived and the fella's said he's sorry."

★

In Love

The honeymoon couple were staying overnight at her mother's house before flying abroad the next day. They retired early, but less than five minutes later, the young girl raced back down the stairs.

"Oh mother," she said, "he's got such a hairy chest."

"That's quite normal," she replied, "now up you go and enjoy yourself."

But a minute later, she was back down again.

"Oh mother, he hasn't just got hair on his chest, it's all over his body."

"Come on girl, that's no problem, now get up there and show him what you're made of."

The young girl went back up to the bedroom just as her new husband was taking off his socks to reveal that part of his right foot was missing.

She ran downstairs again and squealed,

"Mother, he's got three quarters of a foot!"

"What!" exclaimed the woman. "You wait here and I'll go upstairs."

"My darling," he whispered on their honeymoon night. "I would travel to the ends of the earth for you, climb the highest mountain and swim the deepest sea."
Six months later she divorced him. He was never at home.

A man couldn't decide who to marry. The beautiful young girl, full of fun, but a bit dumb, or the more mature plainer woman who was a famous opera singer. He eventually chose fame and fortune and went for the older woman. At breakfast on the morning after their wedding, he looked her up and down critically and said, "Sing, for goodness sake, sing."

To encourage her naive young husband to be more exciting in bed, the young wife bought a pair of crotchless knickers. At the time he was due home from work, she lay on the bed with her legs apart and said to him as he came through the door, "Hello darling, fancy a bit of this?"
"Agh! no thanks!" he said horrified. "Just look what it's done to your panties."

★

It was their honeymoon night and the new bride and her husband both had an awful secret. He suffered from very smelly feet and she had halitosis (dreadful bad breath). They prepared themselves for the wedding bed. He threw his socks in the bin and she ate a packet of mints. But it was no good, each of them knew they couldn't start their married life keeping secrets from each other.

The man began, "Darling, I have a confession to make. I suffer from smelly feet."

"It doesn't matter," she said bravely. "In fact I think I ought to tell you..."

But before she could say anymore, he interrupted her, saying, "I know, I know, you're going to tell me you've swallowed my socks."

Poor Tracy! She'd only been married a few months but her husband, Dave, had already forsaken her for the pub. No matter how hard she tried – from wearing see-through nighties and provocative perfume –

he would come in from work, get changed and disappear down the pub until the early hours of the morning. However all this changed one night when she heard him arrive home well before midnight.

"Come on girl," he said, "get yourself upstairs and let's have all your clothes off."

Tracy could hardly believe it. At long last her husband had come home for a night of passion. She scampered upstairs and stripped off.

"Right, now do a handstand," he said.

Anticipating wonderful things, Tracy did a handstand in front of the mirror. Dave then put his head between her legs and looking in the mirror, he remarked, "Yeah, perhaps the guys were right when they said a beard would suit me."

A man went to the doctor's, three weeks after getting married. "I'm really fed up, doctor, my wife and I haven't consummated the marriage because she says it hurts too much. What can we do?"

"No need to get too worried," replied the doctor, "this problem is not uncommon. I suggest, before you start, to drop your manhood into a beaker of Vaseline."

"What!" exclaimed the man, "are you telling me you can get yours into a beaker?"

A young woman, who'd only been married a month, went to the doctor's complaining of exhaustion.

"It's nothing to worry about," said the doctor. "It's not uncommon for newly weds to overdo their lovemaking. May I suggest that for the next month you confine your sexual activities to the days of the week which have an 's' in them. So that would be Tuesday, Wednesday, Thursday, Saturday and Sunday and the other two days you would rest."

So the girl went home and told her husband what the doctor had said and they agreed to follow his orders. Everything went according to plan the first week, but on the Monday night the husband woke up with a huge hard-on. He nudged his wife in the ribs to wake her up.

"What is it?" she yawned. "What day is it?"

"Monsday," he replied.

"What's wrong Cindy?" asked her mother when she saw her newly married daughter in floods of tears. "Oh mum," she cried. "Stan's gone out shooting pool and I can't find out how to cook it in any of my recipe books."

Gerald decided to marry for a second time. He'd been a successful businessman and lived a very happy life but his wife of 35 years had died and he was lonely. For some time, he'd been dating a girl 20 years his junior and he felt the time was right to pop the question.

"Well..." she hesitated. "There are a few things I'd insist upon."

"Just name them, my dear," he replied.

"First of all, I'd want my own monthly account."

"It's yours," he replied.

"And I'd like my own car."

"Certainly," he said.

She paused for a moment and then said "And what about sex?"

"Oh infrequently," he replied, blushing.

She mused on this for a moment or two and then continued, "Is that one word or two?"

A man kept begging his girlfriend to marry him, but he was a lazy swine and wouldn't get up off his arse to go and find work. "How can I marry you?" she would ask. "What would we live on?"

"Love, my darling, love," he would always reply. Eventually he wore her down and she agreed to marry him. On the evening of their wedding he walked in to find her sitting naked on the electric fire.

"What are you doing!" he exclaimed.

"Just heating your dinner," she replied sweetly.

A naive young girl was taking the library trolley around the hospital wards when she noticed a man who had his penis heavily bandaged. "Oh you poor thing," she remarked. "Did you break a bone?"

"A bone!" he replied astonished. "Are you married?"

"Oh yes," she said blushing. "We've been married for three months."

"Well in that case, you've certainly married quite a stud," he replied.

★

A Scotsman was marrying an English girl and mindful that he didn't want to upset the guests south of the border, he decided to wear something under his kilt. He went along to the outfitters and bought six yards of his own tartan which were to be made up into some special underpants. The day before the wedding, the pants were ready and delivered to his home. "You bought too much," said the seamstress, so there's three yards over which you can keep until you need it."

The day of the wedding dawned. The Scotsman was unbelievably nervous. So much so, that he forgot to put on his brand new underpants. Anyway, it didn't matter. The day was a great success. That night, once the festivities were over, the newly married couple retired to the honeymoon suite. The groom was fairly drunk by this time and lifted his kilt high in the air to show his new wife the special tartan underpants – forgetting that he hadn't put them on that morning.

"What do you reckon to that?" he said proudly. "I bet you've not seen anything like that before?"

She gasped with delight at his impressive tackle.

"Oh lovely!" she said.

The groom smiled with satisfaction.

"Well, there's another three yards of this at home which you can use when we return."

★

The young newlyweds rushed down to the station and just caught the train as it was leaving the platform.

"That was close!" remarked the bridegroom. "I hope we've got everything."

A few moments later, the ticket inspector arrived.

"Tickets please, everyone," he called.

The bridegroom hastily pulled out a piece of paper and handed it to the inspector.

"I'm sorry," said the inspector, noticing the confetti all over their clothes, "but although this piece of paper allows you a lifetime of free rides, it's not valid on the 4.42 to Edinburgh. You see sir," he said, handing back the paper, "this is your marriage certificate."

Chris and Lucy had been courting for three years but they'd never been intimate because he had a wooden leg and could never tell her about it. They decided to get married and on the momentous day, Chris realised he was going to have to tell Lucy the truth, but still he chickened out. That night, when they got into the bedroom, Chris turned to Lucy and said,

"Lucy, darling, I've got a big secret and I guess it's time I told you what it was."

With that, he switched off the light, stripped off, and detached his wooden leg.

"Here," he whispered, handing her the leg.

"Oooh," she chuckled. "You old devil, now this is what I call a surprise."

Out of Love

Two men were talking over a pint of beer. "Me and the wife had a terrible argument last night," said Alf. "She's a bloody stubborn woman. But I got the last word in."

"Good for you, Alf," said his mate, "and what was that?"

"Okay, buy the damned thing," he replied.

The King was due to set off for the crusade and knew he would be away for more than a year. Not trusting his knights who would be left behind, he had a special chastity belt made for the queen containing a little guillotine.

A year passed and when the King returned, he asked the knights to bare all and every single one of them except one had lost their manhood.

The King turned to the Knight who was still intact, saying, "You are the only one who has remained loyal to me. You may pick their punishment. Come on, speak up, or have you lost your tongue?"

★

The man went for his annual check up and was given a clean bill of health by the doctor.

"There is just one thing," he said. "You are a bit smelly down below, if you know what I mean."

Exceedingly embarrassed, the man went home and as he walked through the door, he shouted to his wife.

"Hold on," she called out from upstairs. "I'm so busy, I haven't even got time to wipe my bum."

"That's what I want to talk to you about," he said.

The man turned to his wife in anger and said
"You silly cow, locking the dog in the boot of the car has got
to be the most stupid thing ever."
"Oh yeah," she retorted, "wait till I tell you about the car
keys."

The couple had been married for seven years and were going through a bad patch. They agreed to see a marriage counsellor and a few minutes into the interview, the counsellor took the wife in his arms and kissed her passionately.

"Now, that's what your wife needs," he explained to the astonished husband. "More passion. Tuesday, Thursday and Friday every week."

The husband thought for a moment and replied grudgingly,

"Well, okay then. But I can't bring her in on Fridays, it's darts night."

A married couple are driving down the interstate doing 55
mph. The wife is behind the wheel. Her husband looks over at
her and says,
"Honey, I know we've been married for 15 years, but, I want
a divorce."
The wife says nothing but slowly increases speed to 60 mph.
He then says, "I don't want you to try to talk me out of it,

because I've been having an affair with your best friend, and she's a better lover than you."

Again the wife stays quiet and just speeds up as her anger increases.

"I want the house," he says.

Again the wife speeds up, and is now doing 70mph.

"I want the kids too," he says.

The wife just keeps driving faster and faster – now she's up to 80mph.

"I want the car, the checking account, and all the credit cards too," he continues.

The wife slowly starts to veer toward a bridge overpass piling, as he says,

"Is there anything you want?"

"No, I've got everything I need," says the wife.

"What's that?" he asks.

The wife replies, just before they hit the wall at 90mph,

"I've got the airbag!"

The husband was coming up to retirement age, and his wife decided they should celebrate by taking a week's cruise to the continent.

"We can pretend we're young again," she said coyly, "and do all the things that we used to do when we first met."

The husband agreed and while his wife made the arrangements, he visited the local chemist for a box of condoms and a packet of seasick tablets. However, when he returned, his wife greeted him with the news that if they booked up for one week, they'd get another week free. So back to the chemist he went, to get another packet of condoms and more seasick pills. Saturday night arrived and to the couple's joy, they won £1 million on the lottery.

"Oh Charles," beamed his wife, "now we can do what we've always wanted to do, and take our dream round-the-world cruise."

"Yes dear," replied Charles as he put on his hat and headed for the door.

"Won't be long," he shouted.

"Twelve packets of condoms and six bottles of seasick pills, please," he asked the chemist.

"You know sir," said the chemist, "I don't mean to pry, but if it makes you that sick, why do you keep on doing it?"

★

Randy Ron, his workmates called him. He just couldn't get enough.

One afternoon he came home early from work, went straight up to the bedroom to change and found his wife in bed with the covers pulled right over her head. Not one to miss a chance, he stripped off, crept under the covers and hastily made love to her. Later he got up and went downstairs, only to discover his wife in the garden.

"How can you be down here?" he demanded, "I just left you in bed."

"No, that's my mother, she wasn't feeling so well so I told her to lie down."

The man turned pale and sat down shaking.

"Bloody hell, I've just made love to your mother!"

"Oh no," she gasped, running upstairs. "Mum, Mum, why didn't you say something?"

Her mother replied with affront, "I haven't spoken to that randy bugger for three years and I'm not about to start now."

The old couple had been married for more than 40 years and their sex life was sadly lacking. Hoping that a change of scenery might do the trick, they took a holiday to North Africa and while Bob dozed in bed, Mabel went shopping in the local markets. On one occasion she was fascinated to watch a snake charmer. As he played the flute, the snake would emerge from the basket until it was standing straight in the air. I must have that, she thought, so after a great deal of haggling she finally bought the flute and hurried back to the hotel. Bob was fast asleep when Mabel returned, so she quietly got out the flute and started to play it. Slowly, slowly, the bedclothes started to rise until they were nearly a foot above her sleeping husband. Overcome with anticipation, Mabel tore her clothes off and threw back the bedclothes, to find her husband's pajama cord standing to attention.

An old country couple visit the doctor in the nearby town. Neither of them had been inside a surgery for more than 20 years, so it was all a bit strange.

"Right, Mrs Crotchitt, before I do the examination, I'll need a specimen. If you'll just return to the waiting room, it won't be long," said the doctor.

Baffled, she returns to her husband and tells him about the

specimen.

"What can it be?" she asks puzzled.

"I don't know," he replies. "Why don't you see if you can find that nice nurse who showed us in here. I'm sure she'll tell you."

So the old lady goes off and after a few minutes, an almighty noise breaks out. There are sounds of broken glass and raised voices. Suddenly the old woman returns looking very dishevelled.

"Bloody hell, woman, what happened to you?" asks her husband.

"I don't rightly know," replies the distraught wife. "I went and asked the nurse what a specimen was. She told me to piss in a bottle, I told her to crap in a bucket and then things just got out of hand."

★

The marriage of the two celebrities had become public property, so it wasn't a surprise that the intimate details of their divorce were splashed across the tabloid press. The most juicy piece of news for the readers was that they'd split up because his todger was too small to satisfy the needs of his beautiful wife. The rowing couple met for the last time in court, their hostility to each other was plainly obvious. As she got up to leave she turned to him and putting her little finger in the air, hissed, "Good riddance, creep."

He responded immediately. He put a finger in both sides of his mouth and stretched it as wide as possible. "So long, bitch," he snarled.

The middle-aged couple stopped overnight in an hotel and just after midnight, as they were lying in bed, they heard terrific noises from the room next door. A girl seemed to be pounding the bed and moaning loudly.

"Ooh Marvin, it sounds as if she's having a fit," said Agnes.

"Oh yes," replied Marvin, thinking back to their early days of marriage, "and it sounds like a bloody tight one too."

Martin arrived back from the doctors feeling very miserable. The doctor had told him that unless he lost two stone in weight, he was in danger of having a heart attack.

Now his wife loved him very much and realised that it was going to be very hard for him to cut down on his eating. So she decided to shame him into it.

"I bet you won't do it," she sneered, "you're too weak willed. Look at Geoffrey, he's given up smoking, but then he's much more determined."

Martin was angry. "Right," he blustered, "if that's what you think of me, I'll show you. Not only will I lose two stone but until I do, sex is out."

To her dismay, Martin moved into the spare room that night and two weeks later he was still there. His wife was so miserable. She missed her husband terribly, so on the following night, after he'd gone to bed, she knocked on the door.

"It's only me, can I come in a moment," she said.

Martin couldn't believe his eyes when she walked through the door. There she stood in a silky dressing gown which fell open as she moved to reveal her nakedness underneath. She looked at him coyly from beneath her long eyelashes and whispered huskily,

"Hello Martin."

"What do you want?" he replied, gasping for breath.

"I just wanted to let you know that Geoffrey's started smoking again."

The woman picked the phone up and a voice said,

"Hello Sandy, fancy a drink tonight?"

"No, I'm working late," she replied.

"Well, how about tomorrow?"

"No, I'm meeting friends for dinner."

"Okay, let's make it this weekend?"

"Sorry, I'm off to my mother's."

"Oh for goodness sake. Sometimes I wonder why we ever got married!"

Watching her husband dish up second helpings onto his plate, she said scornfully,

"Sometimes, I think you like food more than you like sex."

"Now why would you think that?" he replied tucking happily into his breakfast.

"We're the only couple I know who have mirrors on the dining room ceiling!"

**Three men discussing what to buy their wives for their birthdays.
"I'm going to get my wife some sexy underwear and a pair of
Italian shoes, then if she doesn't like one, hopefully she'll like
the other."**

**"That's a good idea," says the second man. "I'll get my wife two
presents as well and maybe one of them will be alright. Let's
see – I think I'll get a gold necklace and an evening dress."**

**"What about you Jack?" they say, turning to the third man who
has remained morosely quiet.**

**"Oh, I know what I'm getting Doreen, a mink coat and a dildo.
If she doesn't like the coat she can go fuck herself."**

"Oh sure," said the frustrated wife. "My husband's a winner all right!
When it comes to lovemaking, he always finishes first."

**A disappointed husband said to his wife, on seeing he put her
bra on, "I don't know why you bother, you've nothing to put in
it."**

**"Listen, you, I don't complain when you buy underpants," she
snapped back.**

"Now listen, son, you'll look back on this time as the happiest in your
life," confided the boy's father.

"But dad, I'm not getting married for another week."

"That's what I mean, son," he nodded sadly.

In Love

★

Did you hear about the girl who advertised for a husband in the personal column of the local paper?
She had over 200 replies saying, "You can have mine."

★

A woman comes back from the doctor's smiling all over her face.
"You're in a good mood," remarks her husband. "What's happened?"
"The doctor has just told me I've got the boobs of a 21-year-old."
"Oh yeah, what did he say about your 50-year-old arse?"
"Nothing," she retorted. "We didn't mention you."

★

A reporter from the local newspaper was interviewing a couple who were celebrating their 25th anniversary.
"And after all this time, can you still say you're in love?" he asked.
"Oh yes," said the husband "I'm in love with her sister and she's in love with the man next door."

Overheard on a bus:
"I'm worried about my wife. It's her appearance, she's let me down."
"Oh, how come?" replied the other.
"Well, I haven't seen her for three days."

"Do you know I found a great way of getting my husband to increase the housekeeping. Last week I went shopping with him wearing a low-cut blouse with no bra on. When I bent down to get something from the bottom shelf one of my boobs fell out. He was so angry until I told him it was because I didn't have enough money to buy a good bra, so he increased the housekeeping straightaway."

"What a great idea," said her friend, "I'll have to try something like that."

The two women met up the following week but her friend looked very downcast.

"What happened, didn't it work?"

"I remembered what you said and just before we went out on Saturday night I lifted up my dress and said, "Look Alf, I'm wearing no knickers cos I can't afford to buy any, and you'll never guess what the old bugger did. He gave me a couple of quid to buy myself a comb, telling me that at least I could look tidy."

Two men talking in the bookies:

"What's wrong Charlie? You don't look so good this morning."

"It's the bloody wife; she's keeping me awake at night dreaming of this driving test she's taking next week. Every so often she grabs hold of my cock and moves it around like a gear stick. It's no joke."

"I've got an idea Charlie. Next time she starts, turn her over and stick it up her backside – maybe that will stop her."

The next night, Charlie does as his mate suggests, turns her over and gives her one up her arse.

"£5 of 4-Star, please," she says.

★

Coming home from work earlier than planned, the husband found his wife in the kitchen, bending over the oven. She looked so desirable, he immediately dropped his trousers and took her from behind. After it was finished, he gave her a sharp smack on the bum.

"What the bloody hell was that for?" she asked, indignantly.

"That was for not looking round to see who it was!" he replied.

★

"You know Bob, I don't know how much longer I can stand it. My wife is just a dirty good-for-nothing. The house is a tip, she never cooks and the whole place is filthy. I've just got to get rid of her."

"Listen Steve, I've got an idea," said his mate. "I read somewhere that people can die from having too much sex. Why don't you spend the whole weekend in bed with her and see what happens."

So Steve followed Bob's advice and spent the whole weekend in bed with his wife

. On Monday morning, he was so knackered he could barely get himself to work. That night, he arrived home to find out how successful the plan had been, but as he walked in, he couldn't believe his eyes. The house was gleaming, everything was spotlessly clean and a roast was cooking in the oven.

Standing in the kitchen with a glass of champagne in her hand was his wife in a sexy negligee.

"You see lover," she said smiling. "You do right by me and I'll do right by you."

★

A woman went to the doctors' complaining of a total lack of energy. After being examined, he told her she was on the edge of a nervous breakdown and should give up cigarettes, gin and sex for 3 months. But after a week, the woman returned saying she was even closer to a breakdown through not smoking.

"OK, have 5 cigarettes a day."

Another week went by and she returned saying she missed her glass of gin so much, it helped to relax her.

"OK, just one glass a day," said the doctor.

Two weeks later she returned again and before she could say anything, the doctor quickly interrupted.

"OK, OK, but only with your husband – there must be no excitement."

★

"Doctor, doctor," said the frustrated woman. "How can I improve my husband's performance in bed?"

"Well, first of all, you must tell him what you want," suggested the doctor. So in bed that night, the wife turned towards her husband and whispered, "Darling, caress my breasts and tell me how much you love me."

So the husband did as she asked.

Then, she whispered again, "Lower."

So in a very deep voice he said,
"I love you."

In the middle of the night, the woman nudged her husband saying, "Jack, I think I heard a noise downstairs. Are you awake?"

"No," he replied.

A man sat at the end of the bar looking sadly into his pint of beer.

"You don't look so good Bob, what's wrong?" asked the barman.

"It's the bloody wife," he moaned. "She makes my life so miserable, nag, nag, nag, all the time."

"Well, I've got a bit of advice," offered the barman. "There was a fellow in here not long ago who had the same problem and he was told that if he made love to his wife for five hours every night, she wouldn't be able to take the strain and in two months, she'd be dead."

"Was she?" asked Bob, with interest.

"You bet she was," replied the barman. So Bob went off home and for the next six weeks he made love to his wife every night for five hours. One evening, he staggered into the bar looking 10 years older and completely knackered.

"How's it going?" asked the barman, looking somewhat concerned.

"Well, the wife may be smiling a lot more and enjoying life to the full, but I console myself with the knowledge that she's only got two more weeks to live."

Do you know what it means to come home at night to someone who gives you love, affection and understanding? It means you're in the wrong house.

★

A man said, "Was that your wife who answered the door?"
"Of course it was," replied the husband. "You don't think I've got an au pair that ugly?"

★

My wife gets so easily upset that she cries when the traffic lights are against her.

★

Moaning man:
"Is there anything worse than a wife who never stops talking about her last husband?"
"Yes – a wife who never stops talking about her next husband," his friend replied.

★

Two mates were talking about marriage.
One complained that his wife never felt like sex, but the other replied, "I know what the trouble is, you need a good technique. Tonight after supper open a bottle of champagne, put on some sexy music, slowly undress her, fondle her breasts, stroke her thighs ..." "Yes, then what?"
"Call for me."

★

"Oh my darling, drink makes you look so sexy."
"But I haven't been drinking."
"No, but I have."

★

The couple had been married for many years and all romance had gone out of their marriage. One day, as his wife was getting ready for bed, he grabbed her boobs and her bum saying, "If these were firmer you wouldn't need so much scaffolding!"

The wife was very upset and the next day when the husband stripped off to have a shower, she grabbed hold of his todger and said, "If this was firmer, I wouldn't need the man next door."

★

A woman comes home to find her husband crying his eyes out.
"My goodness, what's wrong?" she asks.
He looks up at her and says,
"Do you remember 15 years ago when I got you pregnant? Your father was so flamin' angry he said I had to marry you or go to jail?"
"Yes, I remember," she replies, "but why are you thinking of that now?"
"Well today is the day I would have been released!"

★

Romance

"I love you very much," said the ardent young lover. "I may not have much money, like my mate Martin, I may not have a sports car or a cottage in the country like him. But I love you with all my heart and everything I have is yours."

"Very nice," she replied, preoccupied, "but just tell me a little more about Martin."

★

"Sweetheart," said the young man, "since I met you, I can't eat, I can't drink, in fact I can't do anything."

Thinking he was lovesick, she replied confidently,

"Why's that?"

"Because I'm flat broke," came the reply.

★

"Sir," said the young man to the girl's father, "your daughter has told me she loves me so much, she can't live without me and she wants us to get married."

"I see. So you want my permission."

"No. I want you to tell her to leave me alone."

★

An arrogant man loved to show-off in front of his mates. He saw this girl coming down the street and swaggered up to her.

"Hey, darling, what do you say to some ass?"

"Hello ass," she replied, walking away.

★

The young girl stormed back into the flat looking very angry.

"What's up with you?" asked her friend.

"It's my new boyfriend, Colin. I had to slap his face four times tonight."

"Really?!" she exclaimed, "trying it on all the time, is he?"

"No," she retorted. "The bugger keeps falling asleep."

★

"Darling, quick in here," said the Italian woman excitedly. She dragged him into the bedroom and began to remove his clothes.

"I have discovered you can get special sprays for here," she said, pointing to her pussy. "They come in lots of different flavours – chocolate, banana, strawberry..."

He interrupted her impatiently.

"What flavour did you get?" he asked with anticipation.

"Anchovy," she replied.

★

"Mr Howard, your daughter is going to marry me."

"Well, that's your fault for hanging around here too much."

★

A public school boy fell deeply in love with the barmaid at the local pub. He desperately wanted to marry her but was afraid to take her home to ma and pa because of her working class background. He saved up all his substantial allowance and sent her off to a finishing school in Switzerland for a month's intensive course. When she returned, her whole demeanour and conversation were impeccable. He was delighted. The following day they set out for the family estate, so happy in each other's company. Suddenly, she turned to him and said, "Darling, while I was away did you get blue?"

"Tut, tut," he replied. "You've only been back a day and already you're getting your tenses mixed up."

"Gloria, when did you first realise you loved me?"

"When I got upset at people saying you were ugly, fat and fucking useless."

One Sunday morning, a young couple decided to take a walk through the nearby forest. It was such a lovely day, that they stopped for a while in a clearing, one thing led to another and soon they were writhing around on the ground. Suddenly the girl cried out in pain.

"What's wrong?" asked the man, looking concerned.

"I think I've got a pine needle stuck in me," she replied. "Will you get it out?"

As the man looked, he saw the pine needle had embedded itself in the girl's very private spot.

"Oh no," he replied, "I can't. This is Forestry Commission land and it says over there on that notice board that no timber must be moved from recreational areas."

★

"It's not fair," moaned the young woman to her elderly aunt.

"We've been married for three years and I still can't get pregnant. Yet all you ever hear about is girls who sleep with men once and get caught."

"Very true," replied her aunt thoughtfully, "but that only happens if you're single."

★

For three months, the young ambitious executive had been secretly having an affair with the dynamic managing director of an international company. Whenever it was possible, they would go to his flat in the city and spend some hours tumbling among the sheets. One day, as he walked out of the shower back into the bedroom, she looked at him and asked,

"Why is it that you're going grey on top but down below it's still a deep rich brown?"

"Quite simple, my dear," he replied arrogantly. "I've never had any worries down below."

★

"It's no good," said his new girlfriend.

"I can't feel a thing, I'm afraid your organ is too small."

"Is that so?" he retorted, "perhaps that's because I didn't realise I'd be playing in a cathedral."

The newly married wife was not happy with her husband's lovemaking technique. The trouble was that he was too rough – in, thrash about, all over. She decided to try and teach him gentler ways. When they went to bed that night, she persuaded him to try a different method.

"I'm going to put 10 pence on each shoulder, 50 pence on your back and 5 pence on your bum. As you say each coin, I want you to move the corresponding part of your body."

"Okay," he agreed. "10 pence, 10 pence, 50 pence, 5 pence." As he said these words, he moved accordingly and the lovemaking was much more gentle.

"10 pence, 10 pence, 50 pence, 5 pence," he said, repeating it over and over again.

"Oooh, that's wonderful," whispered his wife joyously.

"10 pence, 10 pence, 50 pence, 5 pence," he gasped.

"Oh yes, oh yes," she cried.

"10 pence, 10 pence, 50 pence, 5 pence," he panted.

"Again, again," she cried.

"10 pence, 10 pence, 50 pence... oh bugger it," he cried, "75p, 75p, 75p ...."

★

The young girl and her father were at loggerheads about who she should marry. The father wanted her to wed Lionel – short, fat but very rich. She wanted Troy – tall, dark and handsome. Eventually, the father decided that the two men would have to compete against each other in a race and whoever won would marry his daughter.

First the men would have to run 1500 metres, then complete a gruelling obstacle course and finally swim across the river. The great day dawned and as 8 o'clock chimed, the two men set off. By the time they had completed the first two stages, Troy had a comfortable lead, but the daughter was anxious. To spur him on, she stripped off and standing on the other side of the river, she beckoned to him provocatively. At first, he lengthened his stroke but suddenly he began floundering and to her horror, Lionel caught up, passed him and eventually won the race. Later, as Lionel and the daughter prepared for marriage, she saw the defeated Troy and said angrily, "You silly prat, what happened? You were winning easily."

"I know," he replied sadly. "It was all going well until you took your clothes off and then I started picking up weed!"

Every day for six months, Colin had passed the local Chinese take-away time and time again, just to get a glimpse of the beautiful girl behind the counter. He couldn't eat, he couldn't sleep. All he could think about was his little eastern delight. One day, he had a couple of neat whiskies and plucked up the courage to go in and invite her out to the cinema. And she agreed! He was ecstatic. The following week, they went to see a romance at the local flicks, they walked back under the moonlight and he invited her in for coffee. Later, he put his arm around her, nibbled her ear and tentatively put his hand on her breasts. She didn't push him away so he was encouraged to go further. Soon, they were shagging away in bed, not once but three times. Eventually she started to fall asleep but Colin was still full of lust. He leant over and

whispered in her ear,

"How about a 69 before we go to sleep?"

To his amazement, she sat up angrily and replied,

"Listen, you selfish prat. I've put up with you pawing me all night. I've let you screw me three times, and I have to say you're not very good, there's no bloody way I'm starting cooking at this time of the morning!"

Karl was God's gift to women, or so he thought. Clubbing it every night, he would pick up a different girl three or four times a week and in no time at all smooth-talk them into bed. On Friday night, he arrived home with his latest catch, a young girl called Sandra. Soon, they were in the bedroom and as he began stripping off to reveal his perfect body, Sandra noticed two tattoos. One on his right shoulder, the other on his lower back.

"What's that then?" she said, pointing to his shoulder.

"Oh that's a lily," he replied. "I used to go out with a girl called Lily. She was all right, so I got this to remind me of her."

"So what's that?" she said, pointing to his back.

"That's a tiger. It reminds me of another girl who loved me. Her nick name was Tiger because she was really feisty. Cor what a girl!"

By this time Sandra was a bit fed up with talking about his ex's, but she gasped in astonishment when he dropped his pants to reveal a strange symbol on his todger.

"Don't tell me that's another of your girlfriends?" she sneered.

"Oh no, love," he said smiling, "that's a BT symbol."

"What d'you mean?"

Karl lunged towards her and said,
"It's for yoo-hoo."

The couple had been courting for almost a year when they decided to get married. James was over the moon. He had always wanted to marry a true blonde and although they had saved themselves for the big day, she assured him she was blonde, through and through. Some months after the wedding, James happened to notice one day that his wife's pubes were turning black.

"Hey!" he cried. "You told me you were a true blonde."

"But I am," she lied, thinking quickly. "It's like this James. You know when you hit your nail with a hammer, it goes all black?"

"Yeah," he replied suspiciously.

"Well, come on James, you can't deny you've been giving this some hammer these last few months."

The man had had a bad day at work and now his girlfriend was late meeting him in the pub. Eventually she arrived looking flustered.

"Oh Geoffrey," she said, "I've got some good news and some bad news."

"Cut the crap," he replied angrily. "I'm in no mood for games. Just tell me the good news."

"Okay," she said. "The good news is that you're not firing blanks."

"Go on, Julie," coaxed the man. "If I get this car up to 100, will you take your clothes off?"

She finally agrees and when he hits 100, she starts to strip. Unfortunately his eyes linger on her just a little too long and the car careers off the road and crashes into a ditch. The girl is thrown clear but the man is trapped.

"Go and get help," he gasps.

"I can't," she says. "I haven't got any clothes on."

"Just go," he urges. "Look, my shoe's lying over there, use it to cover yourself and hurry."

Just round the corner she spots a garage and runs up to it in great distress.

"Oh please help me," she cries, on seeing the mechanic. "My boyfriend's stuck."

The man looks down at the shoe covering her crotch and replies, "I'm sorry love, there's not a lot I can do, he's too far in."

John sat down and put pen to paper.

"My dear Lucy, can you ever forgive me? I'd had a lot of pressure at work and I wasn't thinking straight when I broke off our engagement. Of course I love you more than anything in the world. Let's not let my moment of madness spoil our future happiness.

Hugs & kisses

John

P.S. Congratulations on winning top prize on the lottery."

"Doctor, doctor, I think there's something terribly wrong with me," said the agitated man. He went on to describe his symptoms.

"The first time I made love, I felt warm and restful and comfortable all over. But the second time I couldn't stop shivering, I was so cold and covered in goose pimples."

"Mmm," replied the doctor, "that sounds very unusual, I'd better give you a thorough examination."

But nothing seemed amiss so the doctor sent for the man's wife and told her about the odd complaint.

"He felt warm and comfortable the first time, but cold and shivery the second."

The wife snorted with contempt. "I'm not surprised," she said. "The first time was in summer and the second time was in mid-December!"

A young man had been going out with his girlfriend for two months and decided he would like to buy her a present, but something that was not too personal in case she thought he was getting too serious. Unsure of what to buy, he asked his sister to go with him to the shops and after looking around, he decided to buy some gloves. As the young man made the purchase, his sister also did some shopping and bought a pair of knickers. Unfortunately, in wrapping up the two purchases, the attendant got them muddled up so the young man got the knickers. He never thought to check, he simply wrote a letter to go with the gift and posted the parcel that evening. His letter read: "My darling Debs,

Hope you like this little gift. I bought them because I noticed you didn't wear any when we go out in the evenings. My sister would have chosen the long ones but I think the shorter ones are easier to get off. I hope the colour's to your liking. The shop assistant had a pair the same colour and she showed me the ones she'd been wearing for the past two months and they were hardly soiled. She was very helpful. She tried yours on for me so that I could see what they looked like. I wish I could be there when you first put them on, but as I'm not meeting you until Saturday I suppose others will see them before I do. Until then, all my love

Dave.

P.S. The shop assistant also gave me a little tip. When you take them off, blow in them before putting them away as they will be a little damp from wearing, of course."

Two middle-aged bachelors had shared a house for many years and it was with great sadness that one day they realised they had hit hard times.

"It's no good, Jack," said Marvin. "We'll have to get rid of our last remaining chicken, we'll eat her for lunch tomorrow."

The following day dawned and it was Jack's turn to cook, so he prepared the bird and put it in the oven. However some hours later Marvin arrived home to find the kitchen full of smoke, the bird blackened and charred, and Jack nowhere to be found.

Marvin searched the house and eventually found Jack in the garden shed, with his head between the legs of their faithful

old cleaner, Janet.

"Damn it, Jack," snarled Marvin, "you really are a first-class prat. First you fuck the only bird we've got to eat, and now you're eating the only bird we've got to fuck."

As a 'thank you' to his father's estate workers, the eldest son would dress up as Father Christmas each year and visit every house with a sackful of toys. This year, he arrived at the third house and tiptoed into the bedroom, only to be confronted by a beautiful young woman who sat up in bed when she heard his footsteps.

"Oh, I'm so sorry," said Father Christmas. "I thought this was Bobby's room."

"No, he's next door," she whispered. "But don't go, stay awhile," and with that she dropped the sheet to reveal a see-through nightie.

"No, no," said Father Christmas blushing, "I've got a busy night ahead of me."

"Oh, come on," she urged, slowly disrobing. "A few more minutes won't make that much difference."

"I'm sorry I can't," he replied, now feeling very hot under the collar.

"Oh please," she said, jumping naked out of bed.

"Oh bugger it!" he exclaimed, putting down the sack of toys. "I wouldn't get back up the chimney like this anyway."

Karl met a woman in a pub and asked her if she would like a drink.

"No thanks," she replied. "I don't drink alcohol."

"How about a cigarette?"

She shook her head. "I don't smoke," she replied.

"Packet of crisps?"

Again she shook her head. Secretly congratulating himself on spending so little, he asked her if he could see her home and when she said 'yes,' he was delighted.

They arrived at her front door, and in the hall was a dead horse. Seeing the look on his face, she said, "Well I didn't say I was tidy."

★

For 20 years, a man has been writing to a woman in Norway but they have never met. At long last, the man decides they ought to do something about it and he suggests that she should fly over and he'll meet her at the airport.

"I think that's a wonderful idea," she replies, "but I think I ought to tell you that I'm completely bald, I suffer from a nervous complaint and don't have any hair on my body."

"No problem," he replies.

Another letter arrives soon after and in this she says, "I think you should also know that I don't have any arms, I write by putting the pen between my toes."

A little startled to receive this news, he still tells her to come, but by return of post she writes that she meant to tell him she only has one eye in the middle of her forehead.

It's too late for him to back out, so he writes to say he's looking forward to seeing her and could she wear a carnation in her buttonhole so that he will recognise her.

★

She was so naive the man tricked her into marrying him by telling her she was pregnant.

★

Mother was trying to console her daughter who was crying her eyes out because her boyfriend had dumped her.

In case it was sex that had caused the split, mother told her about the birds and the bees but was suddenly interrupted by daughter.

"Oh no mum, I can fuck and suck with the rest of them, but he says I'm a useless cook."

★

A couple were fooling around in the back of the parked car. She said, "Do you mind taking your ring off? It's uncomfortable."

"That's not my ring," he laughed, "That's my watch."

★

First man to second:

"How did your date go last night? Did you have a good time?"

"Yes great. Funny thing is she likes it in her ear," he replied.

"Are you sure?"

"Oh yes, 'cos when I tried to put it in her mouth, she kept turning her head."

★

"Darling," whispered Jack in Flo's ear, "it's only a week before we get married; can't we fool around a bit?"

"Now, Jack," she replied. "We said we'd wait till we were married; can't you just wait another seven days?"

"Oh Flo, it's going to be the longest seven days of my life. Can't you just give me a hint of what's to come? How about unbuttoning your blouse and letting me have a quick feel of your tits?"

"Oh Jack …. I suppose so, if you're that desperate."

So she unbuttoned her blouse and Jack had a quick feel. He was barely able to contain himself.

"Oh Flo, just one other little thing, please, please let me have a quick sniff of your pussy. I promise I won't touch. Go on, there's only a week to go."

So Flo relented, dropped her knickers and let Jack have a quick sniff.

"Golly, Flo," he said "Are you sure it's going to last another week?"

★

The snow was thick on the ground when May and her boyfriend, Tom, got stranded miles from anywhere with engine trouble.

"Don't worry," said Tom. "I know about cars, I'm sure I can fix it."

After tinkering around with the engine for a few minutes he got back into the car and put his hands between her legs saying, "My hands are so cold I can't work on the engine properly, so I'm just warming them up."

A few minutes later he got back out and continued to mend the car but every so often got back in to warm up his hands between her legs. When some time had passed and he got in the car again she turned to him and said, "It's a pity your ears never get cold."

★

A courting couple in Lover's Lane have been kissing feverishly for quite some time when the man, unable to contain himself any longer, sticks his todger in the girl's hand. She immediately gets out of the car shouting loudly, "I've only two words to say to you – piss off!"
The man screams back, "I've got two words to say to you – let go!"

★

A young courting couple went out into the countryside and after some passionate kissing she sat astride him as he lay on the grass. Suddenly they heard someone coming so she remained where she was but quickly covered him up with hay.
"Well, hello," said the local doctor. "What brings you out here?"
Quickly thinking, she replied, "I was just looking at my uncle's farm. When he goes, it's promised to me so I'm going to build a new barn there." She wriggled around and pointed east, "A new house there." she wriggled around and pointed west, "And turn that piece of land into a garden centre," and she wriggled around again to point south.
"Hmm, that's very interesting, and what's more interesting is that I recognise that pair of boots as belonging to my son."
"Thanks a lot, dad," came a muffled voice, "And due to your bad timing she'll need to build a nursery and somewhere to keep the pushchair as well."

A young man had a special party piece where he would put two fingers in his mouth and give a whistle that could be heard half a mile away.

This man started courting and one night took his girl out into the country where they spent a couple of enjoyable hours. However, their fun made them late back and as they got to the bus stop the last bus was moving off.

"Quick, stop him, whistle," she said, The man put his two fingers to his mouth, paused and said, "It's a lovely night, let's walk, it won't take long."

Parked down Lover's Lane, but failing to get into the right kind of mood, the man finally disentangles himself from the girl, saying, "You've got no tits and your hole's too tight."

She replies through clenched teeth, "Get off my fucking back."

"My blind date was so boring," said the girl to her friends, "that in the end I had to sit on his face just to keep him quiet."

★

It's Lovers Lane and a passing policeman goes up to a parked car, looks through the window and says, "What's going on here, then?"

"Just a little necking," replies the man.

"Well, put your little neck back in your trousers and bugger off out of it."

★

After an evening in a Newcastle nightclub, a local girl who'd been chatted up all night by a rather attractive man, suggested they go back to her place.

They were sitting on the sofa when the bloke's hand started to wander up the girl's thigh. Suddenly she slapped his face and shouted indignantly, "Where's yer manners, like? Tits first!"

★

A girl turns to her friend and says, "Do you prefer watching TV or going out with your boyfriend?"

"There's not a lot of difference," said her friend. "Either way, I get a lot of interference."

★

Out on their first date, a young man drove his girlfriend out into the country in his old sports car. However, after labouring slowly up a steep hill, the car suddenly made some strange noises, and came to a halt.

"Shall we get out and push it up?" he said.

"OK, but will it be alright to leave the car here?"

★

A young man began courting a girl from a high-class family and one evening they invited him to join them at the opera. Worried about making a good impression, he calmed his nerves by downing a few pints beforehand. When it was time for the performance, they were shown to their seats – the first row of the balcony, but halfway through the first act the man needed to pee. The longer he sat, the more agonising it became, yet he was too embarrassed to disturb the whole row by getting out to go to the toilet. Eventually he hit upon an idea. Covering his lap with the programme, he slid out his dick and peed over the edge of the balcony. Such a relief! But a moment later, a voice was heard from below,

"For goodness sake, wave it about a bit."

★

Tom was so shy he'd never had the courage to ask a girl out so his mate Jack decided to take him out on the town and get him laid. Halfway through the evening they were drinking in a nightclub when a girl at the other end of the bar winked at Tom.

"Hey Jack," he stuttered, "that girl over there winked at me. What shall I do?"

"Wink back," said Jack.

A little later she smiled at him.

"Hey Jack, she's smiling at me now."

"Well smile back," said Jack.

A moment later he turned to his mate again and gasped,

"Jack, Jack, she's just leant forward and shown me her tits. What should I do?"

"Show her your nuts," said Jack who was busy chatting up someone else.

So Tom turned to face the girl, put one finger in his ear, one finger up his nose and hollered like a jackass.

★

Dancing together for the first time, the man turned to his partner and said, "My dear, do you know the minuet?"

"Good gracious, no, I don't even know all the men I've laid."

★

A rather shy young man went along to the village dance and met up with a rather pretty girl. His chat up lines were sadly lacking, so in blind panic he said the only thing he could think of.

"You're Scottish, aren't you?"

"Ay, I am, how did ye know that?"

"It's the way you roll your R's."

"Oh no," she said. "It's these high-heeled shoes that do that."

★

The young couple had just got down to business when the girl suddenly stopped.

"What's wrong sweetheart, am I hurting you, shall I take it out?"

"Yes," she murmured. "Would you mind taking it out and then putting it in a few times until I make up my mind?"

★

"Hello Colin, what are you doing riding around on that woman's bicycle?"

"Well it's a long story," replied Des. "I was on my way into town when this lady passes me on a bicycle. She stops, waits for me to catch up, gives me a kiss and then takes her clothes off!"

"You can have anything you want" she says, so I took the bicycle ... Well I'm not a pervert, I don't wear women's clothes."

★

"Oh my darling," whispered the passionate young man. "Am I the first man you've ever made love to?"

"Yes, yes," she replied looking bored "Why do men always ask the same silly question?"

★

What is an outdoor girl?
One with the bloom of youth in her cheeks and the cheek of youth in her bloomers.

★

A bloke was walking through the park late at night when he stood on a man's bottom.

"Oh thank you," said a girl's voice.

★

It was 11.30 at night as the young couple made their way back from the pub. Suddenly they could contain their passion no longer and stopping by a fence he took her there and then. Unfortunately their excitement was so boisterous that the fence was knocked down and the sound brought the householder storming down the garden.

"What the hell's going on?" he yelled. "I want £60 now to

repair that bloody fence!"

The man paid up and later when they were alone, he turned to his girlfriend and said,

"Come on Sylvie, you're always on about equal rights, how about giving me half towards the fence?"

"Get stuffed!" she answered. "You were the one doing all the pushing."

★

The village idiot was getting a lot of teasing from the local boys.

"Hello Jake," they said. "We hear you've been practising a lot of sexual positions."

"That's right," he said proudly. "I hopes to try them on girls soon."

★

A rather reticent young girl was asked how she got on with her new boyfriend.

"Let's just say my legs are my best friends," she replied mysteriously.

"Oh come on," said her mate "What does that mean?"

"It means he came on too strong so I walked home."

A few weeks later the two friends were talking and the girl's mate asked her how her new date went on the previous night.

"Pretty much as before," she replied "My legs are my best friends."

Time went by and on the third time they met up the girl looked radiantly happy.

"You're looking well," commented her mate. "Something's

doing you good."
"Oh yes," replied the girl "I've met this wonderful bloke and let's just say even the best of friends must part."

★

Overheard in a parked car down lovers lane:
"Suck, Beryl, suck ... blow is just a figure of speech."

★

Did you hear about the young girl who swallowed a pin when she was 10 and never felt a prick until she was 19?

★

"Now don't forget," said mother as her daughter went out on her first date "say no to everything he suggests."
Later on in the evening after they'd been out to dinner he turned to her and asked, "Do you mind if we go back to my place for a bit of sex?"

★

"Hey darling, what do you think of this photograph, it's me posing for the centrefold – good ain't it?" boasted the young man.
"Mmm," replied the girl. "If I were you, I'd get it enlarged."

★

The boy was so frustrated. He'd been seeing this girl for over a month but apart from some kissing and cuddling, he'd never made a move on her because he was embarrassed at the small size of his willy. Eventually, he plucked up all his courage took it out and placed it in her hand.

"No thanks," she said. "I don't smoke."

After thrashing away for a good five minutes, the man lay back on the bed smiling smugly.

"How was it for you darling, good?"

"Quite painless really," she replied. "I never felt a thing."

Mum walks into the bedroom to find her daughter in fits of tears.

"Oh mum, it's so unfair. Yesterday, Derek said he'd buy me a diamond ring if I stayed the night with him. So I did, but all he bought was a cheap trinket."

"My darling," says Mum. "Always remember this and you won't fall into the trap again. When they're hard they're soft and when they're soft, they're hard."

A young hitchhiker got a lift with a lorry driver but halfway through the night they found themselves stranded on top of the moors. The driver told her they'd have to wait till morning before getting help so she could have his bed in the cabin and he would sleep on the seat. After a while, the girl whispered, "It's a shame you have to give up your bed, why don't you come in with me, there's plenty of room."

So the man got in beside her.

"It might be nice if we slept 'married'," she giggled.
"Whatever you like," he said, and he turned his back to her and went to sleep.

If only the young man had been more sexually experienced! When she asked him if he fancied something from the Karma Sutra, he replied, "Thanks, but not for me. Indian food has me on the toilet all night."

"Hi handsome! Is that a gun in your hand or are you just pleased to see me?"
"It's a gun," he replied.

The man was desperate.
"But Julie, the size of a man's tackle isn't everything. Don't you think a man's personality is more important?
She replied, "But you haven't much of a personality either!"

"Oh my darling, do you always kiss with your eyes closed?"
whispered the smitten young man.
"Only when I have to kiss you," she replied.

"Oh Tracy, I love you," he simpered. "Please tell me there's no one else in your life."

"Of course there's no one else," she replied, "do you think I'd go to the cinema with a nerd like you, if there was someone else?"

Three men are discussing how best to drive women wild. The first says he nibbles their ears and their toes and it really turns them on. The second says he kisses them all over and it drives them mad. The third says that after he's made love to them he wipes himself on their curtains – now that really does drive them wild!

A couple have been apart for nearly six months and when they eventually embrace again at the railway station he says,
"FF," but she says "No, EF."
He replies, "FF" and at that point the ticket inspector taps him on he shoulder and says, "I couldn't help but overhear, what's going on?"
The man replies, "She wants to eat first."

At the Tuesday coffee morning the ladies got into a heated argument about which of their husbands had the biggest member. The Mayor's wife said it was her husband and was so insistent that in the end she was told she had to prove it. On arriving home she told her husband, who looked aghast.
"Dorothy, you know mine is only small. What are we going to do?"
Fortunately they had a friend whose member was enormous

and they asked him if he would do them a favour.

"Don't worry, no one will know because you'll be hidden behind a screen and you'll put it through a hole."

The day came and the friend stuck his enormous member through the hole. The Mayor's wife smiled smugly, sure she had won. However, suddenly a woman's voice was heard to say, "Hold on, that's not the Mayor's, that's the vicar's, I recognise the wart on the end."

A man dyes his hair jet black because it had been going grey and is so pleased with the results that when he's buying a paper in the newsagent's, asks the shopkeeper how old he thinks he is.

"Oh, about 32," he says.

"No, I'm 40," laughs the man very pleased.

Then he goes into the chip shop to buy some fish and asks the woman behind the counter how old she thinks he is.

"Oh, about 34."

"No, I'm 40," comes the smug reply.

Later he sees an old woman at the bus stop.

"How old do you think I am?" he says.

"Well," says the old woman, "I'll have to feel your willy before I can tell you."

"What!" gasps the man. "That's the only way I can tell," she says.

"OK then." He unzips his flies and she puts her hand in.

"Oooooh," she says. "You're 40."

"How can you tell?" he says.

"I was standing behind you in the chip shop."

★

An emergency call was made to the local police station.

"Come quickly!" gasped the voice. "A burglar is trapped in the bedroom of an old spinster."

"We'll be right there," said the desk sergeant. "May I ask who's talking?"

"It's me, the burglar, help!"

★

The young couple had been out on their first date and as they drove home, passions were running high. Then disaster struck. Just as they got to the top of a steep hill, the engine stalled and they came to a sudden halt. Steve jumped out and crawled underneath the car to see what was wrong and a few minutes later, Sandra joined him. As they lay there, side by side, lust took over and soon they were in the throes of unbridled passion.

"It's all right," he whispered, "no one can see us under here."

But a few minutes later, a big pair of boots came into view and as Steve looked up he saw a policeman, looking down.

"Now what's going on here?" he demanded.

"Well... er... the car stalled," stammered Steve, trying to pull his clothes together. "And I was just trying to find out what caused it."

"Well, if I was you, I'd take a look at the brakes at the same time, your car's about half a mile down the road."

Men on Women

"I can't go out with you tonight, I'm getting married."
"OK. How about tomorrow night then?"

Two old men sitting in the park. One says to the other "When I was young I never slept with my wife before we got married. Did you?"
"I'm not sure" says the other. "What was her maiden name?"

My wife is so neat, in the middle of the night I got up to get a drink and when I returned, the bed was made.

"I'm getting a divorce," said Jack to his mate, Bill. "The wife hasn't spoken to me for six months."
Bill thought about this for a moment and then replied, "Just make sure you know what you're doing, Jack. Wives like that are hard to find."

A married couple are in bed one night when he turns to her and says, "Darling, I've got a new position for us to try. We must lie back to back."
"But I don't understand," she says, "how can that be?"
"It's OK. We've got another couple joining us."

★

"Drink makes you look beautiful and very sexy."
"But I haven't been drinking."
"No, but I have."

★

She was only an architect's daughter but she let the borough surveyor.
What's the difference between a virgin and a light bulb?
You can unscrew a light bulb.

★

You know John, as soon as I get home I'm going to tear the wife's bra off – the elastic's killing me.

★

Do you know the definition of a hen-pecked man?
One who is sterile but daren't tell his pregnant wife.

★

What's pink and moist and split in the middle?
A grapefruit.

★

How do you get rid of unwanted pubic hair?
Spit it out.

"Hey, Jack, what do you grow in your garden?"
"Tired."

★

What do you call a man with a one inch willy?
Justin.

★

What is a woman's belly button for?
It's somewhere to put your chewing gum on the way down.

★

Is it true that a man who goes to sleep with a sex problem on his mind
will wake up in the morning with the answer in his hand?

★

A brassiere is a device for making mountains out of molehills.

★

A lady is a woman who doesn't smoke or drink and only swears when
it slips out.

★

What do video games and Men Only have in common?
They both improve hand-to-eye co-ordination.

★

What does an ugly girl put behind her ears to make her more attractive?
Her legs.

★

What's the definition of indefinitely?
When your balls are bouncing off her arse, that's when you're in – definitely.

★

What do you say to a girl who can suck a marble through a hose pipe?
Will you marry me?

★

What have ugly girls and mopeds got in common?
They're both fun to ride as long as no one sees you.

★

Why is virginity like a balloon?
One prick and it's gone.

★

What do you do if a bird shits on your car?
Never take her out again.

★

And don't forget – if you shake it more than three times, you're playing with it.

Did you hear about the poor old spinster who dreamt she'd got married but when she woke up there was nothing in it?

How many fish do you get in a pair of tights?
Two soles, two eels and a wet plaice.

Overheard on the top deck of a bus:
"I'm knackered, Bill; it's been a hell of a day at work, You know, compared to us, women have it so easy. Why, they even sit down to take a piss."

How can you tell if a woman is wearing pantyhose?
When she farts her ankles swell up.

What's the similarity between cabbage and pubic hair?
You push them both to one side and continue eating.

Do you know why it's called sex?
Because it's easier to spell than Ahhhhm ooohmm, uggghh,
eeeeee....

★

What's the difference between a penis and a bonus?
Your wife will always blow your bonus.

★

What's the smartest thing ever to come out of a woman's
mouth? Einstein's dick.

★

Why are wives like condoms?
They both spend too much time in your wallet and not enough time
on the end of your dick.

★

What's the difference between a battery and a woman?
A battery has a positive side.

★

Why do women rub their eyes when they wake up in the morning?
They don't have balls to scratch.

★

What's the difference between Mm-m and Ahhh?
About 3 inches.

★

Why don't women like having sex with an SAS man?
They slip in and out unnoticed.

★

Overheard on the top deck of a bus:
"Do you know, Jack, if girls are made of sugar and spice and
all that's nice, how come they taste like fish?"

★

What do you say to a woman with no arms and no legs?
Nice tits sweetheart.

★

What's the difference between an egg and a wank?
You can beat an egg.

★

What's the difference between a woman and a fast food chicken take
away?
Once you've had the breast and leg all that's left is a greasy box to
stick your bone in.

★

What's the definition of a yankee?
It's like a quickie, only you can do it yourself.

In Sickness & Health

At the Chemist's

A man goes into a chemist's and asks the lady assistant for a packet of condoms, but he's not sure what size he needs. "That's no problem," replies the lady. "Just pop into the back where we have a board with a number of different holes and that way we'll know your size."

The man does as he's told and sticks his willy in the different holes, not knowing that each time he does so the lady assistant, hidden on the other side, is fondling him.

Eventually he discovers his size and returns to the shop.

"Did you find your size?" she asks.

"Oh, yes, but bugger the condoms, how much do you want for that board?" he replies.

A young man out for a good time pops into the local chemist's to stock up. The shop is empty.

"Anyone there?" he shouts and from the back room comes the chemist's wife, a bitter and unhappy woman.

"Four French letters, please, Miss."

"Don't you Miss me," she replies.

"Oh, sorry, make that five then, please."

The woman rushed into the chemist's, crying.

"Do you realise what you've done?" she wailed. "You gave my husband rat poison instead of stomach salts."

"Oh dear," said the chemist. "That is awful, you owe me another £2."

★

Two men become firm friends when they found themselves in the same hospital ward. Both had had their tongues removed through a serious illness and when they were better, they decided to go out on the town and pick up a couple of girls to celebrate their recovery. After a few drinks, they found two girls and by a series of graphic hand signs, managed to get them to agree to go for a ride with them. As they parked up in Lovers' Lane, one of the men signed to the other, "Have you got any condoms?"

"No," signed the other. "You'd better get down the all-night chemist and buy some."

He handed the man a £10 note and off he went.

Five minutes later, the man returned and made signs explaining that the chemist couldn't understand him.

"That's easy," signed the other. "Just get your dick out and put it on the counter. He'll understand."

Another two minutes went by and the man returned crestfallen.

"What happened?" they asked.

The man signed, "I did what you suggested. I put my dick on the counter and showed him my £10. He then put his dick on the counter. It was bigger than mine, so he pocketed the money."

The dog breeder was advised that if she wanted a 'champion', some of the dog's hair needed to be removed from its underside. She went along to the chemist and asked for some hair remover.

"This is the most efficient product," said the chemist, showing her a small tube of cream, "but it's advisable to keep your arms up in the air for at least two minutes before taking it off."

"Oh no, you misunderstand me," said the woman, blushing. "It's for my Chihuahua."

"Oh I see," he replied, "that's no problem, just don't ride a bike for a couple of hours afterwards."

The man rushed into the chemist's and asked,
"Have you got anything to stop a terrible bout of hiccups?"
Without warning, the chemist immediately slapped him hard across the face.
"There," he said triumphantly. "I bet that's stopped them."
The man stood there stunned, his cheek turning bright red and replied,
"It's for my wife waiting outside in the car."

What does a man and a packet of condoms have in common? They both come in three sizes; small, medium and liars.

A man walked into a chemist's shop complaining angrily,
"I bought a gross of condoms here on Friday but it turned out

to be only 130."

"I'm so very sorry, sir," apologised the chemist, and he immediately wrapped up another 14.

"I hope it didn't spoil your weekend."

★

The C.O. walks into a chemist's and enquires the price of a condom. "Well, we don't usually sell them singly but it would be 30p," says the assistant.

"And how much would it cost for one to be repaired?"

"Oh sir, it wouldn't be worthwhile, there's so much work involved. It would cost at least £20."

The officer leaves and returns the next day.

"I've had a word with the men, we'll buy a new one."

★

Chemist to young man:

"Sir, I would recommend these condoms; they're guaranteed by the makers."

"Ah, but what if they break?"

"Then sir, the guarantee runs out."

★

At the Doctor's

"Doris," said Fred. "I don't rightly know too much about this sex thing, I guess we'll have to go and see the Doctor."

So the newlyweds visited the surgery and asked the doctor to show them how it was done. The doctor agreed, told Doris to take all her clothes off and then he got down on top of her and performed enthusiastically. When it was over he said,

"That's what sex is, now do you understand?"

"Yes thank you doctor," said Fred, "and how often do I have to bring her in to see you?"

"Doctor, doctor, I'm so worried," said the anxious man. "Both my wife and I have black hair, but our son's just been born with red hair. Do you think something funny has been going on?"

"Not necessarily," replied the doctor. "How many times do you have sex?"

"About 5 times a year."

"Well there's your answer then, you're just a little rusty."

"I'm a little stiff from rugby, doctor."

"That's OK, it doesn't matter where you come from."

A man went to the doctor about his best friend.

"It's Bob, doctor, he's been told to give up smoking because of his bad health, but he just can't seem to do it. Have you got any ideas, I'd really like to try and help him."

The doctor thought for a moment and then said "Yes, I've got an idea that could cure him. Before he smokes his packet of cigarettes, stick each one up your arse first, without him knowing, and then put them back in the pack. That should do the trick."

And indeed it did. After a week had gone by, the man's friend told him he'd definitely given up fags because they left a foul taste in the mouth.

Pleased with his success, the man happened to bump into the doctor the following day in the street. He told him the good news but then continued, "The trouble is doctor, how do I stop this dreadful need to stick cigarettes up my arse?"

"How did you get on at the doctor's, Pete?" asked his old mate, George.
"Well, he thinks he can do something for me," replied Pete. "He's told me to drink a glass of this medicine after a hot bath."
"So do you feel any different?"
"Not yet, I've only managed to drink half the bath water up to now."

"Mrs Smith, I have some very bad news for you, concerning your husband. We've had the tests back and it shows that he has only hours to live. I'm afraid he'll probably be dead by tomorrow morning."

The poor woman goes home in a terrible state of shock but she is determined to make his last few hours the best he's ever had. That night, she suggests they go upstairs early and wearing her sexiest nightie, she lures him into bed and makes love to him like he's never experienced before. After 2 hours, they lay back exhausted and fall asleep. But half an hour later, the husband wakes up, nudges his wife and tells her it was so wonderful, can they do it again. Now this happens all night long until the poor wife hardly has the strength to move. As dawn breaks, he whispers yet again,

"Just once more, darling, please."

"It's alright for you," she snaps back at him, "You don't have to get up in the morning."

★

"Doctor, you've got to help me. My dick isn't big enough to satisfy my wife," said the distraught man.

"Do you drink special brew?" asked the doctor.

"Yes."

"Well, that's your problem, special brew tends to keep it small, you'd better try some brown ale."

A few weeks later, the doctor bumped into the man in the off-licence.

"Was it a success? I see you've got some brown ale there," said the doctor.

"Oh yes, the sex is great now. Thanks, doc. I don't drink the brown ale, though; I give it to my wife."

★

A young couple, finding themselves with nowhere to go to do their loving, had taken to using the local cemetery. He would take his amour up against a gravestone, and in this way they would find their mutual pleasure.

However, after a week or two, the girl's back had become very painful, so she went to the doctor.

The doctor got her to strip, and examined her thoroughly.

"Well, doctor?" she asked, as she got dressed. "What's wrong with my back?"

"I don't know about your back," replied the doctor, "but your arse died in 1904."

A woman went to the doctor's because she was feeling tired and listless. He asked her to strip off and noticing she was somewhat overweight said, "Why don't you diet?"

She looked down and replied, "Do you think so? What colour do you suggest?"

★

"Mr Jones, you're health is very poor," said the doctor. "Try going on a healthier diet: eat more fruit".

"But, doctor, I have three cherries in every martini."

★

A girl goes to the doctor's because she's found two green marks on the inside of her thighs. After examining her, the doctor asks a few questions.

"You're not a prostitute, are you?"

"How dare you? No I am not," she says.

"Do you have a boyfriend?"

"I am engaged."

"Ah, would he happen to be a gypsy?"

"Yes, he is."

"Then just tell him that his earrings aren't real gold."

"Doctor, doctor, I've got a penis growing on my forehead, what can I do?" said the distraught young man.

"I'm afraid there's not much that can be done, it would be too risky to surgically remove it."

"Does that mean that everytime I look in the mirror I'm going to see a penis staring back at me?"

"Well, er... no," said the doctor hesitantly. "You won't see the penis because you'll have a pair of bollocks hanging over your eyes."

A man goes into the doctor's, takes his dick out and lays it on the table. After looking at it for a few minutes, the doctor says,

"Well, it looks alright to me."

The man smiles, "Yes, it's nice isn't it?"

The doctor pointed to a jar on the shelf in his surgery and said, "I want you to fill that."

"What!" gasped the patient. "From here?"

★

"Just go over to the window and stick your tongue out," said the doctor to his patient.
"Why?"
"Because I don't like the man across the road."

★

A very small woman went to the doctor's complaining that her fanny was painful. After a complete examination, the puzzled doctor could find nothing wrong.
"Do you have this pain all the time?" he asked.
"No, only when it's wet outside."
"OK, well next time it's wet come and see me," he suggested. The following week it had rained heavily and the woman appeared once more at the surgery. Again the doctor examined her and immediately discovered the problem.
"Just lie there a moment," he said, "while I find some scissors."
A moment later she sighed with relief.
"Oh doctor, the pain's gone. It's wonderful, what did you do?"
"Oh, quite simple really. I just trimmed an inch off the top of your wellingtons."

★

A man takes a girl back to his flat but after some heavy petting, he suddenly stops and says, "It's no good, I'm so frightened of getting

AIDS, would you mind if I used my toe?"

She doesn't mind, so he sticks his toe up and she sits astride him.

A few days later, he notices something wrong with his toe, so he goes to the doctor.

"My goodness, I'm getting some odd cases at the moment," says the doctor. "You've got thrush on your toe and only yesterday I had a woman in who had athlete's foot in a most unusual place."

A man went to the doctor because he could not get an erection. Some weeks passed but none of the treatments worked so finally the doctor gave him an ancient remedy which involved injecting him in his member.

It was such a success that the man had a permanent erection, so he went back to the doctor to ask if it could be reduced.

"I'm sorry, it's impossible," said the doctor.

"But surely you can do something. All drugs have antidotes."

"I agree," said the doctor, "but this injection wasn't a drug. Just three of sand to one of cement!"

A man went to the doctor's covered in blood and bruises.

"What happened?" asked the doctor.

"It's my wife; she had another nightmare."

"But surely she couldn't have done this.

"Well, doctor, when she shouted out, 'Get out quick, my husband's home!', I automatically jumped out of the window."

A man goes to his doctor because he has not been able to have an erection for five years. The doctor tells him that after such a long time the condition has become very serious and there's only one pill that can help. But beware, the pill is so powerful that once taken the man will have three huge erections and that will be it for the rest of his life. He also tells him that the pill is voice-activated and will only work when the man says, "Ding dong." Once the man has had his erection it will return to normal by saying, "Ding dong" again.

It's a hard decision to make, knowing that these three erections will be the last he ever has, but he reasons it's better than not at all, so he takes the pill.

On the way home, he starts to have doubts as to whether it works, so he decides to try it out.

"Ding dong," he says, and this huge todger comes hurtling out of his trousers.

"Blimey!" says the man and quickly says "Ding dong" to return back to normal.

Now full of anticipation, the man races home and crosses the road without looking properly.

"Ding dong," goes the ice cream van and once again this huge appendage appears, frightening the passers by.

"Ding dong" and it goes back to normal.

Thankfully he gets home without any mishap, knowing he's only got one left. He rushes into the house, pushes his beautiful, but frustrated wife to the floor, tears her clothes off and says, "Darling , darling, I love you so much, ding dong."

"What's the ding dong for?" asks his wife.

A man goes to the doctor and tells him he swallowed three 10p pieces four weeks ago.

"Can you get them out?" he asks.

The doctor looks at him puzzled.

"You swallowed the money four weeks ago and it's only now you're coming to see me?"

"That's right," replies the man. "I didn't need the money then."

The man was so bad in bed, when he masturbated, his hand fell asleep.

A man goes to the doctor with a most unusual complaint. His penis is so big it drags his vocal chords down and causes him to stutter. The doctor tells him he can be cured but it will mean an operation to take away eight inches from his very large member. The man agrees and the operation is a complete success.

However some weeks go by and the man misses his extra long penis – after all, it made him quite a celebrity. So he goes back to the doctor to ask if it can be put back on.

"S-s-s-orry," says the doctor, "that's not p-p-ppossible I'm af-f-fraid."

★

A woman went to the doctor to tell him that every time she went to the toilet, pennies, ten pence pieces and fifty pence pieces came out.

"Don't worry," said the doctor. "You're just going through the change."

★

A buxom young lady goes to the doctor and he asks her to undress. When she's completely naked, he starts to feel her thighs.

"Do you know what I'm doing?" he asks.

"Yes, you're checking to see if there are any abnormalities."

Then he starts to fondle her breasts.

"Do you know what I'm doing now?"

"Yes, you're checking to see if there are any strange lumps."

Then the doctor lays her down on the table, jumps on top of her and starts making love.

"Now do you know what I'm doing?" he asks.

"Yes," she replies. "You're catching herpes."

★

The doctor told the old deaf man he needed a sample of his urine, a stool specimen and a sperm specimen.

"What's he saying?" said the old man to his wife.

"He wants you to leave your underpants here."

"You've got to cut down on your smoking, drinking and sex life, otherwise your heart is going to give out on you," said the doctor to his 70 year old patient. "Only two cigarettes a day and one pint of beer."

"What about sex?" asked the man.

"Only with your wife," replied the doctor. "You mustn't get excited."

★

"Doctor, doctor, my balls have turned green."
"Well, you've heard of cauliflower ears, those are brothel sprouts."

"Doctor, every bone in my body hurts."
"Then be thankful you're not a kipper."

A doctor is the only man who can get women to strip and then send their husbands the bill.

I have a great doctor. If you can't afford the operation, he touches up the x-rays.

★

A man goes to the doctor, upset because every night he has the same dream where two gorgeous women are trying to get into bed with him but he keeps pushing them away.
The doctor asks what the man would like him to do and the patient replies, "Break my arms."

The old woman says to her next-door neighbour who she knows is suffering from piles, "Put some tea leaves up there. It's a good remedy."

So she does, but it's no better. In fact, it gets worse so she goes to the doctor. As she's bending over, she says to him, "Can you see anything?"

The doctor replies, "No, but you're going to meet a tall dark handsome man on Monday."

A man was asked to send a sample of his urine to the surgery before the doctor could complete his examination. Unfortunately, the man had to go to work, so asked the young boy next door to drop it in for him. On the way, however, the boy spilled most of it and fearing trouble, topped it up with a cow's in a nearby field. It wasn't long before the doctor called for him to come to the surgery as soon as possible, and when he returned home later he was furious with his wife.

"So much for all your fancy positions!" he snarled at his wife. "Now I'm pregnant, and it's all your fault!"

"I am very sorry to say that I have two bad pieces of news for you," said the doctor to his patient.

"Oh dear, what is it?" asked the patient.

"You have only 24 hours to live," came the reply.

"Oh no, what other piece of bad news could there be?"

"I tried to get you on the phone all day yesterday."

★

A man went to the doctor and said he couldn't stop farting. It was dreadful. He just couldn't stop.
The doctor went away and came back with a huge long pole.
"Oh no," said the man.
"It's alright," replied the doctor, "I'm only going to open the window."

A young wife went to the doctor's complaining that her husband never made love to her. She wanted to know if it was her fault. After a complete examination, the doctor concluded it was not her – it must be her husband.
"Give him two of these pills every morning and by evening you should be happily satisfied. But let me know how it goes because these pills are still experimental."
Only one day had passed before she stormed back into the surgery.
"I am so angry," she said. "One minute we were sipping tea, the next moment he lunged at me, lifted my dress, pulled down my knickers and took me on the table there and then."
"But isn't that what you wanted?" puzzled the doctor.
"Yes, but not in the middle of the coffee shop; I'll never be able to show my face in there again."

"Doctor, I'm so overweight, I've tried hundreds of different diets but nothing seems to work. Can you help me?" asked the fat man.
The doctor gave him some pills and told him to come back in

a month. This he did, having lost over a stone in weight.

"It's wonderful," said the man. "Every night I'd take a pill and then all night I dream of being stranded on this desert island with 20 beautiful girls, each one of them demanding sexual satisfaction. No wonder I've lost weight."

"That'll be £40 then," said the doctor and the man went away very happy.

Now this man had a friend, a miserly sort of fellow who was also having trouble losing weight so he was recommended to go along and see the same doctor and get similar treatment. However, after a month had gone by he returned in a very disgruntled mood even though he had lost a stone in weight as well.

"What's wrong," asked the doctor, "the pills have worked, haven't they?"

"Oh sure, every night when I went to sleep I dreamt I was in the jungle being chased by wild savages brandishing machetes. Every morning I was knackered. But how come I get this nightmare and my mate is surrounded by beautiful women?"

"Well what did you expect? You insisted you have it on the NHS," said the doctor.

★

"Doctor I want to get married but I think my cock's too small. What shall I do?"

He replied, "Go and stay down on the local farm, dip your cock in fresh milk every day and have it sucked by a calf."

Some weeks later, they met in the street and the doctor asked him how his marriage was going.

"Oh, I didn't bother in the end, I just bought the calf."

Doctor to woman patient:

"You have acute appendicitis."

"Thank you, you have a real neat bum," she replied.

A man took his wife to the doctor's complaining about her sex drive. It was non-stop, whatever time of the day, whatever place, she was always hankering after sex.

"I'll see what I can do," said the doctor and he asked her to go into the consulting room and strip off. As soon as he started to examine her, she began to make little groaning noises, and tempt him forward with her open legs. It was too much for him and in no time at all he was astride her.

But all the noise attracted the attention of the husband waiting outside, so he opened the door to find out what was happening.

"What the hell's going on here?" he shouted.

"Oh er... nothing to worry about, I'm taking your wife's temperature" said the sweating doctor.

"Really?" said the man taking a flick knife out of his pocket. "When that thing comes out it better have numbers on it."

Did you hear about the man who went to the chiropodists and put his willy on the table?

When the chiropodist told him it wasn't a foot, he replied,
"I know, but I'm proud it's 11 inches."

A woman walked into the dentist very nervously and said,
"I'd rather have a baby than have my teeth checked."
"Okay," said the dentist, "if that's what you want, I'll have to adjust the chair."

A man went to the dentist with a raging toothache.
"It'll have to come out immediately," said the dentist, taking hold of his drill.
The patient grabbed hold of the dentist's balls and replied,
"We're not going to hurt each other, are we?"

★

The local Mayor decided to do something useful for the community so went along to the sperm bank to make a donation.
"Have you been before?" asked the receptionist.
"I believe I have," replied the Mayor. "You've probably got my notes from last time."
"Oh yes," replied the girl. "You're going to need some help so I'll put you in our category D area."
"Wait a minute, what do you mean category D! I don't need help."
"I'm sorry Sir, but it says in your notes that you're a clueless wanker."

Jack's wife went along to the optician's for her annual check up.

"Right," said the optician "Can you read the bottom line?"

After a few moments she shook her head.

"OK, try the next line."

Again she shook her head. This went on until they got to the largest letter at the top but she still shook her head. By this time the optician was so frustrated he unzipped his trousers, pulled out his willy and shouted,

"Well can you see this?"

"Oh yes," she replied.

"Well there's the trouble," said the optician. "You're cock-eyed."

★

A very rich woman reaches middle age and decides to have a face lift to keep her looking young. She goes along to the most famous and wickedly expensive surgeon in town and he explains he has discovered a new and revolutionary technique.

"Once I have performed the operation, I will put two little screws behind each ear and whenever you see a little wrinkle appear, you just gently turn the screws and it will disappear."

The technique is a wonderful success and for over 10 years the woman keeps a wrinkle-free face by turning the screws when necessary. However one day she notices she has bags under her eyes but when she turns the screws, no matter how many times, the bags will not go away. In a blind panic she rushes back to the surgeon.

"Look what's happened," she wails "I can't get ride of them."

The surgeon replies,

"Madam, you have used the screws so much that those bags under your eyes are your breasts and if you continue to turn the screws, you'll end up with a beard."

★

"It's no good Mabel, I can't find anything wrong with you, it must be the effects of drinking," said the doctor.
"Well in that case I'll come back when you're sober!" exclaimed the woman.

★

A very obese man went to the doctors and was told he would have to lose at least 7 stone.

"It's no good," wailed the man. "I've tried all sorts of diets and they never work."

"Well this one is different," said the doctor. "You will take nothing by mouth, everything you eat will be through your rectum."

A month went by and the man went back to the doctors looking very happy.

"Well done, you've lost nearly 4 stone, carry on like this and you'll soon be down to the correct weight. Do you have any problems?"

"None at all," said the man. "I'll see you in a month's time."

As the man walked to the door, the doctor noticed that he was walking in an odd way.

"Are you sure there's nothing wrong?" asked the doctor. "You seem to be walking in a curious way."

"No, everything's fine, doc," said the man "I'm just chewing some bubble gum."

★

"Doctor, doctor, I'm so embarrassed, I've got several holes in my willy and when I go for a pee it sprinkles out all over me and over anyone standing close by. Please say you can do something."

The doctor considered the man for a few minutes and then wrote something down on a card.

"Here," he said, "take this card, on it is the name of a man who can help you."

"Oh thanks doc, will he be able to cure me?"

"No, but he's one of the country's finest flute players and he'll show you how to hold it properly."

★

At first Johnny was embarrassed to find a lady doctor waiting for him in the surgery. She asked him to strip and then began examining him. As she put her soft, gentle hands on his body she said,

"Say 99 please."

Johnny smiled and then as slowly as he could began 1 ... 2 ... 3 ...

A man suffering from constipation was given a course of suppositories by his GP. But a week later he was back complaining they hadn't worked.

"Are you sure you've been taking them regularly?" asked the doctor.

"Of course I bloody well have," he answered angrily. "What do you think I've been doing, sticking them up my arse?"

★

A very worried woman went to the doctors to complain about the male hormone she was having to take.

"Oh doctor, I'm growing hair in all sorts of places."

"Don't worry, that's not unusual in a case like this. Where in particular is the hair?"

"On my balls," she replied.

★

A man goes to the doctor for his 5 yearly check up and after the examination the doctor says,

"Mr Biggins, I have some good news and some bad news."

"Oh doctor, tell me, what's the bad news?"

"The bad news is that I've diagnosed you have homosexual tendencies," replied the doctor.

"Good heavens, what's the good news?"

"Well, I find you rather cute."

★

"Doctor, doctor, I think I may be impotent. When I try and make love to my wife nothing happens."

The doctor thought for a moment and then said,

"Make an appointment for both you and your wife to come to the surgery and I'll see what I can do."

So the following week they both turn up at the surgery. The doctor takes the wife into another room and asks her to undress. Then he asks her to walk up and down, twirl around and jump in the air.

"Thank you very much Mrs Smith, you can get dressed now."

The doctor goes back into the other room and takes the husband to one side.

"Don't worry Mr Smith, there's nothing wrong with you, your wife doesn't give me a hard-on either."

There are only two men in the doctor's waiting room. One has his arm bandaged up and the second is covered in food – potatoes in his hair, a lamb chop sticking out of his pocket, gravy running down his trousers and peas up his nose. The second man turns to the first and asks him what happened.

"Oh it's my own fault," he replied. "I was looking at this beautiful girl instead of watching where I was going. I tripped over a step and I think I might have broken my arm. What about you?"

"Oh it's nothing much, I'm just not eating properly."

★

A man went to the doctor's feeling run down.

"What you need is a holiday" said the doctor. "You need to get away from the routine, could you go abroad?"

"I sure could," replied the man. "What's she like?"

A woman took her son down to the doctor's surgery.

"Doctor, tell me please, can a boy of 13 take out his own appendix?" she demanded.

"Indeed not," said the doctor.

"There you are, I told you so!" she yelled at her son. "Now put it back immediately."

★

A woman went to the doctor's with her son because she was concerned that his penis was too small and not growing normally.

"Nothing to worry about," replied the doctor. "Every night, before he goes to bed, give him a cup of hot milk and put in a teaspoon of this special B16 powder. That'll soon put things right."

A few evenings later, the little boy walked into the kitchen to find his mum putting three tablespoons of the powder into a mug of hot milk.

"But Mum," said the boy, "the doctor only said a teaspoon."

"Oh this isn't for you," she replied, "this is for your father."

★

The doctor examined the wife's husband thoroughly before he turned to her and said,

"I'm sorry, I don't like the look of your husband."

"Neither do I," she replied, "but at least he's useful around the house."

★

A man goes to the surgery feeling sick, but the doctor is unable to diagnose what's wrong with him, so he takes some blood tests and tells him to return the following week. However, he's too ill to leave the house so his wife goes along to get the results.

"Oh dear, oh dear," says the doctor, shaking his head, "it

seems I have two patients by the name of Jack Brown in forblood tests this week and the tests have been muddled up. It means your husband either has VD or Alzheimer's disease." The poor wife is very distressed.

"What shall I do?" she asks.

"Don't worry, it's quite simple," replies the doctor. "Take your husband on a long journey, go by bus and train, then leave him there and see if he can find his way home. If he does get home alright, don't let him fuck you."

"Every time I sneeze, I have an orgasm," said the girl to her doctor.

"What do you take for it?" he asked.

"Pepper."

A man is suffering very badly from severe headaches, dizziness and spots before the eyes.

"I'm sorry to say," said the doctor, "that you have got an infection in your testicles and unless you have them removed, the symptoms will spread."

Unwilling to accept this dreadful diagnosis, the man consults two other doctors but they both give the same opinion. So resigned to his fate, the man has both testicles removed.

Some days later, in an effort to cheer himself up, he decides to go shopping. 'At least I can look good even if I don't feel it' he thinks to himself, so he visits the most exclusive gentlemens outfitters for miles around.

"Ah yes," says the tailor. "You're a 34" waist, 32" inside leg and 15" collar size."

"That's very impressive," says the man. "How can you be so accurate?"

"Years of training sir," replies the tailor. "I also know that you are a 40" chest, take size 11 in shoes and wear medium sized underpants."

"Absolutely correct," says the man, "except for the underpants. I take a small size."

"Then may I suggest you change the size, sir, otherwise you'll eventually start to suffer from severe headaches, dizziness and spots before the eyes."

★

A simple old woman fell and badly hurt her leg.

"You'll have to rest for a few days," said the doctor, after he'd bandaged it up, "and please don't use the stairs until I give you permission."

The following week, she returned to the surgery for a check-up.

"Your leg is almost healed," said the doctor, "You can start using the stairs again."

"Oh thank goodness for that," she replied happily. "Shinning up the drain pipe was wearing me out."

★

"Every time I look in the mirror, I see an old man, tired and haggard."

"Well there's nothing wrong with your eyesight," replied the doctor.

★

A woman is so upset about her flat chest, she tells her husband she wants to go to a plastic surgeon.

"Hold on a minute," replies the man, "before you go, try rubbing toilet paper on your nipples for the next few days."

"But why? I don't understand. Will it make them bigger?"

"Well it certainly worked for your arse, didn't it?"

★

"I'm sorry, my glasses have broken again," said the man to the optician.

"Oh dear," replied the optician. "It's becoming a bit of a habit. What happened this time?"

"Well, I was kissing my girlfriend when it happened."

"Really?! I can't see why that should break your glasses."

"She crossed her legs," he replied.

★

There were only two people in the doctor's waiting room. Robert had come for a blood test and was sitting opposite a man who was constantly mumbling to himself,

"Please let me be ill, please, please let me be ill."

Unable to contain his curiosity any longer, Robert asked the man,

"I'm sorry, I couldn't help but overhear you say you hoped you were sick. Why is that?"

The man replied sadly, "I'd hate to be well and feel like this!"

"Doctor, doctor," shouted the distressed receptionist, "that man you pronounced fit and well a few minutes ago has dropped down dead outside the surgery."
The doctor replied calmly,
"Don't worry Beth, turn him round so he looks as if he's just coming in."

The great consultant looked down his nose at the scruffy man who shuffled into the room. After a quick examination, he asked
"Have you been to see anyone else before coming to see me?"
"Yes, Dr Peek," he replied warily.
"Dr Peek! That charlatan!" exclaimed the consultant, "and I suppose he fed you lots of useless pills and doled out some pathetic advice?"
"I don't know, he told me to come and see you."

The professor was lecturing his students on plastic surgery. At one point he asked them what they would do if someone was born without a penis. A hand shot up at the back and a boy answered,
"Wait until she'd grown up and then give her one."

★

"Doctor, doctor," cried the man in despair. "I've got such terrible bad breath. It's having a dreadful effect on my love life. I can't get a girl to come near me. What shall I do?"
The doctor thought for a moment and replied,

"You have two chances. You either stop scratching your arse, or you stop biting your nails."

★

"Oh doctor," said the distraught patient. "Why do so many people take an instant dislike to me?"
"Saves time," came the reply.

★

An arrogant man went to the doctor's and after a complete examination was told he either had V.D. or mumps. The doctor told him to come back the following day for his test results when he told him "I'm sorry Mr Squires, I'm afraid you have V.D."
"Well I knew that," said the man scornfully. "How on earth would I come in contact with the mumps?"

★

A woman goes to the doctor's because she's at her wits end. For months she's tried to get a boyfriend but no one is interested, and her need to have a loving relationship is making her desperate. Having spent a fortune on good clothes and evocative perfume to no avail, she tells the doctor of her plight. The doctor soon realises that she needs to see a sex therapist so he refers her to Doctor Choy Nang.
"Harro," says the doctor, "what can I do for you, prease."
The woman relates her sad story and the doctor tells her he will have to run a series of tests.
"Preese take off your clothes," he says. She does this and

stands in front of him while he looks at her very carefully.

"Now preese, on hands and knees and crawl around the room."

Although astonished at his request, she does as he wishes.

"Ah ha," he says, smiling broadly. "I know what problem is, you have Ed Zachany disease."

The woman gasps, "Oh no, what's that?"

"It mean your face look Ed Zachany like your arse."

A young couple were about to get married. The husband-to-be was ecstatic that such a gorgeous creature would want to marry such a boring old fart as himself. First they had to get the all clear from the doctor's. A few days after the examinations, the doctor asked the young man to come in for the results.

"Ah Mr Brownall, do come in. I have some good news and some bad news."

"Oh no," replied the poor man. "What's the bad news?"

"Your wife-to-be has herpes."

"Bloody hell!" he exclaimed. "What's the good news?"

"She didn't get it from you."

"Come in Mr Burton," said the doctor solemnly.

"I've had the results of your tests and I've got some good news and some bad news."

"What's the bad news?" asked the man anxiously.

"I'm afraid you have a rare illness picked up from your

expeditions into the jungle. There's no cure. In fact, within the next 24 hours, you'll go into a coma and die."

The man gasped in pain. "Then what the hell's the good news?" he asked.

The doctor's face lit up with anticipation.

"You know my new receptionist out, the one with big tits? I've just asked her out and she said 'Yes'!"

A man went for his annual examination at the hospital and as he removed his trousers he revealed his penis was the size of a little "pinkie." Unfortunately, the nurses weren't quick enough to hide their amusement and the man retorted angrily,

"Hey, it's the uniforms, I can't help getting a hard-on when I see them."

A bloke went to a specialist because his todger had turned bright red. "Mmm, we'll soon put that right," said the doctor, and after messing around with it for a few minutes, it was back to normal.

"That's great," said the man. "How much do I owe you?"

"Just £20."

The following Sunday he was telling his mate about it in the pub.

"Well, to be honest," confessed his mate, "I think I've got something similar, only mine is a yellowy green colour. He sounds good, and cheap, I think I'll go and see him."

"Mmm," said the specialist thoughtfully. "Well I can do something for you, but it's quite a complicated treatment and will cost you £3,000."

"What!" exclaimed the man. "You only charged my mate £20."

"Yes, indeed," replied the specialist, "but he just had lipstick on his.

You've got gangrene."

★

**An old woman goes to the doctor's to get the results of her tests.
"Sit down, Mrs Chivers," says the doctor kindly, "I'm afraid
the news isn't very good."
"Tell me the worst," she replies.
"Well, there are two things. First you have cancer..."
"Oh no," she gasps.
"...and secondly, you have Alzheimer's disease."
"Oh thank goodness for that," she says smiling, "for a moment
I thought you were going to tell me I had cancer."**

★

Which is worse, Alzheimer's disease, or Parkinson's disease?
Parkinson's; I'd rather forget a beer than spill one.

★

In Hospital

Although divorced five years previously, the couple had remained friends for the sake of their daughter. One day, the ex-wife learns that her ex-husband has been taken ill and will have to stay in bed for at least two weeks. Because he's on his own, she decides to go round to see if there's any way she can help and she volunteers to take over from the nurse who has been popping in for an hour each day. The ex-wife learns to give him his medicines, cook his food and generally look after him. One day, she's giving him a bed bath when she notices he has a huge erection. "Oh my goodness," she remarks. "Look John, he still remembers me."

Two simple lads were working in the sawmill when Jack accidentally cut his arm off. As quick as lightning his mate, Pete, put it in a plastic bag and rushed them both to hospital. After four hours the brilliant surgeon had sewn the arm back on and within three months Jack was as good as new. That winter Jack was so cold, his concentration slipped and he cut off his right leg. Quick as a flash Pete wrapped up the leg in a plastic bag and rushed them to hospital. Although the operation was more difficult, the surgeon, once again, miraculously attached the leg back to Jack's body and after six months he had fully recovered. The months went by until one day Jack fell asleep at work and cut his head off. Ready for every emergency, Pete got the head in a plastic bag and rushed them to hospital.

"This is a very difficult operation," said the surgeon, "it's touch and go." He told Pete to come back the following morning to see how things were progressing. The next day Pete arrived at the hospital and met a very serious looking surgeon.

"I'm sorry, your friend didn't make it."

Grief stricken, Pete replied, "I know you did all you could doc, but you did warn me it might not work."

"Oh it wasn't the operation," said the surgeon "that was successful; Jack had suffocated in the plastic bag."

The man came into work, one arm in a sling, a bandage round his head, two black eyes and a painful limp.

"And what time do you call this?" asked his boss. "You're very late."

"I'm sorry sir, I tripped over the garden step," said the poor man.

"Oh yeah, and it took a whole hour to do that, did it!" replied the boss scornfully.

Three surgeons were relaxing in the bar after a conference and the first one said, "I had a pretty easy time last week. I had to operate on a computer analyst and when I opened him up, all the parts were filed and labelled and the retrieval system was very competent."

"Well, my week was even easier," said the second surgeon. "I had to operate on an electronics expert, all the different systems were colour-coded so you could see what was wrong

459

immediately."

"Yes, that sounds good," said the third surgeon. "But I had the easiest of all. I had to operate on an estate agent. They've only got two moving parts – the mouth and the arsehole – and they're both used for the same thing."

'Simple Sam' is the local odd-job man in the village, not too bright but always willing to have a go. One day, he hears there are vacancies going in the local sawmill, so he goes along in the hope of getting a job. Reluctantly, the boss takes him on, emphasising how dangerous the job is and how he must always think 'Safety.' However, only two hours into the job and Sam stumbles over a plank of wood, puts his hands out to save himself and gets all his fingers and thumbs sawn off by a giant blade. There's no one else about, so he runs off in shock to the local hospital, where he faints on the doorstep. Later, as he regains consciousness, he hears the doctor's voice.

"Sam, Sam, if only you'd brought your fingers in with you we might have been able to sew them on before it was too late."

"I would have," cried Sam, "but I couldn't pick them up."

A young, rich lawyer had a very bad car crash. The car was a write-off but even worse, the lawyer's arm had been severed. When the paramedics arrived, they heard him whimpering "My BMW, oh no, my BMW."

"Sir," said one of the helpers, "I think you should be more concerned about your arm."

The lawyer looked round and seeing just his shoulder, exclaimed
"Oh no, my Rolex, my Rolex."

"Hey, haven't we met somewhere before?"
"Yes, I'm the nurse at the VD clinic."

Young nurse in nurses' home knocks on matron's door while she's having a bath.
"Yes, who is it?" asks the matron.
 "I have Mr Thompson to see you."
"Come, come nurse", responds matron. "I'm naked in the bath."
The nurse continues, "Mr Thompson, the blind man."
"OK, bring him in" says matron.
The door opens and the nurse and Mr Thompson enter the bathroom. Looking at the matron, Mr Thompson says, "Nice tits matron. Now where do you want these blinds?"

A young nurse is walking along the corridor with one of her boobs hanging out of her uniform. Matron appears and on seeing this is outraged. She asks for an immediate explanation. The nurse, with a resigned air, replies, "Sorry, Matron, it's these young house doctors. They never put anything back where they found it."

Two nurses locked out of the nurses home late at night, shinned up the drainpipe and in through an open window. The first nurse turned to her friend and said, "Doing this makes me feel like a burglar."

"Me too," said the second, "but where will we find two burglars at this time of night?"

A woman is visiting her sick aunt in hospital and as she's leaving, she notices a ward completely enclosed by glass.

"Excuse me, nurse, what's that for?" she asks.

"That's the Isolation Ward. The man in there has got distemper, the plague, hepatitis and AIDS."

As they look, they see a man going towards the glass pushing a trolley.

"Is that his lunch?"

"Yes, he has Ryvita, After-eight chocolates and dried sheets of lasagna."

"Goodness, will that make him better?"

"No," replied the nurse, "but it's all we can slide under the door."

★

An unscrupulous young man decided to embarrass the new student nurse so when she came round to make his bed, he asked, "Excuse me nurse, where does a woman's hair grow blackest and thickest and curliest?"

The poor nurse turned scarlet and went off to find the Sister. A little later, Sister came over to the young man's bed and said, "Mr Jenkins, I hear you've been upsetting one of our nurses. Just exactly what did you say to her?"

"All I asked was where does a woman's hair grow blackest, thickest and curliest, Sister?"

"Indeed, and where might that be?" she said, glaring at him.

"Why, in Africa of course."

★

"Doctor, we have had to buy three new operating tables this month alone. Will you please try not to cut so deeply?"

★

She must be the unluckiest person in the world.
She's just had a kidney transplant from a bed wetter.

★

A very rich young man, hearing about the amazing advances in body part transplants, decided he would like a new brain. He went to the specialist to find out what was on offer.

"Well, at the moment we have a computer analyst for £10,000; a university professor for £15,000 and a high court judge for £20,000."

"Money is no object," said the young man.

"Tell me, what is the best and most expensive brain you have?"

"Well," said the specialist, "We do have an MP's on offer at £50,000."

"I don't understand," said the young man, "why is that one so much more expensive?"

"That's simple," said the specialist. "It's hardly ever been used."

★

A man went into hospital to have a penis transplant, having lost his own in an industrial accident. After the operation, he immediately asked the surgeon how it went.

"Well," hesitated the surgeon, "mixed results really. The transplant was a success. I think you'll agree it's an impressive member, but unfortunately your hand has rejected it."

★

How do patients in a burns unit pick their noses?
From a catalogue.

★

Did you hear about the unlucky man who had a wet dream and had to go to the VD clinic?

★

Do you know how Alcoholics Anonymous practises Russian Roulette?
They pass round six glasses of tonic water – but one of them is a gin and tonic.

★

There's one definite way of giving a person amnesia.
Lend them money.

★

A London man had an awful time last week when he didn't realise the difference between fixative and laxative.
His teeth have been stuck on the lavatory for three days.

★

Did you hear about the gynaecologist who papered his hall through the front door letter box?

★

A plastic surgeon was complaining to his colleague about one of his regular patients.

"I'm being sued by Cynthia Prighorse. I told her she was unwise to have so many facelifts."

"Why, what happened?" asked the colleague.

"She's got a beard."

★

A young man goes to a plastic surgeon because he's got a very small dick. The surgeon tells him he could be helped but it would mean implanting part of a baby elephant's trunk. The man agrees and the operation is a great success.

A few days later, he decides to celebrate and takes out an old girlfriend for a romantic meal to tell her how everything could be different between them now.

Suddenly, his new appendage flies out of his trousers, grabs a bread roll and disappears.

"Wow, that's quite a trick!" says the girl. "Do it again."

But the young man, with a pained look on his face, replies, "I'm not sure if my arse could stand another bread roll."

★

A woman's face was so badly injured in an accident it required plastic surgery.

"We can do it," the surgeon said, "but it will cost you £2,000 and we will need to take skin off your backside."

The man agreed and the operation was a great success. His wife was even more beautiful. A few days later the plastic surgeon rang the husband to tell him he had paid £500 too much.

"Oh no," said the husband, "the extra is for the extra pleasure I get everytime I see my mother in law kiss my arse."

A man went back to the plastic surgeon to complain about a new hand he had grafted on after his own hand had been smashed up in an accident.

"Well, it looks alright to me," said the plastic surgeon.

"It is most of the time. Trouble is you gave me a female hand and every time I go for a slash, it won't let go."

A woman goes to the doctor to tell him she wants a baby but she doesn't want a relationship with a man.

The doctor tells her it's no problem. Just take her clothes off, lie on the couch with legs wide apart and he'll go and get a bottle of semen. However, coming back from the storeroom he catches sight of her on the table and is overcome by her beauty and stunning body. He leaves the bottle behind, drops his trousers around his ankles and comes back into the room saying, "Sorry, but we're out of bottles. You'll have to have draught."

★

A man went to a sperm bank but found the whole atmosphere of the place made it impossible for him to perform. So he asked one of the young nurses who was new to the clinic if she would help him.

Some time later, he emerged with a very small sample and was asked by the doctor why he had been so long.

"Sorry, doc," he replied. "I would have been out sooner but it took ages to get your nurse to cough it back up."

★

Of all the sperm that lived in Jack's body, one was fitter and more active than the rest. It was determined that when the time came, it would fertilise the egg and make the woman pregnant.

Some time later, all the signs showed that the moment was coming and off they raced, the fittest one out front. But suddenly, it stopped dead, turned round and tried desperately to swim back the other way.

"What's wrong?" they shouted.

"Quick, get back! It's a blow job."

★

Did you hear about the gay ENT surgeon?
He was known as the Queer nose and throat specialist!

★

The Mayor and the Lady Mayoress were visiting the local hospital. They were very impressed with what they saw, until they came upon a cubicle where a man sat wanking over a copy of 'Razzle'.

"What's going on here?" demanded the Mayor, covering the Lady Mayoress' eyes.

"Oh, that's okay," replied the doctor, "this is the sperm donor's ward, and he's just making a donation."

Mollified by this, the tour continued, but in the next room they found a pretty young nurse in her underwear, giving a patient a blow job.

"Oh my God!" yelled the Mayor, "this is disgusting! Doctor, explain at once!"

"Oh that's nothing," replied the doctor, "he's a sperm donor too, the same as the other patient, except this man here has private health insurance."

It was Monday morning and the great but absentminded rectal surgeon was on his rounds. Halfway round the ward the nurse nudged him and whispered in his ear.

"Sir, you have a suppository behind your left ear."

"Oh damn," cursed the surgeon. "That means some bum's got my pencil."

A gorgeous shapely girl was lying naked in a hospital bed with just a sheet covering her. Suddenly a young man in a white coat came in, pulled back the sheet and examined her closely.

"What's the verdict?" she asked.

"I don't know," replied the man slowly, "you'll have to ask the doctor that. I'm just here to clean the ward."

"Oh Carol, you'll never guess what I've just seen," said the plain nurse to the pretty nurse. "The man in cubicle 7 has "NOON" tattooed on his willy."

"Oh no," replied Carol, "it's not NOON, its Northampton."

★

One of the fielders got hit in the crotch by a cricket ball, the pain was so severe he collapsed unconscious on the ground and woke up in hospital.

"Hey doc," he croaked, "am I alright? Will I be able to play again?"

The doctor replied, "Yes, you'll be able to play again .... if you've got a women's team at the club, that is."

★

A man went to the doctors with a bad wrist and after a quick examination, he was transferred to the accident and emergency unit at the local hospital. Immediately on getting there, the nurse asked him for a urine sample which he thought was a very odd thing to ask for, considering it was his wrist that hurt. However, nurse insisted, so he did as she wished. Fifteen minutes later, he was ushered in to see the doctor who told him he had dislocated his wrist.

"Don't tell me you learnt that from the urine sample?" laughed the man.

"Oh yes we did," insisted the doctor, "there have been such great developments in medicine and we now have a fool-proof way of diagnosing many complaints just by taking a urine sample."

After the man was patched up, he left for home. An appointment was made to see him in six weeks time, when he had to bring along another sample. On the day of the next visit, the man decided to test just how good the new method was so he peed in the jar, got his wife and daughter to do the same, as well as the cat, and also wanked into it. This time, the analysis took much longer, but eventually he got in to see the doctor.

"Well? What's the verdict?" he asked.

The doctor looked at him very seriously and replied,

"Your wrist is much better, but your wife has VD, your daughter is pregnant, the cat has fleas and if you don't stop wanking, your wrist will just get worse."

Three women at an antenatal clinic were asked what position they were in when they conceived.

The first said he was on top.

"In that case you'll have a boy," said the doctor.

The second said she was on top.

"In that case you'll have a girl," came the reply.

But before the third woman could reply she burst into tears.

"Oh no, please tell me I'm not going to have puppies."

In the Dentist's Chair

The dentist looked at his patient and gave his verdict. "For the best results, your treatment will cost about £5,000, but," he added hastily, "you will have perfect teeth for the rest of your life."

"Oh dear!" exclaimed the patient, "that's an awful lot of money. I couldn't pay it all in one go."

"No, no, I quite understand, we could arrange monthly payments."

"I see. I suppose it would be a bit like buying a luxury item, like a yacht," mused the man.

"That's right," replied the dentist. "I am."

"Come in Donald," said the dentist, "take a seat. Now, I wonder if you'll do something for me. Before we start, would you mind screaming very loudly?"

Donald looked puzzled. "Well, I suppose so," he replied, "but can you tell me why?"

"By all means," replied the dentist. "My team's got through to the FA Cup Final, and I'm never going to get there if I don't get rid of that lot out there."

"I wish you hadn't left it for so long before coming to see me," said the dentist to his patient. "But your teeth are way past being saved, so I'll have to take them all out and make you a set of false ones."

The patient looked terrified.

"I can't," he gasped. "I just can't stand the pain."

"Come now," said the dentist impatiently. "Just imagine how nice it will be again to be able to eat your food properly. And I can assure you there'll be very little pain."

The man still didn't look convinced.

"I tell you what," said the dentist, who'd just had an idea, "why don't you talk to Mr Taylor. He lives down your street and I did the same for him not so long ago. If you ask him about the pain, I'm positive he'll reassure you."

So later in the week, the man contacted Mr Taylor and asked him about the pain.

"Mmm," mused Mr Taylor, "let me put it this way. I had my teeth done four months ago and last week I was repairing our garden gate when I accidentally hammered a nail into my hand. And that was the first time in four months my teeth didn't hurt!"

"Kate, listen to me," pleaded her dentist. "We've got to stop this. It'll only end in tears."

"But why?" she asked. "We've had great sex for over a year and my husband's never found out. He's not even suspicious."

"But he will be soon. Don't you realise you've only got one tooth left in your mouth?"

Instead of opening his mouth, Colin pulled down his trousers to expose his todger.

"Now hold on a minute," said the dentist looking alarmed. "I'm not a doctor, I can't help you down there."

"Oh yes you can," replied Colin, "take a closer look. I've got a tooth stuck in it."

★

"Thanks for seeing us so quickly," said the grateful man to the dentist. "As I said on the phone, it's a bit of an emergency because this toothache's come just as we were flying out to the Bahamas at 6 o'clock tonight. Please take it out as quickly as possible. Don't worry about pain killers or anything like that, just yank it out."

"Well, I think I ought to warn you that it will be very painful if I don't use anything."

"Not to worry. Just get a move on."

"Okay. I think you're very brave. Just pop up into the chair for me please."

The man turned to his wife and said

"You heard what he said, Ruth, sit up in the chair."

★

"I'm not paying this outrageous bill," yelled the man. "You've charged me four times over."

"Maybe so," replied the dentist calmly, "but you made so much noise during your treatment, that the other three patients in the waiting room, cancelled their appointments and have gone elsewhere."

★

"You don't have to open your mouth that far, madam," said the dentist. "I expect to stay outside while extracting your teeth."

In the Grave and Beyond

It was Bob's funeral. His wife and three children were sitting in the front row listening to the vicar as he spoke enthusiastically about the man's life.

"He was a wonderful father, a hard-working man and a great asset to the community ...."

At this point, the widow suddenly jumped up flustered and shooed her children out of the door, saying, "Oh dear, I think I must have got the wrong time, because this can't be my Bob's funeral."

The devil tells a man who's just arrived in hell that he must choose one of three doors to enter and in the room beyond he will spend eternity.

The man is very worried that he will choose the wrong door so eventually persuades the devil to let him have a quick look behind the doors before making his choice.

Behind the first door he sees everyone standing on their head on a wooden floor. He doesn't fancy doing that for eternity but the second door is even worse. Everyone is standing on their head on a stone floor. However in the third room everyone is standing around drinking tea, ankle deep in manure. Oh well, thought the man, at least I'm not standing on my head, so he tells the devil his choice is room 3.

He goes into room 3 and just as the door slams shut behind him he hears the devil shout out, "OK everyone, tea break's over! Get back on your heads."

★

Two neighbours, one upright and a pillar of the church, the other a drinker and fornicator. Eventually the wicked one dies from his excesses, a few years later the other one dies goes up to heaven and is astonished to see the wicked one with a large barrel of beer and a naked angel on his lap. The upright man is outraged and complains to St. Peter.

"I denied myself all the good things in life so that I could come to heaven and when I get here I see him enjoying himself when he should be in hell."

"Don't worry, he is in hell. The barrel's got a hole in it and the angel hasn't."

★

A woman returns from her husband's cremation and tips his ashes onto the kitchen table. She then says to them, "You see this beautiful fur coat which I always asked for and never got. Well, I've bought it myself. And you see this pearl necklace I always longed for. Well, I've bought that too. And you see these exclusive leather boots, the one's I always wanted – I've bought them as well."

Then she stands up, leans over the table and says and blows her husband's ashes all over the floor.

"And there's that blow job you always wanted and never got."

Did you hear about the suicide club that held a special meeting? It was the only one.

Did you hear about the wife who couldn't afford a headstone for her husband ? She left his head out.

Two men are walking through a graveyard when they stop to read the writing on one of the headstones which says, "Not dead, just sleeping."
One man turns to the other and says, "He ain't fooling nobody, only himself."

"I'm sorry to hear you buried Jack yesterday," said the neighbour.
"Had to," replied Joan. "He was dead, you see."

A man goes to a fortune teller because he fears he's going to die.
"Don't be silly," replies Gypsy Rose. "You'll live till the ripe old age of 95."
"But I'm 95 now," he replies.
"There, you see, I'm always right."

★

Did you hear about 'good time Sal'?
When she died they had to bury her in a Y-shaped coffin.

★

Three nuns at the pearly gates were being questioned by St. Peter before being allowed to enter.

He said to the first nun, "Who was the first man?"

"Adam," she replied, the gates opened and in she went.

To the second nun he asked, "What was the name of the first woman?"

"Eve," came the reply and in she went.

Then to the third he said, "What were the first words spoken by Eve to Adam?"

"Wow, that's a hard one!" replied the nun and at that the gates opened and she disappeared inside.

Did you hear about the woman who wore black garters?
To commemorate those who passed beyond.

A woman died, went to heaven and asked if she could be reunited with her husband.

"What's his name?" asked the angel.

"Smith."

"Oh dear, we have thousands of Smiths. Is there anything you can tell me about him that would make him easier to find?"

"Well, not really," she replied, "except that he did say just before he died that if I was unfaithful to him, he'd turn in his grave."

"Ah yes," said the angel. "You'll be wanting 'Spinning Smith.'"

A man died with a full erection and no matter how hard the

undertakers tried to put the coffin lid down, it would not close. Eventually they rang up the wife and told her their problem.

"I'll tell you what to do," she said. "Cut it off and stick it up his backside."

The day of the funeral came and as the wife passed the open coffin she looked down at the pained expression on his face and hissed, "There you are you bugger, I told you it hurt."

A new group of men had arrived in heaven and were told to get into two lines. One was for henpecked men, the other for independent, liberated men. However, only one man stood in this second line and when asked why, he replied, "Because my wife told me I had to."

A man arrived in heaven and had to answer a few questions before he was allowed to stay.

"Have you ever done anything good in your life?" asked the angel.

"Well, um... I once gave a blind beggar 5p."

"Anything else?"

"I put 15p in the charity box when they were collecting for the local hospital."

At this the angel turned to the gatekeeper and said, "Give him his 20p back and tell him to go to hell."

An estate agent named Bill Strange was making out his will and one of the instructions he put in was to have his gravestone inscribed with the words "Here lies a truthful man."

"But they won't know who it is," replied the lawyer.

"Oh yes, they will," he smiled, "When people pass by and read the headstone they'll say, 'That's strange!' "

★

A lawyer and the Pope die on the same day and arrive in heaven together. St. Peter takes the Pope to his room which is quite small, poorly furnished and only has a skylight. He then takes the lawyer to his quarters, which are 5-star in comfort and outside is his own swimming pool set in landscaped gardens.

"Wow, I can't believe it!" he gasps. "Why have I got this when the Pope has so little?"

"It's like this; we have many popes up here and it gets a little boring, but we've never had a lawyer before."

★

At the funeral of his wife, Bob was absolutely distraught, his hands over his eyes, moaning and crying. The vicar thought he'd better go and comfort the poor man, so went over, put his arms around his shoulders and said, "Come on Bobby, time will help heal the loss and who knows, maybe one day you'll meet someone new."

"So what?" cried Bob. "Where am I going to get a fuck tonight?"

Two men arrive at the gates of heaven together and get asked some questions by the gatekeeper.

"Right, Mr White. I see from your records that you've lived an exemplary life. You've done a lot for your community, you've been a good husband and a loving father. Just one question, have you ever been unfaithful?"

"Never," replied the man.

"In that case, I grant you a BMW and free petrol to get you around heaven."

The gatekeeper then turned to the second man.

"Well, Mr Black. I see you've not had a bad life, you've been good to your parents, you've worked hard and lived fairly modestly, but just one question, have you ever been unfaithful?"

Mr Black had to admit that he'd been unfaithful on four occasions.

"In that case, I grant you a mini for your transport around heaven."

Some days went by and the two men happened to meet up. Mr White was sitting dejectedly at the wheel of his car.

"What's wrong?" asked Mr Black. "You've got a lovely car, free petrol, why are you looking so down in the mouth?"

He replied, sadly, "I've just seen my wife riding around on a bicycle."

★

An old couple in their eighties die and both go to heaven on the same day where they are met by one of the angels.

After signing in, the couple are shown to their new house. It is magnificent – wonderful views, plush interior, all mod cons and push button controls, plus a limousine in the garage outside. The old man turns to his wife and says, "Bloody hell, Flo, if you hadn't made us stop smoking, we'd have been here enjoying this years ago."

★

One of the world's best wicket keepers had just taken his place on the field when he was struck by a bolt of lightning and died instantly. When he got to heaven he was met by St Peter, who showed him to his new quarters saying,
"If you look out of your back window, you'll see our cricket pitch being prepared for a very important game tomorrow against Hell. It would make us winners of the ashes."
"That's amazing," said the wicket keeper. "I didn't know there was cricket up here."
"Of course, why do you think we sent for you!"

A woman asked her friend at work if she would look after her budgie while she was away on holiday. Unfortunately, the bird was quite old and died within a couple of days. Arriving back at work, the woman asked how her budgie was and her friend replied bluntly, "It's dead, dropped off its perch and that was that."
The poor woman collapsed in floods of tears. "You could have broken it more gently to me, you could have said one minute he was singing his heart out and then all of a sudden he lay quietly down and went to sleep with a smile on his face. At least I could have imagined he

died happy. Anyway, I bet my mum next door was sad to hear the news as well."

"Yes, the day after it happened she was singing merrily in the garden when all of a sudden...."

★

Flo goes along to the local seance to try and get in touch with her late husband.

She's in luck and it's not long before she's asking him how he spends his time in heaven.

"Well, I get up in the morning, have something to eat, do a bit of bonking, take a nap, have something to eat, do a bit more bonking, go for a walk, eat, bonk, eat again and then go to bed," he said.

"But, Alf, you were never like that down here," said Flo, quite amazed.

"No, but I wasn't a rabbit then."

"Doctor, doctor, was the operation successful?"

"Sorry, I'm not the doctor, I'm the Angel Gabriel."

The funeral was halfway through when the vicar got up to talk.

"Come on, someone must have something nice to say about our departed brother," he said.

Silence.

"He must have done something good during his life, can't

anyone remember anything?"

Still there was silence.

"Perhaps he once helped an old lady across the street ... or put some money in a collecting box. Come on, someone say something," he pleaded.

All of a sudden, a man stood up at the back and said, "His brother was worse!"

An old fellow in Yorkshire died of a bad chest and on the day of the funeral, they got him into the coffin and took him up to the cemetery at the top of the hill. Unfortunately, just as they got there the hearse doors opened and the coffin slipped out back down the hill, across the main road and smashed through the door of the chemist's shop. It hit the counter and the top burst open.

"What's going on?" asked the lady in the shop.

The old man in the coffin sat up and said, "Can you give something to stop me coughin'?"

★

The Chairman of a leading travel agency dies and finds himself sitting alone on a cloud. Along comes an angel and says, "Hello, we're having trouble deciding where you should go, whether it should be heaven or hell. So we've decided you can choose for yourself from these brochures."

The angel gives the man some brochures containing pictures and descriptions of both places. Heaven looks very nice and peaceful with lots of lovely scenery and people sitting around

reading or listening to music. Hell looks a lot more lively. Scantily clad girls are frolicking in pools, there are pictures of tables sagging under the weight of sumptuous food, there's dancing, drinking and generally 'a good time' feel. It doesn't take long for the Chairman to decide he'd like to go to hell and with that he's whisked away. A month goes by and the angel happens to be passing Hell's gateway when he sees the Chairman chained to a rock with a pair of bellows in his hand, frantically keeping the flames of Hell burning. He spots the angel and says bitterly, "This is nothing like I thought it was going to be."

"Ah well," said the angel. "You of all people should know better than to believe all it says in the brochures."

A man was lying on his death bed, time was running out and his family were standing round about.

"Joe, Joe," whispered his wife, "is there anything I can do for you? Do you have a last wish?"

Joe lifted his head slowly from the pillow and sniffed the air. He could smell his wife's baking in the oven.

"Can I have just a last slice of the wonderful cake you're baking?" he croaked.

"I'm afraid not Joe, that's for the funeral."

The two men had just reached the 10th hole when a funeral procession went slowly by. The first man stopped playing, took his hat off and bowed his head.

"That was very good of you," said the second man.

"Well it's only right. We were married 27 years and she was a good wife to me," he replied.

★

On the death of her husband, Doris placed a notice in the local newspaper.

"Robert Percy, aged 62, died of VD on June 7, at 3pm."

The next day, she met her friend in the street and her friend asked her somewhat puzzled.

"But Doris, I thought you told me he died of a bowel complaint?"

"He did," she replied "but I'd prefer people to remember him as a great lover rather than the little shit he really was."

★

One of Ireland's greatest footballers died and went to heaven where he was met by an angel at the Pearly Gates.

"Is there any reason why you think you should not be allowed in?" asked the angel.

The footballer thought for a moment and then replied,

"Actually there was an international match that I played in, Ireland against England and I purposefully fell over in the box so that we were awarded a penalty. It helped us to beat England 2-1."

"Well it's not the most serious mistake I've ever heard so you may come in."

"Oh that's wonderful, I've always regretted that moment ….

thank you so much St Peter."

"Think nothing of it," said the angel. "Incidentally, I'm not St Peter; it's his day off today. I'm St Patrick."

"Hello John, how are you?" asked the barman. "How are you managing since your wife died?"

"Not too bad" replied John, "the sex is just the same, but the washing up clogs the sink."

A very successful businessman was lying on his death bed. Just before the end he whispered.

"Beryl, are you there?"

"Yes Jack, I'm here."

"Tom, are you there?"

"Yes dad, I'm here."

"Richard are you there?"

"Yes dad" he sobbed "I'm here."

Suddenly Jack jerked himself up and shouted angrily,

"So who's minding the business then?"

An old woman had been going to the same doctor for over 50 years and during that time had made his life a living hell by constantly complaining about one thing after another.

Eventually, however, she died and was buried in the local churchyard, but it was less than a month later that the doctor also died and was buried in the next plot to her. For a few minutes after the mourners had gone all was quiet and then the doctor heard tapping on the side of his coffin.

"What is it now Mrs Mowner?" he signed.

"Can you give me something for worms doctor?"

It was the funeral of Big John Nowall, the most arrogant man in the district. As his coffin passed into the church one of the spectators turned to the other and said,

"I can't believe Big John's in there, the coffin looks so small."

"Oh that's easy to explain," came the reply. "Once they let all the bullshit out of him, he fitted perfectly."

Asked to identify her missing husband, Beryl went along to the morgue but on pulling back the sheet she shook her head sadly.

"No that's not him," she said looking at the man's well endowed parts, "but some poor woman's lost a good friend."

Two Scotsmen were talking in the pub and one turns to the other saying,

"Now Mick, if I should die first, will you pour a bottle of the finest malt whisky over my grave?"

"That I will," says Jock, "but do you mind if it goes through my kidneys first?"

The beautiful young girl was sitting on the park bench, crying her eyes out. When Matthew saw her unhappiness, he went over and sat down, asking what was wrong.

"Everything," she wailed. "I've just lost my job so I can't pay the mortgage and I'm going to be evicted. Then this morning I discovered I had a fatal hereditary disease which means I'll die in middle age."

"Oh dear," he said kindly, "why don't I try to cheer you up. How about coming out to dinner with me on Friday night?"

"I can't," she sniffed, "I'm going to kill myself on Friday night."

"Well all right then. How about Thursday night instead?"

"Please come in and sit down Mr. Morton," said the doctor, looking grave. "I'm afraid your test results have come back and it's very bad news. You only have a year to live."

Mr. Morton put his head in his hands and gasped,

"Oh no, oh no, what shall I do?"

"Well if I were you," replied the doctor, "I'd move out into the country, to a very quiet place, and marry an ugly, nagging woman. I assure you, it'll be the longest year of your life."

"It was a dreadful shock to us all," sobbed Mrs. Maggs. "Poor old dad!"

"Please don't upset yourself too much," comforted the vicar, "we'll make sure he has a memorable send-off. How old was he, by the way?"

"98," she replied.

"98!" exclaimed the vicar, "so why were you all so shocked?"

"We didn't know he had a bad heart till he went bungee jumping yesterday."

★

Laying on his deathbed, the old man's eyes rested on the face of his sorrowful wife.

"Dear Agnes," he rasped, "we've been through a lot together. When I was just 20 my parents were killed in a car accident, and you were there for me. Then we had the terrible floods of '64 when we lost all our possessions and you helped me through it. Now I've caught this fatal disease and here you are by my side. Do you know," he continued with a spark of anger, "I'm beginning to think you're fucking bad luck for me!"

★

"Hello children," said the new teacher.
"Let's get to know each other better. Tell me what your fathers do for a living."
"My dad's a greengrocer," said Matthew.
"Mine's a doctor," said Jane.
"My dad works in an office," said Becky.
"And what about your father, Simon?"
"My dad's dead, miss," came the reply.
"Oh dear. What did he do before he died?"
"He grabbed his chest, groaned a lot and then fell onto the floor, miss."

★

As the wife watched her husband's coffin disappear into the ground, she turned to her friend and said,
"You know, Ethel, I blame myself for his death."
"Oh why's that then?"
"Because I shot him," she replied.

A 'diddle' of antique dealers are tragically killed in a plane crash and the group of 10 find themselves outside the Pearly Gates.
"Mmmm," said St Peter, scratching his head, "we don't usually let in such a lot of antique dealers at the same time. I'll have to go and ask God."
St Peter went off and found God, hard at work in his office.
"There's a group of antique dealers at the gates, shall we let them in?" he asked.
"Just this once," replied God, "if there's so many of them, they'll be too bothered about each other to cause havoc anywhere else."
St Peter went back to the entrance but returned moments later in a panic.
"They've gone!" he exclaimed breathlessly.
"What? The antique dealers?"
"No," replied Peter, "the Pearly Gates."

Arthur was lying on his deathbed, his wife had been told he only had days to live. As she sat with him on one of his last evenings, he whispered to her, "Oh Rose, now that my life is coming to an end, would you do one last thing for me. It's something that's never happened throughout our married life so please, as a last request, will you give me a blow job?"

Shocked, but caught up in the emotion, Rose agreed and did it there and then. The next day, Arthur seemed slightly better and this improvement continued throughout the week until he started to sit up in bed and take food. The doctors hailed it as a miraculous recovery. Rose just sat there and cried.

"What's wrong?" asked the doctor anxiously, "your husband is going to live, you should be happy."

"I was just thinking," she sobbed. "I could have saved my handsome next-door neighbour."

"Number 11, legs eleven," shouted the bingo caller.

"Bingo!" came the reply, and as the balls were set up for the next game, the caller recognised old Flo sitting miserably in the corner. He walked over and said,

"Hello Flo. What's up? You've got a face like a wet weekend.""Hello Ron," she replied. "My husband died three days ago."

"Oh, I'm so sorry," he said. "So have you come here on your own?"

"I have," she replied, "and the worst thing is that no one can pick me up till much later today, after the funeral is over."

★

On the Couch

A worried wife sent her rugby-mad husband to see a psychiatrist. "Now Mr Owen, let's try some word association. What do you think of if I describe something as smooth, curvy and sometimes difficult to handle?"

"A rugby ball," came the reply.

"Good. Now what about the act of coming up behind someone who is bending down and putting your arms round their waist?"

"A scrum."

"Excellent. And lastly – firm, athletic thighs?"

"A top class rugby player."

"Well, Mr Owen, I can see no problem there. Your reactions are absolutely normal considering some of the silly answers I get in here. Don't worry about it, and I'll see you at the game on Saturday, in our usual seats."

"Hello, is this the right number for the Downside Psychiatric Hospital?"

"That's right."

"May I speak to the man in Room Four?"

"I'm sorry, sir, there is no man in Room Four."

"Hooray, I've escaped !"

A man walks into a bar, orders a pint, drinks it and then wets himself, leaving a puddle all over the floor. The landlord is livid but the man is so embarrassed and so apologetic, he allows him to stay. But after another pint the man does it again – pisses all down his leg. That's it, the landlord throws him out of the pub, telling him never to come back.

A month later, however, he sees the man walk through the door.

"You're banned!" he bellows across the room and the poor man is so embarrassed he rushes out sobbing. Six months go by and one lunchtime the same man appears again.

"Hold on landlord, everything's sorted out now, it was a nervous affliction."

"Well, OK," says the landlord who could see that the man had changed, and he serves him a pint of beer. No sooner had he drunk it than he weed all down his leg onto the carpet.

"You bastard!' roars the landlord. "You told me you had it sorted."

"I have," smiles the man. "I went to a psychiatrist and he taught me not to be embarrassed and upset about it. I'm quite confident now, in fact I feel proud."

★

"I think I know what's wrong with you," said the psychiatrist to his patient.

"You're feeling all screwed up."

"Yes, that's right, how did you know?" replied the patient.

"Well, ever since you walked in, you've been trying to get into the waste paper basket."

★

Did you hear about the psychiatrist who was so busy, instead of a couch he used bunk beds?

A man goes to the psychiatrist. The psychiatrist says, "You're mad".
The man says, "I want a second opinion."
"OK," answers the psychiatrist. "You're ugly too."

A therapist is trying to find out if there is any link between the number of times people have sex and the way they live their lives.
He gathers together a group of people and asks, "How many have sex four times a week?"
Half the class put their hands up.
"How many have sex four times a month?"
Ten hands go up.
"Four times a year?"
Two hands go up.
"And once a year?"
Up pops a hand at the back of the group, belonging to a man who is jumping up and down and smiling all over his face.
"Well," says the therapist, "You're very happy considering you only have sex once a year."
"I am," he cries, "tonight's the night!"

A man goes to see a sex psychologist because he has a fetish about eggs.

"Just look at this, doc," he says, pulling an egg out of his jacket pocket.

"Look at these beautiful curves, the smoothness of the shell, the beautiful colour..."

The psychologist is amazed.

"Do you really believe all this?"

The man whispers quietly to him, "No, not really, but you've got to say these things if you want to get them into bed!"

"Doctor, it's my husband, he thinks he's a chicken."

"Good gracious," replied the doctor. "Why didn't you come to me me sooner?"

"Well, we needed the eggs."

To assess Bob's state of mind the psychiatrist told him he was going to make some random marks on the paper and Bob was to tell him what he saw.

After the first mark Bob replied,

"That's Madonna in the nude."

For the second mark he said,

"That's my next door neighbour stark naked."

and for the third mark,

"That's my wife's knitting circle with no clothes on."

The psychiatrist looked up exasperated.

"The trouble with you, Bob, is that you're obsessed with sex."

"Get off!" retorted Bob angrily. "You're the one drawing the dirty pictures."

★

Did you hear about the psychiatrist who kept his wife under the bed? He thought she was a little potty.

★

"Oh doctor, doctor," said the embarrassed woman. "I think I suffer from being sexually perverted."

"Can you tell me about it? "asked the psychiatrist kindly. "I'm sure it's not as bad as you think."

"I can't possibly," she replied, blushing madly. "It's too awful."

After a few minutes of gentle persuasion the doctor eventually said, "You know many people have strange perversions, even I do. So if you show me yours, then I'll show you mine."

"Well ..." she stammered. "I like my bottom to be kissed."

"Oh goodness that's not much," said the doctor "Pop round behind the screen and then I'll show you mine."

A couple of minutes later, the doctor called her round and he's sitting there looking very smug.

"I thought you were going to show me your perversion?" she says, puzzled.

"I am," replies the psychiatrist. "Look, I've shat in your handbag."

★

A couple went to the psychiatrist and asked him if he minded watching them have sexual intercourse. The psychiatrist was used to odd requests so he agreed and after it was over he charged them £35. The following week they returned and asked him again. He assured them that there was nothing wrong with their technique, but they were so insistent that he relented. Again, he charged them £35.

However, when they came back a third time, the shrink became very suspicious.

"Why are you doing this?" he asked.

"You're doing us a big favour, doc" they said. "I'm married, my girlfriend lives with her mum, and the hotels are very expensive. If we come here it only costs us £35 and I can claim it back on my private health insurance."

★

"I'm very disappointed," said the psychiatrist to his patient. "If you're committed to curing this nervous problem, you must come and see me on a regular basis. Yet it's nearly a month since you missed your last appointment."

The man replied sullenly, "I was only doing what you said."

"What's that supposed to mean? What did I say?"

"You told me to keep away from anyone who got on my nerves.

"And what about your love life?" the psychiatrist asked the woman.

"Well, it's like Bonfire Night," she replied.

"I see. You mean it's full of fun, coloured lights and lots of big bangs?"

"No," she said scornfully. "It happens once a year."

★

"What's up Jack?" asked his mate.

"It's the wife. She introduced me to her psychiatrist this morning. She said 'This is Jack, my husband, one of the men I was telling you about.'"

★

One of the benefactors of the local lunatic asylum is walking around the wards when he sees a man sitting bolt upright in bed pretending to drive and making car noises.

"How are you?" asks the visitor.

"Knackered," replies the patient. "I've had to drive all the way to Scotland to deliver a load of steel."

In the next bed, the patient is frantically moving up and down underneath the covers.

"Everything all right?" he asks, pulling back the bedclothes to reveal a naked man lying face downwards.

"You bet," grins the man. "I'm shagging his wife while he's in Scotland."

★

The woman went for her weekly appointment with the psychiatrist.

"So Mrs Freelot, what have your dreams been about this week?"

"I haven't had any," she replied."

Oh dear," he said sighing deeply. "How can I help you, if you won't do your homework?

★

The man lay down on the psychiatrist's couch and unburdened his problems.

"It all started when I was a teenager. At 15, I really wanted a girlfriend. Then when I found one at 17, she was so dull, I couldn't bear it. I needed a bit of passion in my life, so I dated this girl at work but she was so emotional – crying with happiness, crying with sadness – that it wore me out. I dumped her and went out with someone a little less demonstrative. But she was boring. I decided I needed excitement in my life, so I found a girl who was a real party animal. We'd be out every night, never getting back till dawn and I was really knackered. Half the time I didn't know where she was or who she was with! It was all too much, so I decided to look for someone much more focused, someone who was going places. I found her all right. We got married, but she wanted better things, so she divorced me and took everything I owned. So, doc, all I want now is a girl with big tits."

★

A man was referred to a psychiatrist who decided to start off by testing him with word association.

"I'm going to repeat the same word over and over again and I want you to tell me what comes into your mind. Are you ready? Good. The word is breasts."

"Melons," replied the man.

"Breasts."

"Grapefruit," said the man.

"Breasts."

"Oranges."

"Breasts."

"Windscreen wipers."

"Hold on a minute. Windscreen wipers? I don't understand."

"It's easy," smiled the man. "First, this one, then that one, then this one...."

A man went to the doctor's because he was having trouble with his sex life. He hoped the doctor would be able to cure him of premature ejaculation. The doctor advised him that when he was getting to the point of no return, he should give himself a shock and that would help prolong his lovemaking. Eager to try it out as soon as possible, the man bought a starting pistol and rushed home immediately. To his delight his wife was in bed, naked, waiting for him. Without a second thought, he jumped into bed and they were soon having oral sex. Then as he felt ejaculation coming on, he reached for the gun and fired it. The following day, the man went back to the doctor. He was asked whether it was a success.

"Not really, no," he replied. "When I fired the gun, my wife had a heart attack and bit the top of my penis off, while our next-door neighbour came out of the wardrobe with his hands in the air."

Over the Hill

A little boy and his grandpa were sitting in the garden when the little boy said, "Grandpa, grandpa, see that little worm over there. I bet I can put him back into his hole."

Grandpa accepted the bet and they agreed on £5.

"You'll never be able to do it lad, the worm is too limp to be pushed back."

The little boy disappeared inside and came back and with a can of hairspray. He sprayed the worm until it became as stiff as a board and then quite easily stuck it back in the hole.

"See Grandpa, I win my bet."

Grandpa handed over £5 and said,

"I'm just popping into the house, I'll be with you in a little while."

Sure enough, 10 minutes later he reappeared and handed the boy another £5.

"But Grandpa, you've already paid me," said the boy.

"Ah yes," smiled Grandpa, "but this is from your Grandma."

What's the difference between a stick-up and a hold- up?
Age.

When do you realise you're getting old?
When you have dry dreams and wet farts.

A young journalist was asked to go and interview a celebrated old colonel who had moved into the area. Now the old colonel's reputation for bravery was well documented and the journalist decided to try and get a different angle on the interview. After chatting for about 20 minutes he then asked the colonel if there had been any time when he was really frightened.

The colonel thought for a moment and then replied,

"There was a time when we were deep in the jungle, on the track of a bunch of renegades when suddenly a lion jumped out at me and roared 'Aaarrgh', bloody hell, I shit myself."

The journalist was thrilled with the story.

"When was that?" he asked. "When did that happen?"

"Just now when I went 'Aaarrgh'," replied the colonel.

The social worker was doing the rounds at the local residential home and she stopped to talk to Bob who was 92. After she'd helped him to cut up his food, she noticed a bowl of nuts on a small table next to him. "I was given them as a present," he said, "but I don't like them much. You're very welcome to have them."

Now the social worker was very fond of nuts so she nibbled away on them as she continued to chat to old Bob. As she was about to go she commented,

"Thanks for the nuts, it's an odd present to give to someone with no teeth."

"Oh no," he said. "When I was given them, they had chocolate on."

An old man decides he would like to join a nudist colony so he goes along to spend a day there, before joining up. He strips off, spends half an hour walking around and then, feeling tired, sits down to rest on a park bench. Moments later a beautiful young woman comes along and in no time at all he finds himself with a raging erection. On seeing this, she gets down on her knees and gives him a blow job. 'This is wonderful,' he thinks to himself and immediately goes along to the office to sign up. The rest of the day passes pleasantly and just before he goes home, he drops his cigarette. Bending down to pick it up, a young man comes up and takes him roughly from behind.

Immediately the poor old man returns to the office to cancel his subscription.

"I'm so sorry you've changed your mind," said the owner, "you seemed to like it so much."

"That's true," said the old man, "but at my age I only get excited once a month, but I'm always dropping cigarettes."

★

Two old ladies were on holiday in Greece and had landed up at one of the local museums. As they wandered around they came across a magnificent 12' statue of a greek god, naked apart from a fig leaf. One of the old ladies stood transfixed.

"Come on Mabel," said the othe.r "What are you waiting for, Christmas?"

"No, just autumn," she replied.

An old man hobbled up to the ice cream counter and asked for a chocolate cornet.
"Crushed nuts?" asked the salesgirl.
"No, arthritis," he replied.

"Doctor please help me," begged the old man. "You've got to give me something to lower my sex drive."
"Oh come now Mr Smith, it's all in your head."
"Exactly," moaned the man. "Can't you lower it a little?"

Did you hear about the old man who went to bed and reached across for his wife's hand?
She replied,
"Not tonight Bill, I'm too tired."

What are the signs of growing older?
At the beginning it's tri-weekly, then 20 years later it's try weekly, but after 65 it's try weakly!

A very old man went to the doctors to find out if he was in good working order to enjoy an active sex life.
"OK, I'll have to examine you then," said the doctor, "drop your trousers."
"No need for that," replied the man, sticking out his index finger and his tongue.

★

What's blue and fucks grannies?
Hypothermia.

★

It was the day of the over 60's social club outing to Scarborough. They all boarded at Sheffield and after half an hour Bert had to get up to go to the toilet. On the way back to his seat, the bus lurched and he was thrown onto the lap of an old woman, accidentally elbowing her breasts as he tried to save himself.
"I'm so very sorry," he stammered, "but if your heart is as big as your breasts, I'll see you in heaven."
She replied,
"Well, dear, if your cock's as hard as your elbow, I'll see you in Scarborough."

★

What does an 80 year old woman have between her knees that a young 20 year old doesn't?
Her nipples.

★

"It's no good Doris," said her husband. "I know we've been married for 40 years, but I'm going to move in with Alice next door."
"But why, Alf? Haven't I always been a good wife, kept you happy?"
"Yes ... but Alice gives me oral sex."

"But I give you oral sex as well," exclaimed Doris.
"I know, but you don't have Parkinsons Disease."

An old married couple stopped at a roadside cafe to have a cup of tea before resuming their journey. Thirty minutes later, the man realised he'd left his glasses on the cafe table, so they had to turn round and drive back, the woman complaining all the way about his forgetfulness. They arrived back at the cafe and as he got out of the car she said,
"While you're in there, you might as well get my umbrella too."

Did you hear about the dirty old yachtsman?
He took a young girl out to sea and asked her to toss him off.
The lifeboat is still searching for the body.

Two old ladies are waiting at the bus stop when it begins to rain. The first woman, Doris, is smoking, so she takes a condom out of her bag, snips the end off and puts it over her cigarette to stop it getting wet.
"That's a great idea," enthuses Mabel, "I must do the same, where do you get them from?"
"Just pop into the chemists," Doris replies.
So when they arrive in town, Mabel heads for the chemist shop and asks for a packet of condoms.
"What size would that be Madam?" enquires the assistant.
"I'm not sure," she replies, "One that fits over a Camel please."

★

Two old men were sitting on a park bench commenting on life when one turned to the other and said,

"Now here's an interesting thing, when I was in my 20's and got a stiffie, I couldn't bend it at all. Then in my 30's, I could bend it an inch, in my 40's, I could bend it 2 inches, 3 inches in my 50's and now I'm going to be 60 next week. Doesn't it make you wonder how much stronger I'm going to get!"

★

"Let me tell you," said old William, slurring into his pint of beer.
"Alchohol's a dreadful thing, dreadful. It killed my wife, you know."
"I'm so sorry," replied his listener, "alcoholic was she?"
"No, no, I came home pissed and shot her."

★

A short-sighted spinster was ill in bed and got a visit from what she thought was the vicar. After he had been with her for some time, he left as her friend arrived.

"That was nice of the vicar to call wasn't it?" said the spinster.
"No dear, that was the doctor."
"Oh," replied the spinster. "I thought the dear vicar was very familiar."

A rich but sleazy old man picks up a young girl in the local pub. He buys her drinks all night and then suggests they go somewhere for a late supper. To his astonishment, she agrees and suggests they go to

one of the classiest clubs in town, where she orders all the most expensive food and eats the lot with gusto.

"Goodness me, do you always eat so much?" he asks.

"Only when someone's trying to get into my knickers!" she replies.

An old couple are sitting in deck chairs enjoying a few rays of sun when all of a sudden, a seagull flies overhead and drops his load on top of the man's head.

"Just a moment dear," says the wife. "I think I've got some tissue paper in my bag."

"Don't be daft, Dora, it'll be miles from here by now," he replies.

Three men were moaning about the problems that old age brings.

"Look at me," said the 70 year old. "Every morning I'm woken by the urge to have a pee but when I get up and go to the bathroom I have to stand there ages before anything happens."

"I wish I had your problems," said the 80 year old. "Every morning I go for a shit but I'm so constipated I end up being there for over 2 hours."

"Well you're both bloody lucky," said the 90 year old. "Every morning at 7 o'clock, I have a good piss, and shit like an elephant. The problem is ... I don't wake up until 8.30."

Two women were in the kitchen listening to their husbands' conversation.

"It's incredible," said the first lady, "that all they can talk about is golf and sex."

"Oh I don't know," replied her friend. "You must remember at their ages that's all they can do – talk about it."

★

Two friends meet up at the over 60's social club.

"I haven't seen you in here for a few weeks," commented the first man.

"No, I've been in jail."

"In jail! Whatever did you do?"

"Nothing. It just so happened that I was walking in the park when a beautiful young girl and a policeman rushed up and the girl accused me of sexual assault. Well at my age, I was so flattered, I didn't deny it."

★

Two old men reminiscing about the old times.

"Do you know Sid, when I was just a lad I never slept with my wife before we got married. Did you?"

"I can't remember," said Alf. "What was her maiden name?"

A very old woman is walking down the lane when she sees a frog waving to her.

"Oh Miss," he calls. "Please help me. If you give me a kiss I will turn into a handsome film star and I promise to stay with you forever."

The old woman picks up the frog and puts it straight into her handbag.

"Hey!" shouts the frog. "Aren't you going to kiss me?"

"Oh no," she replies. "When you get to my age what good is a handsome man? A talking frog is much more exciting."

★

An old woman who'd been living on her own for many years was burgled one night. They tied her up, ransacked the house and were just about to leave when the boss turned to his accomplices and said, "Wait outside, I reckon I'll just give her something to remember me by."

"Oh, come on boss," whined the others, "Let's just get out of here before there's any trouble."

Hearing this, the old woman interrupted,

"Now hold on, he's the boss, he'll decide what to do!"

★

Two old ladies talking over half a mild in the local pub.

"Did you hear old Sid had a massive stroke?" said one.

"Oh yes," said the other. "Everyone knew, that's why he was to popular with the ladies."

★

"Look Flo," said the old spinster, "they're selling 3 cucumbers for 60p."

"Well I can always eat the other two," came the reply.

★

He was so old that when he asked the doctor how long he might live, the doctor replied, "Don't go buying any green bananas."

★

An old widower of 80 married a young girl of 26 and not long after astounded the vicar by telling him he would soon be needed for a christening. Recovering from the news, the vicar congratulated the old man and asked him if this was going to be the first of many.
"Oh no vicar, you see my eldest son is going abroad."
Of course the vicar thought the worse but said, "I don't understand. What's your son got to do with it?"
"Well, you see, he used to lift me on and off."

★

A feisty spinster reached 100 years old and attracted the attention of the press.
"How's your health?" asked one.
"Let me tell you, I've never been to a doctor in my life," she replied.
"That's incredible – do you mean to say you've never been bedridden in your life?"
"Of course I have, young fella, in fact table-ended as well, but there's no need to put that in the paper."

★

One resident at the Green Fields retirement home is sitting outside enjoying the early afternoon sun. Every now and again he leans over to the left and immediately a care helper rushes

over and straightens him up. Later that day his son comes to visit and the son asks his father if the home is treating him well.

"Yes and no," comes the reply. "The beds are comfortable, the food's tasty, but they won't let me fart."

★

He has such a bad memory, the only thing to stay in his head for longer than 12 hours is a cold.

★

You know you're getting old when you bend down to tie up your shoes and look around to see if there's anything else needs to be done while you're down there.

★

An old man stopped to comfort a little boy who was crying on a park bench.

"What's wrong, son?" he said.

"I'm crying because I can't do what the big boys do."

So the old man sat down and cried too.

★

Getting old is when you don't comb your hair, you just start re- arranging it.

★

Grandma was 102. She didn't have wrinkles; she had pleats.

(Dennis Wolfering)

★

He's so old that when he asks for a three-minute egg, they ask for the money up front.

★

"I don't understand," said the young widow's friend.

"You say your husband was killed by the bells. What does that mean?"

"Well, my husband was 75 and he would save up all his strength for us to make love on a Sunday to the rhythm of the church bells. He would still be here today if it hadn't been for that blasted ice cream van going past."

★

An old man of 85 was sitting hunched up over his pint, crying his eyes out.

"What's wrong?" asked a fellow drinker.

"I got married two weeks ago to a beautiful curvaceous young redhead who's a gourmet cook, a wonderful conversationalist and fantastic in bed," replied the old man.

"That's wonderful; you're a very lucky man. I don't understand why you're so upset."

"I can't remember where I live!" he cried.

★

It's good to exercise. My grandpa started walking 5 miles a day when he was 60. Today he's 95 and we don't know where the hell he is.

First prize at a fancy dress party for nudists went to a young girl who wore black gloves and black shoes and went as the five of spades.
The second prize went to a 98-year-old man for the best dried fruit arrangement.

You know old age has overtaken you when the phone rings and a sexy voice at the other end says, "Do you know who this is, lover?" And you say "No" and put the phone down.

You know it's old age when you try to straighten out the wrinkles in your socks and realise you're not wearing any.

You know you're getting old when the phone rings on a Saturday night and you hope it isn't for you.
(Ogden Nash)

★

They say life begins at 40. But so does lumbago, rheumatism, deafness and repeating oneself more than three times to the same person.

Two old men sitting on a park bench. One turns to the other and says, "Do you remember when we used to chase the girls down the street?" The other replied, "Yes, I remember chasing them but I can't remember for the life of me why."

An old lady went to the doctor complaining of constipation. "I sit there for hours," she said. "Ah yes, but do you take anything?" asked the doctor. "Oh yes, I take my knitting."

Four very old ladies were walking through the park when a man approached and flashed at them. Two of the ladies had strokes but the other two weren't quick enough.

"Are you sure it's a good idea to marry such a young, energetic girl?" said the doctor to his elderly patient. "You know, such energetic sex could prove fatal." "Oh well," said the old man, "if she dies, at least she dies happy."

Old man looking at his withered penis: "We were born together, we've lived through childhood together, had adventures together, known marriage together, even played together.

So now, why now, did you have to die first?" he sighed.

What is the similarity between men and old age?
They both come too soon.

A rich old man of 88 married a beautiful young girl of 23 and it wasn't long before she was expecting a baby. Overjoyed at the news, the old man was taken aside by his kindly doctor, who had known his patient for a long time and was concerned for his well-being.

"Listen, Jack, it's about the baby. Let's see if I can explain what I mean. There was a big game hunter who'd spent all his life in Africa but was now really too old to last the distance. He decided to go out one last time but being so absentminded, instead of his gun, he took his walking stick with him. Some time went by when suddenly a man-eating lion confronted the man. He lifted his stick and shot the animal dead."

"But, that can't be!" cried his patient, "Someone else must have shot it."

"Absolutely," replied the doctor. "That's what I'm trying to tell you."

The interfering old busybody from next door was complaining that her neighbour's old husband was chasing all the young girls.

"I think it's disgusting," she said.

"Oh, there's nothing to it," replied the wife calmly. "After all,

you've seen dogs chasing cars many times but you never see them catch one, and even if they did, I doubt whether they could drive."

Rosie was bored. In her younger days she'd been known as 'Good time Rose', but since moving to the retirement home there was nothing to do. Then she had a great idea and on the door of her room pinned a notice saying, "The Good Times are back. £30 in bed, £10 on the table."

Nothing happened for a couple of days and then one night there was a knock on the door and old Alfred was standing there.

"I've got £30 here," he said.

"OK, hop into bed."

"Not bloody likely, I want three on the table."

An old retired colonel was invited to a reunion dinner and halfway through the proceedings he rang his wife.

"Agnes, this reunion is turning out to be more than I bargained for. They've got naked girls dancing on the table and then giving their favours to anyone who's interested. What do you think I should do?"

She replied, "If you think you can do anything you'd better get home straightaway."

It's the old man's 100th birthday and as a special treat, all his mates pay for a naked lady to come over and do the business. The doorbell goes and when he opens the door she's standing there in her coat which she lets fall open to reveal that she's totally bare underneath. "Hello, darling," she says seductively. "I'm here for 'Supersex'."

"I'll just have the soup, thanks," says the old man.

Jack and Flo went to stay for a weekend with his parents. There wasn't much room in the tiny flat so Jack ended up sleeping with his dad. In the middle of the night he got an elbow in the ribs.

"Jack, Jack," whispered his dad, "I'm going next door to give your mum a good rogering!"

"What! Dad, it's the middle of the night and you're 75 years old."

"Yes, but I've got such a mighty fine erection – the first for 15 years – and I don't want to waste it, son."

"Well, in that case, I'll have to come with you," said Jack. "You're holding my cock."

A woman knows when she's getting old.

It's when her girdle pinches, but her husband doesn't.

★

"Now, remember, Bert, let that bald man go ahead of you in the toilet. I've heard that hair loss and incontinence usually start at the same time in men over 50."

★

A man of 75 retires to a golfing community and spends every day out on the course. But as time passes, he realises he can't see where the ball is going after a particularly long tee shot, so he goes to visit the eye doctor. The doctor examines him and says, "There's nothing wrong with your eyes except the fact that you're getting on in years. It may be a good idea if you hired a caddy who could spot the ball for you."

The old man follows the doctor's advice and places an ad in the local newspaper. Early the next day the doorbell rings and standing there is a man of 85.

"I've come about your ad in the local paper," he says.

"Gosh!" says the golfer. "Are you sure you'll be able to see the ball at such long distances?"

"No problem at all, I've got the eyes of a hawk," he replies.

So the next day they go out onto the course and the golfer tees off, sending the ball flying down the fairway.

"Did you see where that went?" asks the golfer.

"Sure did," replies the old man.

"Good," says the golfer. "Where?"

"I forget," he replies.

★

An 85-year-old man married a young girl of 25 and the event made headline news on the local radio. The old man was interviewed and asked about his sex life.

"Oh, it's nearly every night," he replied. "Nearly on Monday, nearly on Tuesday …."

★

Old Jack hadn't been feeling too well but had to go out to collect his pension. All went well until he set off for home when suddenly he felt an eruption in his stomach and knew he had to get to the toilet as soon as possible. He wasn't too far from the public toilets, which was lucky really because all hell was about to break loose. He raced into the cubicle backwards to save time, pulling his trousers down as he did, sat down and relaxed .... But as he looked down, he saw two pairs of shoes.

"Bugger me!" he cursed, jumping up quickly. "Sorry mate, I didn't see you there, I didn't mean to shit all over you, it was an emergency." "Oh that's quite alright," replied the man. "It's a good thing I saw you coming and pulled your trousers up before you sat down."

With a few hours to kill before the pubs open a man limps into a faith healing meeting and finds a seat on the front row. After the 30-minute service, the faith healer comes down from the platform and starts to touch some of the people. To the first one he puts his hands over the woman's eyes and she jumps up shouting, "I can see, I can see!"

He then lays his hands on a man who cannot walk and to everyone's delight he gets up out of his wheelchair and begins to dance. And so it goes on, people are being healed left, right and centre. Suddenly, the healer is standing in front of the newcomer and is just about to put out his hands when he shouts, "No, no, don't touch me! I've waited weeks for the orange disability stickers for my car, and they only came this morning."

★

Three old women were having tea on the lawns of the retirement home and the subject turned to memory.

"I may be 75," said the first old lady, "but I can still remember lying in my cot, just days after being born."

"Oh that's nothing," said the second woman scornfully, "I can remember being born. Horrible it was. Going from a nice warm dark place into blinding light and getting my bum smacked. Aagh!"

Not to be outdone by the other two storytellers, the third woman piped up, "I'm 86 and I can remember going to Blackpool with my father and coming back with my mother!"

★

Two old ladies were chatting over a cup of tea in the old people's home.

"It's no good Doris," said one sadly, "Every night I wear my see-through nightie but they're all too old to see through it!"

★

The 85-year-old man went to the doctor's complaining about his love life slowing down.

"When did you first notice this?" asked the doctor.

"Three times last night and twice this morning," he replied.

★

Two old spinsters were catching up on the local gossip.

"I see old Violet Henshaw has just cremated her third

husband," said one.

"So I see," replied the other. "Some of us can't get a husband at all, and Violet's got husbands to burn!"

★

The old couple went to Eastbourne for their two week summer holiday but alas, the day before they were due to return, Maurice collapsed and died. He was brought home by special delivery and the funeral took place a few days later. As friends and relatives filed past his coffin, Rose turned to the widow and remarked,

"Gosh, Ethel, he looks wonderful."

"Oh yes," agreed Ethel, "those two weeks in Eastbourne did him a power of good."

★

An old man had just lost his wife. All he had left was his cat and because he was lonely and had no one to talk to, he thought he would try to teach the cat to talk. He decided to feed his cat the best food and speak to him every day for an hour.

Wonderful salmon, the very best rabbit, an endless variety of birds, this, and much more, was fed to the cat every day. The animal obviously enjoyed the gourmet menu but never said a word. Then one day, the man had just served up a plate of specially prepared mice when the cat shouted suddenly,

"Look out!"

The old man was so dumbfounded, he just sat there with his mouth open and the next moment the ceiling collapsed on top of him, killing him stone dead.

"Silly bugger," said the cat. "Spends two years trying to get me to talk and then when I do, he takes no bloody notice!"

★

The old man was addressing the class of 14-year-olds as part of 'people in the community' week.

"I'm fighting fit," he said. "I've never smoked, I've never had a drink, I don't eat between meals and I've been faithful to my wife for fifty years. Tomorrow I'll be celebrating my 80th birthday."

A voice from the back called out,

"How?"

★

"It's funny how old age affects you," said one old man to the other. "Do you know, it's made my wife's arms shorter."

"Really?"

"Yeah, when we were first married, she could put her arms right round me."

★

An old couple were lying in bed when the woman turned to her husband and said

"Oh Ben, do you remember when you used to nuzzle my neck?"

"Sure do," he replied.

"Will you do it again, for old times sake?"

"Okay," he said, jumping out of bed.

"But where are you going?" she asked, puzzled.

"To get my teeth," came the reply.

Two old men talking over a pint of beer in the local pub. One turns to the other sadly and says,
"You know, George, I'm sick of getting old. I've become so forgetful. First, I forgot people's names, then their faces... then I forgot to pull my zip up and now, heaven help me! I forget to pull it down."

Two old men were sitting on the beach watching the bikini-clad girls walking by, running into the water and playing beach volleyball.
"Do you think all this exercise, keeps you fit?" asked one.
"I should say so," replied the other. "I walk two miles every day just to watch this."

Two old men were sitting in the park talking over past times. They'd got onto the subject of pubs.
"They're more like restaurants, these days," said one.
"And the beer's not so good," replied the other.
"But its the spittoons that I miss," continued the first.
"You always did," came the reply.

★

A very old man would take his daily walk around the garden and that would be the most exercise he could manage before collapsing in his well-worn armchair for the rest of the day. One morning he was halfway round his stroll when to; his surprise he found an old golden idol sticking out of the bushes.

"I say, what have we here?" he murmured and to his further astonishment the idol spoke back.

"Please help me," it said. "I'm not really an idol, I'm a beautiful young girl but many years ago a spell was put on me and it can only be broken if I have sex with a man."

"Oh no," said the man. "I can't manage that sort of thing anymore." She begged him again,

"Oh please, please help me. I've been lost in this undergrowth for years it may be such a long time before another man finds me."

The man thought for a moment and then replied, "Okay, I've got an idea. I'll just go and call my son, he's an idle fucking bastard."

Three aged women were sitting in the park when they heard the sound of the ice cream van and decided to have a cornet each. They played eeny, meeny, miney mo to see who should go and the task fell to Beryl. She took their money, struggled to her feet and set off. It was more than an hour later when Cath turned to the other woman and commented,

"I don't know where our Beryl's got to, I think the old bugger's run off with the money."

"Don't you bloody start," came Beryl's voice from a few yards behind the bench, "or I won't go at all."

★

Gerald returned home from the retirement party his friends had arranged at work and he felt very depressed. Long endless days stretched out before him, nothing to do and no money to spend.

"Come on, cheer up love," greeted his wife. "I've got a surprise for you." She took him by the hand and led him down to the bottom of the garden.

"Look over there," she said, pointing to a luxury apartment block down by the river. "All that is ours."

"What!" he exclaimed. "The whole building? But how, I don't understand."

"Well, do you remember how I used to charge you £50 every time we made love?"

He nodded.

She continued, "I saved up all the money and bought the building for our retirement."

"Oh that's fantastic," he gasped, but then a look of sadness passed over his face.

"Oh Doris, if only I'd known, I would have given you all my business."

Two old blokes were talking.

"Come on Bert, cheer up," said Alfred. "Let's go and have a pint of the dark brew, I hear it puts lead in your pencil."

"No thanks, if it's all the same to you," replied Bert. "I haven't really got anyone to write to."

Two old men were sitting in the park watching the girls walking by in their skimpy outfits.

"By golly, Bernie," said one, "doesn't it make you want to sit them down on your knee and kiss and cuddle them."

"Oh yes," replied the other, "but wasn't there something else we used to do as well?"

★

A very old couple in their 80's went to the doctor for their annual check-up. All seemed well apart from the fact that the wife was worried they were both getting very forgetful.

The doctor replied "If it's worrying you that much, I think I have an idea. Keep a pad and pencil close by and whatever you do, or are planning to do, just write it down on the pad to remind yourselves."

So the couple returned home and later that afternoon, the wife said to her husband,

"Jack darling, I fancy a nice cup of tea. Put a slice of lemon with it, please and also bring me a couple of digestive biscuits."

The husband got up to go to the kitchen when she said suddenly, "Oh and don't forget to write it down."

Her husband laughed. "Come off it, Doris, I'm not so forgetful that I'd get a cup of tea and a plate of digestives wrong."

He disappeared into the kitchen and it was 20 minutes later before he reappeared with a glass of orange and a lightly boiled egg.

"Oh Donald," she reproached him, "I told you you should have written it down. You've forgotten the toast soldiers."

★

Two blind old ladies walk into the gents toilet by mistake to freshen-up. Two men had also just gone in and on seeing the ladies find themselves in a very embarrassing position. Hoping not to be noticed they stand very still. The first lady mistakes one of them for the washbasin. She grabs hold of his willy, pulls it a couple of times and, unable to stop himself, the man begins to pee.

"At least they have nice warm water in here," she remarks to her friend.

"Well this is even better," replies the second, "it dispenses soap as well."

The delicatessen was the most popular venue in town because the pretty young shop assistant was known to wear no knickers. All day long the men would file in and out, always asking for something on the top shelf so that she had to climb up the ladder and reveal all.

In recent weeks there'd been a box of raisin shortcake on the top shelf and, of course, they'd never been so popular! Dozens of times a day she'd be up and down the ladder and was just reaching for another tin when an old man came into the shop. "I suppose yours is raisin too," she called down to him.

As he looked up and saw the delights on view he replied, "Not yet, but it's beginning to stir."

Two old women limp towards each other along the pavement. As they pass, one points at her foot and says, "Bad arthritis, had it ten years."

The other replies, pointing at her foot, "Dog shit, got it round the corner a minute ago."

★

A vain man was determined to get an all-over suntan, but when he looked in the mirror he saw he was bronzed everywhere except for his penis. Then he had a great idea. He found a deserted, out-of-the-way part of the beach, buried himself completely in sand apart from his penis which he left sticking out to catch the sun's rays. Later on that afternoon, two old women happened to walk by and one said to the other. "You know Doris, it's so unfair. When I was eight, I didn't like it, when I was 18, I was very intrigued by it, then when I was 25, I loved it. In my 40's I went looking for it, in my 50's I yearned for it and now in my 70's I've almost forgotten about it. But look Doris, look at that, the bloody things are growing wild now."

★

An old spinster was getting married for the first time and the thought of sex was troubling her. When her friend heard about her fears she advised the spinster to get a cucumber and practice with it. The spinster took up the idea and a few weeks passed before they met again.

"Are you more confident about the wedding now?" asked her friend.

"Oh bugger the wedding," came the reply, "I've bought a stock of cucumbers instead!"

She's Gotta Have It

What's the difference between a cockerel and a nymphomaniac? The cockerel says "Cock-a-doodle-do" while the nymphomaniac cries "Any cock'll do."

What's the first thing a nymphomaniac learns when she starts taking driving lessons?
You can also sit up in a car.

Did you hear about the nymphomaniac who robbed a bank?
She tied up the safe and blew the guard.

Why is a nymphomaniac like a door knob?
Everyone gets a turn.

Did you hear about the nymphomaniac who when asked how many husbands she'd had, replied, "Shall I count my own?"

Have you heard about the nymphomaniac in the newsagent's?
When asked by the man if she kept stationery she replied, "I do up to the last ten seconds and then I go absolutely mad."

What's the difference between a nymphomaniac and butter?
Butter is difficult to spread.

What do you get if you cross a nymphomaniac with a dictionary?
A fucking know-it-all.

A priest went to see sweet Mary O'Sullivan who was in hospital for appendicitis.
"Hello Mary, I prayed for you last night," he said.
"Oh there's no need for that," she replied. "Just look me up in the phone book."

★

What's a nymphomaniac's great dilemma?
Meeting a man with V.D. who has got an enormous dick.

★

A nymphomaniac went to buy her latest boyfriend some cricket equipment.
"How much are the stumps?" she asked.
"£15 Miss."
"And the bat?"
"£20."
"Well I can only afford one, so I'll take the bat."

"How about a ball for the bat?" persisted the pushy salesman.

"No thanks," she replied, "but I'll blow you for the stumps."

★

A 'good time' girl went up to a man leaning on the bar and whispered in his ear

"Hey, big boy, I'm all yours for just £100."

"Blimey, that's a lot of money," the man replied.

"Yeah, but for that you get anything and everything you desire," she cooed, pressing her voluptuous body against his. "And I mean anything!"

She saw he was getting interested so she continued,

"Yes, any fantasy you like, come on, just whisper three little words in my ear and it'll be done for just £100."

"Just £100," he mused.

He thought for a moment and then said, "Decorate the house."

★

It was almost a disaster when the blonde accidentally made two dates on the same night.

But it was all right in the end... she managed to squeeze both of them in.

★

What do you get when you cross a nymphomaniac with a Dry Cleaning specialist?

Someone who'll suck your laundry.

★

"You just wouldn't believe it," said the dumb blonde to her friend. "Men always assume you're going to spend the night with them. I'm sick of it. Take last night for example. I was over at this bloke's flat and he took it for granted I was stopping. Well! that was the last straw! I was so insulted, I put my dress back on and left."

★

A young girl, not inexperienced in the ways of sex, was browsing through the big department store when she spotted the most beautiful pair of shoes she'd ever seen.
"Oh, I must have them," she said to herself, but the price was outrageous. However, not discouraged she sought out the manager who happened to be a young buck in his 30's and thought he was God's gift to women. It wasn't long before they came to an agreement that she would have the shoes in return for a few favours in the storeroom.
"I'll soon have you screaming with delight," he boasted.
They went into the back, he proudly revealed his todger and off they went. But no matter how much effort he put into it, she hardly reacted. She just lay there looking at her prize shoes lying at her side.
Now the man's pride was at stake, so he went at it for a second time. But he still didn't get the reaction he was looking for. So he tried a third time and to his immense relief, she began to move, lifting her legs higher and grabbing him tighter around the neck.
"That's my boy," he said to himself and then smugly remarked to the girl, "You see, I told you it would be the

best you've ever had."

"Oh, don't be daft," she replied. "I'm just trying on my new shoes."

★

What does a nymphomaniac say after sex?
Thanks guys.

★

Simon had such a bad throat, he could hardly speak. So he decided to pop round to the doctor's surgery.
He knocked at the door and it was opened by the doctor's beautiful young daughter.
"Is he in?" he whispered.
"No," she whispered, looking around. "Come on in."

★

Why is a nymphomaniac like a doorknob?
Everyone gets a turn.

What happens when a group of nymphomaniacs have a party?
Everybody comes.

What's the four letter word a nymphomaniac usually screams out during sex?
Next.

★

The nymphomaniac looked at the strapping young man and said "Hey, big boy, can you make love to me and hurt me?" "Sure can," he said.
So he fucked her and then hit her over the head with a blunt instrument.

★

A nymphomaniac is out to have a good time and meets up with three blokes in the local nightclub. She can't decide which one to make a play for, but noticing they all stutter, she devises a plan. "Look chaps," she says. "If one of you can tell me where you come from, without stuttering, I'll give them a blow job."
The lads agree enthusiastically.
"I come from L-L-Liverpool," says the first.
"Oh shame," she says.
"I come from B-B-Birmingham," says the second.
"Never mind," she replies.
"I come from London ...."
"Great," she says and in a flash has his cock out of his trousers. But just as she's about to perform he says,
"..d-d-derry."

★

A nymphomaniac was doing her gardening one Sunday afternoon when the wind blew her skirt up to reveal her bare arse. At this moment a dog appeared in the garden and stuck his tongue in her crotch. Without looking around she whispered, "Whoever you are, I do the gardening three times a week, Sunday afternoon, Friday and Saturday mornings."

Did you hear about the young girl who failed her driving test?
When the car stopped, she automatically got into the back seat.

Did you hear what happened when the nymphomaniac went to the library?
She got a book out called 'How to Hump' and didn't realise until she got home that it was vol.4 of the encyclopaedia.

On the Field
of Play

Football

This Glasgow Celtic fan was such a fanatic even the house was painted green and white.

His wife said, "I'm pissed off, you think more of Celtic than you do me."

"Christ Almighty, woman," he said. "I think more of fucking Rangers than I do you."

Who is the most unpopular person on the terraces at Borussia Monchengladbach?

The guy who stands up and shouts, "Give us a B."

A block of flats is on fire and a woman with a baby is trapped on the eighth floor. She is leaning out of the window, screaming for help.

Below her on the pavement, the crowd are urging her to throw down the baby, saying they will catch it, but she is afraid it might be dropped. Then along comes Peter Shilton who persuades her that the baby will be safe in his hands. So at last convinced all will be well she throws down the baby and to much cheering and clapping he catches the baby ... bounces it twice and boots it up the street.

★

On holiday, Bob was amazed when he went to see the local football team and halfway through the match they all suddenly stood stock-still except one, who put the ball behind his back.

**"What's going on?" he asked the supporter next to him.
"They're just posing for this week's 'Spot The Ball'
competition."**

The nymphomaniac volunteered to put up some of the men from the
visiting football club. Six of them should have arrived after the match
but one called Dix injured himself during the game and had to go to
hospital.

On hearing the doorbell, she opened the door and greeted them
enthusiastically.

"So how many do I get?" she said. "There are five of us here without
Dix," they replied.

And she slammed the door in their faces.

★

**A professional footballer was out on a first date and after the
pubs closed he invited her back to his place. Removing his
jacket, she noticed UMBRO tattooed on both arms and he
explained it was part of an advertising campaign and he
received £1,000 for each arm. When he saw how impressed
she was he removed his shirt and there across his chest was
the word PUMA.**

**"I got £1,500 for this," he said. "And £800 each for these"
and he dropped his trousers to show the word KAPPA
tattooed on both ankles.**

**"But this is the best," he laughed and with that he showed her
his penis.**

"Oh!" she exclaimed. "Why SLAG?"

"No, no," he replied, "I got £8,000 for this and if you stay around a while you'll see it says SLAZENGER."

Who says girls can't make the football team?
Suzie did! She's so athletic, she'll play ball with anyone.

"I'm transferring you to North Nogoland," said the boss to his salesman.

"But, sir, all you ever get there are whores and footballers."

"My wife comes from there!"

"Really, what position did she play?"

"Football, football, football! I'm sick of it. If you took me out on Saturday afternoon instead of going to the match I think I'd die of shock."

"Now, now, dear," said her husband. "It's no good trying to bribe me."

Did you hear about the two football managers of a local derby? They promised their players a pint of beer for every goal scored. The result was 50-49.

It was the women's football league final and a large crowd had turned out to watch. But 10 minutes into the game, the goalkeeper was thrown against the post and knocked to the ground. Immediately, all the linesmen and officials rushed over to give her help but after five minutes and no sign of recovery, the referee walked over to find out what was going on.

"We're trying to give her the kiss of life," explained one of the officials, "but she keeps trying to get up and walk away."

★

"Hey ref, are you blind or what?" shouted the angry fan in the crowd as he saw his team's striker fouled yet again. The ref walked over to the heckler and shouted, "What did you say?" "Bloody hell," replied the man, "he's deaf as well."

★

Two men went to watch Bradford City. When they got to the ticket booth, one of them handed over £20, and said "Two, please". "Certainly, sir," replied the ticket seller. "The home dressing room's down that way; take your pick."

★

A man walks into the local pub with a parrot on his shoulder to watch Wales playing Albania on TV. The match soon starts to go Albania's way and after 10 minutes they score from a free kick. All of a sudden, the parrot starts to make awful moaning noises.

"Sorry," says the man, "he's a fanatical Wales supporter, so

he's obviously quite upset."

The score remains the same until half-time but Albania score a second goal only 5 minutes into the second half. This time the parrot is besides himself with anguish – moaning, stomping up and down and burying his head in his feathers. When a third Albanian goal is scored, there's absolute chaos. The bird starts pulling out all his feathers until there is a pile of them on the floor.

"Jesus!" says the barman, "if he reacts like this when they lose, what's he like when they win?"

"I don't know, I've only had him a few years."

★

"Now, listen son, we can't afford for you to get injured before the Cup match next week, so I'll put you on for the first 45 minutes and pull you off at half-time."

"Wow, thanks Boss, all I got at my old club was a slice of orange at half time."

★

While David Beckham is hanging around in a department store one day, waiting for Posh to finish trying on frocks, he wanders into the kitchen department, and sees a cylindrical metal object which he finds very intriuging.

"What's this?" he asks the assistant.

"It's a Thermos flask," she replies.

"But what does it do?" asks the Boy Wonder.

"It keeps hot things hot, and cold things cold," the assistant tells him.

Thinking this is marvellous, David buys one, and takes it to training with him next day.

"Look what I've got," he tells the lads, proudly. "It's a Thermos flask." The lads are impressed.

"What does it do?" they ask.

"It keeps hot things hot and cold things cold," replies David.

"And what have you got in it?" asks Gary Neville.

"Two cups of coffee and a choc ice," says David.

★

A famous footballer was asked if he would appear nude in a glossy magazine.

"We'd like you to pose holding a ball," explained the editor.

"OK, but what do I do with my other hand?"

★

Two Manchester United fans are walking along the street when one of them sees a mirror on the ground. He picks it up and says, "Hey, I recognise that bloke."

The other man takes it from him and replies,

"Of course you do, you wanker, it's me."

★

Which 3 league teams have swear words in their names?

Arsenal, Scunthorpe and Manchester fucking United.

A Plymouth Argyle fan is walking through the park one day when he stumbles over an old lamp. A genie pops out and tells him he has just one wish, what would he like. The man looks down at his dog and tells the genie he would like his dog to win the Crufts Dog Show to become supreme champion.

"You've got to be joking!" replies the genie. "Just look at him. He must be on his last legs, he's a flea bitten old mongrel with half a tail."

"OK," sighs the man, "in that case can you make Plymouth win the FA Cup?"

The genie looks at him for a moment and then says,

"Let's have another look at this dog then."

A footballer got kicked in his vital parts and lay doubled up on the ground holding himself and moaning.

"Are you alright mate?" asked the first-aid man, rushing up to him.

"For God's sake," groaned the man, "don't worry about rubbing them, just count them!"

Every weekend, her husband would be out playing football with his local team and while he was away, Gloria would entertain her lover. However, disaster struck one afternoon when the pitch was so waterlogged that the husband came back early.

"Quick," whispered the wife, "crouch down behind the sofa, it's too late to get away."

Unfortunately, the husband settled himself down and didn't look as if he was going to move.

"Bugger this," muttered the lover to himself, and he stood up wearing only jockey shorts and a vest saying, as he walked out of the door, "Bloody weather, can't see a thing, you didn't see which way the cross country runners went?"

A motorist is stopped for going through a red light and is asked to take a breathalyser test.

"I can't blow," says the man. "I suffer from asthma," and he shows the policeman his asthmatics card.

"OK, then we'll have to take you down to the station for a blood test."

"I can't. I'm a haemophiliac," and he produces a doctor's card.

"In that case, it'll have to be a urine test."

Once again, the man produces a card from his wallet. It reads 'Manchester City Supporters Club – Please don't take the piss'.

Coventry CIty suffered a break-in recently when thieves stole the entire contents of the trophy room. Police are looking for a man carrying a roll of sky-blue carpet.

"Did you notice the football team ogling that girl as she walked by?" the wife asked her husband.

"What football team?" came the reply.

Two football fans were down at the front of the crowd when some hooligans towards the back started to throw beer cans. One of the fans got very agitated and couldn't concentrate on the game properly.

"Don't worry," said his mate. "It's like the war, if it's got your name on it..."

"That's the trouble," interrupted the other. "My name's Foster."

Two rival football supporters travelled home from the match in the same railway compartment. As Tony got up to go to the buffet car, he asked the other if he could get him anything.

"Thanks mate," replied the man. "A glass of lager please."

When Tony had gone, the rival fan gobbed in Tony's football cap which was lying on the seat. Then Tony returned and handed over the glass of lager, which he drank down greedily. At last it was Tony's stop and as he got up to leave, he put his cap on and immediately realised what had happened.

"You know mate," he said looking at the smirk on the other's face, "we really should stop doing all this – gobbing in caps and pissing in lager."

The Manchester United players are all in the dressing room ten minutes before kick-off, when Roy Keane comes limping in, looking in pain.

"Sorry boss, it's my back," he says to a worried Alex

Ferguson, "I pulled a muscle in training yesterday, and I won't be able to play unless I get a cortisone injection."

"Hey!" says David Beckham, "if he's getting a new car then I want one as well!"

★

Golf

"What happened to you?" exclaimed his mates, as Jack walked into the bar with a black eye.

"I got it playing golf," he said rather sheepishly, "and before you ask, it wasn't a golf ball it was a club."

Laughing into their beer, his mates insisted on hearing the full story.

"Well, I hit a bad shot and my golf ball landed in a field of cows. When I went to retrieve it, one of the women golfers was in there also looking for a lost ball. Luckily I found mine quite quickly and was about to leave when I noticed one of the cows frantically flipping its tail. I walked over, lifted the cow's tail and saw a golf ball wedged in its crack. So I called the lady over, raised the tail and said 'This looks like yours'. That's when she hit me with the club."

Angry wife to husband:

"You were twice as long on the golf course today. Why's that?"

"A slight problem," replied the husband.

"Old Jack died on the ninth hole and from then on in it was play the hole, drag Jack, play the hole, drag Jack, play the hole..."

★

Two skinflints decided to put a small wager on their game of golf. £1 to the winner was agreed and they set off. By the end of the sixth tee, all was equal, but then Clive hooked his ball into the rough. Try as they could, there was no sign of his ball, and it would mean that Clive would drop at least two strokes. Thinking of the wager they'd put on the game, he waited for Gerald to turn his back, then took out a second ball, dropped it on the grass and shouted in triumph.

"Ah, found it at last, here it is."

"Clive, you're a bloody cheat," said Malcolm angrily. "That's not your ball, there's no length you won't go to just to win the bet."

"Now look here," blustered Clive. "How do you know it's not my ball?"

"Because I've been standing on it for the past five minutes," replied Malcolm.

★

An Englishman, Scotsman and Arab were talking about their families.

"I have 10 children," said the Englishman. "One more, and I'll have my own football team."

"I have 14 children. One more, and I'll have my own rugby team," replied the Scotsman.

"Well, I have 17 wives," said the Arab. "One more and I'll have my own golf course."

★

Two men were playing golf on the eighth hole when a funeral procession went by. One of the men stopped playing, put down his club and bowed his head.

The other said, "That was very decent of you."

"Well she was a good wife to me you know," replied the first.

For more than six months a woman had been having golf lessons but still couldn't hit the ball more than a few yards down the fairway.

Unable to take it any longer, her coach shouted, "You're not holding the club properly! Hold it like you hold your husband's cock!"

So the woman did and the ball flew through the air landing on the green.

"That's terrific," said the stunned coach. "You can take the club out of your mouth now."

A golfer was returning to the clubhouse after a disastrous day on the links. He'd been over par on every hole, lost three balls, and eventually thrown away most of his clubs in a fury.

As he stamped up to the clubhouse, he stood on a rake and yelled, "That was the best two balls I've hit today."

★

A young couple meet on holiday and after a whirlwind romance decide to get married.

"I must warn you," says the man, "that I'm golf crazy. I like to play every day, you'll hardly ever see me."

"Don't worry," she says. "I have something to confess as well. I'm a hooker."

"That's OK," he says. "You're probably not keeping your wrists straight."

★

It was competition day at the local golf club and the retired colonel found himself paired up with the bishop.

They set off and it wasn't long before the colonel forgot who he was playing with and on missing a short putt exclaimed, "Shit! Missed the bastard!"

The bishop shook his head reproachfully.

A little later, the same happened again, and the colonel missed an easy putt.

"Shit! Missed the bastard!" he shouted loudly, at which point the bishop was forced to tell him that the Almighty would not be pleased with his language and that something dreadful might happen to him. But almost immediately on the next hole the Colonel missed his drive and was so incensed he shouted and swore for a good half minute.

All of a sudden the skies opened, there was a terrible clap of thunder, and lightning struck the Bishop dead.

After a short pause a voice was heard from above,

"Shit! Missed the bastard!"

★

Each week the vicar and retired colonel played a round of golf and no matter how well he did, the vicar was never able to beat him. After one very close defeat the colonel turned to him and said, "Don't worry Vicar, you win in the end. You'll be burying me in the not too distant future."

"That's true," said the vicar dispiritedly. "But even then it'll be your hole."

★

A group of men, very competitive when it came to golf, were arguing on the ninth tee. When the Captain arrived and asked what was wrong they replied,

"See my partner Bob over there lying in the bunker? He's just died of a stroke and these buggers want to add it to my score."

★

It was the honeymoon night and the happy couple strip off as quickly as possible and jump into bed. But just before they start, she whispers to him, "Before we start, I feel I must tell you that one of my previous lovers was the Captain of our local golf club."

"Listen love," he replies. "Whatever went on before doesn't matter; we're married now, and nothing will come between us." And for the next 30 minutes they vigorously do the business. Afterwards the husband lights a cigarette and picks up the phone.

"What are you doing?" she asks.

"I'm going to get us some smoked salmon and pink champagne - we deserve it," he says smiling.

"Oh no," she says, "the Captain of the golf club would have made love to me again."

So once again they have 30 minutes of unbridled passion and then once again he calls for room service.

"No, no," she cries, "he would have done it a third time."

Again, they do it but by this time the husband is feeling knackered.

He reaches for the phone and before she can say anything, he

says wearily, "I'm just ringing the golf Captain to find out what the par for the hole is."

"Molly, would you get married again if I died?" asked her husband.
"Probably," she replied.
"And would you share with him all the little things we did together?"
"I expect so," she said.
"And would you let him have my prize golf clubs?"
"Oh no," she replied, "he's left handed."

A local golf club was being built for the less well off in the district and it was agreed that the women's team would practise once the men had finished and they would share the same equipment. That night, once the men had gone, the ladies walked out to the first hole when they suddenly heard an anguished voice behind them.
"Hold on," shouted Doreen. "I've got the clubs but the men have gone home and taken their balls with them!"

★

"My doctor has told me I must give up golf."
"Oh, I see he's played with you too!"

★

Every Sunday afternoon when her husband was away on the local golf course, the wife would entertain her lover on the sofa. The two were humping away so passionately one afternoon that they didn't notice how bad the weather had got until they heard her husband walking up the garden path. In blind panic, the man jumped off and hid behind the sofa as he walked in.

"Couldn't play in that weather," he complained. "Can't see a yard in front of you." And with that he settled down to read the newspaper. An hour passed and the man behind the sofa had such bad cramp he couldn't take it any more. He stood up, picked up the husband's clubs and strode confidently to the door remarking, "Bloody weather, you didn't happen to see a ball coming this way?" And with that, he was gone.

The local golf club was having an 'Open Day' to attract new members and one man from the wrong side of town asked the official, "Is this where the changing rooms are at?"

"My dear, sir, you do not finish a sentence with a proposition, I'll have you know."

"OK, by me," replied the man. "Is this where the changing rooms are at, fuck face?"

A man joined the local golf club and before taking a walk round the greens, he decided to have a couple of drinks in the bar. When he tried to pay he was told,

"That's alright Sir, it's on the house for new members."

He then decided to have lunch and again they refused his money.

Feeling well pleased with himself, the new member decided he'd have a go at a few practice shots so he went too the club shop for some golf balls.

"That'll be £5 each – £30 please Sir."

"Christ," commented the man, "they've got you by the balls round here."

An old man knocked at the door of the solicitors' offices and asked one of the partners if his grandson, an articled clerk, could have the afternoon off to accompany him to the last day of the Open at Wentworth.

"I'm afraid you're out of luck. He's taken the afternoon off to go to your funeral," came the reply.

★

Three blokes met up to play golf on Sunday morning and compared notes on how they managed to get their wives to let them go. The first said he'd brought his wife breakfast in bed, taken the dog for an early morning walk and washed the car.

"She was so pleased, she was delighted to let me go" he said. The second man recounted how he'd prepared everything for Sunday lunch and cleared up the kitchen from a dinner party the night before.

"She reckoned I'd earned a round of golf," he said.

The third man looked at his mates and said,

"I woke up, belched twice, scratched my balls and let rip with a real stinker. Then I said to her 'Come on then, intercourse or golf course?' She couldn't wait to see me go."

On his tour of the world's best golf courses, a man ends up on a course in Africa. As he sets off for the first hole, he is accompanied by a caddie who carries a shotgun.

"Surely we don't need that," he says.

"Believe me, we do," replies the caddie.

All goes well until they get to the 7th hole and the man's tee shot lands in the bunker. As he steps into the sand a huge cobra suddenly looms up and as quick as a flash, the caddie aims his gun and shoots the snake dead.

"Bloody hell, I see what you mean," says the golfer, sweating profusely.

Then at the 12th hole, the ball lands in the rough and as the golfer goes over to hit it, a lion appears unexpectedly.

Again, the caddie immediately takes aim and frightens the lion off with a gun blast. The rest of the holes are played without interruption but on the 18th the golfer finds he's hit the ball close to the water. As he steps up to take the shot a crocodile rears up out of the lake and grabs hold of him.

"Quick man, do something!" he yells at the caddie.

"Sorry, sir, I can't give you a shot at this hole."

★

For a whole week, the golfing instructor has been giving lessons to a new female member of the club and at the end of the session he invites her out for a drink. She accepts and they

go off into town. After a couple of drinks, he invites her to dinner, then to a club and finally back to his place.

"Look, Ron," she says as they sit close together on his sofa, "I think I ought to tell you that I'm not really a woman, I'm a transvestite."

"Why you awful, you dreadful, you... you... immoral..."

"Come on, Ron, we are living in a more tolerant society."

"But it's unforgiveable. You've been playing off the women's tee all week!"

★

Jack and his wife were playing a round of golf but on the seventh tee, Jack's ball landed behind the maintenance shed.

"Don't worry," said his wife, "there's no need to take a penalty shot, if we open both doors and take out the mowers you can drive straight through."

They did as she suggested and he gave the ball a mighty hit. Unfortunately he missed the far opening and the ball ricocheted back and hit his wife in the head, killing her stone dead.

A couple of days later he was playing a round of golf with his friend and to his astonishment, ended up in a similar position.

"No need to take a penalty shot," said his friend, "just open the doors at either end of the shed and hit the ball through."

"Not bloody likely," replied the man. "I tried that a couple of days ago and ended up with a double bogey."

★

An irritable old man was taking a short cut across the golf course when he got struck by a golf ball.

"I'm terribly sorry," said the player, running up to him.

"That's not good enough. I've got a weak heart, anything could have happened. I demand £500 in compensation."

"But I said fore!" exclaimed the player.

"OK, done," replied the man.

"I really want to give this my best shot," said Jack to his mate. "My mother in law is watching from the clubhouse balcony."

"Oh get away!" replied his friend. "It's too far away, you couldn't possibly hit her from here."

A man drives his Rolls Royce into the Golf Club car park and as he's getting his clubs out of the boot a fellow member comes up to him.

"That really is a beautiful car," he says. "May I ask how much it cost you?"

"Oh about £250,000," replies the man looking pleased.

"And how long have you had it?" he continues.

"About 4 years, I work for Cunard you know."

"So what!" retorted the man "I work fuckin' hard too, but I still couldn't afford a Rolls Royce."

The pompous club pro was challenged to a round of golf by one of the less experienced members for a prize of £100. The pro, smiling to himself, immediately took up the challenge, "but" said his partner "as long as you agree that I can have two 'geronimos'." Not knowing what these were, but confident in his own ability, the club pro agrees. At the end of the round, the other members are astonished to see the pro handing over £100.

"We can't believe it," they said. "What happened?"

"Well, I was just swinging my club down for the first hole, when my partner grabs me by the bollocks and shouts 'geronimo!'." Imagine trying to play the next 17 holes, waiting for the second one."

Beryl had been moaning at Jack for ages because he wouldn't teach her golf. Eventually it got him down so much he gave in and took her out one Monday afternoon. After spending some time explaining the finer points of the game they stepped up to the 1st tee and Beryl hit a mighty drive which landed straight onto the green and disappeared into the hole.

"OK," said Jack, "I'll take a practice shot now, and then we'll begin."

The men were talking in the Clubhouse bar after spending a day on the greens. Each was recounting their golfing experiences.

One said,

"If I'm going round on my own, the dog comes to keep me company and if I go one over par on a hole he somersaults backwards."

"That's incredible!" responded the others.

Warming to the subject, the man continued.

"And if I go 2 over par at a hole, he does a double somersault backwards."

"Amazing," came the response, "that's quite a feat, how does he do it?"

"Oh, I kick him twice."

★

Two lady golfers were teeing off on the 7th hole when the second player's shot went so wide it hit a man on the 8th tee. He clasped his hands to his crotch in agony as he fell to the ground.

"Oh I'm so very sorry," said the woman as she ran over to help him. "Is there anything I can do? I'm a masseuse so I might be able to ease the pain."

With that, she ordered the man to lay out on the ground, put his hands by his side, undid his trousers and started to massage his manhood. "There, is that helping?" she asked looking very concerned.

"That's great," he replied, "but my finger is still throbbing."

★

"What's wrong Beryl?" asked Joan, seeing her friend in floods of tears.

"It's Jack, he's left me."

"Oh get away, he's always walking out on you."

"No, no, you don't understand. This time it's for good, he's taken his golf clubs."

★

This businessman arrives for a conference in Japan, and on the first night is taken to one of Tokyo's most exclusive brothels. He is soon closeted with a charming young thing, and before long he is banging away at her.

"Ohhh, push 'arder, push 'arder!" she moans, so he does his best to satisfy her.

"PUSH 'ARDER, PUSH 'ARDER!" she continues to cry out, as she writhes around on the bed.

The man redoubles his efforts to shove every last inch into her, and soon he is slumped on the bed, gasping for breath, utterly exhausted, but well satisfied.

The next day he is invited to play a round of golf with Mr Sakamoto, the managing director of a big Japanese firm. Mr Sakamoto tees off, and slices the ball so badly, that it flies off at right angles, and ends up in the adjacent 18th hole.

"Damn it!" exclaims Mr Sakamoto in irritation. "Push 'arder!"

"Push 'arder?" asks the businessman, puzzled. "What does that mean, exactly?"

"Wrong hole," replies Mr Sakamoto.

★

"I say James, did you take my advice and get those new bifocals?"

"Yes, thanks Martin, I did, and it improved my golf dramatically, just as you said it would. When I looked down I saw two balls, a big one and a little one, and when I looked at the green, I saw a big hole and a little hole. So I just hit the small ball into the big hole and hey presto! Worked like a dream."

"So why aren't you wearing them now?"

"Bit of a faux pas," replied James. "Wet my trousers, don't you know. After the game I went to the toilet, looked down and saw one small 'fellow' and one large. Well I knew the big one couldn't be mine, so I put it away again."

★

A husband was being asked by the coroner's court the circumstances surrounding his wife's death.

"It was a dreadful accident," he said.

"I was teeing off at the seventh hole, when I hooked it badly and it hit my wife on the head. She died later, in the ambulance."

"Yes," agreed the coroner, "that seems to explain the injuries, but could you please tell me why she had a golf ball stuck up her arse?"

"Well, the first shot had been so bad, I decided to take it again."

★

"It's no good Bernard, I can't play anymore, it's the old stomach, not so good," said Lewis as the two friends walked onto the ninth fairway.

"That's a shame," replied Bernard. "Are you sure?"

"Very. To tell you the truth, I farted at the last hole."

"Well that's no big deal."

"No, but you see, the trouble is, I followed through."

★

Two blokes were in the Clubhouse having drinks. One turned to the other and said, "I say, did you hear about poor old Malcolm? Pressure got to him, you know. Went berserk yesterday and beat his wife to death with a golf club."

"Poor show," replied Gerald, "but just for the record, how many strokes?"

★

Out on the Cricket Pitch

Three cricket managers meet up to talk over the previous cricket season and as they are strolling back to their hotel they notice a sign saying 'Come and find out what the future has in store for you – speak to Mystic May now.' They've had a bit to drink, so decide to go in and have some fun.

"We'd like to know if God's a cricket fan, and if so, can he tell us how our teams will do in the future?" says one of them, winking at the other two.

But Mystical May takes them very seriously and asks them which teams they manage and what they want to ask.

The first says, "When will Somerset win a major trophy?"

After a moment's silence, a loud voice is heard: "2040."

"Damn, I'll have gone by then."

The second man asks the same question for Lancashire and the voice says, "2038."

"Oh no, I won't be here either."

Then the third man, one of the England Selectors, asks, "When will England win the Ashes?"

This time, there is an even longer silence before the voice booms out. "Bloody hell, I won't be around either."

A man found himself hurtling to earth after his parachute failed to open. Thinking this was the end, he was suddenly amazed to see a group of men standing in a circle shouting to him, "Don't worry, you'll be alright, we'll catch you!"

Unable to believe his luck, he was just about to relax when looking down again he realised they were the English cricket team.

He was the laziest boy in the class. Only yesterday, the children were asked to produce an account of a cricket match. All the others spent an hour writing while he took 30 seconds.

When the teacher saw it later she read, "Rain stopped play."

A very famous cricketer who could play right-handed or left-handed was asked how he decided which way to play that day. The man explained.

"If my wife is lying on her left side, I play left-handed and if she's lying on her right side, then I play right-handed."

"Ah, but what if she's lying on her back?"

"In that case, I ring up and tell them I'll be late that morning."

A passer by happened to see a coffin being brought out of the church, with a cricket bat and pads on it's lid. He turned to one of the mourners and said, "Like his cricket, did he?"

"Still does," replied the mourner. "He's straight off to a match after this, once they've buried his wife."

Did you hear about the fanatical cricket fan?
On the day his pregnant wife was rushed to hospital he was to be found in the waiting room listening to the test match on a Walkman. Suddenly, his anxious mother in-law arrived and asked him for the latest news.
"It's going well," he replied enthusiastically. "They've got five out in this session, and there's only two more to get out", whereupon the mother-in-law fainted on the spot.

The finest batsman the county had ever had was killed in a bad car crash and one of the substitute cricketers thought it was time he showed what he could do.
"Listen boss, how about me taking his place?" he asked.
"Well, I'm not sure," replied the manager. "We'll have to see what the undertakers say first."

Why did the battered wife decide to live with the English cricket team?
They don't beat anybody.

Two men were down in Hell, stoking the fire the way they had done it for the past twenty years. Then one day, to their astonishment, it began to snow. And the snow got heavier and heavier till eventually the fire went out and the icy wind blew.
"Bloody hell," said one, "what's going on?"
"It looks as if England have won the Ashes," replied the other.

★

A horse was walking by the village green when he spotted a game of cricket in progress. He went over to the Captain and asked, "Any chance of a game?"

The Captain looked dumbfounded when he heard the horse talk but it so happened that one of his team had just retired injured so he agreed to put him in at number 7. The horse was sensational. He hit a four or a six off every ball in the over and the crowd were going wild. However, when the bowler changed ends, batsman 6 hit a single.

"Run," he shouted to the horse, "run, quick." But the horse didn't move an inch and the batsman was run out.

"Why didn't you run?" he demanded, as he left the field.

"Listen," said the horse angrily. "If I could run I'd be at the racecourse now, not stuck in some bloody village cricket team."

★

This Sporting Life

The steward at the local cross-country race asked one of the competitors what time he pulled out.

"I didn't," replied the runner, "and now I'm really worried."

Two men are changing in the dressing rooms after playing a game of badminton. After showering, one of them puts on bra and pants.

"Hey, what's going on here?" asks his mate. "How long have you been wearing these?"

"Ever since my wife found them in my car," he replies.

A world class gymnast, away from home at an athletics meeting, spends a night of passion with one of her fellow athletes. On returning home she's overcome with guilt and goes off to confession. When the priest gives her absolution she's so relieved she comes out of church doing handstands and double somersaults just as Mrs O'Neil is going in.

"Oh no," murmurs the woman.

"What a day to do that as the penance and me with no knickers on."

My girlfriend is a real athlete.
Always ready to play ball with me.

★

A devout church woman happened to see a scruffy looking man sitting on a park bench and as she went past him she pressed £5 into the palm of his hand, saying, "Have faith, young man, have faith."
Two days later, she walked through the park again and sitting on the bench was the same scruffy man. When he saw her his eyes lit up and he ran to meet her.
"Here you are, Ma'am, Have Faith came in at 10-1", and with that he stuck a wad of notes in her hand.

Two blokes meet up on the river bank to do a day's fishing. One turns to the other and says, "Haven't seen you around for a while; have you been away?"
"Yes," says the man looking glum, "I've been on my honeymoon."
"Congratulations. Is she pretty, your wife?"
"No, she's plug ugly, she can't cook and she's bad in bed."
"Then why on earth did you marry her?"
"She's got worms."

Did you hear about the world's worst boxer?
He had advertising on the bottom of his boots. He eventually gave up when he saw a face in the third row that he recognised and after two minutes realised it was his own!

Jack had just played a gruelling game of tennis down at his local club when he looked at his watch and realised he was going to be late for his mother's cocktail party.

"Damn," he muttered to himself as he hastily changed and rushed off home forgetting about the two tennis balls that he'd put in his pocket.

In fact he didn't realise anything was wrong until he started getting very odd looks from a lovely young girl.

Blushing madly, he stammered, "Oh er... they're just my tennis balls."

"Golly," she replied. "I bet that's even more painful than tennis elbow."

Why do men enjoy fishing so much?
It's the only time people will say to them
"Cor! that's a big one."

Two women watching Rugby League.
"Great tackle," called out one.
"Nice bum, too," added the other.

★

It had been a long and gruelling wrestling match. The advantage swung from one contestant to the other with no one getting the upper hand. Then, out of the blue, the champion managed to get his opponent into his favourite hold and for the crowd, it looked as if the whole match was over. But suddenly, to everyone's amazement, there came a mighty roar and the champion went flying through the air, lay on his back stunned, and was counted out. After the match, the winning trainer came over to his man and said, "I can't believe Ken, I thought it was all over when he got you in that hold."

"So did I," agreed the man, "but when I opened my eyes and saw this pair of balls in front of my face, I bit them as hard as I could and do you know, it's amazing how much strength you have when you bite your own balls!"

The local tennis club was having its annual competition and Steve had just beaten Malcolm, a notoriously bad loser. In the bar afterwards, Malcolm passed Steve and running his hand over Steve's bald head, remarked, "My goodness, your head feels just like my wife's backside."

Quick as a flash Steve stroked his head and replied "Well I never, it does, doesn't it?"

Smart Alecs

What's the difference between men and women when they fill the car up with petrol?
The men always give the hose a few shakes when they've finished.

★

Did you hear about the man who lost two fingers in the sawmill?
Strangely enough, he didn't notice they were missing until he waved goodbye to the foreman.

★

Why is pubic hair curly?
Because if it wasn't, it would blind you.

★

Did you hear about the shy musician out on his first date?
He was so backward, when the girl told him she wanted to play with his organ, he took out his harmonica.

★

Women's Lib is making him sleep on the wet bit.

★

Have you heard about the frigid woman?
Every time she opened her legs, the central heating went on.

★

Ladies:
What do you call a man doing the washing up?
A start.

★

Did you hear about the Irish tourist officer who got sacked after one week in the job?
His first leaflet was entitled,
"Why not Bangor this weekend."

★

How do you make a bull work very hard?
Give him a tight Jersey.

★

What do you get when you cross a really offensive person with a celebrity?
Dick Van go fuck yourself Dyke.

★

What do you call Einstein masturbating?
A stroke of genius.

★

"Have you lived in this house all your life?
"Not yet."

★

"Julie," he said arrogantly, "did you know that all really great lovers are slightly deaf?"

"No," she replied, "I didn't."

"What?"

When do men act like gentlemen?
The time before they get to fuck their new girlfriends.

Why did the girl have her postcode tattooed on her thigh?
She hoped for some male in her box.

Why did the man put 10p in his condom?
If he couldn't come, then at least he could call.

What can the average Englishman do in four minutes?
Sup a pint, fart and make love to his wife.

Did you hear about the man who drank a bottle of spot remover by mistake?
He dropped out of sight.

He's so thin, when he drinks a tomato juice he looks like a thermometer.

★

Why is a male stud like a drugs' officer?
They're both crack investigators.

★

How does a girl avoid pregnancy?
She uses her head.

★

Did you hear about the man who was so bowlegged, they hung him over the door for good luck?

★

Why don't women have hair on their chests?
You don't get grass growing on a playground.

★

Why do most men never wear short-sleeved shirts?
They've got to have somewhere to wipe their noses.

★

Did you hear about the man whose mistress kept demanding such expensive presents?
He ended up having to marry her for his money.

★

What did the dumb woman do when she read a notice in the public conveniences saying,
"Don't put anything down the toilet but toilet paper?"
She shat on the floor.

★

Have you heard about the new clockwork doll?
It's called the 'dole doll'. When you wind it up, it doesn't work.

★

Having feasted magnificently on a stray bull, the lion roared with satisfaction. However, the sound carried to a group of hunters who tracked him down and shot him.
So please beware: If you're full of bull, keep your mouth shut.

★

Why do so many mothers cry at weddings?
It's because the daughters usually marry someone like their fathers.

★

The man had got such a huge spare tyre, he used to leave tread marks on his girlfriend.

★

What's the definition of sex?
One damp thing after another.

★

Have you noticed that people who have irritating coughs never go to the doctor's... they go to the theatre, the cinema, the concert...

★

What's the difference between hard and dark?
It stays dark all night long.

★

Girls, what can you do to be sure you get something hard between your legs?
Buy a motorbike.

★

Scrawled on a toilet wall:
Always aim high... then you won't splash your shoes.

★

Did you hear the sad story about the karate champion who joined the air force?
On the first day, he saluted his commanding officer a little too enthusiastically, and killed himself.

★

Did you hear about the man who was so lazy, he eventually had to go to hospital to have his chair surgically removed from his arse!

★

The woman was so fat that one day when she hung her bloomers out to dry, a family of gypsies moved in.

★

Have you heard about the revolutionary birthday cake made out of beans?
It blows out its own candles!

★

Why do the female black widow spiders kill the males after mating?
To stop the snoring before it starts.

★

What's the difference between a blonde and a mosquito?
A mosquito stops sucking when you slap it.

★

What's the definition of obscenity?
Anything that gives the judge an erection.

★

Have you ever wondered why kamikaze pilots wore helmets?

★

How do you know if a girl is too fat to fuck?
When you pull her knickers down, her arse is still in them.

★

"No, no, no," exclaimed the female centipede, crossing her legs, "a thousand times no."

★

He must be the unluckiest ex-husband alive!
He missed two maintenance payments on the trot, and she repossessed him.

★

What is virgin wool?
A sheep the farmer hasn't caught yet.

★

"How do you prepare your turkey?" asked the trainee chef.
"Very honestly," came the reply. "We just come right out and tell them they're for the chop."

★

How do you know when your first date is going to be really successful?
When you ask your girl to dance and she gets up on the table.

★

How did Captain Hook die?
Jock itch.

★

Did you hear about the prisoner found unconscious in his cell?
He'd tried to hang himself with a rubber band.

★

What have you got if you have pieces of glass in a condom?
An organ grinder.

★

What's the similarity between masturbation and a game of solitaire?
If you've a good hand, you don't need partners.

★

Why are women and rocks alike?
You skip the flat ones.

★

Did you hear about the man who swallowed a Viagra tablet too slowly?
He got a stiff neck.

★

What is making love?
It's something a woman does while a man is fucking her.

★

Why is Adam known as the first accountant?
He turned a leaf and made an entry.

★

You know you're getting old when you have a party and the

neighbours don't complain.

★

What do you call a man who wants sex on the second date?
Slow.

★

Why did the rubber fly across the room?
It got pissed off.

★

How do we know God is a man?
Because if God were a woman, sperm would taste like chocolate.

★

Why do men have a hole in their penis?
So their brains can get some oxygen now and again.

★

What's the best thing about a blow job?
A few minutes peace and quiet.

★

What's the difference between a woman of 40 years and a man of 40 years?
The woman thinks of having children, the man thinks about dating them.

★

Out on the Tiles

Down the Pub

A man goes into a bar with a cat and a heron and orders two pints of beer for himself and the cat, and a glass of wine for the heron.

"That'll be £4.20," says the barmaid.

"You get these, heron," says the cat, so the bird pays.

A little later, they order another round and this time the cat says to the man, "Your round, mate," so the man pays up.

The three stay at the bar all night drinking heavily but never once does the cat pay for a round, always having some excuse. Eventually, the bemused landlord cannot contain his curiosity any longer and asks the man what he's doing with the cat and heron.

"Well," says the man, "my fairy godmother appeared to me last week, and told me she would grant me one wish. I think she must have been having a bit of a joke with me though, because this wasn't what I had in mind when I asked for a tall bird with a tight pussy."

The man staggered into the bar and shouted,

"A double whisky bartender, and a drink for all your customers... and have one yourself."

"Well, thank you sir."

Moments later, the man shouted again,

"Let's have another drink all round and one for yourself, bartender."

"Excuse me sir, but I think you ought to pay for the other round first."

"But I haven't got any money."

The bartender was beside himself with rage.

"Then fuck off out of here and don't ever come back!" he roared.

However, ten minutes later, the man reappeared, and once more staggered to the bar.

"Double whisky," he slurred, "and a drink for all my friends."

"I suppose you'll be offering me a drink as well," growled the bartender sarcastically.

"Oh no," replied the man, "you get nasty when you drink."

The man stormed into the bar and yelled,

"Okay you bastards, which prat just painted the back of my car pink?"

From the corner, a huge Hells Angel stood up and growled,

"I did. You got a problem with that?"

"No, no," stuttered the man. "I just thought you'd like to know, the first coat is dry."

An Englishman, an Irishman and a Scotsman walked into a bar and each ordered a pint of beer. However, when the drinks arrived, all three pints had a fly swimming around in the froth. The Englishman looked at it disgustedly and pushed it away. The Irishman picked his out with his fingers, threw the fly on the floor and then drank the beer. The Scotsman also picked his fly out of the froth, then began shaking it over the top of the pint, saying, "Spit it out now y' little bastard!"

★

Three Englishmen are looking for a fight. As they walk into their seventh pub of the night, they spot an Irishman sitting in the corner. "Hey, watch this," says the first Englishman winking. He goes up to the Irishman and says, "I hear St Patrick was a shirt-lifter."

"Is that so?" replies the Irishman, sipping his beer. Seeing this, the second man goes over and adds,

"I hear S. Patrick was a shirt-lifter and a pervert."

"Is that so now?" comes the reply.

"I've got it lads," says the third Englishman. "Listen to this." He walks over to the Irishman and growls, "I hear St Patrick was an Englishman."

The Irishman looks up at him and replies, "Yes, that's what your mates have been telling me."

★

A drunk staggers into a bar and spots a man drinking in the corner. He goes up to him and says at the top of his voice, "I've just shagged your mum, it was great."

There's a hushed silence as everyone waits to see a reaction, but the man ignores the comment and the drunk wanders away. But 10 minutes later he shouts at him again from the other end of the bar,

"And I'll tell you now, your mum's the best lay for miles."

Again, everyone waits with baited breath but nothing happens. They all return to their drinks but by now the drunk can't leave it alone. He staggers over to the man once more and yells, "And another thing, she says she wants it from me every night!"

Sighing audibly, the man puts down his beer and places his hand on the drunk's shoulder.

"Just go home dad, you've had enough."

★

Two old men had drunk a pint together, every day for over 20 years. Sadly, one day Tom died, and Albert was left on his own. The last words that Tom had ever uttered were "Albert, me old buddy, in memory of me, have an extra pint each day."

Albert kept his promise and each day he ordered an extra drink. Then one day, to the amazement of the bar staff, he only had one drink.

"What's up, Albert, no drink for your friend?"

"Oh yes, I've just had the pint for Tom, but I can't have one myself. The doctor's told me my liver's packing up."

★

"If you don't keep the noise down, I'm going to have to arrest you," advised the policeman to the drunk who was staggering down the road singing at the top of his voice.

"Oh, have a heart officer," slurred the man "it's the works' outing."

The policeman looked round him, "where are the others then?"

"There aren't any others," he replied. "I'm self-employed."

★

Two drunks missed the last bus home so ended up trying to walk. But as they reached open countryside, one of them sank to his knees in the middle of the road and refused to go any further. He laid down, closed his eyes and was soon fast asleep. The other drunk eyed his mate in astonishment.

"You silly bugger, you'll end up like a squashed hedgehog," he remarked as he settled himself on the grass verge and fell asleep as well. Just after midnight, a car came down the road, swerved to avoid the man asleep in the road, and ploughed straight across the grass verge.

A drunk sets out to go fishing. He gets his tackle box, rods and net, and staggers off to look for a likely spot. Soon, he comes across a huge area of ice and starts to saw a hole. All of a sudden a booming voice speaks from nowhere, "There are no fish under that ice."

The drunk looks round but can't see anyone so he continues to saw. Again the voice booms,

"I've told you once, there are no fish under that ice. You're wasting your time."

The drunk looks up, there's still no sign of anyone so he continues sawing.

"That's enough!" shouts the voice. "Pick up your gear and get out of here, or there'll be trouble"

"Where are you?" yells the drunk. "If you're a ghost trying to scare me, then bugger off."

"No," replies the voice. "I'm the manager of this bloody ice rink."

A man walks into a pub and is greeted by a crocodile.

"What'll it be?" asks the crocodile.

The man just stares at him open-mouthed.

"Come on," he says, "haven't you seen a crocodile before?"

"Oh sorry," he stutters, "it's just that I never thought the horse would sell this place."

★

You know you must be drunk when somebody says 'Go fuck yourself' and you ask for the telephone number.

★

A bloke who's well known for challenging people to dares walks into a pub with an alligator. He picks up a bottle, hits it over the head of the alligator, which stuns the beast into slowly opening its mouth. At this point the man drops his trousers and puts his knob in the alligator's mouth, leaving it there for 10 seconds and removing it just as the jaws of the alligator snap shut.

"Now," said the man addressing the stunned onlookers. "Is there anyone here who will take on this dare?"

The room remains silent for a few moments and then an old lady stands up, saying, "I'll have a go, but please don't hit me too hard with the bottle."

★

Every day a man in the local bar would be surrounded by beautiful women – like bees round a honey pot.

"I don't understand it," said the barman. "It's not as if he has

a lot of money or he dresses expensively, all he does is just sit there licking his eyebrows."

A man walked into a bar with a tiny pianist on his shoulder. The pianist could only have been a foot tall. During the evening the pianist entertained the customers with his wonderful playing and eventually the barman asked the man where he got this wonderful entertainer. "Well, I was walking in a wood and came across an old bottle. In the bottle was a genie who offered me anything I wanted, but I think she was a little hard of hearing, because I didn't ask for a twelve inch pianist."

What a landlord!
I asked him for something cold, tall and full of gin and he introduced me to his wife.

A man thought up a clever way to make some money. His friend had an unusual anatomy in that he had three balls.
"We can make a fortune," he told him. "Come on, I'll show you."
They went into the local pub and the man got everyone's attention by standing on a chair and shouting, "I'll bet anyone in this bar that my friend and the barman there, have five balls between them."
People rushed forward and soon a lot of money had changed hands. At that point the man turned to the barman and said, "I hope you don't mind taking part in this bet."

"Not at all," replied the barman "It's amazing to find a man with 4 balls to go with my one."

★

A lady at the far end of the bar waves her arm in the air to get the attention of the waiter and in doing so shows a good hairy underarm.

Down the other end of the bar is a very drunk man.

"Hey waiter, get that ballerina a drink!" he shouts.

"How do you know she's a ballerina?"

"Well, no one else would get their leg so high."

★

A ranch hand goes into the saloon and orders a shot of whisky. He drinks it down in one gulp, rushes outside, kisses his horse's arse and comes back in again.

Another whisky is ordered and drunk before he rushes outside and kisses his horse's backside again.

After he has done this half a dozen times, the bartender's curiosity gets the better of him and he asks the man why, after each drink, he rushes outside to kiss the horse's bum.

"Chapped lips," replies the man.

"Oh, does that cure them?" asks the surprised bartender.

"No, but it sure as hell stops me licking them."

★

I saw this white horse standing behind a bar.
I said, "Do you know there's a whisky named after you?"
He said, "What, Adrian?"

A man walks into a bar with a weasel on his shoulder.

"Hey, what's this all about?" asks the bartender.

"Let me tell you, mate, this weasel gives the best blow job ever."

"Give me a break, now get out and take it with you."

The man persists. "No, really. Why don't you take it out the back and see?"

The bartender is intrigued by this, and decides to give it a go, and he disappears out the back.

A little while later, he comes back again.

"That was fantastic, I'll give you £100 for it."

"No way," replies the man. They haggle for a while but the man eventually sells for £500. After closing time, the bartender takes the weasel home and finds his wife in the kitchen.

"Mabel, teach this weasel to cook and then get the fuck out of here."

A man is trying to decide what to call his new bar when he spots Lisa coming up the street. Now this man is really keen on Lisa, who's not only gorgeous looking but has legs that go on for ever. That's it, he thinks, I'll call my new bar Lisa's Legs. The next day three men are waiting outside the bar when a cop stops to ask them what they are doing.

"We're waiting for Lisa's Legs to open so we can go in and satisfy ourselves," they reply.

★

A man walked into a pub carrying a red, long-nosed, short-legged dog.
"Ugh, that's an ugly dog," commented a man standing at the bar with his prize bull terrier at his feet.

"Maybe," replied the first man, "but she's a mean bitch."

"Oh yeah? Listen, I'll bet you £50 my dog will have chased her off in less than a minute."

"OK, it's a deal," and with that they lined the two dogs up. On the word 'Attack' the two dogs flew at each other and in no time at all, the bull terrier has been bitten in half.

"Bloody hell!" sobbed the owner, aghast. "What the fuck kind of dog is that?"

The man replied, "Well, before I docked her tail and painted her red, she was a crocodile."

★

"Same as usual, Jack?" asks the bartender as he sees one of his regulars walk up to the bar.

"No thanks, just an orange juice, please," replies the man dejectedly. Taken aback the bartender asks him why.

"It's my wife. She says if I come home one more time legless and covered in puke, she'll pack her bags and leave."

The bartender tells him he has a way to get around the problem.

"Have a £10 note handy and when you arrive home in your usual state, insist it was someone else who threw up all over you. Show her the money and say he offered to pay for the dry cleaning."

Jack's well pleased with the idea and spends the evening drinking pint after pint until he's blind drunk. Sure enough, by the time he's got home, he's thrown up on himself but still remembers the little trick. As soon as his wife starts shouting at him he shows her the money and explains what happened.

"But that's a £20 note," she retorts.

"Er ... yes, that's right," says the man "the same guy shat in my pants as well."

★

A man walks into his local and finds a seat at the bar next to a drunk. For some five minutes the drunk looks at something in his hand and eventually the man's curiosity gets the better of him and he asks what it is.

"It's odd," replied the drunk. "It looks like plastic but feels like rubber."

"Here, let me see," said the man.

He takes the object and begins to roll it between his fingers.

"You're right" he says "It does feel like rubber but looks like plastic. Where did you get it from?"

"My nose," replies the drunk.

★

A giant of a man, very drunk and very mean, throws open the doors of the pub and shouts loudly, "All you on the right side are cock-suckers and all you on the left are mother-fuckers!"

Suddenly a man runs from the left side to the right.

"Where are you going, wimp?" roars the drunk.

"Sorry sir, I was on the wrong side," he replies.

★

After gulping down a Scotch in the local bar, the man bets the bartender £50 he can piss in the empty glass. Eager to make some easy money, the bartender agrees, so the man drops his trousers and starts to piss everywhere – on the floor, the bar, the tables, even the bartender himself. But nothing goes in the glass. The bartender chuckles to himself and demands the £50.

"Just a second," replies the man who goes up to two guys sitting in the corner and comes back moments later with £200 in his hand.

"Here's your £50," he says and hands over the money.

Puzzled the bartender asks, "What was all that about?"

"Well you see, I bet them £200 that I could piss all over this pub, and over you, and you'd still be smiling at the end of it."

★

It has just been announced that Bob Swillall has been elected Chairman of Alcoholics Unanimous. He will be notified of this as soon as he comes round.

A man goes into a bar and asks for a pint of bitter. The barman serves him and the customer drinks it very quickly and then says, "Do you have any brown ale?"

"Of course, sir." And he's served the drink.

A little later the man again asks, "Do you have any lager?"

"Of course, sir. That's what pubs are for."

And a little later still he asks, "Have you got any stout?"

"Naturally," replies the barman.

The barman is pestered all night by these ridiculous questions until finally his temper snaps.

"Sir, this is a pub. We have everything you could wish for – dark ales, light ales, ciders, four kinds of beers, bottled drinks, red wine, white wine ... so please, enough of these stupid questions."

A moment goes by before the man asks, "Do you have shorts?"

"Look, fuck face, I've just said we have everything, so YES, we have shorts."

"Thank goodness for that," replied the man. "I'll have a pair in a large size, 'cos I've just pissed myself."

Jack was sitting at the bar gazing dejectedly into his beer.

"What's up?" asked the barman.

"It was last night," he replied. "I got so drunk I don't remember what I did but when I saw a woman in bed with me I naturally gave her £50."

"Well, that's reasonable, even if you don't remember it," consoled the barman.

"It's not that," said Jack. "It's the fact that it was my wife and she automatically gave me £10 change."

A man walked into the pub with a dog.

"I'm sorry, sir, no dogs allowed in here."

"Yes, but he's a really intelligent dog, ask him to do anything and he will."

"OK," said the barman. "Tell him to go and get me a newspaper."

The man hands the dog £5 and off he goes. Two hours go by and there's still no sign of the dog, so the anxious owner goes looking for him. After roaming the streets, shouting his name, he eventually finds him in a back alley with a bitch, doing the business.

"What's all this about?" asked the owner. "You've never done this before."

"No, but I've never had so much money before," replied the dog.

A bloke goes into a pub and orders a triple whisky and a pint of beer. As soon as the barman puts them in front of him he drinks them all down in one gulp.

"I shouldn't be drinking all this," he says.

"Why's that?"

"Because I've only got 20p on me."

A gambling man goes into a pub and bets the customers that he can smell any wood and tell them what it is, blindfolded. They take on his bet, blindfold him and get him to smell the table. After a moment he says, "That's mahogany."

Next, they get him to smell the top of the bar.

"Yes, I know that, it's oak," he answers confidently.

"OK, it's double or nothing."

They put a snooker cue under his nose. A minute goes by and then he replies, "I would say that's Canadian maple."

Feeling very dispirited, the regulars have one more trick up their sleeve. They get hold of old Meg – the village's oldest tart – lay her out on the table, pull down her knickers and get the man to smell between her legs. After a good sniff, he asks them to turn it over, which they do, and he has another good sniff.

"Can you just turn it back again?" he asks, and again he has a good smell.

This goes on for a couple of minutes with the regulars turning Meg over time and time again.

"OK, your time's up," they say at last.

"Right," says the man. "I would say it's a shit-house door made out of fish boxes."

A man walked into a pub boasting that he could identify any drink blindfolded. Would anyone care to take up the challenge?

Half a dozen of the regulars agreed to the bet. They each put down £10 that he could not identify all six drinks offered to him. Along came the first. The man tasted it and said, "Yes, that's a famous brewery called Jenkins and it's their special bitter."

He was correct.

Another was put before him.

"This is a tequila and is Jose Revello."

Correct; and so it went on. Each time the man was able to name the drink and the manufacturer. By the time the sixth drink came along the punters were getting desperate. This time when they put a drink before him, he tasted it, spat it out and swore profusely.

"Bloody hell, this is urine, this is just plain piss."
"Yes," said a voice, "but whose is it?"

A man goes into a bar and asks the barman if it would be alright to tell an Irish joke.

"I think you ought to know," said the barman, "that my name's O'Riley and many of my fellow countrymen use this pub. That group over there is the local darts team – they're Irish. Those two men over there are Irish, they work round the corner on the building site, and (lowering his voice) that big Irish bastard in the corner is the local hard man."

The newcomer thought for a moment and then said, "Okay. It would take too bloody long to explain the joke to you lot anyway."

★

An anti-drink campaigner walks into a local bar and calls for the customers' attention.

"I would like to show you all something about drinking," he announces and at that point he puts two jars on the table. One he fills with whisky, the other with water. Then he produces two earthworms and drops one into each jar. The one in the whisky jar breathes his last and sinks to the bottom while the other swims happily around in the water.

"So what does this show you about drinking?" asks the campaigner and a voice at the back replies, "If you drink, you won't have worms!"

★

A man goes into a pub carrying an octopus.

"Sorry, mate, you can't bring that in here," says the barman.

"Hold on a minute," says the man, "this isn't just any old octopus. This one can play every single musical instrument you care to put before him. How about a small wager? If he can play all the instruments you can produce, I get free drinks for the night. If not, then I'll buy everyone in here a drink."

The barman agrees and the wager begins. First, the octopus plays the piano and it's beautiful, then it plays the trumpet – a superb piece of jazz – followed by the double bass, violin and the harp. In fact, the harp is so well played it brings tears to the eyes of the customers.

"I'm not beaten yet!" thinks the barman. He goes upstairs into the attic and finds his old bagpipes. They haven't been played for years but he dusts them down and hands them to the octopus. It looks at them, feels them but doesn't start to play.

"Gotcha," smiles the barman triumphantly. "Time to pay up."

"Just a moment," replies the man confidently. "When he realises he can't fuck it, then he'll play it."

A man walks into a bar with a toy poodle on a lead.

"No dogs allowed in here," says the barman. "Only guide dogs for the blind."

"But I am blind," insists the man.

"Well, that's not a guide dog."

"Why, what is it?"

"It's a poodle."

"Bugger, I've been conned."

A very attractive woman walks up to the bar in a local pub and, smiling seductively, signals for the barman to come close to her. When he does, she starts to run her fingers through his hair and whispers, "Are you the landlord?"

"No, I'm sorry, he's not here at the moment" And he gasps with delight as she brings her fingers down through his hair and begins to gently stroke his beard.

"Is there anything I can do?" he whispers.

"Yes, will you please give him a message?" By this time, she's put her fingers in his mouth and he's sucking on them sexily.

"Will you please tell the landlord that there's no toilet paper in the Ladies."

★

Two men were sitting at the bar talking over past times. One said to the other,

"I'll never forget the day I turned to the bottle as a substitute for women."

"Why's that then?" replied the other.

"I got my dick stuck in it."

A man had a very clever parrot whose memory was second to none. One day, the man came up with a foolproof way of making lots of money. He got the parrot to learn the National Anthem and then took it down the pub where he told the customers.

"I bet £10 that my parrot can sing the whole of the National Anthem."

Some interest was shown and the money was placed on the bar. Sadly though, the parrot never uttered a note and the man lost the lot. When he got home, he was besides himself with rage.

"You bloody stupid, half witted bird. You've lost me a fortune today."

"Hang on, hang on," said the parrot. "Just imagine the interest you'll get tomorrow when we go back."

A man walks into a pub and orders a pint of beer and a pasty. "How much will that be?" he asks.

"Nothing Sir, it's on the house."

A little later, he orders another beer and again is told it's on the house. After a third pint, he questions the barman.

"Why are all the drinks free today?"

"Oh, it's quite simple really, Sir" replies the barman. "The owner of this pub doesn't know that I know he's upstairs with my wife. So I'm doing to him down here, what he's doing to me up there."

A fire engine came racing around the corner and disappeared up the road, bells clanging wildly. As it passed 'The Flying Horse', a drunk staggered out and started chasing it, but after a minute or so he collapsed on the ground breathing heavily.

"Bugger it!" he gasped. "You can keep your bloody ice creams."

A man walked up to the bar and asked for a pint of less.

"Less?" questioned the barmaid, "I've never heard of it, is it a new beer?"

"I don't know," replied the man. "When I went to the doctors this morning, he told me I should drink less."

★

"Whisky on the rocks bartender please," says the man, and as he gulps it down in one go he takes out a picture from his back pocket. "Another whisky please," and again he gulps it down and looks at the picture in his back pocket. For the next 2 hours he goes through the same routine, time and time again. By the end of the night he turns to stagger out when the bartender taps him on the shoulder.

"Sorry mate, but I have to ask," said the bartender. "You've ordered whiskies all night and each time you've drunk one, you've taken out a picture in your back pocket and looked at it. Can I ask why?"

"Sure," replied the man sounding very pissed. "It's a picture of my wife and when I think she's looking good, then it's time for me to go home."

★

A man walks into a pub, orders a pint of beer and asks the barman if he can borrow the pub's newspaper and do the crossword.

The barman thinks for a moment and then replies, "I'd just like to ask you a couple of questions first. Tell me, when a sheep dumps why does it come out in little dottles?"

The man shook his head. "I don't know."

"OK," said the barman. "What about cows, why does it come

out in a round 'pat'?"

Again the man shook his head.

"Listen mate," said the barman scornfully. "You don't know shit, so I don't reckon you'll be able to do this crossword!"

★

The bar was empty except for two men and very soon they got talking and commenting about 'life'.

"Let me tell you something, you can find out a lot about a person very quickly if you know the right question to ask," said the pompous one.

"Is that so?" replied the dimwitted man. "Tell me more."

"Well, say for example that I ask you if you have a dog."

"I do," he replied.

"Well in that case I assume you have a backyard to keep it in."

"I do," he replied.

"Then I also assume you have a house to go with the backyard."

"I do, I do," he replied quite amazed.

"And if you have a house, I think you're probably married."

"I am."

"So I assume you're not gay."

"No, I'm not."

"So there you are," said the pompous man. "Just by asking you whether you have a dog I'm able to deduce that you are married, not gay, and live in a house."

"That's astounding," replied the other, "truly astounding."

A couple of weeks went by and one Thursday lunchtime the dimwitted man found himself back in the same bar. Again it was very quiet apart from a stranger sitting close by.

"Excuse me," said the man who had been eager to put his newly acquired knowledge to the test. "May I ask you whether you have a dog?"

"No I don't," replied the stranger. At that, the man quickly pushed back his chair and headed for the door saying as he went,

"Then I'm not hanging around here chatting to poofs all night."

Two mates were talking over a pint of beer.

"What's wrong Jack? You don't look so good," said Bob.

"It's this bloody toothache, been driving me mad, I just can't get rid of it."

"Well maybe I can help you there. I had a toothache a couple of months ago and believe it or not my wife gave me a blow job and I was cured. Why don't you try it?"

"Thanks Jack, I'll have a go. Will your wife be home tonight?"

A man walks into a pub and the locals ask him if he would like to play bar football.

"Yes," replies the man, "but what do I have to do?"

"Oh it's quite easy – drink beer, piss and then fart."

So the man does as he has been told. Then one of the locals tells him, "If you can do it again, you'll get an extra point."

So the man obliges. He drinks the beer, pulls down his trousers to take a piss but before he has time to fart one of the locals shoves his finger up the man's arse.

"Hey! What the hell's going on?" asks the man.

"Just blocking the point," comes the reply.

★

A man walks into a bar with a Cornish pasty on his head and asks the barman for a pint of beer. Unable to conceal his curiosity the barman hands the man the beer and says,
"Excuse me Sir, I couldn't help but notice that you have a Cornish pasty on your head."
"That's right," replies the man. "I always have a Cornish pasty on my head on a Thursday."
"But Sir, it's Friday today."
"Oh no," says the man. "I must look a right prat."

★

A man went into a bar and ordered a gin and tonic. When it was placed before him, he exclaimed,
"Hey, an ice cube with a hole in it, that's new."
"No it isn't," commented a sullen looking man sitting next to him. "I married one."

★

Two men chatting over a pint.
Bob turns to John and says, "You're looking down in the dumps, what's wrong?"
"It's the wife, since she's started this high powered job she's cut our sex down to 3 times a week."
"You're lucky," remarked Bob. "She's cut me out completely."

A man is drinking at the bar when a huge ugly woman sits down on the stool beside him. He ignores her completely and they drink away quietly for over an hour. Suddenly, the woman turns to him and slurs "If I have another drink, I'm really going to feel it."

He replies, "To be honest, if I have another drink I probably won't mind."

"I'm fed up, Steve," sighed his mate, Jack. "Bloody sex, it's a minefield. If you go out with girls you might get some sort of VD. If you go out with boys, you get AIDS. In fact, you can't even go out with yourself anymore for fear of getting RSI."

"You know Fred, I gave up booze and sex once," said Jack.

"Never, I don't believe you," came the reply.

"It's true. It was the worst 40 minutes of my life."

"If I don't do something soon, our marriage is down the Swanee," said Bill to his mate.

"What is it then? The eternal triangle?"

"Yeah," he nodded sadly.

"Listen Bill, I had that problem once but we managed to get back on track."

"Yeah? How come?"

"We ate the sheep."

Jack sat quietly nursing his pint of beer.

"Hello mate," said Bob, coming to sit beside him, "you're quiet tonight, anything wrong?"

"It's me and Angie," he replied, "our sex life is so boring, sometimes I wonder why we got married in the first place."

"Come on, cheer up," replied Bob. "I think I've got the answer. You just need to spice it up a bit. Catch her unawares, that often does the trick."

When Bob saw Jack a couple of weeks later, he looked much happier. "So it worked then?" asked Bob.

"You bet," smiled Jack. "The following afternoon I bought her a big bunch of roses and a box of chocolates, rushed into the house, grabbed her from behind, pulled down her knickers and did it there and then on the living room carpet."

He paused, then added,

"Mind you, I don't know what the vicar thought, he was taking tea with her at the time."

Saturday morning at the library, Martin spots Kevin over in the non-fiction section.

"Hello Kevin, been away? Haven't seen you for a while."

"Oh hello, Martin. As a matter of fact I have. I went on a weekend course to that big hotel off the A1. It was all about reincarnation. Very good. Mind, it cost £400."

"Phew! That's a bit steep."

"Yes, I suppose it was. Still, you only live once."

A man walks into the bar with a monkey and asks for 2 pints of beer.

"We don't serve monkeys in here," replies the barman. "You'll have to go elsewhere."

"Oh come on, you can see how quiet he is, there'll be no trouble," urges the man.

Eventually the barman gives in and 2 pints are placed on the bar. However it's not long before the monkey starts to feel the effects of the beer and he begins to get quite boisterous. All of a sudden he swings over to the snooker table, picks up the black ball and swallows it. The barman is outraged and orders them both out immediately.

"Hey look, I'm really sorry mate. That ball will have to come out at some point and then I'll bring it straight back." True to his word, a couple of days later the man returns, accompanied by the monkey on a lead and of course the black snooker ball. He hands back the ball and orders a couple of pints.

"No way," says the barman. "Who knows what trouble that monkey of yours will cause this time."

"No, no, I've got him on a lead now, nothing will happen," replies the man, so the barman serves them. The monkey sits quietly on the stool, supping his beer and occasionally taking a peanut from the dish on the bar. Each time he picks one up, he first sticks it up his backside before putting it in his mouth. The barman looks on astonished and turning to the man he asks, "What's with your monkey, why does he keep doing that with the peanuts?"

"Oh it's simple really. After the trouble with the black snooker ball he likes to test the size of his food before he eats it."

★

A man spends the evening in the pub and by the end of the night he's so drunk he can hardly walk home. But he sets off and in a befuddled haze decides to take a short cut through the park and climb over the wall. All goes well until the final gate which is topped by sharp glass and shinning over this he badly rips his backside. By the time he gets home, he's in agony so quietly, without waking the wife, he heads for the bathroom to inspect the damage, clean up the wounds and do a bit of safety first. The next morning he crawls out of bed with a king-sized hangover and an aching arse.

"What did you get up to last night?" accused his wife "you were well pissed when you got in last night."

"No I wasn't," he replied. "What makes you think that?"

"I'll tell you why. I found all our plasters on the bathroom mirror this morning," she retorted.

A man walks up to the bar and asks for an entendre.

"Would you like a single or a double?" asks the barmaid.

"A double please," he replies.

"OK Sir, so yours is a large one."

A lady sitting alone in a bar gets pestered all night long by men trying to proposition her, but she sends them all away with a flea in their ear.

Then, towards the end of the evening, an alien walks in, sits down, orders a drink and completely ignores her. She is intrigued and asks him why he is not interested in her.

"On our planet we have sex in a different way and it's much more powerful. Would you like to try it?"

He then puts his middle finger on her forehead and she immediately begins to feel quite stimulated. This feeling gets more and more powerful until she reaches an orgasm never experienced before by any human being. It was so wonderful, she begs for more, but he holds up his limp finger and says, "Give me half an hour."

★

A bloke walked into the pub and was astounded at the sight of the barman. He was built like the side of a brick shithouse with muscles bulging out all over, tattoos everywhere, unshaven and sweaty.

After a moment or two the barman became aware of the looks he was getting and said,

"What the bloody hell are you looking at?"

"Sorry mate, it's just that you look just like someone I know. You're almost identical ... if it wasn't for the moustache ..."

"But I haven't got a moustache," said the barman.

"No, but my wife has."

★

In the Altogether

There were mixed reactions when Lady Godiva rode side-saddle through the town. Those on the right cheered, shouted and whistled, those on the left were strangely quiet.

★

How can you tell a short-sighted man in a nudist colony?
It isn't hard.

★

Who's the most popular man in a nudist colony? The one who can carry two teas and a couple of doughnuts all at the same time.

★

A family went on holiday to the coast and wandered accidentally onto a nudist beach. The little boy ran off to play but returned a few minutes later saying,
"Mummy, Mummy, I've just seen some women with boobs much much bigger than yours."
Mummy replied,
"Son, the bigger they are, the more stupid the women."
The little boy went off again but soon came running back.
"Mummy, mummy, I've just seen some men with much bigger willies than daddy has."
As before, Mummy replied,
"The bigger they are, the more stupid the men."
Five minutes later, and the little boy came back very excited.

"Mummy, Mummy, I've just seen Daddy talking to the most stupid lady I've ever seen, and as he was talking to her, he started to get more and more stupid as well."

★

A married couple decided to join a nudist colony and after their initial embarrassment, they settled down quite happily. At dinner that night, she said to her husband, "I'm glad we chose to do this. It feels right, it gives me a nice warm feeling."
"I'm not surprised," he replied. "You've got your tits in the soup."

★

Doctor, do you agree with eating everything raw?
No, always keep your clothes on.

★

A nudist never has to hold his hand out to see if it is raining.

★

Did you hear about the dwarf who was expelled from the nudist colony?
He was always poking his nose into other people's business.

★

In the Wild

Johnson the intrepid explorer, is making his way through the jungle, when suddenly a party of natives appear in front of him. "Hold it right there, white man!" snaps the leader. "What are you taking from the jungle?"

They search Johnson's baggage, and soon discover a large supply of walnuts.

They march him into their village, strip him naked, and tie him to a stake in the middle of the village square.

"This will teach you to steal from the jungle," says the chief, and he begins to stuff the walnuts up Johnson's arse, saying, "This is the only way you will leave here with our property."

On hearing this, Johnson breaks out in fits of laughter, to the chief's astonishment. "How can you laugh?" he demands. "There must be 30 pounds of walnuts here, and they're all going up your arse. Is that funny?"

"Oh, it's not that," says Johnson, "it's just that I can't stand my boss."

"So why is that funny?" demands the chief.

"Well," says Johnson, "he's two days behind me on the trail with a consignment of pineapples."

★

After a long and tiring day's hunting in the jungle, the group of men made their way back to the camp for their evening meal. That night they had plenty to celebrate, having shot some good trophies, so they laid into the whisky quite heavily. At one point, Martin staggered off to have a pee and being so drunk he failed to do his fly up again. As he sat down, Gerry turned to him and said,

"Hey, Martin, I just saw a big snake in that chair when you sat down."

"Really?" he replied, somewhat dazed.

"Yes, I can still see it. Keep still and I'll knock it on the head with this empty bottle."

Thump, there was an almighty thwack which brought tears to Martin's eyes.

"Quick man," he said, "do it again, the bugger's just bitten me."

★

A man and his wife went on safari and having lost the rest of the sightseeing party, they found themselves alone in the jungle. Suddenly the wife screamed as they were confronted by a huge gorilla. He grabbed her by the arse and began tearing her clothes off. "Help, Fred, help me, what shall I do?" she yelled.

"Tell him you've got a headache and you're too tired," he replied.

★

Three men, one of whom is a bit simple, are captured by savages in the deepest part of the jungle and are told they have one last wish before being killed. The first man asks for a crate of bourbon which he drinks until he collapses unconscious on the ground. The savages then kill him and eat him, but keep his skin to make a canoe.

The second man asks for a dozen women, all of whom he

screws in turn until he collapses exhausted on the ground. The savages then do the same to this man.

Finally, it's the turn of the 'simple' man to pick a wish and he asks for a fork, which he then starts stabbing himself with all over his body. Puzzled, the savages ask him what he is doing and he replies,

"You're not making a fucking canoe out of me!"

A young couple went on a safari to Africa, accompanied by the woman's mother. On the second day, they got separated from their party and found themselves in a remote part of the jungle. Suddenly, a lion jumped out of the undergrowth and stood growling ferociously in front of the mother-in-law.

"Quick George!" screamed his wife, "do something!"

"Not bloody likely," he replied, "that lion got himself into this mess, he can get himself out again."

Two hunters are walking through the jungle, one is carrying a concrete post and the other is carrying a wooden shed.

"Why have you got that shed with you?" asks the first hunter.

He replies, "Well you see, if we get attacked by a wild animal, I can take refuge inside the shed."

They walk on a bit and the second hunter enquires,

"So why are you carrying a concrete post?"

"Well, if we get attacked by a wild animal, I can drop the post and run faster."

★

"Jack, what happened?" gasped his friend on seeing him in the intensive care unit of the local hospital. "I thought you were touring in South America."

"I was," replied Jack weakly, "but it all went horribly wrong. Three weeks into the tour, our band played in this remote village and we went down such a storm that the Chief ordered all our instruments to be filled with fabulous jewels. Unfortunately, I was playing the flute at the time, so I didn't do quite so well out of it."

Jack stopped while the nurse mopped his fevered brow and then continued.

"Anyway, later we found ourselves in another out of the way village and this time the Chief hated our music so much, he ordered all the instruments to be shoved up our backsides."

"Wow!" exclaimed his friend, "it's a good thing you were playing the flute."

"Well, that's the trouble," said Jack, sadly. "After I missed out on the jewels, I'd switched to the tuba."

★

There's been a severe shortage of food in the jungle, so when a missionary appears, two cannibals start to fight over who will take the prize. Eventually, too weak to argue, they decide to share him – one starting at the top, the other at his feet, until they meet up in the middle. After eating for some minutes, one cannibal turns to the other and says, "How's it going?"

"Fantastic!" replies the other. "I'm having a ball."

"Oh no!" exclaims the first, "slow down, you're eating too fast."

★

Two athletes are on a safari holiday in deepest, darkest Africa, when they get separated from the rest of the party. All of a sudden they look up to find themselves face to face with a very angry lion. The first athlete immediately bends down to put his running shoes on.

"What the hell are you doing?" screams the second, "you'll never outrun him!"

"I know," says the first, "but I can outrun you."

★

How do you know when you've passed a rhinoceros?
You can't close the toilet lid.

★

A randy old gorilla was walking through the wildlife park when he saw a lion bending over, drinking from the water hole. Unable to restrain himself, he came up quietly behind the animal, grabbed him by the front paws and gave him a good rogering. Once free, the lion went berserk, determined to take revenge on his attacker. Meanwhile, the gorilla had raced back into the undergrowth where he came across a lone hunter. Deciding to disguise himself, he knocked the man out, took off his clothes and put them on himself, covering up his fur with a long coat and pulling a hat low down on his forehead. In the man's belongings there was also a newspaper which he held up in front of his face and started to read. A moment later, the lion came along, saw the 'hunter' and asked him if he'd seen a gorilla.

"You mean the one that molested a lion by the watering hole?" he said.

"Bloody hell!" said the astonished lion. "Don't tell me it's in the papers already!"

★

Two men on safari were cooling down by dangling their feet in the river. Suddenly, one of them screams. "Aaarghh, an alligator has just bitten off my foot."
"Which one?"
"I don't bloody know, when you've seen one, you've seen them all."

★

Out in the middle of the jungle a hunter spots a gorilla standing in a clearing. He takes aim and fires but when he goes to collect his prize, there's no sign of the animal.

Suddenly there's a voice behind him,

"I'm fed up being target practice for you lot. Now get down on your knees and give me a blow job."

The hunter has no choice but to comply, thankful he has got off with his life. However, the next day he returns with a bigger and better gun, spies the gorilla and fires. Again he misses and again he is forced to see to the big brute.

Determined to succeed, the man returns on a third day, this time with telescopic sight, and tries again.

Once more he fails and as he gets down on his knees to give the gorilla another blow job the animal says to him, "You know, I'm beginning to think it's more than the hunting you're after."

On safari in darkest Africa, a bishop got separated from his party and came face to face with a huge lion. Knowing his gun was empty the hunter got down on his knees to say a last prayer and was amazed to find the lion praying.

"Praise the Lord! A Christian lion!" exclaimed the bishop joyously.

"Quiet!" roared the lion, "I'm saying grace."

An elephant and a monkey were strolling through the jungle when suddenly the elephant fell down a large hole.

Quickly the monkey ran for help and waved down a Rolls Royce on a nearby road. Hearing of his friend's plight, they hurried back to the hole, dropped a rope down and pulled the elephant out.

Some months later the monkey fell down a steep hole but was rescued quite easily when the elephant dropped his donger down for the monkey to climb up.

So it just goes to show that you don't need a Rolls Royce if you've got a big dick.

A bear and a rabbit find themselves squatting down side by side in the woods. The bear turns to the rabbit and asks, "Do you find that shit sticks to your fur?"

"Why yes, now that you ask, it does," says the rabbit.

"Oh good." And with that the bear picks up the rabbit and wipes his arse with him.

A man goes hunting with his two dogs and a monkey and his fellow hunters ask him what the monkey is for.

He replies "When the dogs have cornered the animal up a tree the monkey goes in and shoots it at close range."

Later in the day they hear the dogs barking so a gun is handed to the monkey and he shins up the tree only to return a few seconds later. He jumps to the ground and immediately shoots the dog dead.

"Christl!" exclaims one of the hunters. "Why did he do that?"

The man replied, "If there's one thing he can't stand, it's liars."

A dedicated professor of music decided to go deep into the African jungle to test his theory that wild animals could be tamed by playing them beautiful music. Sure enough, his theory proved to be true. As he began playing a beautiful piece of classical music on his violin, he soon had an appreciative audience – two giraffes, three snakes, four zebras and a host of monkeys. All of a sudden, a lion roared into the middle of them and bit off the professor's head.

"Why did you do that?" complained the other animals. "That was beautiful music and you've gone and spoilt it."

The lion put a paw to his ear and said, "What?"

In the Gay Bar

The young man finally made up his mind to tell his mother he was gay. He could no longer keep it a secret so one evening when she was in the kitchen making supper, he took, the plunge and told her.

"Mum, I have something to tell you, I'm gay."

Immediately, his mother replied,

"Does being gay mean you have men's dicks in your mouth?"

"Well...." stammered the young man. "Yes, it does."

"In that case," she said angrily, "don't you ever criticise my cooking again."

★

A gay walks into a pub carrying a small bag and announces to the crowd,

"If anyone can guess what's in my bag, I'm yours for the night."

A big, burly man stands up, thinking he'll have a laugh and shouts, "OK, I guess you've got a 10 ton truck in there."

The gay looks into his bag and smiles.

"Well done, we have a winner."

★

Arthur was such an unlucky man. One day he approached a prostitute and she said she had a headache.

★

There was a convention on in town and all the available

accommodation was taken up by the visiting delegates.

"I'm sorry Sir, there isn't a room anywhere, the only bed I've got left means you'll have to share a room with one of our local residents and he snores so loudly you won't get any sleep at all."

The weary traveller considered it for a moment and then smiled.

"No problem," he said, "I don't mind sharing."

The next morning, the man went to check out.

"Well sir, you look well rested, you must have slept well, how did you manage it with all that snoring?"

"I wasn't disturbed at all," replied the man. "Before I went to sleep I blew the other man a kiss and said 'sleep well darling.' He stayed awake all night watching me."

A young man moves into a new neighbourhood, alone and without any friends. He's only been there a couple of days when there's a knock on the door.

"Hi," says the visitor. "I'm Colin, I live just down the hall from you and I thought I'd come and introduce myself."

"Thanks," says the young man. "I'm Mike".

"Well Mike, would you like to come to a party over at my place on Saturday night? There'll be plenty of booze, great music and lots of sex."

"Wow, that sounds good, what do you reckon I should wear?" says Mike.

"Oh, come as you are, there'll just be the two of us."

★

Two retired gentlemen met up in their club for drinks. The first said, "How's that son of yours getting on, Bernard?"

"Oh, very well, thank you. This year his company made record profits so now he's bought himself a country estate. In fact, he's given away his flat in Mayfair to one of his friends."

"What about your son?" asked the second man.

"I'm pleased to say, he's also doing well. He's just finished a very successful film and with the proceeds, he's given away his 2-seater plane and bought himself a company jet."

As the two men sat there, contemplating their sons' good fortune, another man joined them.

"Good evening Bernard, hello Geoffrey, may I join you?"

"Certainly," they replied, "we were just catching up on news of our sons. How's yours doing, by the way?"

"Well, mixed fortunes really," he said. "Last week he confessed to my wife and I that he was gay. But it's not all bad news. He's made some lovely friends. One's given him a flat in Mayfair and the other's presented him with a 2-seater plane."

Alan and Cyril went to Blackpool for the weekend and because the weather was so hot, they decided to spend the afternoon on the beach. While Alan sunbathed, Cyril took the lilo into the water but after half an hour the wind suddenly blew up and he found himself floating out to sea. Luckily, the lifeguards spotted the danger and took immediate action. A few minutes later, he was dragged gasping from the sea as Alan rushed up.

"Cyril, Cyril, are you alright? It's me, Alan."

"Indeed I'm not!" gasped Cyril. "I was on that Lilo for ages and not once did you look up and blow me a kiss."

★

"I'm sorry dad, I think I've let you down."

"Why's that son?"

"Yesterday we had to do our first parachute jump and when it came to my turn,

I just froze, I couldn't make myself take that final step."

"So what happened."

"The instructor told me if I didn't jump, he'd fuck me up the arse." "So did you jump?"

"I did a little, at first."

★

One of the most beautiful girls in the region had all her clothes stolen when she went sunbathing in what she thought was a secluded spot. Realising that the evening was coming and it would get cold she knew she'd have to take a chance and get home as soon as possible. At that moment she saw a young man pedalling along the road, flagged him down and told him of her plight. He readily agreed to take her home and she jumped on his bicycle. After 10 minutes she couldn't believe he wasn't affected by her appearance and said, "Haven't you noticed I'm completely naked?"

"Oh yes," replied the young man, "but haven't you noticed that I'm riding a girls bicycle?"

Two gay boys were having a terrible row.

"Fuck off!" screamed the first.

"Go to hel!l" retorted the second.

"Kiss my arse!" replied the first.

"Oh you want to make up now," smiled the second.

How many gays does it take to screw in a light bulb?

One, if he takes it slowly and uses plenty of lubrication.

Have you heard? There are now special pool tables in lesbian bars – no balls.

Police were called today to break up a fight at the drag races.

Two gays arrived wearing the same dress.

In the gay shop down the road they're selling a strong kind of condom.

It's called seal-a-meal.

A young man was introduced to the Queen as the new royal photographer.

"How amazing!" she said, "My uncle is a photographer."

"Well that is a coincidence," he replied. "My uncle's an old Queen."

★

The social climber confided to her friend over a cup of coffee.
"It's awful, my son's just told me he's gay...oh well, at least his boyfriend's a judge."

★

Do you know the difference between a general rodeo and a gay rodeo?
At a general rodeo they all shout, "Ride that sucker!"

★

In a smoky old night-club the pianist leant over to a man on the front table and said, "You see, I told you I could make you forget about that girl."
"You sure did," he replied. "Play with it again, Sam."

★

Remember, if you are a bisexual, it doubles your chance of a date on a Saturday night.

★

Did you hear about the woman who married a bisexual?
She didn't know which way to turn.

★

Apology from the latecomer:
"Sorry. I'm late. I met a man on a narrow path and didn't know whether to toss him off or let him block my passage."

★

A very small guy walks into a bar and finds himself standing next to a huge man. The man turns to him and says,

"Hi, I'm 6'6", 240lbs, 12" penis, Turner Brown."

The small guy immediately faints. When he comes around he is being helped to a chair by the big man, who asks, "What's wrong with you, man?"

"I'm sorry, can you repeat what you said before?"

"Sure, 6'6", 240 lbs, 12" penis, Turner Brown."

The small guy sighs with relief,

"Oh, thank God, I thought you said turn around."

Four gay guys walked into a pub but there was only one barstool.

It was no problem, though, they turned it upside down.

Do you know the difference between a general rodeo and a gay rodeo? Advice to prison inmates – never volunteer to play the female role in the Christmas panto.

After travelling for some hours, the motorist realised he was completely lost, so it was with a sigh of relief that he saw a little village nestling in the valley. Arriving on the main street, he knocked at the door of the first house.

"Excuse me, sir, can you tell me the name of this village?"

"Of course, you're in Little Poofsville."

"That's a strange name. Why's it called that?"
"I don't know, I'll just call the wife. Hey, Bob, why's it...?"

★

"Doctor, doctor, I think I might be gay," said the young man.
"What makes you think that?"
"My father was gay, my grandfather was gay, my two uncles and my older brother."
"Good gracious," said the doctor. "Is there no one in your family who likes women?"
"Yes," replied the man. "My sister does."

★

What did one Lesbian say to the other?
Your face or mine.

★

What do you call a lesbian dinosaur?
A lickalotapuss.

★

A Lesbian goes to the gynaecologist and after being examined, he says, "Well, this is meticulously well kept."
"Oh yes," she replies, "I have a woman in three times a week."

★

On Holiday

A man fishing off the end of the pier is suddenly amazed to see an old wizened woman in a wheelchair hurtling down towards the edge. To his dismay he realises she is determined to go over, so just in time he stops her and asks what's wrong.

The old woman, who's wrinkled, half bald and toothless, starts to cry and tells him she's nearly 90 and has never been kissed. The man looks at her, hides his repulsion and gives her a kiss, although it's almost too much to stomach when she sticks her tongue down his throat. However she goes away happy. But a couple of hours later he sees her again, hurtling down towards the pier's edge. "What's wrong now?" he asks. Tears streaming down her face, she tells him she has never been hugged. So he closes his eyes takes a deep breath and just manages to give her a big hug. The man returns to his fishing and after another hour he manages to catch a very big fish which he has trouble reeling in. At that crucial moment the old woman returns, hurtling down the pier, and losing concentration for a moment he loses his prize catch. He turns to the tearful old hag who, this time, tells him she's never been fucked. So the man gently lifts her out of the wheelchair, and smiling toothlessly at him she tells him to lie her on the sand under the pier where they won't be disturbed. The man agrees, takes up two loose planks from the floor of the pier and drops her through to the sand below. The woman laughs excitedly, again saying, "I've never been fucked before."

Well you will be now," replies the man. "The tide comes in in 15 minutes," and with that he walks away.

★

Two men fell overboard when they were out at sea and only Jim could swim.

"Jump on my back, John, and we'll try swimming for shore," Jim said.

For the next 2 hours Jim swam towards land. Twice he was ready to give up but urged on by John they eventually made it.

"Bloody hell, I'm fucked," panted Jim as he crawled up the sand.

"Yes, sorry about that," said John "It was the only way I could hang on."

★

The small guest house was full, but taking pity on the stranded traveller the owner agreed to the man sharing a bed with his daughter. However, when the man tried some hanky panky she replied, "Stop that at once or I'll call my father."

Some time went by and he tried again but got the same reply:

"Stop that or I'll call my father."

Then to his amazement, third time lucky, she agreed and they spent a passionate 20 minutes bonking.

Five minutes later she tapped him on the shoulder and asked for more. He obligingly agreed and away they went. Exhausted afterwards, he was just about to go to sleep when she tapped his shoulder again. This was repeated half the night until he was so knackered he turned to her and said, "Stop that or I'll call your father."

A young man, finding himself stranded in the middle of nowhere, comes upon a little cottage. On knocking, the door is opened by a Chinaman who allows him to stay the night as long as he goes nowhere near his daughter. Disobey and the three most horrible tortures will be inflicted upon him.

However, the young man is rather stupid and when he sees the Chinaman's beautiful daughter he forgets all about his promise. That night when everything is quiet he steals into the daughter's room and they enjoy a night of non-stop rollicking, before he creeps back to his own bed at dawn.

A couple of hours later he wakes to find a boulder on his chest and pinned to it is a little note which says, "Beware, large boulder on chest – torture 1."

The young man is arrogant enough to dismiss the whole thing and he throws the boulder out of the window. As he does so he notices another note which says, "Beware boulder tied to left testicle – torture 2."

Quickly thinking that the lesser of two evils was to break a few bones jumping out of the window, he did just that before the rope tightened. However as he went through the window, he saw another sign reading: "Beware, right testicle tied to bedroom door – torture 3."

Two young men go on holiday together to Spain and spend all day on the beach and go clubbing at night. By the time they leave the beach each day Bob has usually made a date with one of the many pretty girls round about, but Des never has any luck.

"What am I going to do, why can't I score?" he asks Bob.

His mate looks at him critically – he is rather a poor example of manhood – and says, "Tomorrow, when you come to the beach, stick an orange down your swimming trunks."

The following day, Bob is late joining Des and it's not until lunchtime that they meet up.

"Hi Des, how's it going?"

"Still not pulled anyone," he replies dejectedly.

Bob takes another good look at him and whispers, "Next time Des, put the orange down the front of your trunks."

A couple popped into the local hotel bar for a drink but when the man went to the gents he found it infested with flies. Returning to the bar, he complained to the barman, who said to him reassuringly, "Don't worry, sir, the bell for lunch will be rung in five minutes."

"How will that help?" asked the puzzled man.

"They'll all come up to the dining room," he replied.

Did you hear about the beautiful blonde hitchhiker?

A passing motorist picked her up and asked her what she did for a living.

"I'm a magician," she said.

"Never! Go on prove it," he replied.

So she touched him on his leg and turned him into an hotel.

When in Madrid, a man is recommended to go to a special local restaurant that serves the testicles of the slain bull from the local bull fight. When he gets there, he sees written up outside the restaurant, "After the killing in the ring, the testicles are on your plate within 30 minutes."

Sitting at table, the man orders the hot testicles, but on arrival, the chap is slightly disgruntled, it looks like two pickled walnuts covered with tomato sauce.

"This is very disappointing," he says to the waiter. "I've seen bulls' knackers and usually they're huge. What's wrong with these?"

The waiter smiles and says, "Ah yes, sir, but sometimes the bull wins."

A pretty American girl on holiday in Scotland said to a man wearing a kilt, "I've often wondered what you have under your kilt."

He replied, "I'm a man of few words. Give me your hand."

★

A jumbo jet full to capacity is flying across the Atlantic when the pilot suddenly makes an announcement.

"I must apologise, ladies and gentlemen, one of our engines has packed up but we've got three others, so we'll reach our destination, but it will be a little later than scheduled."

Some time passes and then he makes another announcement:

"I'm sorry for the inconvenience; we've lost another engine, so we'll be an hour late getting to our destination."

Then some minutes later he announces the loss of another engine and tells his passengers the delay in landing will be two hours.

At this point, one of the passengers turns to the person next to him and says, "Bloody hell, if we lose another engine, we'll be up here all night."

Two strangers in a train compartment, a handsome young biologist and a pretty young girl. As they are travelling through the countryside they pass field after field of animals, many of them doing what comes naturally.

The young girl starts to get hot under the collar and turning to the man, asks him if he could tell her what attracts the animals to each other.

"It would be a pleasure," he says. "At certain times in the year the female gives off an odour attracting the male to her and heightening his sexual awareness".

At last they reach their destination and on parting the man says he hopes they'll meet again one day.

"Only if the cold in your head is better," she replies.

An American seaman working on a trawler around the Far East takes shore leave and spends the whole week fucking everything in sight. Alas, he picks up a very serious strain of VD and is forced to go along to an American doctor.

"I'm afraid there is not much we can do for you," says the

doctor. "We'll have to cut your penis off or you may die."

The man is dumbfounded, but determined to get a second opinion, he visits a European doctor. The diagnosis is exactly the same.

Dismayed beyond belief, he goes to see a local doctor tucked away in the backstreets of the city. The doctor tells him there is no need for the operation, it is just a way for these foreign doctors to make more money. The man is overjoyed.

"You mean I don't have to have it cut off?"

"Not at all," replied the doctor. "Just wait a few days and your cock will fall off by itself."

Stranded miles from home after an all-night party, 'Good Time Lil' flags down a passing taxi and says to the driver, "Look mate, I'm out of money but if you'll take me back to Brighton, we can do the business on the back seat."

The unscrupulous driver agrees, takes her home and then gets into the back seat with her. He takes down his trousers, she takes off her knickers and sits astride him, when he suddenly complains.

"You haven't got anything smaller by any chance!"

No matter what you do, you can't please everyone. Take the old couple who went away on a weekend break and couldn't find anywhere to stay. As a kindly gesture the manager of a 4-Star hotel offered to let them stay in the bridal suite.

"What the heck do we want that for, I'm 75 years old."

"Excuse me Sir, I've allowed people to stay in the snooker room before now but I haven't expected them to play snooker all night."

★

"I've just had the most fabulous holiday in St Tropez," said the office girl to her friends. "I met this dishy masseur."

"You mean monsieur, don't you?" said Doreen. "A masseur is someone who gets you to strip and rubs you all over..."

"So this dishy masseur...."

★

A couple were staying overnight at a country hotel but were unable to get to sleep because of the loud noise coming from downstairs. Eventually, the man could stand it no longer and rang down to reception.

"What the hell's going on? The noise is deafening."

"My apologies, sir, they're holding the Policeman's Ball."

"Well for fuck's sake, tell them to let go of it!"

★

A woman from the city stops overnight at a B&B in the heart of the country. The toilet is at the bottom of the garden and after using it she comes back in and complains to the owner.

"There's no lock on that toilet." "No need," he says. "Who'd want to steal a pail of shit?"

President Bush and a monkey get sent up to space to look for life on another planet. They eventually land many light years away on an unfamiliar world and each has an envelope with a set of instructions. The monkey opens his envelope, and inside is a thick sheaf of papers, which give him detailed instructions to study the terrain, take readings of the air pressure, rocks and minerals and finally, make contact with any alien inhabitants. George 'Dubya' opens his envelope and finds a scrap of paper which just says, "Feed the monkey, George."

Bob was so excited. He'd never been up in a plane before but today he was having a special trip in a two seater. At 3 o'clock, they took off and were soon travelling high up in the sky when all of a sudden, the pilot collapsed and died of a heart attack. Bob was petrified. After some minutes of total panic he found the radio.

"Mayday, mayday, somebody help me, the pilot's dead and I'm up here on my own."

"Receiving you, loud and clear," came a voice from the control room. "Try and keep calm, can you tell me where you are?"

"I don't know!" he yelled. "But we're flying upside down."

"And how do you know that?"

"Because crap's running out of my collar."

Flying for the first time, an old man was having trouble with his ears, so the stewardess brought him some chewing gum.

As he was leaving, he turned to her and said, "Thanks for the chewing gum, but how do I get it out of my ears?"

The man was angry.

"Look, I booked a room with en suite facilities."

"But this isn't your room, sir, this is the lift."

A van driver picks up a young female hitchhiker and after they've travelled some distance he propositions her. She agrees and suggests they get into the back of the van but he tells her it's full of plumbing equipment.

"I know," he says. "Let's do it on the bonnet." So throwing all caution to the wind, they climb aboard and start bonking away. The passion is getting stronger and stronger, the van is swaying from side to side and at the crucial moment he flings himself away and hits his back on the aerial. The next day, it's still very painful so he goes along to the doctor's.

"Mmm... that's the worse case of Van Aerial disease I've ever seen."

★

A man stops overnight at an hotel and rings down to reception asking for one of their local girls.

"How disgusting," says the owner's wife. "Go and tell him we don't allow that sort of thing here."

But the husband thought she was making a lot of fuss about nothing.

"OK, I'll go and tell him," she said and off she stormed upstairs.

Half an hour passed and the man appeared downstairs and said to the owner, "The girls round here are a bit feisty aren't they? The one you sent me was a real tough one but I got her in the end."

★

A group of ladies are travelling in a railway carriage that only has a door onto the platform. As it pulls into one of the stations, a drunk climbs aboard, sits himself in the corner and immediately falls asleep. Some time later he wakes up dying for a pee.

"Excuse me, ladies, this is a bit of an emergency. Would you mind if I peed out of the window?"

The women are broadminded enough and tell him to go ahead. However a little further on he needs another one, so he asks the ladies again.

"Go ahead," said the spokeslady, "but I think we would all prefer it if this time you peed in the carriage and farted out of the window."

The couple and their son had set up camp and the boy had wandered off to play. A few minutes later he returned carrying the top half of a bikini in his hand.

"Now son," said the dad thoughtfully, "just show me exactly where you found this."

Two teachers are returning home from a two-day course when their car breaks down and they are forced to spend the night at an hotel. Unfortunately, all the single rooms are taken so they have to share a double. The woman gets ready for bed changing in the bathroom, then the man does the same. Later, as they areboth lying there, the woman realises she's got the hots for her colleague but is too shy to do anything about it. Instead, she makes idle conversation.

"Listen Derek, it sounds as if we have a dripping tap."

Derek turns to her and replies,

"I have an idea Doreen," he says. "How about just for tonight we pretend we're man and wife."

"Oh yes," she says excitedly, "that's wonderful. I'd love to."

"Good," he says, "go turn that tap off, will you?"

A tourist staggers out of the bar after ten pints of beer and strays onto the nudist beach where he is confronted by a naked woman. He stands and stares at her for a few moments, until she looks up and sees him.

"What do you want?" she demands angrily.

"My wife's got an outfit just like yours," says the drunk.

A wealthy man was travelling through Egypt by camel but had been having a lot of trouble finding a top class animal to suit his needs. Eventually, he was advised to visit the best camel breeder in the district, Ali Bari, who would have what he wanted.

"Good day, Ali Bari," he said. "The next stage of my trip is going to last four weeks so I need an animal that won't let me down. I don't care how much I pay."

"Very well," replied the dealer, and he took him to see a magnificent camel in his courtyard.

"This camel will get you there quite safely. Just remember to give him plenty of water before setting out."

So the wealthy man followed instructions and then travelled into the desert. But alas, after two weeks the camel dropped down dead. Fortunately, the man was rescued and was able to finish his journey soon after.

It wasn't until a year later that the man found himself back in the town when he had bought the camel from Ali Bari. He accosted the dealer saying, "How dare you sell me such a poor animal. It only lasted two weeks before dropping dead. You swindled me."

The dealer protested,

"Did you give it plenty of water."

"Of course I did."

"And did you give him the two-brick treatment?"

"The two-brick treatment? What's that?"

Ali Bari replied, "When you think he's just about to stop drinking, you bang his balls between two bricks and he sucks in enough water to last another two weeks."

★

Two spinsters went on holiday together and once they'd booked into the hotel, they made their way down to the beach. As one went to dip her toes in the water, the other noticed a man sitting on his own. He'd obviously just arrived because he was deathly pale. Plucking up courage, she went over to talk to him.

"Hi, I'm Mildred. Have you just arrived, you look rather pale?"

"Yeah," he snarled. "I've been inside for the past 15 years."

"Oh really? What for?"

"Five years for burglary, two years for deception..."

"Oh my!" she exclaimed.

"...and the last eight years for killing my wife."

Mildred's face brightened and she called over to her friend, "Hey Flo, he's single."

★

A man walked into a massage parlour and was taken to a small room told to undress and lie face down on the bed. He'd just done this when a beautiful blonde entered the room, dressed in a shimmering, but skimpy bikini, her massive breasts threatening to fall out of her bra at any moment. As he lay there, she covered him with sweet smelling oils and gently rubbed down his body.

Unable to control himself, he was soon sporting a huge erection and as she asked him to turn over, it was revealed in all it's glory.

"I see sir may want to do something about that," she said smiling, as she walked seductively out of the door.

He lay there in a state of ecstasy. Any minute she'd return and administer to his every need. She'd probably gone to change into another little sexy number.

Five minutes later she opened the door and said gently, "Have you finished yet?"

A mini-cab driver had an attractive fare in the back when suddenly the engine failed. He got out and lifted the bonnet to see what was wrong. The attractive girl got out too and came over to see what he was doing.

"Do you want a screwdriver?" she asked.

"In a moment, Miss. I'll just finish up here first."

On the Game

A prostitute is knocked down by a car and a man runs over to help her.

"Are you alright?" he asks.

"I don't know," she replies. "I don't think I can see."

"Well, how many fingers am I holding up?" he says.

"Oh no!" she wails, "I'm paralysed as well."

Definition of a prostitute:
A busy body.

A man arrives at the door of the whorehouse and asks for the services of Doreen. Sure enough Doreen appears and they disappear upstairs. Afterwards he gives her £200. The next day he asks for Doreen again, they do the business and he hands her another £200. This is repeated on a third and fourth day by which time Doreen has become very attached to the man.

She says, "Come back tomorrow and you can have it for nothing."

"I'm sorry I have to return to Scotland tomorrow. By the way I know your brother; here's the rest of the £1000 he asked me to give you."

A man went to a brothel and asked how much they charged.
"£30 when you start and £40 when you finish," he was told.
That sounded all right to him, so he went in and did the business.

The following week he returned for a repeat performance.

"£30 when I start and £40 when I finish. Is that right?" he asked and on confirmation he handed over £30 and was taken upstairs to see Lil. Nearly two hours later he was still on the job and Lil began to complain loudly.

"Now listen," she said. "You're taking the mickey here. Ain't it about time, you scarpered."

"Oh no, dear lady," he replied, "I can't. You see, I'm broke."

Two prostitutes talking over a cup of tea.

"What's your day been like, Gloria?"

"Exhausting, but good business. I've climbed up and down those stairs more than 70 times today."

"Oh your poor feet!"

It was his first time in London and the American decided to search out the best brothels. At last he found one that was slightly less seedy than some of the others that he'd looked at and he went in to be 'serviced'.

Before taking his clothes off he thought he'd try some small talk to ease the tension he was feeling.

"Do you know I come from the other side," he said.

"Wow," she replied. "Hurry up and get your clothes off: this I want to see!"

The girl was asked to put down her occupation on the passport application form.

"That'll be 'prostitute'," she replied.

"Oh no, you can't put that!" exclaimed the clerk.

"How about 'brothel worker'?" she suggested.

"No, that's no good either."

She thought for a moment and then said,

"I know, put 'chicken farmer'."

"Pardon?" he asked.

"Well I did raise over 500 cocks last year."

A midget went into a whorehouse and demanded service. After much discussion amongst the girls, Sylvia drew the short straw and disappeared upstairs with him. But it was only a moment later when they heard a loud scream and running upstairs to the room, they found Sylvia in a swoon. Standing next to her was the midget, naked and sporting the longest dick the girls had ever seen.

After a moment of astonished silence one of the girls asked,

"Wow, that's fantastic, do you mind if we touch it?"

"No, go ahead," said the midget, "but whatever you do, no sucking, I used to be 6'5" tall."

Negotiations are still continuing over a new pay deal for the Soho girls. They are demanding more money on the table, even more money on the floor and danger money on top of the piano.

A man goes to a brothel, hires one of the girls and spends the next couple of hours giving her the best fuck she's ever had. He returns the following night, gets the same girl and gives a repeat performance. By the end of the third night the girl is so impressed she offers him a session on the house and it's absolutely wonderful.

"You're the most amazing thing that's ever happened to me" she tells him "if I pay you £200 will you do it again, now?"

The man agrees but as he looks down at his small and lifeless manhood he sneers at it and says,

"You can spend it alright, but when it comes to earning...!"

PC Jenkins was doing his nightly rounds when he discovered a woman in an alleyway. Her blouse was open, her knickers were round her ankles and she was eating a packet of sweets.

"What's going on here?" asked PC Jenkins.

"Bloody hell, has he gone?" she replied, looking around.

An old man went back to the whorehouse a year later and staggered up to the door. He was very fragile and extremely shaky on his legs, and when Madam saw him she said, "Hey old man, you've had it."

"Oh bugger," he replied confused, "how much do I owe you?"

★

Another old man goes to a whorehouse and asks how much it will be.

"Prices begin at £100," she says.

"You're putting me on!" he gasps.

"Then that'll be an extra £20 on top of the price," she replies.

★

Throughout his teenage life, John had been warned by his God-fearing father that brothels were the ultimate places of sin and that anyone going to them would die a dreadful death. However, one night out on a stag party John and his mates ended up in the red light district and banishing all thoughts of his father from his mind, John went into a brothel. He was taken upstairs by Madam and ushered into a bedroom where a beautiful girl lay naked on the bed. Suddenly as he looked at her, all the warnings came back to him and he cried aloud, "Bloody hell, my dad was right, I can feel myself going stiff already."

★

A husband and wife went to Manchester for the day. He had a meeting in the morning and she went off to do some shopping. Now the meeting finished much earlier than expected so the man went off into the centre of town and landed up in the 'better part" of the red light district. As he was passing one of the 'ladies' flats, a beautiful hooker came out and before he knew what he was doing, he asked her how much she charged a session. The hooker looked at him disdainfully and told him it would be £150.

"Bloody hell, that's daylight robbery!" he exclaimed. "I've only got

£30." and feeling very disappointed he left to meet his wife for lunch. Just as the meal was over, the same hooker and a client entered the restaurant and on seeing the man and his wife she whispered to him as she passed,

"There you go, that's what you get for £30."

The God of War comes to earth and enters a brothel in London where he is attracted to one girl in particular. He stays for 3 days spending most of the time engaged in mad passionate love but then he gets a message from the heavens ordering him home. As he's about to leave he realises he's never really spoken to the girl. He hasn't even told her his name.

"I'm Thor," he says.

"You're sore! I can't even walk," she replies.

Jack was sitting at the bar looking dejectedly into his pint of beer.

"Hey Jack, what's up?" asked the barman.

"Everything," he replied. "I got so drunk last night, I can't remember what I did, but when I woke up to find myself in bed with a woman, I naturally gave her £50."

The barman laughed. "Don't worry mate, it happens to all of us. Just accept that you spent the money and can't remember what it was like."

"No, no, you've got me wrong," replied Jack. "The fact is that the woman in bed with me was my wife, and she automatically gave me £10 change."

After a long time at sea, the old captain comes ashore and goes straight down the whorehouse. He's taken upstairs by one of the girls, they agree a price and he gets to work. Pleased with his performance, he says to the girl, "How's it going? I'm not too fast am I? How fast am I going?"

The girl yawns and says, "You're doing about three knots, Grandad. You're not in, you're not stiff and you're not getting your money back!"

A man travelled all around London looking for a prostitute with the pox. Finally, one of them agreed to help.

"There's only one girl I know who has the pox ...."

"Oh thank you, thank you, please take me to her and I'll pay her and you well."

"But why?" she asked.

"Let me explain. If I catch the pox I can go home and give it to the dairy maid, who'll give it to the gardener, who'll give it to my mother, who'll give it to my father, who'll give it to the Mayoress, who'll give it to the headmaster – and that's the bugger I'm after."

Did you hear about the man who was so tight with his money he rang up a hooker and asked her what night she was free?

A brothel is like a circus, except that a circus is a cunning array of stunts.

The local Soho police have just raided the local whorehouse and lined the girls up along the street ready for taking down the nick. At that moment an old woman comes along and when she sees the queue, asks the girl at the end why they are all there. "We're queueing up to get our free ice lollies," replies one of the girls sarcastically. The old woman takes it literally and joins the end of the queue. Time passes as the coppers question each of the girls and when one sees the old woman he says, "You're a bit old for this sort of thing aren't you?" "Indeed not," replies the old woman angrily. "I may not have any teeth but I can still suck."

A man with both his arms and legs in plaster knocks at the door of the local brothel.
"I'm looking for a woman," he says when the Madam opens the door.
"And what can you do in that state?" she asks.
"I knocked on the door, didn't I?"

★

"When I grow up I want to be a prostitute," said the lush young girl to the Reverend Mother. The Reverend Mother threw up her hands in horror. "What did you say?"
"I said I want to be a prostitute."
"Oh praise the Lord!" replied the Reverend Mother. "I thought you said a Protestant."

Two dwarves who had just done a season with the travelling circus, land up in town with wallets full of money, out for a good time. After doing a round of the bars they end up at the whorehouse and get taken upstairs by two of the working girls. Sadly, however much he tries, the first dwarf cannot get an erection so he spends the night feeling very miserable particularly as he can hear his mate next door repeating time and time again

'One, two, three up', 'one, two, three up'.

The next morning they make their way back to the circus. The second dwarf asks the first how it went.

"Bloody awful," he replies. "I couldn't get it to stand up to save my life. What about you?"

"Waste of time," he answers. "I couldn't even get onto the bed."

A man went up to town and engaged the services of a young lady. After doing the business she asked for £75.

"Good gracious, you're expensive."

"Well, haven't you heard of me? I'm Polly, the best in town."

"Did you say your name was Polo?"

"No, Polly. Why?"

He replied, "Because you've definitely got a hole with a mint in it."

"Hey dad," teenage son says to his father. "I've got this homework problem. I've got to show the difference between theoretical and real."

"Well, son, here's what you do. Go and ask your mum if she would sleep with Mel Gibson for a thousand pounds. Then go and ask your sister if she would sleep with Leonardo di Caprio for a thousand pounds and come and tell me the answer."

Son goes off to his mother, who replies she would (but keep it to himself) and to his sister, who's wild about the idea. He then returns to his Dad and says, "I see what you mean. Theoretically, we're sitting on a possible £2,000, but in real terms we're living with a couple of whores."

A man invited a prostitute back to his hotel bedroom and with only a few words spoken, immediately got her down on the bed and started giving her a good seeing to. After a good hour of very energetic sex he suddenly got up and said, "Just one moment, please" and walked into the bathroom. He returned a moment later, jumped in the bed and began again. Another hour of passion went on, when he suddenly got up again and disappeared into the bathroom, only to return a moment later and begin again. Hour after hour went by and the prostitute was feeling very knackered and needed a breather. She jumped up, saying, 'Won't be a moment' and going into the bathroom she found the man's three brothers.

A good time girl went into the DIY store to buy some hinges. When she was paying the storekeeper asked, "Need a screw for those hinges?"

"No, but how about a blow job for the shelves over there?"

★

A man landed up in a very seedy part of town where the whore houses were the lowest of the low. Knocking at one of the doors, he shouted, "Come on, let me in." And a voice replied, "Put £50 through the letter box first."
He did this but nothing happened.
"Hey," he bellowed, "I want to be screwed."
"What! Again!" came the reply.

★

What did the nymphomaniac say after having sex? "So which football team do you guys play for?"

★

A panda goes down to the local brothel and demands sex with their best girl. It's a bit unusual but business hasn't been very good, so they agree and choose Big Rose to see to him. However, just as they're about to go upstairs the panda requests something to eat. Anything to please the customer, so Big Rose prepares a snack for him – after all she'll put it on the bill – and then they get down to the main business. After an hour of strenuous bonking the panda gets up and heads for the door.
"Hold on a minute, haven't you forgotten something. I'm a prostitute and that means you pay me for all that sex."
"So what?" replies the panda. "You should know by now that the definition of a panda is an animal that eats, shoots and leaves. Bye."

★

"How much will it cost?" the man asked the streetwalker.

"£15 up the alley, £120 if we spend the night in a comfortable hotel."

"OK, here's £120."

"Good, it's cold out here tonight. I could do with a nice hotel room."

"Not bloody likely!" replied the man. "I want it eight times up the alley."

★

Bob had been away at sea for six months and was desperate for a woman. As soon as he came ashore, he went to the nearest whore house and demanded their best girl. Once upstairs, he immediately stripped off and jumped straight into bed.

"Okay love," he said to the waiting girl, "I hope you've eaten recently."

"Yes, I have. But why?"

"'Cos you won't get another chance for the next two days," he replied.

An old couple living off a small pension find themselves down to the last few pennies and unable to pay their bills. In one last desperate attempt to keep the bailiffs from the door the old girl decides to go on the game. She takes her curlers out, puts her teeth in and struggles into a mini skirt before disappearing into the night.

Just before dawn, she staggers home to her husband who asks her how much she's made.

"£120.50," she replies.

"Bloody hell, who was the prick who gave you only 50p?"
"They all did!" she cries.

A man goes into a brothel and tells the Madam that he's only got £20, what can she offer him? The Madam gives him a duck and off he goes to one of the rooms where he shags it for 25 minutes. The following week, he goes back but this time he's only got £10. After some discussion, the Madam gives him a chicken, and sends him on his way.

On his next visit, he is down to his last fiver, but asks the Madam hopefully if he can get something – anything – for it.

The Madam shows him into a room where there are a line of blokes looking through peepholes. He takes his turn and through the peephole he sees three women and one man up to all sorts of things on a trapeze.

"It's good this, isn't it?" he says turning to the bloke next to him.

"Not bad," replies his neighbour, "but you should have been here last week, there was a bloke shagging a chicken."

A huge, 6'6", 18 stone man was having great trouble finding anyone who would have sex with him because one look at his gigantic penis frightened the girls away. The poor man roamed London seeking satisfaction but with no luck. He ended up sitting in a boozer looking sadly into his beer.

"What's up, mate?" said a man sitting down opposite. "You look as if you've got the problems of the world on your shoulders."

The big man told him of his fruitless search.

"I know just the answer," replied the newcomer. "If you come with me I'll take you to Madam Cyn, she's got girls who've seen and done everything."

They arrived at the whorehouse door and the big man explained his problem.

"Just how big is it?" Madam asked.

"Five inches" he replied.

She laughed, "Five inches long! Goodness, that's a lot of fuss about nothing."

"Five inches thick, madame," replies the man.

A man was very surprised that on visiting a foreign whorehouse he was given £500 on leaving. Unable to believe his luck, he returned the following day and again on leaving was given £500. However on the third day he left without anything and disappointed, asked why.

"We're not filming today, sir," came the reply.

Three men are walking around Soho looking for a screw when they see a prostitute hanging round the street corner. The first man goes over and asks her what she can do for a tenner. She beckons him into an alley where they stay for ten minutes before he rejoins his mates on the street.

"What did she do, what did she do?" they urged.

"It was wonderful," said the man with a big grin on his face. "She put this doughnut on the end of my knob and then slowly ate it off."

This really got the other two men going. So the second went over to her and asked what she could do with £20. Again, she took him into the alley and he reappeared 20 minutes later full of smiles.

"Wow, she really knows how to turn you on!" he said. "She put two doughnuts on the end of my knob, sprinkled them with sugar and then slowly licked them off."

By this time, the third man couldn't wait to have a go, but he didn't tell the others he had £50 on him. However, after only a few minutes he was back looking very pissed off.

"That was quick, mate," they said. "What's wrong?"

"Well, she had these four doughnuts which she put over my knob, covered them with raspberry jam, sugar, chocolate, whipped cream and amaretto."

"Go on, what happened?"

"Well it looked so good, I ate it myself."

"I've met some disgusting people in my time but you are the worst ever. You're a dirty, dreadful old man," said the prostitute to her client.

"Listen, I've paid you, haven't I? So I'll ask you to keep a civil tongue in my arse."

A high-up banker arrives back home after spending six months on a distant outpost and heads straight for the local brothel. Once inside, he goes upstairs with one of the girls and into a bedroom where she starts to fiddle with his flies.

"Now, now," he says, as he pushes her hand away, "Any more of that familiarity and the fuck's off."

"My dear, what would your mother say if she saw you?" said the kindly social worker to the street corner prostitute.

"She'd kill me," replied the girl. " I'm on her patch."

A soldier, on weekend leave, goes into the nearest town looking for a bit of sex. He ends up staying the night at one of the seedy brothels and next morning, when he wakes up, he groans, "Bloody hell, I feel terrible, you haven't got AIDS, have you?" he says to the girl.

"No," she replies.

"Thank goodness, I wouldn't want that again."

A man visited a brothel in the middle of an African Jungle and a sign inside the door advertised a special 'Jungle Roulette'.

"What's that?" he inquired.

"Well, it's a special service where six girls offer to give you a blow job and you can choose up to three of them."

"Wow, that sounds good. What's the catch?"

"One of the girls is a cannibal."

★

The President's housekeeper was horrified to see the family parrot escape from his cage and fly out of the window. Feeling partly to blame, she rushed down to the local pet shop to buy another that looked exactly the same.

"I've only one like that," said the man, "but it's a bit risky because this parrot has come from a whorehouse and has picked up some foul language."

"Never mind, I'll just have to take a chance."

Later on in the day, the President and his family arrive home and as they enter, the parrot speaks.

"Too young," he says as the daughter comes in.

"Too old," he says of the wife.

Then, as the President enters, he squawks excitedly, "Hello big boy, long time no see."

Why don't prostitutes vote?
Because they don't care who gets in.

A man has only got an hour left before he has to rejoin his ship, so he hurries off to the local brothel for a 'quickie'.

"You'll have to wait," replies the Madam, "we've got the girls, but there isn't a room free."

"Forget the room; we'll find somewhere. Just get me the girl," he replies.

So he and Susie climb up the fire escape and find a space on the flat roof. However they get so carried away that they roll too close to the edge and both of them plunge to the ground entwined, where they are killed stone dead.

Moments later, an old drunk tramp staggers by and seeing the fallen couple he knocks on the door.

"What do you want?" demands the Madam.

He replies slowly, "I just wanted to let you know your sign's fallen down."

★

A young man, out on his first night in Florence, walked up to a young girl on the street corner and asked, "Do you understand English?"

"A leetle bit," she replied.

"How much?" he continued.

"£30."

★

A stranger in town, the man goes to a nightclub to find some action and spots a stunning redhead at the end of the bar, talking to a smug-looking man. As he watches, the man passes her some money and they disappear.

"Hey mate," he calls to the barman. "What's the story on that redhead who was standing at the end of the bar just now?"

"Forget it," replies the barman, "she's a high class pro, and she's well out of your league."

Now the stranger's been on the rigs for several months so he's feeling quite rich. The next night he returns to the bar and sees the redhead standing in the same place but this time, she's on her own.

He saunters over to her and smiles.

"What's it to be?" she asks.

"What's on offer?" he replies.

"Well, I can give you a hand job for £100."

"What!" he exclaims, "you must be joking."

"Look wise guy," she says. "See this club and the casino. They're both mine. Bought by the money I made on hand jobs. That's how good they are."

So the man agrees and it's the best experience he's ever had.

The next night he's back looking for more.

"It was bloody fantastic," he tells her. "What else is on offer?"

"I do a blow job for £300."

"£300!" he gasps.

"You see that Lotus Elan out there?" she says pointing. "That's just one of three cars I've bought from doing blow jobs. It's the best ever."

So he eagerly pays the money and off they go. The man has an ecstatic experience and spends the whole of the next day recovering. Then he's straight back down the club, panting for more.

"I've got to have some pussy!" he tells her. "I don't care what it costs."

She looks at him sadly and beckons him outside.

"You see that?" she says, pointing to a 5* hotel, across the street.

"I don't believe it," he replies astonished. "Is that yours too?"

"It would be, if I had a pussy," she replies.

Old Henry came across his son's bank book and inside saw details of his recent spending. It read 'Cute Carol £40, Juicy Lucy £45 and Lucious Lil £35.'

"Now look here son," said Henry, "if you must pay for it, at least get a better bargain and secondly, be a little more discreet when writing it down in your bank book. You enjoy golf, refer to it in those terms."

Some weeks later, Henry looked at his son's book again and was pleased to see he had taken his advice. The entries read 'green fees £20', 'green fees £25' and green fees £30.' However his satisfaction turned to shame when a fourth entry read 'repairs to putter £200'.

Two drunks picked up a couple of prostitutes and took them down the local sleazy hotel. In no time at all, Tommy was well into the rhythm when his mate Al rushed into the room.

"Hey Tom, do you mind swapping? Only the one I've got is my sister."

It was the first time that the Bishop had visited the small town, and arrangements and celebrations had been planned for weeks. On his arrival, a young journalist squeezed his way to the front of the thronging crowds and called out to him,

"Your Worship, what about the brothels?"

The Bishop looked surprised and replied, "Are there any brothels here?"

The following day the headline in the newspaper read:

"First words spoken by Bishop: 'Are there any brothels here?'"

"Hello darling," said the cocky young man going up to the girl at the bar.

"What do you do then?"

She replied coldly, "I put a stocking on my right leg, then a stocking on my left leg, and between the two, I make a living."

The female lay-preacher went down to the local whorehouse to preach to the girls and try to persuade them to turn their backs on whoring and embrace the Lord.

She began, "At one time you would have found me in the arms of soldiers, sailors and airmen but now I love the Lord..."

"Way to go, Sister," interrupted a woman from the back, "fuck 'em all."

A man went to a brothel and paid £200 for a session with Cindy. Unfortunately, she suffered a fatal stroke half-way through and collapsed on to the floor. The man rushed from the room yelling for the Madam.

"It's Cindy!" he gasped, "she's died on me."

"Now calm down," said the Madam, "she hadn't been feeling well, it's not your fault. I'll call the doctor."

"What the hell for?" he screamed. "I can't fuck the doctor."

A country priest was visiting a convent in the rough area of a big city. Not used to the transport system, he got off two stops

too early so he walked the rest of the way. It wasn't long before a woman approached him and sidling up, she whispered in his ear, "Come on sir, only £10 for a blow job."

He smiled at her, shook his head and continued on his way. Soon, another woman approached, offered him a similar price, but he shook his head and walked on. By the time he reached the convent, he had been stopped more than five times. He went through the gate and spotted a young nun cleaning the windows.

"Hello Sister," he said. "I wonder if you could tell me... what is a blow job?"

"£10," she replied immediately. "That's the going rate around here."

Brian went along to the nightclub for an interview as a bouncer.

"You'll do nicely," said the owner. "The pay's £120 per week, but we do throw in a few extras. Upstairs, is Madame Ruby's whorehouse and after work each night, the staff are allowed to have one of the girls for free."

"Paradise!" thought Brian, and he eagerly accepted the job.

The following Monday, he started work and after his shift went upstairs and was told to visit Mandy. There she sat, in a revealing nurse's uniform, and he couldn't wait to get started. However, all she did was toss him off, nothing more. The next night he tried Lindy but again, to his disappointment, she just tossed him off. And that's what happened all week. After his seven-day stint, the owner asked him how it was going.

"Okay," he said. "I'm a bit disappointed with the girls, though. All they do is toss me off."

"Ah, but you must remember Brian, we work a week in hand here."

★

A rich, but slightly mad old man arranged for a prostitute to come round to his house at 8 o'clock in the evening. When a beautiful curvaceous blonde arrived at the door, she asked him what he would like and he told her he wanted a bath. So she prepared the bath, he stripped off and got in.

"Now, what would you like?" she asked.

"I'd like some thunder," he said, "please bang your fist against the door."

So she did that and after a few minutes asked him again "What would you like?"

"Lightning," he replied. "Lots of lightning, please switch the light on and off."

She did this and he squealed with pleasure.

"Great!" he enthused. "Now I want waves, stormy waves."

So she leant over the bath and made waves with her hands.

By this time, the girl had been there over an hour and was getting very bored.

"Come on," she coaxed. "Don't you want some sex?"

"What!" he exclaimed. "In this weather? You must be joking."

★

Out Shopping

A Scotsman, a bit the worse for wear, staggered into an off licence for some more booze. There were two men in front of him. The first had a huge beard and a big cigar. He ordered £100's worth of spirits and told the shop assistant to put it on the F11 convention bill. After he had gone the second man, also sporting a large cigar and a slightly smaller beard, ordered £200's of sherry and port, and asked for it to be also put on the F11 convention account. So the Scotsman thought he'd try and get away with the same thing.

"Two crates of whisky please, and put it on the F11 convention account my good man," he said, trying to sound very upright and sober. The shop assistant replied, "I'm sorry Sir, I can't do that, you don't have a large beard and cigar."

For a moment the Scotsman looked defeated but then a smile lit up his face as he lifted his kilt and replied, "Ah yes, but I'm working undercover."

"Great news boss," said the salesman.
"You remember that checked suit in bright green and yellow… The one you thought you'd be stuck with forever? Well, I've sold it, and at the asking price."
"Well, that's fantastic," replied the boss, very impressed. "Well done, I think you deserve a bonus for that. By the way, why have you got a bandage on your hand?"
"Oh that's where his guide dog bit me."

A sleazy man ran a pet shop and advertised on the front window that he had a dog for sale, specially reared for spinsters.

It wasn't long before a woman came in asking for more details.

"I assure you Miss, this dog will cater for all your needs," he said as he brought out a huge Alsatian for her to inspect. The woman bought the dog and they went home. However, a week later, he received an angry phone call from here, complaining that the dog was not satisfactory.

"My sincere apologies," smarmed the man. "I'll come round and see you straight away."

When the man arrived, he found the woman in bed and the dog asleep on the carpet.

"Look lively, Brutus," he said to the dog as he took his clothes off, "I'm only going to show you one more time."

The man knocked on his manager's door.

"Excuse me Sir, may I have tomorrow off, the wife wants to go shopping."

"Certainly not," replied the manager.

"Oh thank you sir, you've saved my life!"

A man was strolling around an old antique market when he spotted a long forgotten brass rat pushed into a far corner of one of the shops. A collector of brass objects, the purchase was soon made and the man departed. However, he hadn't gone too far when he noticed a rat running up behind him and within minutes, the whole area was swimming in the vermin. Frightened for his life the man raced down the road to the river and threw the brass rat into the water. Lo and behold all the rats ran into the water and drowned. Some time later, he returned to the antique market and sought out the man who had sold him the rat. When the shopkeeper recognised him, he said, "Back again already Sir, is there something wrong with your figure?"

"Oh no, not at all," replied the man, "I was just wondering if you had any brass figures of lawyers."

★

A bloke goes into a bakers and asks for three pork pies. The assistant picks the pies up with a pair of tongs and puts them in a paper bag. The man then asks for three strawberry tarts and the assistant picks up another pair of tongs and puts three tarts into a bag.

"I must compliment you on such impressive hygienic standards" said the man.

"Thank you," said the assistant. "We're very careful not to touch any of the food."

Just as the man was leaving the shop, he noticed a piece of string hanging from the assistant's trousers.

"Excuse me, what is that piece of string?" he asked.

"That's used when I go to the toilet. So that I don't touch my penis, I pull it out with the string," said the assistant.

"But how do you put it back?"

"Oh, I use one of these pairs of tongs."

The couple had been married many years and it had got to the stage where any romance that might have been, had died long ago. On a shopping trip into town they stop off at the tailors to get the husband fitted for a new pair of trousers.

"What size zip would you like?" asked the assistant.

"Oh, the longest you've got," he quickly replied.

After they'd left the shop the wife turned to him and remarked bitterly, "You remind me of that good-for-nothing brother of yours. Every day he opens the doors of his double garage and wheels out a bicycle."

A very shy man had the embarrassing task of returning a pair of underpants to the shop and being served by a pretty young girl.

"What's wrong with them Sir?" she asked.

"They're, they're ... er unsatisfactory" he said, blushing madly.

"Can you tell me why?"

The man was lost for words but as he was looking wildly around for inspiration, an idea came to him.

"Do you know the old Grand Hotel on Union Street?"

"Yes."

"And do you know the ballroom underneath."

"But there is no ballroom underneath."

"Exactly!" exclaimed the man "and that's just what's wrong with these underpants."

A woman tries on an evening dress in the shop and says to the sales assistant "What do you think, I know the neckline's a bit low cut, is it too daring?"

"Well Madam, have you got hairs on your chest?" said the assistant.

"No, of course not."

"Then I think it's too daring."

"There you are, does it fit properly?" he asked.

"Oh yes, it's great," she replied.

"It doesn't hurt, does it?"

"Not at all."

"Well that's good, because we've only got these shoes in this size."

There was only one supermarket basket left at the door of the shop as a woman and a man approached from separate directions.

"Excuse me," said the woman, "do you want that basket?"

"No thanks," he replied, "I'm only after one thing."

"Typical male," she said to herself as he walked away.

Coming home from work, a man passed a sex shop and on impulse went in and bought a blow-up doll. He couldn't wait to get home to try it out but when he pumped her up, she just went flat again. The next day the man went back to the sex shop and demanded to see the manager.

"So what exactly was wrong with the doll?" he asked.

"I'll tell you what," he replied angrily. "As soon as I'd blown her up, she went down on me."

"Bloody hell," exclaimed the manager. "If I'd known that I'd have charged you twice as much."

★

The man was approached by the most beautiful sales girl he had ever seen.

"Can I help you Sir?" she said "What would you like?"

"What would I like?" he mused. "I would like to take you away from all this. We would go to the most elegant restaurant in town, linger over the port and then head back to my place for soft lights, sweet music and mad passionate love." He sighed, "That's what I'd like, but what I need is a new shirt."

★

I bought my girlfriend a fur coat. I said to her, "Your knickers are coming down." "No they're not" she said.

"Then that coat's going back!"

★

A man goes to the most exclusive shop in Mayfair to buy his wife some exquisite lingerie for their wedding anniversary.

The sales assistant shows him some outfits around £100 but he shakes his head saying, "No, it's got to be more sheer than that."

She then shows him an outfit at £150 but he insists on having something even more sheer. So eventually she brings out some lingerie at £400, extra, extra, sheer.

He takes the lingerie home and asks his wife to go and put it on so that he can see what it looks like. The wife, however, decides to play a trick on him. She is convinced that because it is so sheer he wouldn't be able to tell whether she was wearing it or not, and then she would go back to the shops and pocket the refund.

So she appears before him with nothing on.

"Well what do you think?" she says.

"Crikey!" he replies. "You'd think at that price they'd iron out the creases first."

"Oh no, not another hat? Where will I get the money to pay for it?"

"But sweetheart, you know I'm not nosey."

A woman walks into a pet shop and asks the owner for some wasps.

"I'm sorry, Madam, we don't sell wasps in here."

"But you do," she insists.

"No, I think you're mistaken," replies the owner.

"Well, in that case, why have you got two in the window?"

A Brummie walks into a shop and asks for a kipper tie.

"This is a clothes shop, not a café," comes the reply.

A woman went into a butcher's shop and asked for a Norfolk Turkey. "Just a moment," said the assistant, and he disappeared into the backroom and came back with the bird, which he showed to the woman.

Immediately she put her fingers right up its backside and after a minute exclaimed, "This isn't a Norfolk Turkey, this is a Shropshire. How dare you try to trick me?"

Astonished at her outburst, he apologised profusely and returned to the backroom where he picked up another turkey. On returning, the woman shoved her hands up its arse, smiled and said, "That's better. Wrap it up, please."

After she had left the shop, the butcher came out of his office and asked what all the commotion was about. When the assistant recounted the incident the butcher said, "It's no good trying to fool that old biddy, she knows her turkeys. You should know them too by now. Where have you been?"

Fed up with the butcher's jibes, the assistant turns round and sticks his bum in the air.

"You're the expert, you tell me!"

As the man crossed the street he tripped up and broke his watch on the side of the pavement.

"Damn," he muttered "I must get it mended" and looking around he saw a shop with a huge clock in the window. Thinking it must be a watchmakers he went in and asked the owner to mend his watch.

"I'm sorry Sir, I don't mend watches, I perform circumcisions."

"Then why do you have a huge clock in your window?" replied the man feeling somewhat irritated.

"Well what would you put in the window?" said the owner.

An old woman was handling all the meat on the butcher's slab but not buying anything. Eventually the butcher lost his patience with her and said, "Listen, madam, it's not like your Jack, it doesn't get bigger the longer you handle it."

Women on Men

The mystery in life that's never been solved is why, when men get drunk, someone creeps into their bedroom in the dead of night, pees in the wardrobe and pukes in their shoes

Why do married women have so many wrinkles?
From squinting down and saying, "Pull what?"

What's the definition of a lazy man?
One who marries a pregnant woman.

Why did God create men?
Because a vibrator can't dig the garden.

What are the three most popular female lies?
1. Of course you're the best lover I've ever had.
2. Size doesn't mean everything.
3. Only interested in your money? How can you say that? Of course not.

Have you heard about the man who put a condom on inside out ... and went?

★

After watching a steamy video at work, a man goes home to his wife and asks her why she doesn't moan when they make love.

"If that's what you want, I'll do it tonight," she says.

That night, in bed, he gets on top of her and after a couple of minutes she says,

"When are you going to paint the kitchen? Why can't I have a new dress? Next door have got a far better car than we have ...."

A street busker is trying very unsuccessfully to play his cello and the noise he's making is driving most people away.

"Cor, Flo," said May, as they passed him by, "he reminds me of our Bert. He sits and scratches at his instrument too, instead of learning how to use it properly."

Three women are talking about their husbands and the subject of nicknames comes up.

"My husband's called Big Mac cos he's got the largest, meatiest donger you ever did see," said the first woman happily.

"I call my husband 'Surfing Willy' cos when he gets going I feel like I'm floating on water," said the second.

"Mine's called Cointreau," said the third.

Puzzled, one of the other women asked, "Isn't that some kind of fancy liquor?"

"Yep."

Why do men prefer big tits and tight pussies?
Because they have big mouths and little willies.

"I'd love to get into your knickers," says the lecher to the sweet young thing.
"No thanks," she replies, "One arsehole in there's enough for me."

What's the similarity between a penis and Rubik's cube?
They both get harder the longer you play with them.

Why do Australian men come so quickly?
Because they can't wait to get down to the pub to tell their mates

What's the difference between condoms and coffins?
They both contain something stiff, but one's coming while the other's going.
What is the difference between men and Opal Fruits?
Men don't come in four refreshing fruit flavours.

Did you hear about the man who had five dicks?
His trousers fitted like a glove.

★

What's the similarity between a man and a stamp?
One lick and they stick to you.

What's the similarity between a Hepatitis B injection and sex with a useless man?
A quick, short prick in the bum and it's all over.

What are the two words men don't like to hear?
'Stop' and 'don't.'

Did you hear about the girl who went out with the undertaker?
He only wanted her for her body.

Adam came first.
But then men always do.

Have you heard about the man who's so lazy, instead of taking his teeth out at night he sleeps in a six inches glass of water?

How do you know if a man's a bachelor?
He comes to work every morning from a different direction.

What's pink and hard first thing in the morning?
The *Financial Times* crossword.

★

**What do you get if you cross a rooster with a disobedient dog?
A cock that doesn't come!**

★

The man was so unlucky – one day when he approached a prostitute she said she had a headache.

★

Girls, the best way to drive your fella mad is to smile in your sleep.

★

Why do firemen have bigger balls than policemen?
They sell more tickets.

★

**Why are men more clever than dogs?
So they won't hump women's legs at dinner parties.**

★

What's the definition of female masturbation?
Finishing the job off properly.

Why is it so difficult for women to find caring, sensitive men?
They already have boyfriends.

★

What does a woman have when she's got two little balls in her hand?
The man's undivided attention.

★

What do you call a woman who always knows where her husband is?
A widow.

★

What's the difference between Ooooh.. and Aaaargh..?
Four inches.

★

Lights on – Nobody Home

"Ha, ha," laughed the simpleton. "I've just found out that Jack pays my wife £50 to sleep with him!"

"What!?" exclaimed his friend. "What the hell's so funny about that?!"

"I get it for free."

This Irishman's car broke down and the garage mechanic said, "Yeah, shit in the carburettor."

"How often do I have to do that?" replied the Irishman.

The weather had turned very cold and as a naive young girl was waiting on the platform for the train to arrive, her hands and feet started to go numb. Looking around, she noticed people putting their hands between their legs and when she did the same, her hands warmed up nicely. The following week, the weather was still very cold on the night she went out on her first date. Walking back through the park, they sat down on a park bench and feeling cold, the girl put her hands between her legs. When the boy asked her what she was doing she explained and he told her his hands were cold as well. So in all innocence she put his hands between her legs and said, "There, doesn't that feel better?"

"Oh yes," he said nodding enthusiastically. A short while later he complained his nose was feeling cold so she warmed him up again. Then later still, he told her his willy was so cold it had gone stiff...

The next day, her mates asked here how the date had gone. "Fine," she replied, "but it was such a cold night, I had to warm poor John up, he was freezing! I never realised men's willies made such an awful mess when they thaw out, though..."

A country farmer from Iowa took his son to visit the big city for the first time, and ended up in a big department store. They stared in utter amazement at everything around them, particularly two silver coloured doors which seemed to open and close on their own. As they watched, a wizened old lady pressed a button on the wall and as the doors opened she entered and the doors closed again. Lots of lights started flashing and some moments later, the doors reopened and a beautiful young woman stepped out.
"Well, I'll be damned," said the old farmer. "Son, go fetch your mother."

★

Three men, an Englishman, an Italian and an Irishman are trapped on the roof of a burning building. Below them on the road, the firemen are holding out a blanket for them to jump into.
"Come on," they yell to the Englishman, "jump!"
So he jumps and just as he's about to reach the blanket, they pull it away and he lands on the pavement, stone dead.
"Come on," shout the firemen to the Italian, "hurry up and jump."
"Oh no," screams the Italian, "you'll take the blanket away."
"No we won't. That bloke was a robber and a pickpocket, that's why we took the blanket away. We'll keep it here for you."

So the Italian jumps and again the blanket is removed so he falls to his death.

"Right, come on," they call to the Irishman, "let's have you."

"Holy Mary," shouts the Irishman. "You won't trick me like that. I know you'll take the blanket away."

"No, no," and again they urge him to jump.

"It doesn't matter what you say, I don't believe you," he replies, "just leave the blanket on the ground and walk away slowly."

Did you hear about the bimbo whose boyfriend suffered from dandruff?

When she rang the chemist to ask for something to cure it, he recommended Head and Shoulders. A few days later, she rang back and asked, "How do you give him shoulders?"

When her two cats died, the heartbroken spinster decided to take them to the taxidermist to be stuffed.

"Certainly miss," said the taxidermist obligingly, "and do you want them mounted?"

"Oh no!" she exclaimed "Just side by side."

Three simpletons went on holiday together and ended up sharing a double bed. However it was a bit of a tight squeeze so one of them got out and tried to make himself comfortable in an easy chair. After a few minutes, he got a tap on the shoulder.

"Hey Jake, you can come back to bed, there's plenty of room now."

★

"Oh doctor," cried the naive young girl. "I think there's something wrong with me. My Frank and I have been trying to have a baby for six months but nothing's happened."
"Don't worry," said the kindly doctor. "I'm sure it's not too serious. If you'll just pop onto the bed and take your knickers off..."
"Oh doctor," she interrupted, "I'd rather have my husband's baby."

★

Two girls who'd lived their whole lives up in the mountains, were on their first visit to a big city. Everything was very strange. Round mid-day they spotted a hot dog stand and the delicious smell made them realise how hungry they were.
"I didn't know they ate dogs here," remarked one of them as they unwrapped their purchases.
"Neither did I," replied the other, looking down at her food. "What part of the dog did you get?"

★

Two simple hunters were out in the forest when they spotted a herd of red deer. In their haste to shoot as many as they could, one of the hunters accidentally shot his mate in the stomach. Filled with anguish, he started to drag him through the undergrowth looking for help and fortunately came across a group of walkers. He told them what had happened.

"Do you think he'll be all right?" he asked.

"I don't know," came the reply, "he'd have had a better chance if you hadn't gutted him first."

Two down-and-out robbers decided to break into a bank. They managed to by-pass the security systems and were soon inside. To their surprise, instead of one large safe, there were hundreds of smaller ones so they guessed they were in for a long stint of hard work. After ten minutes, they managed toopen the first safe, only to find it contained nothing more than a bowl of semolina-type pudding. Not having eaten for some days, they wolfed it down and started on the next safe. But again it just contained this pudding which they ate. Eventually they opened all the safes, ate all the puddings but left no richer and feeling slightly nauseous. The next morning on the 9 O'clock News, local radio reported that Ireland's most famous sperm bank had been robbed during the night.

★

The overweight hillbilly returned to the dietician a month later to be told he'd lost a stone in weight.

"Well done," said the dietician, "and you kept strictly to my instructions, did you? Two days of eating, skip a day and just drink fluids, then eat for a further two days, skip a day, and so on..."

"Yes," replied the hillbilly, "but my feet are killing me from all that skipping."

★

All night the naive young Italian man had been smitten by a girl at the bar. He thought she was gorgeous but it took four stiff drinks before he had the courage to go and speak to her. After a few minutes of conversation, she leaned towards him seductively and whispered,
"What I really like is a man who can deliver."
So he went out and brought her back a pizza.

"What a miserable life I've had," thought Bob sadly, as he sipped his beer at the corner of the bar. "Here I am, my 25th birthday today, and I still haven't been out with a girl. If only I wasn't so skinny, if only people would stop calling me beanpole." He ordered another half-pint and suddenly felt a tap on his shoulder. To his amazement, a woman was smiling at him and asking if she could join him. A dream come true! For the next thirty minutes, he was in seventh heaven and he was nearly fit to burst when she invited him back to her flat. When they arrived, she suggested he go into the bedroom and take all his clothes off. She would join him in a moment. He lay there shivering with anticipation when she walked in with a ten year old boy and said, "Now see here Billy, that's what you'll look like when you grow up, if you don't eat your greens."

Posh and Becks have just returned from New York and are taking a taxi home. As is the case with taxi drivers, they have to get into conversation.
"Been anywhere nice, then, guv?" he asks.

"Yeah," replies Becks, "New York."

"Oh nice, very nice," answers the taxi driver approvingly. "Do anything special there?"

"Went to a great restaurant," says Becks.

The taxi driver continues, "I lived in New York for six months, you know. Did an exchange with a New York cabbie. I probably know the restaurant. What was it called?"

Becks thinks for a moment and replies, "I can't remember, give us the name of a London station."

"Euston."

"No."

"St Pancras."

"No."

"Paddington."

"No."

"Victoria."

"Yeah, that's it. Victoria," he says, turning to Posh, "what was the name of that great restaurant?"

Did you hear about the simple man on a picnic?
It rained so hard, it took him two hours to finish his soup.

The two condemned men were taken outside to be hanged. Jake got up on the platform, the rope was put round his neck but as the lever was pulled, the knot slipped and he fell into the river below. Quick as a flash he swam away and escaped.

Brian was then taken up onto the platform and just as they put the rope round his neck, he said vehemently,
"Now, just you be sure you don't mess up with the rope like the last one. I can't swim."

The old country folk had lived up in the hills for as far back as anyone could remember. But the day came when it was necessary to accept a few more up-to-date appliances. A new inside toilet was installed and it was decided that the old outhouse would be blown up by dynamite. The day came to raze the building to the ground and it was the two youngest sons that were given the honour of lighting the fuse. A moment later, the whole building erupted in a mighty bang and to everyone's astonishment, old Grandpa appeared staggering from the rubble. He turned to the two boys and said,
"Whatever you do lads, for Christ's sake, don't eat any of your grandma's friggin' bean stew."

A bloke was walking along the street when he was set upon by two muggers. He put up a terrific fight but was eventually wrestled to the ground and received a black eye, two broken ribs and a bloody nose. When the muggers searched him, they found just 20p in his pocket.
"Hey!" they exclaimed. "Why did you get yourself half killed and all for the sake of 20p?"
"I didn't want people to know I was so poor," he groaned.

A simple country lad was called up for the air force and after some instruction, he was prepared for his first parachute jump.

"After ten seconds, pull this string," he was told, "and if it doesn't work, then pull the string on the other side. When you land, we'll have a truck there to bring you back."

The lad nodded and a few minutes later, jumped out of the plane. But alas, ten seconds later the parachute failed to open. He did as he was instructed and pulled the other string but still nothing happened. The young lad muttered to himself,

"Knowing my luck, the bloody truck won't be there either."

Two men had been drinking all afternoon and could barely stand up. Suddenly, one of them staggered off and disappeared for ten minutes. When he finally returned, the other said to him

"Where the fuck did you go?"

"For a piss," came the reply.

"Do us a favour, go for me now."

"Okay," so the man disappeared again and on his return said,

"You prat, you didn't need to go!"

Just as the prisoner was to be marched out to the gallows, the kindly warden asked him if he'd like a shot of whisky.

"No thanks," he replied, "I've only got to have one glass and I'm all over the place."

Two Irishmen on a train. One turns to the other and says, "I'm sure that fella over there is the Pope."

"Holy Mary," said his mate, "It can't be, go and find out."

The first Irishman goes over to the man and says, "Are you the Pope?"

"Fuck off!" came the reply.

The man went back to his mate.

"He won't say."

And what joke book would be complete without one? An Englishman, a Scotsman and an Irishman were all sentenced to be guillotined. The Englishman was asked if he would like to face upwards to the blade or down to the earth.

He said he would prefer to look down. The knife descended but stuck an inch from his neck, so under the law of the country, he was reprieved.

Next came the Scotsman. He said he wasn't afraid to see what was coming and would look upwards. Again the knife stuck and he was reprieved.

Lastly came the Irishman who said he too was not afraid to see what was coming and he would look upwards.

Just as the knife was to be released he shouted, "Stop, bejeezers – I think I can see what the trouble is here."

When a peasant is caught stealing onions he is given a choice between paying 100 rupees, receiving 100 lashes, or he can eat 100 onions.

He chooses the onions but after eating 20, his eyes streaming, he asks for the lashes. But after 20 lashes he finds it too painful and pays the fine.

When he gets home, he tells his wife, "I really cheated them this time. I only ate a few onions, received only a few lashes and got out of paying the fine as long as I could."

Have you heard about the stupid jellyfish? It set.

Did you hear about the simple-minded tennis player who negotiated a £12 million contract? £12 a year for a million years.

A simple man was pacing up and down in the maternity ward waiting for his wife to deliver their baby when out came the nurse to give him the good news.

"Congratulations, you are now the father of beautiful twins."

"Oh no", he replied. "She's been unfaithful, how could she!"

"What do you mean?" asked the nurse.

"Well, I only had my way with her once, so one of them's not mine."

Three men, two friends and a naive hillbilly, were on top of the World Trade Centre in New York. They were bemoaning the fact that it was so cloudy there wasn't much of a view. One of the friends turned to the hillbilly and said, "I bet you didn't know that when you're up this high these very thick clouds are so solid that if you jump on one you bounce right back up."

"You're having me on?" said the hillbilly.

"No, I'm not. Watch this," and the man jumped off the building, landed on the cloud and bounced back again.

The hillbilly was amazed.

"Look, I'll show you again." And he repeated the action.

Now convinced, the hillbilly decided to have a go himself. He jumped off the building went straight through the clouds and crashed to the pavement below, never to rise again.

The other friend turned to his mate and said, "You know Superman, sometimes you can be a real wanker."

★

A rather naive girl and a cocky young man find themselves waiting at the same bus stop. After some time, they strike up a conversation and he tells her that he works on the local community radio – he does the request show.

"Oh how wonderful!" said the young girl, very impressed. "I would do anything to wish my parents a happy anniversary on the radio."

"Anything?" asks the young man with a gleam in his eye.

"Oh yes," she replies.

So with that he takes her behind the bus stop and whips out his ever increasing member. As soon as she sees it she grabs it with both hands saying, "Hi Mum, hi Dad, Happy Anniversary from...."

Miles out in the middle of nowhere, a motorist suddenly finds himself faced with a fast flowing stream across the road. Uncertain of what to do he notices an old simpleton sitting on a gate watching him.

"Will it be alright if I take my car through the water?" he shouts.

"Ay, no problem," comes the reply.

However, halfway across, the water comes seeping in through the windows and the car stalls.

"I thought you said it would be alright!" yells the angry man.

"Aye," replies the old simpleton, scratching his head. "'Twas all right yesterday when we took the ducks across, it only came up halfway on them."

A young girl, naive to the ways of the world, became a nun but after a year she confessed to the Mother Superior that she was pregnant.

"Why, you foolish girl! Who is this man?"

"Oh Reverend Mother, it's not a man; it's an angel."

"Then you're even more stupid than I gave you credit for."

"Oh, but it's true. When I asked him what his name was he said St Michael and showed me the name tag on his underwear."

The hostess was making a last minute inspection of the dining table before her guests arrived.

"Dodds," she called to her waitress. "For goodness sake,

don't forget the sugar tongs. You know what men are like. They go to the toilet, fiddle with their 'you know what', forget to wash their hands and then, alas, handle the sugar lumps." Halfway through the evening, the hostess called over Dodds again.

"I thought I told you to put out the sugar tongs?"

"But I did Madam."

"Well, I can't see them here."

"Of course not, I put them in the loo."

A bloke goes into the local DIY store and orders 20,000 bricks.

"May I ask what you're building?" says the storekeeper.

"Yes, it's a barbecue."

"Gosh, that seems a lot of bricks for one barbecue."

"Not really; we live on the 18th floor."

Did you hear about the simpleton who stood before the mirror with his eyes closed?

He wanted to see what he looked like when he was asleep.

"Hey Jack, I've just been reading in the paper about this bisexuality. What do you think?"

"Yeah, why not, if you can afford it?"

Two drunks came staggering out of London Zoo, their clothes in tatters and their hands and faces covered in blood.
"That's the last time I try lion dancing," said one to the other.

★

The Antiques Roadshow was coming to the Welsh borders and all the local people were busy looking out any family heirlooms. Simple Sam had lived in one of the outlying villages all his life, and so had his father and grandfather before him.
"I bet you'll have something in the attic that's been there for years. Why don't you go and see?" said Sam's next door neighbour.
"Aye, I'll do that," said Sam.
On the day of the show, many people queued up, carrying all sorts of items and amongst them was Sam dragging a very heavy item wrapped up in brown paper. When it got to his turn, a lot of people took an interest in this mysterious package so it was with bated breath that they waited for it to be unwrapped. Gasps of astonishment went up from the gathering crowd as the expert turned to Sam and said, "You say you found this in the attic?"
"Aye, I did that. It must be very old, I knows it was there when my grandpapa was alive."
"Well, yes, it would have been," said the expert, "it's the water tank."

Did you hear about the yachtsman who took a naive young girl on board his boat and asked her to toss him off?
They're still searching the waters for any sign of him.

A young couple were picnicking in the woods and as they ate they also fed the birds, squirrels and any other inquisitive animals that came to see what was going on.When they'd finished they lay out on the grass and soon fell asleep. What a surprise they got on waking, to see a man sitting on the ground nearby. He told them he had been one of the squirrels they had thrown some crumbs to and that showing such kindness to him had broken a wicked spell and he had been restored to human form. He continued to explain that as a thank you for setting him free, he had three wishes, one for each of them. What two wishes would the couple like?

The husband and wife thought about it for a few moments and then told him that their first wish would be to win the jackpot and the second to become famous Hollywood stars.

"OK," said the man, "your wishes have been granted. Now it's my turn."

He turned to the husband and said, "My wish is to have sex with your wife."

The couple had to agree and after an hour of continuous bonking they lay back exhausted. Then the man turned to the woman and said, "How old is your husband?"

"Thirty-five," she replied.

"He's a bit old to still believe in magic wishes, isn't he?"

★

A man who had lived all his life up in the hills was finally re-housed in a small cottage closer to civilisation. A couple of days after he had moved in a council worker stopped him in

the street and asked how it was going.

"Not bad," he admitted, "but I can't get the hang of this strange contraption in the bathroom – a tank thing with a chain."

"Oh it's quite simple, you just pull the chain and the water flows."

A few days later, they met up again.

"Everything alright?" the council worker asked.

"Not really; as soon as I tried to wash most of the water had disappeared."

Out walking in the countryside one day, a young but 'experienced' girl came upon a youth masturbating by putting his willy between two pieces of best frying steak.

"Hey, my lovely, come home with me and I'll show you what it's all about," she murmured.

So the youth went back to her house and up to the bedroom, where she stripped off, parted her legs and said, "Now you put it in here."

"What, both pieces!" he said.

A man in a Rolls Royce stops to buy petrol at a small country petrol station. Putting his hand in his pocket for the money to pay, he brings out a couple of golf tees.

"What are those for?" asks the garage attendant.

"These are to put your balls on when you're driving off."

"My God, these Rolls Royce people think of everything!"

★

A man went to the doctors to have a medical for joining the services. "Just go behind the screen and strip off," said the doctor. "I'll be with you in a moment."

After he had examined the man he told him that he was in excellent condition.

"There's just one thing that's quite remarkable. Your penis is like a corkscrew."

"Oh yes," said the man. "I've just realised that that's my mother's fault."

"Really? Why's that?"

"When I was small there was only the two of us. I didn't have a dad, and my mum didn't like to talk about certain things so I never knew that when you went to the toilet you should shake it dry and not wring it out."

A young girl travelling on a crowded train asked a man if she could have his seat because she was pregnant. The man immediately jumped up and the girl sat down. As the man looked at her he remarked, "You don't look pregnant, how far gone are you?"

"Oh about 30 minutes," she replied, "but it sure is knackering."

I'm sorry Sir, all our en-suite rooms are taken. Do you mind sharing a bath with another of the male guests?" said the hotel receptionist to the simple man.

"Not at all," he replied, "just so long as he keeps to his end of the bath."

Three men were sitting on a bench high on a cliff overlooking the sea when one of them spotted an old bottle hidden in some undergrowth. He pulled it out, undid the cork and a genie appeared.

"I will grant each of you one wish," declared the genie. "You will fling yourself off the cliff calling out whatever you would like and you will land in a boat full of that wish."

So the first man jumped off and shouted 'Money!' and sure enough he landed in a boat full of £50 notes.

The second man jumped off and shouted 'Beautiful girls!' and sure enough he landed in a boat of beautiful girls.

Then it was the turn of the third man who was a bit simple and had forgotten what he was supposed to do. He took a flying leap off the cliff and as he went down he shouted 'Whee!"

A cat dies and goes to Heaven. God meets him at the gate and says, "You've been a good cat all of these years. Anything you desire is yours, all you have to do is ask."

The cats say, "Well, I lived all my life with a poor family on a farm and had to sleep on hardwood floors." God says, "Say no more." And instantly, a fluffy pillow appears. A few days later, 6 mice are killed in a tragic accident and they go to Heaven. God meets them at the gate with the same offer that He made the cat.

The mice said, "All our lives we've had to run. We've been chased by cats, dogs and even women with brooms. If we could only have a pair of roller skates, we wouldn't have to run anymore." God says, "Say no more." And instantly, each mouse is fitted with a beautiful pair of tiny roller skates. About a week later, God decides to check and see how the cat is doing. The cat is sound asleep on his new pillow. God gently wakes him and asks, "How are you doing? Are you happy here?"

The cat yawns and stretches and says, "Oh, I've never been happier in my life. And those Meals on Wheels are the best!"

★

An American football player from the Deep South was visiting a Yankee relative in Boston over the holidays. He went to a large party and met a pretty co-ed.

He was attempting to start up a conversation with the line, "Where does you go to school?"

The co-ed, of course, was not overly impressed with his grammar or Southern drawl, but did answer his question.

"Yale," she replied.

The UA student took a big, deep breath and shouted, "WHERE DOES YOU GO TO SCHOOL?"

★

A frog goes into a bank and approaches the teller. He can see from her nameplate that her name is Patricia Whack. So he says, "Ms. Whack, I'd like to get a loan to buy a boat and go on a holiday." Patti looks at the frog in disbelief and asks him how much he wants to borrow. The frog says $30,000. The teller asks his name and the frog says it's Kermit Jagger and that it's okay, he knows the bank manager. Patti explains that $30,000 is a substantial amount of money and that he would need to secure some collateral against the loan and asks if he has anything he can use as collateral. The frog says, "Sure, I have this," and produces a tiny pink elephant, about half an inch tall. Bright pink and perfectly formed. Very confused, Patti explains that she'll have to consult with the manager and disappears into a back office. She finds the manager and says, "There's a frog called Kermit Jagger out there who claims to know you and wants to borrow 30 grand. And he wants to use this as collateral." She holds up the tiny pink elephant. "I mean, what on earth is it?" The bank manager replies, "It's a knick-knack Patti Whack, give the frog a loan. His old man's a Rolling Stone."

Three women are about to be executed for crimes. One's a brunette, one's a redhead, and one's a blonde.
Two guards brings the brunette forward, and the executioner asks if she has any last requests. She says no, and the executioner shouts, "Ready . . . Aim . . ."
Suddenly the brunette yells, "earthquake!!" Everyone is startled and looks around. She manages to escape.
The angry guards then bring the redhead forward, and the executioner asks if she has any last requests. She says no, and the executioner shouts, "Ready . . . Aim . . ."
The redhead then screams, "tornado!!" Yet again, everyone is startled and looks around. She too escapes execution.

By this point, the blonde had figured out what the others did. The guards bring her forward, and the executioner asks if she has any last requests. She also says no, and the executioner shouts, Ready . . . Aim . . ."

The blonde shouts, "Fire!!"

★ ★ ★